Chartered
Institute of
Housing

Help with Housing Costs:

Universal Credit and Council Tax Rebates

2021-22

Sam Lister and Martin Ward

D1337543

Shelter

Help with Housing Costs: Guide to Universal Credit and Council Tax Rebates
Sam Lister and Martin Ward, 2014-22

Sam Lister is policy and practice officer at the Chartered Institute of Housing
(email: *sam.lister@cih.org*) and a founding director of Citizens Advice Worcester and
Citizens Advice Hereford. He has specialised in housing benefit and social security since 1993.

Martin Ward is an independent consultant and trainer on housing and benefit related
matters (e-mail: *mward@knowledgeflow.org.uk*). He has provided consultancy services
and training for several national organisations as well as many local authorities and
large and small housing providers across the UK since 1982.

ISBN 978-1-9993510-4-5

Edited and typeset by Davies Communications
(www.daviescomms.com)

Printed by MBA Group Ltd

Chartered Institute of Housing

The Chartered Institute of Housing (CIH) is the independent voice for housing and the home of professional standards. Our goal is simple – to support housing professionals to create a future in which everyone has a place to call home. We passionately believe in the life-changing impact of the work of housing professionals and our purpose is to provide everyone involved in housing with the advice, support and knowledge they need to make a difference every day.

CIH was granted a Royal Charter in 1984. We are a registered charity and the professional body for the housing sector.

> Chartered Institute of Housing
> Suites 5 and 6
> First Floor, Rowan House
> Westwood Way
> Coventry
> CV4 8HS
>
> Telephone: 024 7685 1700
>
> E-mail: *customer.services@cih.org*
>
> Website: *www.cih.org*

Shelter

Shelter helps over a million people a year struggling with bad housing or homelessness – and we campaign to prevent it in the first place.

We're here so no-one has to fight bad housing or homelessness on their own.

Please support us at *shelter.org.uk*

For more information about Shelter, please contact:

> 88 Old Street
> London
> EC1V 9HU
>
> Telephone: 0300 330 1234
>
> Website: *shelter.org.uk*

For help with your housing problems, phone Shelter's free housing advice helpline on 0808 800 4444 (open from 8am to 8pm on Mondays to Fridays and from 8am to 5pm on weekends: calls are free from UK landlines and main mobile networks) or visit *shelter.org.uk/advice*

Contents

Preface

This guide explains universal credit and council tax rebates, focusing on help with housing costs. It gives the rules which apply from 1st April 2021, using information available on that date.

We welcome comments and criticisms on the contents of our guide and make every effort to ensure it is accurate. However, the only statement of the law is found in the relevant Acts, regulations, orders and rules (chapter 1).

This guide has been written with the help and encouragement of many other people. We wish to thank the following in particular:

Liz Davies (Garden Court Chambers), Richard Stanier (Shelter), John Zebedee, Linda Davies and Peter Singer (editing and production) as well as staff from the Department for Work and Pensions and the Rent Service. Their help has been essential to the production of this guide.

Sam Lister and Martin Ward

April 2021

List of tables

Table		Page

Abbreviations

The principal abbreviations used in the guide are given below.

ADM	Advice for Decision Makers (DWP manual)
CTC	Child tax credit
CTGM	Council tax guidance manual
CTR	Council tax rebate
DLA	Disability living allowance
DWP	The Department for Work and Pensions in Great Britain
ESA	Employment and support allowance
ESA(C)	Contributory employment and support allowance
ESA(IR)	Income-related employment and support allowance
GB	England, Scotland and Wales
HB	Housing benefit
HMRC	Her Majesty's Revenue and Customs
HMCTS	Her Majesty's Courts and Tribunals Service
IB	Incapacity benefit
IS	Income support
JSA	Jobseeker's allowance
JSA(C)	Contribution-based jobseeker's allowance
JSA(IB)	Income-based jobseeker's allowance
LCW	Limited capability for work
LCWRA	Limited capability for work and work-related activity
LHA	Local housing allowance
MHCLG	Ministry of Housing, Communities and Local Government
NISR	Northern Ireland Statutory Rules
PIP	Personal independence payment
SAR	Second adult rebate
SDA	Severe disablement allowance
SI	Statutory instrument
SMI	Support for mortgage interest
SPC	State pension credit
SSI	Scottish Statutory Instrument
UC	Universal credit
UK	England, Scotland, Wales and Northern Ireland
WTC	Working tax credit

Key to footnotes

AA	The Social Security Administration Act 1992
art	Article number
CBA	The Social Security Contributions and Benefits Act 1992
C&P	The Universal Credit, Personal Independence Payment, Jobseeker's Allowance and Employment and Support Allowance (Claims and Payments) Regulations 2013, SI No 380
CT(A&E)	The Council Tax (Administration and Enforcement) Regulations 1992, SI No 613
CT(A&E)S	The Council Tax (Administration and Enforcement) (Scotland) Regulations 1992, SI No 1332
CT(ED)	The Council Tax (Exempt Dwellings) Order 1992, SI No 558
CT(LO)	The Council Tax (Liability of Owners) Regulations 1992, SI No 551
CTP	The Council Tax Reduction Schemes (Prescribed Requirements) (England) Regulations 2012, SI No 2885
CT(RD)	The Council Tax (Reductions for Disabilities) Regulations 1992, SI No 554
CTPW	The Council Tax Reduction Scheme and Prescribed Requirements (Wales) Regulations 2013, SI No 3029
CTR	The Council Tax Reduction Schemes (Default Scheme) (England) Regulations 2012, SI No 2886
CTRW	The Council Tax Reduction Schemes (Default Scheme) (Wales) Regulations 2013, SI No 3035
CTS	The Council Tax Reduction (Scotland) Regulations 2012, SSI No 303
CTS66+	The Council Tax Reduction (State Pension Credit) (Scotland) Regulations 2012, SSI No 319
D&A	The Universal Credit, Personal Independence Payment, Jobseeker's Allowance and Employment and Support Allowance (Decisions and Appeals) Regulations 2013, SI No 381
DDO	The Council Tax (Discount Disregards) Order 1992, SI 1992 No 548
DDR	The Council Tax (Additional Provisions for Discount Disregards) Regulations 1992, SI 1992 No 552
EEA	The Immigration (European Economic Area) Regulations 2016, SI No 1052
FTPR	The Tribunal Procedure (First-tier Tribunal) (Social Entitlement Chamber) Rules 2008, SI No 2685
HB	The Housing Benefit Regulations 2006, SI No 213

HB66+	The Housing Benefit (Persons who have attained the age for state pension credit) Regulations 2006, SI No 214
IAA99	The Immigration and Asylum Act 1999
LMI	The Loans for Mortgage Interest Regulations 2017, SI No 725
LGFA	The Local Government Finance Act 1992
IAA99	The Immigration and Asylum Act 1999
NIAA	The Social Security Administration (Northern Ireland) Act 1992
NICBA	The Social Security Contributions and Benefits (Northern Ireland) Act 1992
NIC&P	The Universal Credit, Personal Independence Payment, Jobseeker's Allowance and Employment and Support Allowance (Claims and Payments) Regulations (Northern Ireland) 2016, NISR No 220
NID&A	The Universal Credit, Personal Independence Payment, Jobseeker's Allowance and Employment and Support Allowance (Decisions and Appeals) Regulations (Northern Ireland) 2016, NISR No 221
NIHB	The Housing Benefit Regulations (Northern Ireland) 2006, NISR No 405
NIHB66+	The Housing Benefit (Persons who have attained the age for state pension credit) Regulations (Northern Ireland) 2006, NISR No 406
NILMI	The Loans for Mortgage Interest Regulations (Northern Ireland) 2017, NISR No 176
NIOP	The Social Security (Overpayments and Recovery) Regulations (Northern Ireland) 2016, NISR No 224
NIPOA	The Social Security (Payments on Account of Benefit) Regulations (Northern Ireland) 2016, NISR No 223
NISSO	The Social Security (Northern Ireland) Order 1998, SI No 1506 (NI 10)
NIUC	The Universal Credit Regulations (Northern Ireland) 2016, NISR No 216
NIUCED	The Universal Credit Housing Costs (Executive Determinations) Regulations (Northern Ireland) 2016, NISR No 222
NIUCTP	The Universal Credit (Transitional Provisions) Regulations (Northern Ireland) 2016, NISR No 226
NIWRO	The Welfare Reform (Northern Ireland) Order 2015, SI No 2006 (NI 1)
OPR	The Social Security (Overpayments and Recovery) Regulations 2013, SI No 384
para	Paragraph number
POA	The Social Security (Payments on Account of Benefit) Regulations 2013, SI No 383
reg	Regulation number

RO	Rates (Northern Ireland) Order 1977, SI No 2157
RR	The Rate Relief Regulations (Northern Ireland) 2017, NISR No 184
RRHB	The Rate Relief (General) Regulations (Northern Ireland) 2007, NISR No 204
RRHB66+	The Rate Relief (Qualifying Age) Regulations (Northern Ireland) 2007, NISR No 203
RRLPA	The Rate Relief (Lone Pensioner Allowance) Regulations (Northern Ireland) 2008, NISR No 124
s	Section number
sch	Schedule number
SI	Statutory instrument [year and reference number]
SSA	Social Security Act 1998
SSHD	Secretary of State for the Home Department
SSWP	Secretary of State for Work and Pensions
TCEA	Tribunals, Courts and Enforcement Act 2007
UC	The Universal Credit Regulations 2013, SI No 376
UCROO	The Rent Officers (Universal Credit Functions) Order 2013, SI No 382
UCTP	The Universal Credit (Transitional Provisions) Regulations 2014, SI No 1230
UTPR	The Tribunal Procedure (Upper Tribunal) Rules 2008, SI No 2698
WRA	The Welfare Reform Act 2012

What you can claim

	Working age	Pension age
Renters		
Rent payments	UC	HB
Service charge payments	UC	HB
Renters in supported or temporary accommodation		
Rent payments	HB	HB
Service charge payments	HB	HB
Owners		
Owner occupier payments	SMI	SMI
Service charge payments	UC	SPC
Shared owners		
Owner occupier payments	SMI	SMI
Rent payments	UC	HB
Service charge payments	UC	HB
All		
Living costs	UC	SPC
Council tax (Great Britain)	CTR	CTR
Rates (Northern Ireland)	RR	RR
Other help	DHPs etc	DHPs etc

Universal credit (UC)	volume 1
Housing benefit (HB)	volume 2
Support for mortgage interest (SMI)	volume 1
State pension credit (SPC)	volume 2
Council tax rebate (CTR)	volume 1
Rate rebate (RR)	volume 1
Discretionary housing payments (DHPs)	volume 2

Chapter 1 **Introduction**

- ■ Universal credit and migration to UC: see paras 1.2-13.
- ■ Council tax reductions and rebates: see paras 1.14-20.
- ■ Using this guide, the law and guidance: see paras 1.21-30.
- ■ How decisions are made: see paras 1.31-37.

1.1 Welcome to this guide, which explains the new system of getting help with your housing costs. The guide is used by people claiming benefits, advisers, landlords, mortgage lenders, benefit administrators and appeal tribunals. It gives the rules from April 2021.

UC scheme

1.2 Universal credit (UC) helps meet your living needs if you are working age. For renters it also helps pay your rent. For owner occupiers, support for mortgage interest (SMI) helps pay your mortgage interest.

1.3 UC applies throughout the UK and is replacing six legacy benefits including working age housing benefit (HB) in most cases (para 1.12). During the transition to UC, many people continue to receive these, but once the transition is complete, about seven to eight million households are expected to be on UC.

1.4 Table 1.1 gives the main terminology used in UC, table 1.2 gives statistics, and table 1.3 summarises recent and planned changes to UC.

Who can get UC

1.5 If you are working age:

  (a) you can make a claim for UC at any time;

  (b) but there are exceptions for some under 18-year-olds, students, migrants, prisoners and others.

Chapter 2 gives the details and chapter 3 explains how to claim.

1.6 If you are currently getting one or more legacy benefits (para 1.12):

  (a) the DWP will at some point advise you to claim UC, and in this case you can get transitional protection to stop you being worse off;

  (b) you can claim UC before that, but in this case, you don't get transitional protection;

  (c) in either case, you can't go back to legacy benefits.

This is called 'migration' and is explained in chapter 4.

Table 1.1 **UC terminology**

(a) Family and household terms

Claimant and joint claimant

A claimant is someone who is making a claim for UC or someone who is getting UC. If you are claiming as a couple you are joint claimants.

Working age and pension age

Pension age is 66 or over. Working age is under 66.

Benefit unit

Your benefit unit means you (both of you if you are a couple) and any children and young persons you are responsible for (but not non-dependants).

Couple and single person

You are a couple if you are two people who are married, in a civil partnership, or living together as a couple. You are single if you are not a couple.

Child and young person

A child is someone under 16. A young person is someone aged 16 to 19 who is in secondary education.

Non-dependant

A non-dependant is an adult son, daughter, relative, friend or other adult who lives with you on a non-commercial basis.

(b) Calculation terms

Assessment period

UC is assessed on a monthly basis. Your first assessment period begins on the day you claim UC and the following ones start on the same date each month.

Maximum UC

UC is calculated using your income and capital and your maximum UC. This is made up of a standard allowance and other elements you and your benefit unit qualify for.

Housing costs element

The housing costs element is part of your maximum UC which is for your rent and service charges. Mortgage interest can be met by DWP loans (SMI).

Housing cost contribution

Each non-dependant you have is normally expected to make a housing cost contribution towards your rent and service charges.

The amount of your UC

1.7 How much UC you get depends on your financial and other circumstances, including whether you have a family, are capable of work, are a carer, and/or have childcare costs. See chapters 9 and 10.

UC and your housing costs

1.8 You can get help towards your rent and service charge payments as part of your UC. This is called a 'housing costs element'. It is slightly lower if you have one or more non-dependants. This is explained in chapters 5 to 7.

1.9 You can get support for your mortgage interest (SMI) as a repayable DWP loan. You must be eligible for UC and have no earned income. This is explained in chapters 5 and 8.

Claims, payments and appeals

1.10 You usually claim UC online. If you are claiming as a couple, you make a joint claim. Your claim goes to:

(a) the DWP (Department for Work and Pensions) in Great Britain;

(b) the DFC (Department for Communities) in Northern Ireland.

In this guide, references to the DWP include the DFC.

1.11 UC is based on monthly assessment periods, and you are paid at the end of these. Your landlord and mortgage lender can be paid some of your UC. If you think your UC is wrong, you can ask the DWP or DFC to reconsider and appeal to an independent tribunal. The rules about claims, payments, overpayments and appeals are in chapter 3 and 11 to 14.

The legacy benefits

1.12 The legacy benefits UC is replacing are:

(a) HB for working age claimants (except in supported or temporary accommodation: table 5.2);

(b) income-based JSA (JSA(IB));

(c) income-related ESA (ESA(IR));

(d) income support (IS);

(e) child tax credit (CTC); and

(f) working tax credit (WTC).

Other benefits

1.13   The following benefits continue alongside UC:

  (a) state pension credit (SPC);

  (b) HB for pension age claimants;

  (c) HB for people in temporary or supported accommodation (table 5.2);

  (d) Discretionary housing payments (DHPs);

  (e) Contribution-based JSA/ESA (JSA(C) and (ESA(C)) – also called 'new style' JSA/ESA;

  (f) PIP, DLA, carer's allowance, child benefit and all other state benefits (appendix 2).

Table 1.2 **Households on UC**

	All households	With housing costs element
November 2015	141,142	50,637
May 2016	260,189	98,318
November 2016	398,644	160,105
May 2017	494,852	228,596
November 2017	623,890	315,282
May 2018	837,631	472,416
November 2018	1,265,215	748,288
May 2019	1,820,743	1,126,726
November 2019	2,343,302	1,490,718
May 2020	4,243,465	2,379,734

■ Source: DWP, Stat-Xplore

Examples: Help with housing costs: UC and CTR

1. A single tenant

A single person rents her home. If she meets the conditions:

  ■   she can get UC towards her living needs and her rent;

  ■   she can get CTR towards her council tax.

2. A home owner couple

A couple are buying their home on a mortgage. If they meet the conditions:

  ■   they can get UC towards their living needs;

  ■   they can get SMI towards their mortgage interest;

  ■   they can get CTR towards their council tax.

Council tax reductions and rebates

1.14   Council tax applies in Great Britain (England, Scotland and Wales). It has several kinds of reductions and rebates that you can get whether you are working age or pension age.

Council tax

1.15   Chapter 15 describes:

(a) who gets a council tax bill;

(b) council tax exemptions;

(c) the single person discount.

Council tax rebates

1.16   Chapters 16 and 17 give the details about CTR, including:

(a) CTR if you are on UC;

(b) CTR for other working age and pension age claimants;

(c) variations between England, Scotland and Wales, and between councils in England;

(d) the different kinds of council tax rebate (CTR).

1.17   The family and household terms in CTR are the same as in UC (table 1.1) except:

(a) a claimant is sometimes called an 'applicant';

(b) 'joint claimant' isn't used because in a couple one of you is the claimant for both;

(c) 'family' is used instead of benefit unit.

Claims, awards and appeals

1.18   You claim council tax reductions and rebates from the council that sends your council tax bill.

1.19   CTR is calculated on a weekly basis, and benefit weeks begin on a Monday. Other council tax reductions are awarded for the exact period you qualify for. If you think your CTR or other reduction is wrong, you can ask the council to reconsider and appeal to an independent tribunal. The rules about CTR claims, awards, and appeals are in chapters 16 and 18.

Rate rebates in Northern Ireland

1.20   Northern Ireland has domestic rates instead of council tax. Rate rebates and other reductions are described in chapter 19.

Using this guide

Benefit rules and figures

1.21   The rules in this guide apply from April 2021. The next edition will give the rules from April 2022.

1.22   The UC figures in this guide apply in assessment periods (para 3.38) beginning on or after 6th April 2021. But the coronavirus increase of £86.67 per month (table 9.2) is only expected to apply in assessment periods beginning on or before 6th September 2021.

1.23   The CTR figures apply from 1st April 2021.

UC law and guidance

1.24   The law governing the UC scheme is in the Welfare Reform Act 2012 (in Great Britain), and the Welfare Reform (Northern Ireland) Order SI 2015/2006 9 which is made under the powers in the Northern Ireland (Welfare Reform) Act 2015. The regulations and orders giving the details of the UC scheme are listed in appendix 1. These are called statutory instruments in Great Britain (SIs) and statutory rules in Northern Ireland (NISRs). The main ones are the Universal Credit Regulations 2013 SI No 376 (in Great Britain), and the Universal Credit Regulations (Northern Ireland) 2016 NISR No 216.

1.25   Government guidance on the UC scheme for DWP staff in Great Britain is the responsibility of the DWP. It is contained in its Advice for Decision Makers (ADM). The DWP also issues circulars to local councils which are published.

CTR law and guidance

1.26   The Act of Parliament governing the CTR schemes is the Local Government Finance Act 1992 (as amended by the Local Government Finance Act 2012). The regulations and orders giving the details of the schemes are listed in appendix 1. They are called statutory instruments (SIs). The main ones are the six council tax reduction regulations listed there.

1.27   Government guidance on the CTR scheme is the responsibility of the MHCLG (Ministry of Housing, Communities and Local Government) in England, and of the Scottish and Welsh Governments. In England the Council Tax Guidance Manual (CTGM) is produced by the Valuation Tribunal Service.

Case law

1.28   Case law means judgments made:

(a) in Great Britain by the Upper Tribunal (formerly the Social Security Commissioners) and the courts (the High Court, Court of Appeal and Supreme Court);

(b) in Northern Ireland by the NI Commissioners and the courts.

It interprets the law, and is binding on the DWP/DFC, local councils/NIHE and First-tier Tribunals.

Finding and using the law and guidance

1.29   The law, guidance and case law is available online (as shown in the footnote below). The footnotes throughout this guide show which piece of law applies to particular paragraphs. For CTR they give the law in England, and the law for Scotland and Wales is in Appendix 4.

Abbreviations

1.30   The tables at the front of this guide give:

(a) a list of abbreviations used in the text; and

(b) a key to the abbreviations used in the footnotes.

Table 1.3 **Summary of UC changes from 2020**

13th Jul 2020 SI 2020/611 NISR 2020/107	Change to benefit cap that ensures that the correct amount of national living wage, relating to the time when the work was undertaken, is used to calculate whether a grace period applies.
22nd Jul 2020 SI 2019/1152 SI 2020/826 NISR 2019/152 NISR 2020/165	Two-week run-on of JSA(IB), ESA(IR) and IS introduced for claimants migrating from these benefits onto UC. Technical error corrected by later instrument to ensure the full two weeks is paid.
5th Aug 2020 SI 2020/827 NISR 2020/166	Change to the rule allowing certain disabled students to claim UC to make it clear the claimant must be on PIP/DLA and already be accepted as having limited capability for work.
24th Aug 2020 SI 2020/683 NISR 2020/149	Certain third country (non-EEA) nationals who are the family member of a 'person from Northern Ireland' (whether currently resident in Northern Ireland or not) can acquire a right to reside and therefore entitlement to UC.
23rd Sep 2020 SI 2019/1152 NISR 2019/152	Twelve-month exemption from the minimum income floor introduced for claimants who move on to UC through natural migration.
6th Oct 2020	Raising of state pension age complete. Pension age now 66 for men and women (para 2.9). No further rises expected until 2024 (when it is expected to rise gradually from 66 to 68).

1.29   UC regulations with amendments and CTR legislation: www.legislation.gov.uk

UC guidance (ADM): www.gov.uk/government/publications/advice-for-decision-making-staff-guide

UC operational guidance (House of Commons Library, Deposited Papers):

https://depositedpapers.parliament.uk/depositedpaper/2282591/files, DWP 29th October 2020, DEP2020-0646

DWP 21st October 2019 DEP-0980

CTR guidance (England): www.gov.uk/government/collections/localising-council-tax-support

Upper Tribunal Decisions prior to Jan 2016: https://tinyurl.com/SSDecisions1

Upper Tribunal decisions from Jan 2016 onwards: https://tinyurl.com/SSDecisions2

12th Nov 2020 SI 2020/1156 SI 2020/1201 NISR 2020/227 NISR 2020/242	Temporary coronavirus measures relating to the minimum income floor and prisoners that were due to expire on 12th November are extended until April/May 2021 (see below).
16th Nov 2020 SI 2020/1138 NISR 2020/226	Employed earnings reported via the (HMRC) Real Time Information system can be allocated to a different assessment period so that only one set of earnings is considered for people who are paid calendar monthly rather than two.
25th Nov 2020 SI 2020/655 NISR 2020/119	New UC run-on for claimants transferring to SPC. UC continues until end of assessment period in which the claimant reaches pension age. In mixed age couples the elder member can claim SPC/HB as a single person on reaching pension age even if some other exclusion applies.
31st Dec 2020/ 1st Jan 2021 SI 2020/1209 SI 2020/1309 SI 2020/1372	End of Brexit transition period ('Implementation Period'). EEA nationals without preserved rights are now subject to immigration control in the same way as non-EEA nationals. EEA nationals with preserved rights can continue to use then during the six months 'grace period' that ends on 30th June 2021. See also entry below for 30th June 2021.
27th Jan 2021 SI 2019/1152 NISR 2019/152	Severe disability gateway condition for migration to UC ends. No new claims by severely disabled persons for legacy benefits who must claim UC instead.
6th Apr 2021 SI 2020/1519 NISR 2021/14	LHA rates frozen during 2021/22 at their April 2020 levels.
6th Apr 2021 SI 2021/162 SI 2021/313 NISR 2021/67 NISR 2021/82	Benefits up-rating based on previous September consumer prices index of 0.5 percent. The extra £86.67 per month (£20 per week) in the UC standard allowances introduced in April 2020 due to coronavirus continues until the end of September 2021.
30th Apr 2021 12th May 2021	Coronavirus-related temporary measures relating to the minimum income floor and to allow prisoners on temporary release to claim UC, expire (see also 12th November entry).
30th Jun 2021/ 1st July 2021	EU settlement scheme closes. EEA nationals who have not registered by 23:00 lose their EEA preserved rights and their immigration status changes to an overstayer. (See also entry above for 31st December 2020/1st January 2021.)

Planned changes

2021 – Jun 2024	'Managed migration' of claimants on legacy benefits onto UC on an area-by-area basis resumes, with transitional protection against losses. Claimants living in supported or temporary accommodation continue to get HB.
2023-24	New exemptions to the LHA shared accommodation rate (table 6.4) to be introduced covering rough sleepers aged 16-24, care leavers up to the age of 25, and victims of domestic abuse and human trafficking (HM Treasury, Budget Red Book 2020, paras 1.190, 2.20).
2024 or later	The transfer of pension age claimants from HB to SPC, with SPC meeting housing costs in a similar way to UC (called 'housing credit').

How decisions are made

1.31　When the DWP makes a decision about your UC or the council makes a decision about your CTR, they should:

(a) identify the facts (paras 1.32-34); and

(b) apply the law to those facts (paras 1.35-37).

Deciding the facts

1.32　The DWP/council should only take account of facts that are relevant to your UC/CTR. For example, whether you qualify, how much you qualify for, and who it should be paid to.

Balance of probability

1.33　When there is a disagreement about the facts or the facts are uncertain, the DWP/council should decide taking into account the weight of evidence each way.

Burden of proof

1.34　When there is no evidence about the facts or where the evidence is balanced equally each way, the DWP/council should decide what the evidence is based on and who has to demonstrate what. For example:

(a) when you make a claim, it is up to you to demonstrate you are entitled;

(b) when you are told an overpayment is recoverable from you, it is up to the DWP/council to demonstrate this.

Applying the law

1.35   The words of Acts of Parliament, regulations, orders, etc have their ordinary English meaning. But:

(a) some words or phrases are defined in the law – for example 'child' and 'young person' (paras 3.63-64);

(b) some law has been interpreted by Upper Tribunals and courts in case law (para 1.28) – for example deciding whether two people are a couple (paras 3.54-57);

(c) the Supreme Court has decided that the DWP/DFC, council/NIHE or a tribunal may disapply a regulation, order, etc (but not an Act of Parliament) if it breaches the Human Rights Act 1998 (RR (AP) v SSWP (2019)).

The footnotes throughout this guide give the details of relevant law and case law.

Judgment

1.36   The law uses terms like 'reasonable' or 'special circumstances' to show that the DWP/council has to make a judgment. Examples include:

(a) whether it is 'reasonable' for the DWP to award UC towards housing costs on two homes if you are in fear of violence (para 5.24);

(b) whether you have 'special circumstances' for a delay in reporting an advantageous change (para 11.15).

Discretion

1.37   A discretion differs from a judgment in the sense that the DWP/council may choose what to do. The law usually says that they 'may' do something to show this. Examples include:

(a) whether to pay part of your UC to your landlord (para 12.30);

(b) what method to use to recover an overpayment of UC (para 13.36).

1.35   RR (AP) v SSWP [2019] UKSC 52
        https://www.bailii.org/uk/cases/UKSC/2019/52.html

Chapter 2 **Who can get universal credit**

- Entitlement and age limits: see paras 2.1-13.
- Students: see paras 2.14-19.
- Migrants, prisoners, hospital detainees and religious orders: see paras 2.20-28.
- Presence in the UK: see paras 2.29-35.
- The claimant commitment, earnings thresholds and limited capability for work: see paras 2.36-50.

Entitlement

2.1   To get UC, you must make a claim and meet the basic conditions in table 2.1. You must also meet the financial conditions (paras 9.3-11).

Table 2.1 **Basic conditions for UC**

(a)   You must be working age (under 66).

(b)   You must be aged 16 or more.

(c)   If you are aged 16 or 17 you must be in an eligible group (table 2.2).

(d)   If you are a student you must be in an eligible group (table 2.3).

(e)   You must not be an excluded migrant (paras 2.20-21).

(f)   You must not be a prisoner, hospital detainee or member of a religious order (paras 2.22-28).

(g)   You must in most cases be in the UK (para 2.29).

(h)   You must accept a claimant commitment if required to do so (para 2.36).

Notes:

- If you are a single person, you must meet all these conditions (para 2.2).
- If you are in a couple, at least one of you must meet all these conditions (paras 2.4).
- If you are severely disabled, see also paras 4.60-66.

T2.1   WRA 4; UC 3(2),(3), Part 2; NIWRO 9; NIUC 3(1),(2), Part 2

UC for single people

2.2   If you are a single person (paras 3.47-48), you must meet all the basic conditions to get UC (table 2.1).

2.3   In this case:

(a) you make the claim (para 3.2);

(b) you get the standard allowance for a single person (para 9.14) plus any elements you and your benefit unit qualify for;

(c) your own income and capital is taken into account (para 10.2).

UC for couples

2.4   If you are a couple (paras 3.49-51), you can usually get UC as a joint claim couple, but in some cases as a single person (paras 2.5-8). For polygamous marriages, see paras 3.60-61.

Joint claim couples

2.5   To get UC as a joint claim couple, you must:

(a) both meet all the basic conditions (table 2.1); or

(b) both meet all those conditions except that (only) one of you is:

- over 66, or
- an excluded student.

2.6   In this case:

(a) you and your partner both make the UC claim (para 3.3);

(b) you get the standard allowance for a couple (para 9.14) plus any elements you and your benefit unit qualify for;

(c) you and your partner's joint income and capital is taken into account (para 10.2).

In a couple but claiming as a single person

2.7   To get UC as a single person:

(a) you must both meet all the basic conditions (table 2.1); except that

(b) your partner (but not you) is:

- a 16/17-year-old who is not in an eligible group, or
- an excluded migrant, or
- a prisoner, hospital detainee or member of a religious order, or
- absent from the UK.

2.2   WRA 1(1),(2), 2(1)(a), 3(1); NIWRO 6(1),(2), 7(1)(a), 8(1)

2.5   WRA 1(1),(2), 2(1)(b), 3(2); UC 3(2); NIWRO 6(1),(2), 7(1)(b), 8(2); NIUC 3(1)

2.7   WRA 1(1),(2), 2(2), 3(1); UC 3(3); NIWRO 6(1),(2), 7(2), 8(1); NIUC 3(2)

2.8   In this case:

(a) only you make the UC claim (para 3.2);

(b) you get the standard allowance for a single person (para 9.14) plus any elements you and your benefit unit qualify for;

(c) you and your partner's joint income and capital is taken into account (para 10.2).

Maximum age

2.9   To get UC, you must be working age (under 66) or in a couple at least one of you must be working age. When you reach 66 (or in a couple, both of you do) you can get SPC (para 11.26).

Minimum age

2.10   To get UC you must have reached the minimum age, or in a couple both of you must have reached the minimum age. This is:

(a) 16 if you are in an eligible group in table 2.2; or

(b) 18 in all other cases.

Table 2.2 **16/17 year olds: the eligible groups**

(a) Your benefit unit includes a child or (if you are in a couple) a young person (para 3.62).

(b) You have limited capacity for work or for work and work-related activity (paras 2.47-49).

(c) You are within:

  ■ 11 weeks before your expected date of confinement during pregnancy, or

  ■ 15 weeks after giving birth (including a still-birth after 24 weeks of pregnancy).

(d) You are a carer and meet the conditions for a carer element (para 9.39), even if you share care (para 9.40).

(e) You are without parental support (para 2.13).

Note: Only (a), (b) and (e) apply to care leavers (paras 2.11-12).

2.9   Pensions Act 1995, sch 4 para 1(6); WRA 4(1)(b),(4); UC 3(2)(a);
         Pensions (Northern Ireland) Order 1995, SI No 3213, sch 2 para 1(7); NIWRO 9(1)(b),(4); NIUC 3(1)(a)

2.10   WRA 4(1)(a),(3); NIWRO 9(1)(a),(3)

T2.2   UC 8(2), 26(3)(b)(ii), 30, sch 4 para 4; NIUC 8(2), 27(3)(b)(ii), 31, sch 4 para 4

16/17-year-old care leavers

2.11   If you are a care leaver aged 16 or 17, you can only get UC if you are in group (a),(b) or (e) in table 2.2. And in these cases your UC only covers your living costs, not your rent or service charges.

2.12   You are a care leaver if:

(a) you were in care (looked after by a local authority) for one or more periods beginning after you reached 14 (in Scotland, following a children's hearing);

(b) one of these periods continued past your 16th birthday; and

(c) the periods totalled at least three months, or (except in Scotland) would have done apart from the fact that on your 16th birthday you were in hospital or detained in an institution under a court order.

But periods of up to one month aren't counted towards the three months if you spent them in respite care and then returned to the care of your parent(s) or the person with parental responsibility for you.

Without parental support

2.13   In table 2.2(e) and table 2.3(f), you are 'without parental support' if you aren't in care but:

(a) you have no parent or guardian (i.e. someone acting in the place of your parent); or

(b) you cannot live with them because:

■   you are estranged from them, or

■   there is a serious risk to your physical or mental health or of significant harm if you did; or

(c) you are living away from them, and they cannot support you financially because they:

■   have a physical or mental impairment, or

■   are detained in custody, or

■   are prohibited from entering or re-entering the UK.

2.11   UC 8(1),(2),(4); NIUC 8(1),(2),(4)

2.12   UC 8(4) definition: 'care leaver'; NIUC 8(4)

2.13   UC a definition: 'looked after by a local authority', 8(1)(g),(3),(4); NIUC 2,8(1)(g),(3),(4)

Students

Who is a student

2.14   You are a student if you are undertaking:

(a)   non-advanced education (para 2.15); or

(b)   full-time advanced education (para 2.16).

The DWP can treat any other course as falling within (a) or (b) if it is incompatible with the work-related requirements in your claimant commitment (para 2.38).

Non-advanced education

2.15   This means:

(a)   education or training up to level 3 (A levels or equivalent) that includes more than 12 hours per week of guided learning during term time;

(b)   but not courses provided under an employment contract or government-sponsored work preparation courses.

Full-time advanced education

2.16   This means:

(a)   full-time education above level 3 (degree or equivalent); and

(b)   any other course for which you get a student loan or grant (para 10.39).

The period you count as a student

2.17   You count as a student from the day you start the course to the day it ends or you abandon it or are dismissed from it. This:

(a)   includes all term-times and vacations within that period; but

(b)   doesn't include periods in which:

- you take time out of your course with the consent of your educational establishment because you are (or have been) ill or caring for someone, and

- you aren't eligible for a student loan or grant.

2.18   You also count as a student:

(a)   until 31st August after your 16th birthday, in all cases; and

(b)   until the 31st August after your 19th birthday, if you began non-advanced education before that birthday.

2.14   UC 12(1),(1A),(2),(4); NIUC 12(1),(2),(4)

2.15   UC 5(1)(b),(2)-(4), 12(1A),(1B) definition: 'relevant training scheme'; NIUC 6(1)(b),(2)-(4)
         https://www.gov.uk/what-different-qualification-levels-mean

2.16   UC 12(2),(3), 68(7); NIUC 12(2),(3), 68(7)

2.17   UC 13; NIUC 13

2.18   UC 5(1),(2); NIUC 6(1),(2)

Which students can get UC

2.19   Table 2.3 shows which students are eligible for UC. If you are an excluded student (a student not in the table), you can't get UC. And if you are in a couple, you can't get UC if both of you are excluded students. But if only one of you is an excluded student, you can get UC as a joint claim couple (para 2.5).

Table 2.3 **Students: the UC eligible groups**

Non-advanced education and full-time education

(a)   Your benefit unit includes a child or young person (para 3.62).

(b)   You have a foster child placed with you.

(c)   You have reached pension age.

(d)   You:

-    have limited capability for work or for work and work-related activity (paras 2.47-49); and

-    are on PIP, DLA, attendance allowance or an equivalent benefit (para 10.37).

(e)   You transferred to UC as part of managed migration (paras 4.22-27) and remain on the same course as on your migration day (para 4.55).

Non-advanced education only

(f)   You:

-    are aged under 21, or aged 21 and reached that age while on your course; and

-    are without parental support (para 2.13).

Migrants, prisoners, detainees and religious orders

Migrants and recent arrivals

2.20   Chapter 20 explains:

(a)   who is a migrant (for example this includes many recent arrivals to the UK);

(b)   which migrants are eligible for UC and which are excluded.

2.21   If you are an excluded migrant, you can't get UC. But if your partner is an excluded migrant and you are not, you can get UC as a single person (para 2.7).

2.19   WRA 4(1)(d),(6); UC 3(2)(b), 13(4), 14; NIWRO 9(1)(d),(6); NIUC 3(1)(b), 13(4), 14

T2.3   UC 2 definition: 'foster parent', 12(3), 14; UCTP 60; NIUC 2, 12(3), 14; NIUCTP 61

2.21   WRA 4(1)(c),(5); UC 3(3)(b),(e), 9; NIWRO 9(1)(c),(5); NIUC 3(2)(b),(e),

Prisoners

2.22   You are a 'prisoner' if you are detained in custody (other than hospital: para 2.27). You can't get UC (except as explained in para 2.24). But if your partner is a prisoner and you are not, you can get UC as a single person (para 2.7).

Prisoners on temporary release

2.23   Since 13th May 2021, you count as a prisoner if you are on temporary release, so the rules about prisoners apply to you (paras 2.22, 2.24). From 8th April 2020 to 12th May 2021, a rule introduced for coronavirus (but which applied in all cases) meant you don't count as a prisoner, so you could get UC in the same way as anyone else.

Single prisoners' housing costs

2.24   You can get a UC housing costs element towards your rent and service charges (para 5.3) for the first six months that you are a prisoner if:

    (a) you had already claimed UC before you became a prisoner; and

    (b) you were entitled to UC as a single person immediately before you became a prisoner (including a couple claiming as a single person: see para 2.7); and

    (c) the calculation of your UC included a UC housing costs element; and

    (d) you haven't yet been sentenced or have been sentenced but aren't expected to serve more than six months.

2.25   When you meet the conditions in para 2.24, your UC is recalculated to include just the housing costs element (paras 9.7-8).

2.26   The law doesn't give specific rules for SMI for single prisoners. But you can only get SMI on a dwelling that is your home (para 5.14), so the DWP is likely to follow similar rules to those in para 2.24.

Hospital detainees

2.27   You are a hospital detainee if you are serving a sentence of imprisonment detained in hospital. You can't get UC (even for housing costs). But if your partner is a hospital detainee and you are not, you can get UC as a single person (para 2.7).

Member of a religious order

2.28   You can't get UC if you are a member of a religious order and are fully maintained by them. But if this applies to your partner and not you, you can get UC as a single person (para 2.7).

2.22   UC 2 definition: 'prisoner'; NIUC 2

2.23   SI 2020/409 regs 2, 6; SI 2020/1156 regs 1,2; NISR 2020/63 regs 2, 6; NISR 2020/227 regs 1,2

2.24   WRA 6(1)(a); UC 3(3)(c), 19(1)(b),(2),(3); NIWRO 11(1)(a); NIUC 3(2)(c), 19(1)(b),(2),(3)

2.25-26 WRA 6(1)(a); UC 3(3)(c), 19(1)(b),(2),(3); NIWRO 11(1)(a); NIUC 3(2)(c), 19(1)(b),(2),(3)

2.27-28 UCTP 2(1) definition: 'severe disability premium', 4A; SI 2019/1152; NIUCTP 2(1), 2B; NISR 2019/152

Presence in the UK

2.29   This section gives the UC basic conditions about being in the UK. This means Great Britain (England, Wales and Scotland) or Northern Ireland, but not the Republic of Ireland, the Channel Islands or the Isle of Man.

2.30   To get UC you must be in the UK. This means you must be physically present here. If you are in a couple, and you are in the UK but your partner is not, you can get UC as a single person (para 2.7). Exceptions to this rule are in paras 2.31-35.

Crown servants and HM Forces

2.31   You do not have to be in the UK to get UC if you are absent for the following reasons, nor does your partner if they are accompanying you:

(a)   you are a Crown servant or member of HM Forces; and

(b)   you are posted overseas to perform your duties; and

(c)   immediately before you were posted overseas you were habitually resident in the UK.

Temporary absence abroad: first month

2.32   If you are on UC, you can continue to get UC during a temporary absence from the UK of up to one month (so long as it is not expected to exceed one month) whatever the reason for your absence – for example you could be on holiday.

Temporary absence abroad: a death in the family

2.33   You can then continue to get UC for up to one further month during a temporary absence from the UK, if your absence is in connection with the death of:

(a)   your partner; or

(b)   a child or young person you or your partner are responsible for; or

(c)   a close relative (table 5.4(k)) of you or one of the above.

But this applies only if the DWP considers it would be unreasonable to expect you to return within the first month.

Temporary absence abroad: medical treatment etc

2.34   If you are on UC, you can continue to get UC during a temporary absence from the UK of up to six months (so long as it is not expected to exceed six months) if your absence is solely in connection with you:

(a)   being treated by (or under the supervision of) a qualified practitioner for an illness or physical or mental impairment; or

(b)   undergoing convalescence or care which results from treatment for an illness or physical or mental impairment which you had before you left the UK; or

---

2.30   WRA 4(1)(c); UC 3(3)(b); NIWRO 9(1)(c); NIUC 3(2)(b), 9

2.31   UC 10; NIUC 10

2.32   UC 11(1)(a),(b)(i); NIUC 11(1)(a),(b)(i)

2.33   UC 11(2); NIUC 11(2)

(c)   accompanying your partner or a child or young person you are responsible for, if their absence is for one of the above reasons.

Temporary absences abroad: mariners etc

2.35   If you are on UC, you can continue to get UC during a temporary absence from the UK of up to six months (so long as it is not expected to exceed six months) if you are:

(a)   a mariner with a UK contract of employment; or

(b)   a continental shelf worker in UK, EU or Norwegian waters.

The claimant commitment

2.36   To get UC you must agree to a claimant commitment, or if you are a joint claim couple you both must, unless:

(a)   you lack the capacity to do so; or

(b)   exceptional circumstances make it unreasonable to expect you to do so.

What a claimant commitment contains

2.37   Your claimant commitment contains your duties (e.g. to tell the DWP about changes in your circumstances) and says which work-related requirements apply to you [www].

Work-related requirements

2.38   You may be required to carry out one or more of the following 'work-related requirements':

(a)   a work search requirement;

(b)   a work availability requirement;

(c)   a work-focused interview requirement;

(d)   a work preparation requirement.

If you fail to carry out a requirement you may be subject to a sanction and you may or may not be able to get UC hardship payments: see paras 9.80-88.

Exceptions to work search and availability requirements

2.39   If you fall within any of the exceptions in table 2.4:

(a)   you don't have to meet any work search or availability requirements; but

(b)   in some cases, you may have to meet work-focused or preparation requirements.

If you are a joint claim couple, the exceptions apply to you separately.

2.34   UC 11(1)(a),(b)(ii),(3),(5); NIUC 11(1)(a),(b)(ii),(3),(5)

2.35   UC 11(1)(a),(b)(ii),(4),(5); NIUC 11(1)(a),(b)(ii),(4),(5)

2.36   WRA 4(1)(e),(7); UC 16; NIWRO 9(1)(e),(7); NIUC 16

2.37   WRA 14(1),(4); UC Part 8; NIWRO 19(1),(4); NIUC Part 8
        www.gov.uk/government/publications/universal-credit-and-your-claimant-commitment-quick-guide

2.38   WRA 14; UC Part 8; NIWRO 19; NIUC Part 8

2.39   As table 2.4

Table 2.4 **No work search or availability requirements**

If you are in any of the groups in this table, you don't have to meet UC work search or availability requirements (paras 2.38-39).

Earnings level, work capability, work preparation, unfit to work	(a) You have earned income above (or equal to) the JSA threshold or in certain cases the minimum income floor (paras 2.41-44). (b) You have limited capability for work, or for work and work-related activity (paras 2.47-49). (c) You are carrying out agreed work preparation. (d) The DWP accepts you are unfit for work. This applies for up to two periods of up to 14 days in any 12 months, or for more periods and/or days if the DWP agrees.
Children, fostering, adoption, pregnancy *If you are in a couple, (e), (f) and usually (g) can only apply to one of you: you jointly choose which of you this is*	(e) You are responsible for a child under three years old; or (for up to 12 months) for a child under 16 whose parents can't care for them and who would otherwise be likely to go into local authority care. (f) You are the foster parent of a child under 16 years old. (g) You have adopted a child under 16 years old and it is within 12 months of the date of adoption (or the date 14 days before the expected date of placement if you request the 12 months to begin then), but this does not apply if you are the child's close relative (table 5.4(k)) or foster parent. (h) You are pregnant and it is no more than 11 weeks before your expected date of confinement, or you were pregnant and it is no more than 15 weeks after your baby's birth (including a still-birth after 24 weeks of pregnancy).
Pension age, carers, students, domestic violence	(i) You have reached pension age. (j) You meet the conditions for a UC carer element, or would do so except that you share your caring responsibilities with someone who gets the carer element instead of you (para 9.40), or you do not do so but the DWP agrees you have similar caring responsibilities

T2.4   (a)   UC 90, 99(6),(6A); NIUC 89, 97(14),(15)   (b)   WRA 19(2)(a), 21(1)(a); NIWRO 24(2)(a), 26(1)(a)
       (c)   UC 99(5)(a); NIUC 97(11)(a)   (d)   UC 99(4),(4ZA),(4ZB),(5)(c); NIUC 97(11)(c)
       (e)   WRA 19(2)(c),(6), 20(1)(a),21(1)(aa); UC 86,91(2)(e),(3);   (f)   UC 2,85,86, 89(1)(f), 91(2)(a)-(d);
             NWRO 24(2)(c),(6), 25(1)(a), 26(5); NIUC 85,90(2)(e),(3),91   NIUC 2,84,85, 88(1)(f), 90(2)(a)-(d)
       (g)   UC 89(1)(d),(3); NIUC 88(1)(d),(3)   (h)   UC 89(1)(c); NIUC 88(1)(c)
       (i)   UC 89(1)(a); NIUC 88(1)(a)   (j)   WRA 19(2)(b); UC 30, 89(1)(b),(2); NIWRO 24(2)(b); NIUC 31, 88(1)(b),(2)

	(k) You are a student and you fall within eligible group (f) in table 2.3, or you have a student loan or grant (other than a part-time postgraduate master's degree loan) and fall within any of the groups in that table.
	(l) You have been a victim of actual or threatened domestic violence within the past six months from a partner, former partner, or family member you are not (or no longer) living with. A 'family member' includes any close relative (table 5.4(k)). It also includes a grandparent, grandchild, step-brother/sister or brother/sister-in-law or, if any of them are in a couple, their partner. This applies for 13 weeks from when you notify the DWP about it, but only if it has not applied to you during the previous 12 months. It can apply for a further 13 weeks if you are responsible for a child
Treatment abroad, drug/alcohol programmes, emergencies etc, death in the family	(m) You are temporarily absent from GB in connection with treatment, convalescence or care for you, your partner or a child or young person, and you meet the conditions in para 2.34.
	(n) You are in an alcohol or drug dependency treatment programme and have been for no more than six months.
	(o) You temporarily have new or increased child care responsibilities (including when a child is affected by death or violence) or are dealing with a domestic emergency, funeral arrangements etc, and the DWP agrees.
	(p) Your partner, or a child or young person you or your partner are responsible for, or a child of yours (even if not included in your benefit unit) has died within the past six months.
Prisoners, court proceedings, police protection, public duties	(q) You are a prisoner claiming UC for housing costs.
	(r) You are attending a court or tribunal as a party to proceedings or witness.
	(s) You are receiving police protection and have been for no more than six months.
	(t) You are engaged in activities which the DWP agrees amount to a public duty.

T2.4   (k)   UC 68(7), 89(1)(da),(e); NIUC 68(7), 88(1)(e)   (l)   UC 98; NIUC 96
        (m) UC 99(3)(c); NIUC 97(6)(c)   (n)   UC 99(3)(e); NIUC 97(6)(e)
        (o)   UC 99(4A)-(4C),(5)(b),(5A); NIUC 97(8)-(10),(11)(b),(12) (p)   UC 99(3)(d); NIUC 97(6)(d)
        (q)   UC 99(3)(b); NIUC 97(6)(b)   (r)   UC 99(3)(a); NIUC 97(6)(a)
        (s)   UC 99(3)(f); NIUC 97(6)(f)   (t)   UC 99(3)(g); NIUC 97(6)(g)

Earnings thresholds

2.40   The main earnings thresholds used in UC are:

   (a)   the JSA threshold;

   (b)   the minimum income floor;

   (c)   the 16-hour threshold.

The JSA threshold

2.41   The JSA threshold uses the main JSA(IB) figures plus £5 for single people or £10 for couples. The current amounts are:

   (a)   £79.70 per week (£345.37 monthly) for single people;

   (b)   £127.40 per week (£552.07 monthly) for couples.

2.42   If your earned income is at or above the JSA threshold:

   (a)   you can get UC without having to meet the work search or work availability requirements (para 2.38(a),(b));

   (b)   you may not qualify for transitional protection if your earnings drop after you transfer to UC (para 4.50).

But if you are in the DWP's work pilot scheme, the minimum income floor applies to (a) and (b) rather than the JSA threshold. This scheme affects a small number of randomly selected UC claimants.

The minimum income floor

2.43   Your minimum income floor is what you would earn (after deductions for tax and national insurance) for working 35 hours a week at the national living wage of £8.91 per hour. If you are a joint claim couple this applies to each of you independently. The current amount is £311.85 per week (£1351 monthly). But the DWP can agree that a lower number of hours (and lower minimum income floor) applies to you if you have a disability, ill health or caring responsibilities for a child or adult.

2.44   If your earned income is at or above the minimum income floor:

   (a)   you can get UC without having to meet any of the work-related requirements (para 2.38(a)-(d));

   (b)   you can't normally be treated as having notional income from self-employment (paras 10.79-80).

The 16-hour threshold

2.45   Your 16-hour threshold is what you would earn for working 16 hours a week at the national living wage of £8.91 per hour. If you are a joint claim couple this applies to each of you independently. The current amount is £142.56 per week (£617 monthly).

2.41-42 UC 99(6),(6A); UCTP 56(2); SI 2015/89 reg 4; NIUC 97(14),(15); NIUCTP 57(2)

2.43-44 UC 88, 90; NIUC 87, 89

2.45-46 UC 41(2),(3), 82(1)(a),(4); NIUC 42(2),(3), 82(1)(a),(4)

2.46   If your earned income is at or above the 16-hour threshold:

(a) you can't get an LCW or LCWRA element (para 9.33);

(b) the benefit cap doesn't apply to you (para 9.74).

Limited capability for work

2.47   You have:

(a) 'limited capability for work' (LCW) if your ability to work is limited by ill-health or disability;

(b) 'limited capability for work and work-related activity' (LCWRA) if your ability to work and carry out work-related activity is limited by ill-health or disability.

The work capability elements distinguish between LCW and LCWRA (paras 9.29-32) but for all other purposes LCW includes LCWRA.

Who qualifies

2.48   The DWP decides whether you have LCW or LCWRA (or neither of these) as follows:

(a) if you have one of the medical conditions in table 2.5, you automatically qualify;

(b) if you were on ESA, SDA, IB or IS when you claimed UC, a decision in that benefit also applies for UC (para 9.38);

(c) if you reclaim UC after a break of no more than six months, a decision that applied before the break continues to apply after it;

(d) in any other case, the DWP carries out a work capability assessment (para 2.49).

The DWP changes its decision if your medical condition or capability for work changes (paras 11.24-25).

Work capability assessments

2.49   To get a work capability assessment you have to provide the DWP with a doctor's certificate or other medical evidence. The assessment looks at whether and to what extent you can carry out a fixed list of activities and often includes a medical examination.

How LCW and LCWRA affect your UC

2.50   If you have LCW or LCWRA:

(a) you can get UC without having to meet the work search or availability requirements (para 2.38);

(b) you can get UC if you are under 18 or a student (tables 2.2 and 2.3);

(c) you may qualify for an LCW or LCWRA element in your UC (paras 9.31-32);

(d) you qualify for a UC work allowance (para 10.11).

2.47-50 UC 27(3), 38-44, schs 6, 7; UCTP 19, 20, 20A, 21-27; NIUC 28(3), 40-45, schs 6, 7; NIUCTP 19-28

Table 2.5 **Limited capability for work: medical conditions**

You don't have to have a work capability assessment when these apply (para 2.48).

Limited capability for work (LCW)

(a) You are receiving, or recovering from, treatment for haemodialysis, plasmapheresis or total parietal nutrition.

(b) You are receiving, or recovering from, in-patient treatment in hospital or similar institution.

(c) You are prevented from working by law, for reasons relating to possible infection or contamination.

(d) You have a condition that is life threatening or could cause substantial physical or mental health risk to others.

(e) You are a joint claim couple, and one of you is over pension age and is entitled to PIP or DLA.

Limited capability for work and work-related activity (LCWRA)

(f) You are terminally ill (para 9.37).

(g) You are pregnant and there is a serious risk of damage to you or your baby's health.

(h) You are receiving chemotherapy or radiotherapy for cancer, or likely to receive it within six months, or recovering from it.

(i) You are a joint claim couple, and one of you is over pension age and is entitled to:

- the daily living component of PIP,
- the highest rate of the care component of DLA,
- attendance allowance, or
- armed forces independence payment.

Chapter 3 **UC claims**

- Making a claim: see paras 3.1-11.
- How to claim: see paras 3.12-18.
- Information and evidence: see paras 3.19-29.
- Start dates and backdating: see paras 3.30-37.
- Assessment periods and reclaims: see paras 3.38-45.
- Your benefit unit: see paras 3.46-69.
- Non-dependants: see paras 3.70-77.

Making a claim

3.1 You can only get UC if:

(a) you make a claim for it (paras 3.2-3); or

(b) you are treated as having claimed it (paras 3.4-7); or

(c) someone claims it on your behalf (paras 3.8-11).

Claiming as a single person

3.2 You make your claim yourself if:

(a) you are a single person (para 2.2); or

(b) you are in a couple but claiming as a single person (para 2.7);

(c) in some cases, you are in a polygamous marriage (para 3.61).

You (or a person claiming on your behalf) must provide information and evidence about your claim. In cases (b) and (c) this includes your partner's circumstances.

Claiming as a couple (joint claimants)

3.3 You make your claim jointly with your partner if:

(a) you are a joint claim couple (para 2.5); or

(b) in some cases, you are in a polygamous marriage (para 3.61).

Both of you (or a person claiming on your behalf) must provide information and evidence about your claim.

3.1   AA 1,5; NIAA 1,5

3.2   WRA 2(1)(a),(2); UC 3(3),(4); NIWRO 7(1)(a),(2); NIUC 3(2),(3)

3.3   WRA 2(1)(b),(2); UC 3(4); NIWRO 7(1)(b),(2); NIUC 3(3)

If you should have claimed as a couple or as a single person

3.4   The DWP:

(a) can treat you as having claimed UC as a couple if:

- ▪ you each made a claim as a single person, but

- ▪ the DWP decides you are a couple;

(b) must treat you as having claimed UC as a single person if:

- ▪ you made a claim as a couple, but

- ▪ you are only eligible for UC as a single person (para 2.7).

If you become a couple or a single person

3.5   UC continues without you having to make a new claim when:

(a) you become a couple; and

(b) you or your partner (or both of you) have been getting UC (either as a single person or as a couple with someone else); and

(c) you qualify for UC based on your new circumstances.

This also applies when you are a couple but have (until now) only been eligible for UC as a single person (para 2.7).

3.6   And UC continues without you having to make a new claim when:

(a) you become a single person; and

(b) you have been getting UC as a couple; and

(c) you qualify for UC based on your new circumstances.

This applies whether your relationship has ended or your partner has died. It also applies when you are a couple but are now only eligible as a single person (para 2.7).

3.7   In all these cases (paras 3.5-6), the law treats you as having made a claim. You still have to tell the DWP your new financial and other circumstances (para 3.21).

If you are unable to act: attorneys, appointees, etc

3.8   The following may act on your behalf in connection with your UC [www]:

(a) a person who has power of attorney for you;

(b) a deputy appointed for you by the Court of Protection;

(c) a receiver appointed for you;

(d) in Scotland, a judicial factor or any guardian acting or appointed for you.

3.4   C&P 9(1)-(4); NIC&P 8(1)-(4)

3.5-7   C&P 9(6),(8)(a),(10); NIC&P 8(6),(8)(a),(10); SI 2014/2887 reg 5

3.8   General law about incapacity etc
         See DWP, Agents, appointees, attorneys, deputies and third parties: staff guide – https://tinyurl.com/Unable-to-Act

3.9   The DWP can appoint someone to act on your behalf in connection with your UC (known as an 'appointee') if:

(a) they apply in writing to do so (for example in a letter or online); and

(b) unless they are a firm or organisation, they are over 18 years old; and

(c) you do not have an attorney etc (para 3.8).

They can be someone who already acts on your behalf in connection with HB or a social security benefit. DWP guidance [www] suggests an appointee is appropriate if you have a 'mental incapacity or severe physical disability', but the law does not restrict it to these circumstances.

3.10   Your appointee has all the rights you have in connection with UC, including making a claim, receiving payments, and requesting a reconsideration or appeal. They continue to act on your behalf until:

(a) they resign their appointment (they must give the DWP one month's written notice); or

(b) the DWP ends their appointment; or

(c) the DWP is notified that you now have an attorney etc (para 3.8).

If your partner is unable to act

3.11   If you are claiming UC as a couple and your partner is unable to claim jointly with you, you can make the UC claim yourself on behalf of both of you.

How to claim

3.12   You can make your claim for UC:

(a) online; or

(b) by telephone if the DWP agrees to this.

Once you have submitted a claim you may subsequently be asked to provide evidence to confirm information you have given, to attend an interview, and to agree to conditions set out in a claimant commitment (paras 2.36-39). If you don't, your claim will be treated as 'closed' and no action taken on it ([2020] UKUT 109 (AAC)). Citizens Advice can help with UC claims (para 12.15).

Online claims

3.13   Online claims are made to the DWP [www]. The website tells you what information you should have before you start the claim process. The DWP says that 'you need to allow up to 40 minutes for your online application because you must complete it in one session' [www]. Depending on your circumstances the DWP can provide you with assistance to do this in a DWP office or in your home. Your local council may also be able to help you with claiming UC.

3.9   C&P 2(1) definition: 'writing', 57(1)-(3),(6); UCTP 16; NIC&P 2(1),52(1)-(3),(6); NIUCTP 15
http://tinyurl.com/OG-Appointees

3.10   C&P 57(4),(5),(7),(8); NIC&P 52(4),(5),(7),(8)

3.11   C&P 9(5); NIC&P 8(5)

3.12   C&P 8(1),(2), 35; NIC&P 7(1),(2),34

3.13   C&P 8(1), sch 2; NIC&P 7(1), sch 1
www.gov.uk/apply-universal-credit

Telephone claims

3.14   The DWP can agree to accept a telephone claim from particular groups of claimants or in individual cases. If you are not able to go online yourself you can contact an adviser on 0800 328 5644 or text phone 0800 328 1344 between 8am and 6pm, Monday to Friday (closed on bank and public holidays). Note if the call 'ends suddenly it is up to you to call back'.

Completing your claim

3.15   An online claim is properly completed if you use the online claim form and follow the instructions. You must also submit it and log out ([2020] UKUT 108 (AAC)). A telephone claim is properly completed if you provide all the information needed to decide your claim during the call. You may also be required to provide appropriate authentication of your identity and other information, and maintain records of your claim.

Completing a defective claim

3.16   The DWP must tell you if your claim is defective, in other words a claim that doesn't meet the conditions in para 3.15. In these cases:

(a) if it is an online claim, you should re-submit the claim with the missing information, etc, now included;

(b) if it is a telephone claim, you need only provide the information, etc, that was missing.

If you do this within one month of when you were first informed that your claim was defective, or longer if the DWP considers it reasonable, your claim counts as having being made on the date you originally made it.

Deciding your claim

3.17   The DWP must decide whether you qualify for UC and send you a decision about this (para 14.5).

Amending or withdrawing a claim

3.18   Before the DWP decides your claim you can:

(a) amend it: the DWP then decides your claim on the amended basis; or

(b) withdraw it: the DWP then takes no further action on your claim.

You can amend or withdraw a claim by writing to the DWP (online or in a letter, etc), by telephoning them, or in any other way they agree to.

3.14   C&P 8(2); NIC&P 7(1)

3.15   C&P 8(1),(4), sch 2 para 2; NIC&P 7(1),(4), sch 1 para 2

3.16   C&P 8(3)-(6); NIC&P 7(3)-(6)

3.18   C&P 2(1) definition: 'writing', 30, 31; NIC&P 2(1),29,30

Information and evidence

What you should provide

3.19 You have to provide the DWP with information and evidence about whether you qualify, how much you qualify for, and who it should be paid to. This duty applies:

(a) when you make a UC claim;

(b) when your circumstances change; and

(c) when you are overpaid.

If you are a couple this applies to both of you, even if you are claiming UC as a single person; and information one of you provides can be given to the other.

The information the DWP needs

3.20 The DWP must tell you what information and evidence it needs, and whether you should provide it online, by telephone, or personally by attending the DWP office. If you are making a claim you should provide the information within one month from when the DWP first requests it, or longer if the DWP considers it reasonable (para 3.16).

3.21 The DWP needs to know the following:

(a) your income (paras 3.23-26) and capital;

(b) your rent and service charges (para 3.27);

(c) your national insurance number (para 3.28), child benefit number (if appropriate), and details of your bank or similar account;

(d) who is in your benefit unit (para 3.46);

(e) the details of any non-dependants in your home (para 3.70).

Using monthly figures

3.22 In a break from the weekly tradition of state benefits, UC is a monthly benefit. The 'whole month' approach simplifies administration of UC, and avoids numerous changes to your UC if your circumstances change a lot (paras 3.40-41). UC assessment periods are monthly (para 3.38), as are UC allowances and other figures used in the calculation. The DWP must assess your income and rent on a monthly basis, as explained in the following paragraphs.

Monthly earnings

3.23 If you are an employee and are paid monthly, the DWP uses monthly figures when they are paid. But if your payments are shifted (e.g. to avoid a non-banking day such as a weekend or public holiday) you may receive two payments in the same assessment period. In this case the DWP should reallocate the shifted payment to ensure only one payment is taken into account in each of your assessment periods (ADM memo 27/20). The DWP can't apply the rule automatically, so you normally need to ask them to do so each time this situation arises.

3.19 C&P 37(1),(2),(4),(5),(8),(9), 38(1),(2),(6); NIC&P 36(1),(2),(4),(5),(8),(9), 37(1),(2),(6)

3.20 C&P 35, 37(3), 38(3); NIC&P 34, 36(3), 37(3)

3.23 UC 61(6); NIUC 62(6)

Weekly and other non-monthly earnings

3.24   If you are an employee and are paid weekly, or on any other non-monthly basis, the payments aren't averaged out in any way. Instead the DWP adds together all the payments you receive in each assessment period (para 10.22), even if they include a payment for work you did in the past ([2018] UKUT 332 (AAC)). There are two problems:

    (a) If you are paid weekly, some assessment periods contain four pay days, and some contain five. So, your UC is lower in a month with five pay days than in a month with four. Or your level of income may mean that you don't qualify for UC at all in a month with five pay days. If this happens, you have to reclaim UC. This should be fairly straightforward, because your assessment periods are kept 'open' for six months in these cases (paras 3.42 and 10.13-14).

    (b) If you are paid four-weekly, one assessment period each year has two pay days. The High Court has decided that it is irrational for both to be taken into account (R (Pontelerisco and others) v SSWP) and the DWP is likely to issue new guidance about this.

Self-employed earnings

3.25   If you are self-employed, you have to give the DWP monthly figures for your income and outgoings (para 10.30).

Unearned income

3.26   If your state benefits or other unearned income are paid weekly, or on any other non-monthly basis, they are converted to a monthly figure (para 10.33).

Rent and service charges

3.27   You should provide details of your rent and service charges (para 5.3) and evidence of these (e.g. your letting agreement); or if you can't, the DWP can make an estimate. In practice:

    (a) if you are a social renter, the DWP needs separate figures for rent and services – your landlord can help with this or may give the information to the DWP for you;

    (b) if you are a private renter, the DWP needs one figure for rent and services.

If these are due weekly or on any other non-monthly basis, they are converted to a monthly figure (para 9.59).

National insurance number

3.28   To get UC, you have to give your national insurance number and, if you are claiming as a couple, your partner's. If you don't know it, you must assist the DWP in finding out what it is, or if you don't have one you must apply for one. You should normally apply via the DWP using your online account.

3.24   R (Pontelerisco and other) v SSWP [2020] EWHC 1944 (Admin) www.bailii.org/ew/cases/EWHC/Admin/2020/1944.html

3.27   DBA 39((1),(4); NIDBA 39((1),(4)

3.28   AA 1(1A); C&P 5; NIAA 1(1A); NIC&P 5

Information from a third party

3.29   The DWP can require:

(a) your landlord to provide information and evidence about your rent or related matters;

(b) your childcare provider to supply information and evidence relating to the UC childcare costs element (para 9.47);

(c) a person you are caring for to confirm information relating to the UC carer element (paras 9.39-40);

(d) a pension fund holder to provide information (para 10.82);

(e) a rent officer to provide information (para 6.19).

They have one month to do this, or longer if the DWP considers it reasonable.

Examples: Claims, changes and UC assessment periods

1. A claim

Mason claims UC on 5th May and the DWP decides he qualifies for £375 per month.

- His first assessment period starts on 5th May. He should receive UC of £375 for this assessment period by about 12th June (para 12.10).

- His following assessment periods start on the 5th of each month.

2. A rent increase

Mason's rent goes up on 1st August, and the DWP increases his UC.

- His UC increases for the whole of his assessment period starting on 5th July, and for his following assessment periods.

3. An increase in unearned income

Mason's unearned income increases on 29th October, and the DWP reduces his UC.

- His UC reduces for the whole of his assessment period starting on 5th October, and for his following assessment periods.

4. Weekly earned income with frequent UC reclaims

Margaret is on UC and qualifies for a standard allowance of £324.84 before her earnings are taken into account. She has net earnings of £120.00 per week which are paid to her each Saturday. She doesn't qualify for a work allowance.

- In assessment periods with four Saturdays her net earnings are £480.00. Her UC is reduced by 63% of this (para 9.8), which is £302.40, so she gets UC of £22.44 for that assessment period.

- In assessment periods with five Saturdays her net earnings are £600.00. Her UC is reduced by 63% of this, which is £378.00, so her UC is nil for that assessment period.

- This means that at the end of each assessment period with five Saturdays she has to reclaim UC (para 3.24(a)).

3.29   C&P 37(6),(7), 38(7)-(9), 41; NIC&P 36(6),(7), 37(7)-(9), 38

UC start dates and backdating

Your UC start date

3.30   Your UC starts on your date of claim (paras 3.31-32) except when you make an advance claim, qualify for backdating, or reclaim within six months (paras 3.33-37, 3.43). There are also exceptions when you migrate to UC (chapter 4). Chapter 12 explains when your UC is paid.

Your UC date of claim

3.31   Your date of claim is:

(a) the date the DWP received your properly completed claim (para 3.15); or

(b) the date the DWP received your defective claim if you then complete it within the time allowed (para 3.16).

3.32   There are two further rules:

(a) if you receive assistance making an online claim (para 3.13), your date of claim is the day you first notified the DWP of your need for assistance;

(b) if you phone the DWP to make a claim (para 3.14) but they can't take your call until a later date, your date of claim is the day of the first phone call if the later date is within one month.

Advance claims

3.33   If you do not qualify for UC when you claim but will do so within one month, the date of claim is the day you first qualify. The DWP can agree to apply this rule for particular groups of claimants or individual cases.

3.34   You can also choose to claim UC from a date in the future, for example if you claim in advance of losing a job or some other event. In this case, your date of claim is the day you are claiming from.

Backdating

3.35   'Backdating' means you get UC for a period before you claimed it. UC law calls this 'extending the time limit for claiming'.

3.36   You qualify for backdating if:

(a) one or more of the circumstances in table 3.1 applies to you; and

(b) as a result, you 'could not reasonably have been expected to make the claim earlier'.

If you are a joint claim couple (para 2.5), one or more of the circumstances in the table must apply to each of you (and (b) above must apply).

3.30   C&P 26(1); NIC&P 25(1)

3.31   C&P 10(1)(a),(c),(2); NIC&P 9(1)(a),(c),(2)

3.32   C&P 2(1) definition 'appropriate office', 10(1)(b),(d),(2); NIC&P 2(1), 9(1)(b),(d)

3.33   C&P 32; NIC&P 31

3.34   C&P 10(1); NIC&P 9(1)

3.35   C&P 26(2); NIC&P 25(2)

3.36   C&P 26(2)(a),(b),(4); NIC&P 25(2),(a),(b),(4)

Backdating time limit

3.37   Your UC can be backdated for up to one month, and your UC starts on the day your UC is backdated to. For example, if you claim UC on 25th January, it can be backdated to 25th December.

Table 3.1 **Backdating UC: qualifying circumstances**

To qualify for backdating one or more of the following must have meant you could not reasonably have claimed UC earlier.

(a) You were previously on JSA(IB), JSA(C), ESA(IR), ESA(C), IS, HB, CTC or WTC, and you were not told about the ending of that benefit until after it had ended.*

(b) You have a disability.

(c) You had an illness that prevented you from making a claim and you have given the DWP medical evidence that confirms this.

(d) You were unable to make a claim on-line because the official computer system wasn't working.

(e) You were in a couple and the DWP decided not to award you UC (or ended your UC) because your partner didn't accept the claimant commitment, and you are now making a claim as a single person.

* Note: If you are claiming UC because of moving to a new area (para 4.17(f)), you count as being told about your HB ending when your new local council tells you that you can no longer claim HB ([2020] UKUT 309 (AAC)).

Example: Backdating UC

A single person gets a letter from her local council on 9th February saying her HB will end on 14th February. She is blind, and the friend who normally reads her letters to her is away on holiday from 7th to 21st February. He reads the letter to her on 22nd February. She makes an online claim for UC that day and qualifies for UC. She asks the DWP to backdate her UC.

The DWP's decision: The DWP agrees that from 9th February she meets the conditions for qualifying for backdated UC as follows.

Qualifying circumstances: Her circumstances do not fall within (a) in table 3.1, because the council notified her before her HB ended. But they do fall within (b) in the table, because she has a disability.

Ability to claim earlier: Her blindness, and the unavailability of her friend, meant she could not reasonably have been expected to claim UC earlier.

3.37   C&P 26(2); NIC&P 25(2)

T3.1(a)   C&P 26(3)(a),(aa); UCTP 2(1) definition: 'existing benefits', 15(2); NIC&P 25(3)(a),(aa); NIUCTP 2(1), 14(2)

T3.1(b)-(d) and (f)   C&P 26(3)(b)-(d) and (f)-(g) respectively; NIC&P 25(3)(b)-(f)

T3.1(e)   C&P 26(3)(e); SI 2014/2887 reg 5

Assessment periods and reclaims

Your assessment periods

3.38   UC is calculated and paid for monthly assessment periods, with different people's assessment periods beginning on different days of the month. Yours are decided as follows:

(a) your first assessment period begins on the day your UC starts (para 3.30);

(b) after that, they begin on the same day of each following month, with adjustments for the ends of months (table 3.2).

Table 3.2 **UC assessment periods**

If your first assessment period starts on the day of the month in column 1, your following assessment periods start on the day of the month in column 2 (a), (b) or (c).

1 – Start of first assessment period	2 – Start of following assessment periods		
	(a) Except February	(b) February not in a leap year	(c) February in a leap year
1st to 28th	Same as 1	Same as 1	Same as 1
29th	29th	27th	28th
30th	30th	27th	28th
31st	Last day (30th or 31st)	28th	29th

Assessment periods if your start date changes

3.39   Your UC start date can change due to backdating (para 3.37) or because the DWP used the wrong date. When this happens, the DWP can change the start date of:

(a) all your assessment periods (so they are still one month); or

(b) just the first assessment period (so that it is longer or shorter than one month).

In the second case, your UC is calculated on a daily basis.

Assessment periods when your circumstances change

3.40   When your circumstances change:

(a) your assessment periods don't change; but

(b) in most cases (table 11.1) your new amount of UC is awarded from the first day of the assessment period in which the change takes place; or

(c) if you stop qualifying for UC, your UC ends from the first day of that assessment period.

3.38-39 WRA 7; UC 21(1),(2), 21A; SI 2014/2887; NIWRO 12; NIUC 22(1)-(3), 22A

T3.2   UC 21(2); NIUC 22(2)

3.41   This can affect you financially:

(a) you gain if a change that increases your UC takes place near the end of your assessment period, because the new amount is paid from the first day; but

(b) you lose if a change that reduces (or ends) your UC takes place near the end of your assessment period, because the new amount (or no UC) is paid from the first day.

Keeping the same assessment periods

3.42   Your assessment periods continue with the same start date when:

(a) you become a couple or a single person while you are on UC (paras 3.5-7); or

(b) your other circumstances change while you are on UC (paras 3.40-41); or

(c) you are awarded UC within six months of it stopping because your earnings were too high (paras 10.13-15); or

(d) you reclaim UC within six months for other reasons (para 3.43).

If each case, if you have become a couple and each of you previously had different assessment periods, the DWP uses the assessment periods of whichever of you means your UC starts or increases earlier.

Reclaiming UC within six months

3.43   If you reclaim UC within six months of your (or your partner's) UC ending, you can do so by logging on to your online account. This normally allows you to reclaim more quickly. If you do this:

(a) your assessment periods continue with the same start dates; and

(b) your UC starts at the beginning of the assessment period that contains the date you reclaimed.

Before 20th May 2020 there were further rules about reclaiming when you stop receiving earnings, but these have been superseded by the six-month review period in paras 10.13-14.

Reclaiming UC after six months

3.44   If you claim UC more than six months after your (or your partner's) UC ended, the normal UC rules apply (paras 3.30, 3.38).

Duration of your UC award

3.45   There is no fixed time limit for an award of UC. It continues until:

(a) you stop qualifying for it (para 2.1); or

(b) you stop providing the information and evidence showing you qualify (para 11.2).

3.42   UC 21(3)-(3D); C&P 32A; NIUC 22(4)-(8); NIC&P 31A

3.43   UC 21(3C),(3D); C&P 26(5), 32A; 22(7),(8); NIC&P 25(5), 31A

Your benefit unit

3.46   This section explains who is included in your 'benefit unit'. Your entitlement to UC is based on this (para 9.4)

Single people

3.47   For UC purposes you are a 'single person' if you are not in a couple.

3.48   If you are a single person, your benefit unit is:

(a) you; and

(b) any children or young persons you are responsible for.

Couples

3.49   For UC purposes you are a 'couple' if you are two people who are members of the same household (para 3.52) and are:

(a) a married couple or civil partners; or

(b) living together as a married couple or civil partners (para 3.54).

3.50   If you are claiming UC as a joint claim couple (para 2.5), your benefit unit is:

(a) both of you; and

(b) any children or young persons either (or both) of you are responsible for.

3.51   If you are in a couple but claiming UC as a single person (para 2.7), your benefit unit is:

(a) you; and

(b) any children or young persons you are responsible for.

Members of the same household

3.52   You are only a couple for UC purposes if you are members of the same household. (This applies to married couples and civil partners as well as couples who are living together: [2014] UKUT 186 (AAC).) You are not a couple if you:

(a) live in different dwellings and maintain them as separate homes (R(SB) 4/83); or

(b) live in the same dwelling but lead separate lives rather than living as one household (CIS/072/1994).

And you cannot be a member of two (or more) households at the same time (R(SB) 8/85).

3.47   WRA 40; NIWRO 46

3.48   WRA 1(2)(a), 9(1)(a), 10(1); NIWRO 6(2)(a), 14(1)(a), 15(1)

3.49   WRA 39, 40; UC 2 definition: 'partner'; NIWRO 45, 46; NIUC 2

3.50   WRA 1(2)(b), 9(1)(b), 10(1); NIWRO 6(2)(b), 14(1)(b), 15(1)

3.51   WRA 1(2)(a), 2(2), 9(1)(a), 10(1); NIWRO 6(2)(a), 2(2), 14(1)(a), 15(1)

3.52   WRA 39(1)(a),(c); NIWRO 45(1)(a),(c)

3.53   A 'household' generally means a domestic arrangement involving two or more people who live together as a unit (R(IS) 1/99), even when they have a reasonable level of independence and self-sufficiency (R(SB) 8/85). It requires a settled course of daily living rather than visits from time to time (R(F) 2/81). So if you keep your eating, cooking, food storage, finances (including paying your housing costs), living space and family life separate you are unlikely to be members of the same household.

Living together

3.54   If you are not married or in a civil partnership you are only a couple for UC purposes if you are living together as though you were. This means considering:

(a) your purpose in living together (Crake and Butterworth v the Supplementary Benefit Commission); and

(b) if your purpose is unclear, your relationship and living arrangements.

3.55   What matters is your relationship as a whole (R(SB) 17/81) taking account of the following factors (Crake case and [2013] UKUT 505 (AAC)):

(a) whether you share the same household;

(b) the stability of your relationship;

(c) your financial arrangement;

(d) whether you have a sexual relationship;

(e) whether you share responsibility for a child;

(f) whether you publicly acknowledge you are a couple;

(g) the emotional element of your relationship.

The last two points were emphasised in [2014] UKUT 17 (AAC), which held that 'a committed loving relationship must be established and publicly acknowledged'.

3.56   There are many reasons why two people might live in the same household or same dwelling. They might be a couple. But they might be landlord/lady and lodger, house sharers, etc. Even living together for reasons of 'care, companionship and mutual convenience' does not by itself mean you are a couple (R(SB) 35/85).

Ending a relationship

3.57   If you were a couple but your relationship has ended, your shared understanding that it has ended and your actual living arrangement are more important than any shared responsibilities and financial arrangements you still have (CIS/72/1994). But if you remain married or in a civil partnership, a shared understanding may not be enough by itself to show you are no longer a couple (CIS/2900/1998).

3.54   WRA 39(1)(b),(d),(2); NIWRO 45(1)(b),(d),(2); Crake and Butterworth v SBC 21/07/80 QBD 1982 1 ALL ER 498

If your partner is temporarily absent

3.58   If your partner is temporarily absent from your household you continue to count as a couple, unless their absence exceeds or is expected to exceed six months.

3.59   This means you stop counting as a couple if and when your partner:

(a) decides not to return or decides to be absent for more than six months (whether they decide this at the beginning of the absence or during it); or

(b) has been absent for six months

For absences outside the UK see paras 2.29-35.

Polygamous marriages

3.60   For UC purposes you are in a 'polygamous marriage' if you or your husband or wife are married to more than one person under the laws of a country which permits polygamy.

3.61   The members of the polygamous marriage who live in your household can get UC as follows:

(a) the two who were married earliest count as a couple;

(b) each other person in the marriage counts as a single person.

The earlier rules about entitlement to UC and the benefit unit then apply (paras 3.46-51).

Children and young persons

3.62   Your benefit unit includes the children and young persons:

(a) you are responsible for, if you are:

- a single person, or

- in a couple but claiming UC as a single person;

(b) you or your partner are responsible for, if you are:

- in a joint claim couple.

3.63   A 'child' means someone under the age of 16.

3.64   A 'young person' means someone aged 16 or more but under 20 (other than your partner) who:

(a) is in non-advanced education (para 2.15); and

(b) is not on UC, ESA, JSA, HB, CTC or WTC.

3.58   UC 3(6); NIUC 3(5)

3.60   UC 3(5); NIUC 3(4)

3.61   UC 3(4); NIUC 3(3)

3.62   WRA 10(1); NIWRO 15(1)

3.63   WRA 40; NIWRO 46

3.64   WRA 10(5); UC 4(3), 5(1),(5); UCTP 28; NIWRO 15(5); NIUC 4(3), 5(1),(5)

Responsibility for a child or young person

3.65   For UC purposes you are responsible for a child or young person if he or she:

(a) normally lives with you (paras 3.66-67); and

(b) is not a foster child or being looked after by a local authority (para 3.68); and

(c) is not a prisoner (para 2.22).

3.66   Whether a child or young person 'normally lives with you' is a question of fact and is usually straightforward. For example they could be your son or daughter, adopted by you, a step-child, a grandchild or any other child or young person (whether related to you or not), so long as they normally live with you.

3.67   A child or young person can only be the responsibility of one single person or couple at any one time. If they normally live with two or more single persons or couples, they are the responsibility of the single person or couple with the main responsibility. This is decided taking account of all the circumstances, not just who receives the child benefit or the amount of time spent at each address ([2018] UKUT 44 (AAC)). You can choose ('nominate') who this is to be. But the DWP makes the choice instead if:

(a) you do not choose or cannot agree; or

(b) your choice does not reflect the arrangements between you.

Fostering, pre-adoption and local authority care

3.68   A child or young person is not included in your benefit unit if he or she:

(a) is placed with you as a foster child (also called 'kinship care'); or

(b) is placed with you prior to adoption (but an adopted child is included in your benefit unit); or

(c) is in local authority care, unless this is a planned short-term break to give you time off from caring for them, or one of a series of such breaks.

If a child or young person is temporarily absent

3.69   If a child or young person you are responsible for is temporarily absent from your household they continue to be included in your benefit unit, unless their absence exceeds or is expected to exceed:

(a) six months if they remain in Great Britain during the absence;

(b) one month if they are outside Great Britain;

(c) one further month if they remain outside Great Britain and this is in connection with the death of their close relative (table 5.4(k)) and it would be unreasonable for them to be expected to return within the first month;

(d) six months if they are outside Great Britain in connection with treatment, convalescence or care which meets the conditions in para 2.34.

3.65   UC 4(1),(2),(6); NIUC 4(1),(2),(6)

3.67   UC 4(4),(5); NIUC 4(4),(5)

3.68   UC 2 definition: 'looked after by a local authority', 4(6), 4A; NIUC 2, 4(6), 5

3.69   UC 4(7); NIUC 4(7)

Non-dependants

3.70   This section explains who counts as a non-dependant. If you are a renter or shared owner and have one or more non-dependants living with you, this can affect the amount of UC you get for your housing costs (paras 7.8 and 9.63).

Who is a non-dependant

3.71   A 'non-dependant' is anyone who:

(a) normally lives in the accommodation with you; and

(b) is not in any of the groups in table 3.3.

For example, a non-dependant is usually an adult son, daughter, other relative or friend who lives with you on a non-commercial basis, whether they are single or in a couple.

Table 3.3 **People who are not non-dependants**

(a) You and your partner, whether you are claiming UC as a couple or as a single person.

(b) Any child or young person (para 3.73).

(c) A foster child placed with you or your partner (para 3.68).

(d) A resident landlord/landlady and members of their household.

(e) Anyone who is liable to make payments on a commercial basis on the accommodation including:

- a lodger of yours (paras 3.74-75)

- a joint tenant (you rent the accommodation jointly) (para 3.76)

- a separate tenant of your landlord's (the accommodation is rented out in separate lettings).

(f) A non-dependant of anyone described in (e) above (para 3.77).

'Normally living in the accommodation with you'

3.72   To count as a non-dependant a person must 'normally live in the accommodation with you'. For example:

(a) someone who shares essential living accommodation with you, even if you each have your own bedroom, is likely to count as 'living with you' (CH/542/2006, CH/3656/2005); but

(b) a short-term visitor does not count as 'normally' living with you. Nor does a regular or frequent visitor whose normal home is elsewhere – in the UK or abroad ([2018] UKUT 75 (AAC)). Nor does someone you take in temporarily because they have nowhere else to go (CH/4004/2004), though this may change as time goes by (CH/3935/2007).

3.71   UC sch 4 paras 3, 9(1),(2); NIUC sch 4 paras 3, 8(1),(2)

T3.3   UC sch 4 paras 3, 9; NIUC sch 4 paras 3, 8

Non-dependants and children/young persons

3.73 A child or young person (paras 3.63-64) never counts as a non-dependant, whether you, your partner, anyone else or no-one is responsible for them. The only exception is that a child or young person of a non-dependant counts as a non-dependant (and this can be relevant to the size criteria: para 7.14).

Non-dependants and lodgers

3.74 If you have a lodger who pays you rent on a commercial basis, the lodger does not count as a non-dependant.

3.75 The difference between a lodger and a non-dependant is as follows:

(a) a lodger is someone who makes payments to you on a commercial basis (table 5.5(a));

(b) a non-dependant may or may not pay their way. If they do pay you, it is on a non-commercial basis.

Non-dependants and joint tenants

3.76 If you rent your accommodation jointly, your joint tenants are not your non-dependants. For example, if two sisters, a father and son, three friends (and so on) are joint tenants, they are not non-dependants of each other.

3.77 If you jointly rent your accommodation and there is also a non-dependant living there, the non-dependant is included in the UC claim of only one of the joint tenants, as follows:

(a) the non-dependant may normally live with only one of the joint tenants. In that case, they are included in the UC claim of only that joint tenant;

(b) the non-dependant may normally live with more than one of the joint tenants. In that case, once they have been included in the UC claim of one joint tenant they are not included in the UC claim of any of the others.

3.73   UC sch 4 para 9(1)(b),(2)(a),(c),(g); NIUC sch 4 para 8(1)(b),(2)(a),(c),(g)

3.74   UC sch 4 para 9(2)(d); NIUC sch 4 para 8(2)(d)

3.76   UC sch 4 para 9(2)(d); NIUC sch 4 para 8(2)(d)

3.77   UC sch 4 para 9(2)(f); NIUC sch 4 para 8(2)(f)

Chapter 4 **Migration to UC**

Summary

4.1   This chapter describes what happens when you transfer from legacy benefits to UC. This is called 'migration'. It also explains the transitional protection that stops many people being worse off as a result of migration. You can ask the DWP to reconsider decisions about these and appeal to a tribunal about them (chapter 14).

4.2   This chapter only applies to people who have been getting legacy benefits. The legacy benefits are HB, JSA(IB), ESA(IR), IS, CTC and WTC. If you claim UC in any other case (e.g. after losing a job) see chapter 3.

Migration

4.3   There are two kinds of migration:

(a) 'natural migration' is when you transfer without the DWP sending you a migration notice (para 4.12);

(b) 'managed migration' is when you transfer to UC because the DWP has sent you a migration notice (para 4.22).

Ending your legacy benefits

4.4   When you claim UC:

(a) you can continue to get HB at any time on supported or temporary accommodation (table 5.2);

(b) your HB (on other accommodation) and/or JSA(IB)/ESA(IR)/IS end after two weeks (paras 4.5-8);

(c) your CTC/WTC end straight away;

(d) you can't get HB (except as in (a)), JSA(IB)/ESA(IR)/IS or CTC/WTC in the future.

These apply even if you claim UC by mistake ([2018] UKUT 306 (AAC)).

Two-week HB run-on

4.5   If you are on HB when you make your UC claim, you get a two-week run-on of HB that overlaps with the beginning of your UC. This applies in all cases (paras 4.6-7). It is also called a 'transitional housing payment' in the law.

4.6   When your transfer to UC is part of natural migration (para 4.12), you get 'maximum HB' during the two weeks of the run-on, regardless of the level of your income. This means your eligible rent minus any non-dependant contributions that apply, calculated by the HB rules in volume 2 (so if you have a rent-free week this appears to mean nil for that week).

4.7   When your transfer to UC is part of managed migration (including the pilot scheme: para 4.22), your HB during the two weeks continues at the same amount it is on the first day of the run-on (so no changes of circumstance are taken into account after that first day).

Two-week JSA(IB)/ESA(IR)/IS run-on

4.8   If you are on JSA(IB), ESA(IR) or IS when you make your UC claim:

   (a) you get a two-week run-on of that benefit that overlaps with the beginning of your UC;

   (b) if you are on HB you also get a two-week run-on of HB (para 4.5).

These apply whether your transfer is part of natural or managed migration (either the pilot scheme or the full scheme).

Transitional protection

4.9   If you transfer to UC as part of natural migration (para 4.12), you are eligible for:

   (a) the two-week run-ons (paras 4.5-8);

   (b) the UC transitional element only if you are severely disabled (paras 4.42);

   (c) the protection for some self-employed people (para 10.78(f)).

You can't get any other kind of transitional protection.

4.10   If you transfer to UC as part of managed migration (para 4.22), you are eligible for:

   (a) the two-week run-ons (paras 4.5-8);

   (b) the UC transitional element (para 4.41);

   (c) the transitional capital disregard (para 4.55);

   (d) protection for students (table 2.3(e));

   (e) protection for some self-employed people (para 10.78(f)).

Better or worse off?

4.11   Migrating to UC can make you better off. One example is that if you receive earned income, UC is reduced by a lower amount than JSA(IB)/ESA(IR)/IS are (para 9.8). But it can also make you worse off unless you are eligible for transitional protection. In some cases you may be able to get a discretionary help from the DWP or your council (para 4.67).

4.5-7   UCTP 8A, 8B; NIUCTP 6A, 6B

4.7   SI 2019/1152 reg 5; UCTP 8; NISR 2019/152 reg 4; NIUCTP 6

4.8   SI 2019/1152 reg 5; UCTP 8; NISR 2019/152 reg 4; NIUCTP 6

Natural migration

4.12 'Natural migration' is the term used when you transfer from legacy benefits to UC without the DWP having issued you a migration notice (para 4.28).

4.13 It can occur when you make a claim for UC (usually because one of your legacy benefits has ended 'naturally' due to a change in your circumstances). Or it can occur when you become a couple with someone on UC (paras 4.19-20). For transitional protection, see para 4.9.

Claiming UC by choice

4.14 You can choose to claim UC at any time, and this causes all your legacy benefits to end (para 4.4). This is usually because you are sure you will be better off. One example is that if you have a working non-dependant, UC is reduced by a lower figure than HB (para 9.66). However, claiming UC is risky if you aren't sure, because you could be worse off and not qualify for a transitional element.

4.15 In this case:

(a) your UC starts on the day you make your UC claim or on the day it is backdated to (para 4.35);

(b) your CTC/WTC ends on the day before your UC starts;

(c) your HB (except in supported or temporary accommodation) and JSA(IB)/ESA(IR)/IS end two weeks later;

(d) you aren't eligible for the transitional element or capital disregard.

Claiming UC when a legacy benefit ends

4.16 If your entitlement to a legacy benefit ends (under the rules for that benefit) you can no longer claim other legacy benefits to replace it. So you have to claim UC (or be worse off), and this causes any other legacy benefits you are on to end (para 4.4).

4.17 For example this happens when:

(a) you lose JSA(IB)/ESA(IR)/IS because of starting work or increasing your hours or earnings (see example 1);

(b) you lose JSA(IB) because of being unfit for work;

(c) you lose ESA(IR) because of becoming fit for work (see example 2);

(d) you lose WTC because of ending work or reducing your hours (see example 3);

(e) you lose IS because your child reaches the age of five or you stop being responsible for them;

(f) you lose HB because of moving areas (see example 4); or

(g) you lose a legacy benefit for other reasons.

4.18 In these cases, the details are the same as in para 4.15.

4.14   UCTP 6; NIUCTP 8

4.15   C&P 10, 26(1); UCTP 7, 8; NIC&P 10, 26(1); NIUCTP 9, 10

4.16   UCTP 6; NIUCTP 8

4.18   C&P 10, 26(1); UCTP 7, 8; NIC&P 10, 26(1); NIUCTP 9, 10

Examples: Natural migration to UC

1. Getting a job

A claimant on JSA(IB) and HB gets a new job working 16 hours per week and this means his JSA(IB) ends.

- In the past he could have claimed WTC but he can no longer do so.
- He claims UC so his HB also ends.
- He can't in the future claim any of the legacy benefits.

2. Becoming fit for work

A claimant on ESA(IR), CTC and HB becomes fit for work and this means her ESA(IR) ends.

- In the past she could have claimed JSA(IB) but she can no longer do so.
- She claims UC so her CTC and HB also end.
- She can't in the future claim any of the legacy benefits.

3. Losing a job

A claimant on WTC, CTC and HB loses his job and this means his WTC ends.

- In the past he could have claimed JSA(IB), ESA(IR) or IS (depending on his circumstances) but he can no longer do so.
- He claims UC so his CTC and HB also end.
- He can also claim JSA(C) or ESA(C) (depending on his circumstances).
- He can't in the future claim any of the legacy benefits.

4. Moving home to a new job or for other reasons

A claimant on HB moves to a new area and this means her HB ends.

- In the past she could have claimed HB in the new area but she can no longer do so.
- She claims UC so if she is on any other legacy benefits they also end.
- She can't in the future claim any legacy benefits.

Becoming a couple with someone on UC

4.19   If you become a couple with someone who is already on UC you become part of their UC claim (para 3.5), and this causes all your legacy benefits to end.

4.20   In this case:

(a) you are included in the UC claim from the first day of the assessment period in which you become a couple;

(b) your CTC/WTC ends on the previous day;

(c) your HB (except in supported or temporary accommodation) and JSA(IB)/ESA(IR)/IS end two weeks later;

(d) you aren't eligible for the transitional element or capital disregard.

4.20   D&A sch 1 para 20; UCTP 7; NID&A sch 1 para 20; NIUCTP 9

Remaining on legacy benefits

4.21   If you don't transfer to UC as part of natural migration, you can remain on legacy benefits until managed migration applies to you (para 4.22). For guidance see ADM chapter M7. You can't claim any further legacy benefits, but you can:

(a) get HB on supported or temporary accommodation (table 5.2);

(b) get CTC if you claim it while you are on WTC or get WTC if you claim it while on CTC;

(c) get CTC if you had CTC or WTC in the previous tax year and you make a claim for it for the next tax year;

(d) get other benefits (para 1.13).

Managed migration

4.22   'Managed migration' (MM) is the term used when you transfer from legacy benefits to UC because the DWP has issued you a migration notice (para 4.28).

4.23   It includes a pilot MM scheme and full MM scheme (paras 4.24, 4.27). For transitional protection see para 4.10.

The pilot MM scheme

4.24   The pilot MM scheme is limited to 10,000 cases. It began in July 2019 (in Harrogate JCP area) and was suspended in March 2020 due to coronavirus. It is expected to resume during 2021 and run until some time in 2022. If you are included, the DWP:

(a) sends you a migration notice encouraging you to claim UC and offering to discuss this with you;

(b) only ends your legacy benefits if you claim UC (para 4.26).

Pilot MM: if you do claim UC

4.25   In the pilot MM scheme, if you do choose to claim UC:

(a) your UC starts on the day you make your UC claim or the day it is backdated or post-dated to (paras 4.35-36);

(b) your CTC/WTC end on the day before your UC starts;

(c) your HB (except in supported or temporary accommodation) and JSA(IB)/ESA(IR)/IS end two weeks later;

(d) you are eligible for the transitional element and capital disregard (paras 4.50, 4.55).

Pilot MM: if you don't claim UC

4.26   In the pilot MM scheme, if you choose not to claim UC, you can continue to get the legacy benefits you are on until you fall within the full MM scheme. You can't get any further legacy benefits except as in para 4.21.

4.21   UCTP 5(1),(2)(a), 6(1),(8), 7(5), 8(2),(3); SI 2015/33 art 6(4)-(6); NIUCTP 3(1),(2)(a), 4(1),(8), 5(5), 6(2),(3); SI 2017/190 art 24(5)-(7)

4.22   UCTP 44; NIUCTP 45

4.23-24 SI 2019/1152 reg 2

4.25   C&P 10, 26(1); UCTP 8; NIC&P 10, 26(1); NIUCTP 10

The full MM scheme

4.27   The full MM scheme is expected to begin when the pilot scheme is complete and run until 2024. If you are included, the DWP:

(a) sends you a migration notice giving you a deadline to claim UC (para 4.28);

(b) ends your legacy benefits whether or not you claim UC (paras 4.31-34).

However, it is possible some of the rules may change as a result of the pilot MM scheme.

Full MM: your migration notice

4.28   You don't have to transfer to UC until the DWP issues you a migration notice. In the full MM scheme this tells you:

(a) your legacy benefits will end, and which benefits these are;

(b) you will need to claim UC instead;

(c) your 'deadline day' (para 4.29);

(d) other information relating to how to claim UC and what happens if you don't claim UC.

If you are getting any legacy benefits as a couple (or polygamous marriage), the DWP issues this notice to each of you. If the notice should never have been issued to you or shouldn't have been issued to you yet, the DWP can cancel it.

Full MM: your deadline day and final deadline

4.29   In the full MM scheme:

(a) your 'deadline day' is set by the DWP. It must be at least three months after the date your migration notice is issued.

(b) your 'final deadline' is one month after your deadline day. It is the day by which you need to claim UC in order for there to be no gap between your legacy benefits and UC, and in order to qualify for transitional protection (para 4.40).

Extending the deadline day and final deadline

4.30   The DWP can extend your deadline day if there is 'good reason' to do so. You can ask for this once or more than once, or someone can on your behalf, or the DWP can do it without a request. The DWP decides what is good reason on the merits of each individual case. The following are examples of what the DWP is likely to accept:

(a) you are in hospital or have to go to hospital;

(b) you have a mental health condition;

(c) you have a disability;

(d) you have learning difficulties;

(e) you are homeless;

4.28   UCTP 44(1),(2),(4),(5)

4.29   UCTP 44(3),46; NIUCTP 45(3),47

4.30   UCTP 45; NIUCTP 46

(f)   you have caring responsibilities; or

(g)   you have a domestic emergency.

When your deadline day is extended, so is your final deadline, so it is still one month later.

Full MM: if you claim UC by the deadline day

4.31   In the full MM scheme, if you claim UC on or before your deadline day:

(a)   your UC starts on the day you make your UC claim or the day it is backdated or post-dated to (paras 4.35-36);

(b)   your CTC/WTC end on the day before your UC starts;

(c)   your HB (except in supported or temporary accommodation) and JSA(IB)/ESA(IR)/IS end two weeks later;

(d)   you are eligible for the transitional element and capital disregard (paras 4.40, 4.55).

Full MM: if you claim UC after the deadline day but before the final deadline

4.32   In the full MM scheme, if you claim UC after your deadline day but on or before your final deadline:

(a)   your UC starts on your deadline day but can't be backdated or post-dated;

(b)   your CTC/WTC end on the day before your deadline day;

(c)   your HB (except in supported or temporary accommodation) and JSA(IB)/ESA(IR)/IS end two weeks later;

(d)   you are eligible for the transitional element and capital disregard (paras 4.40, 4.55).

Full MM: if you claim UC after the final deadline

4.33   In the full MM scheme, if you claim UC after your final deadline:

(a)   your UC starts on the day you make your UC claim or the day it is backdated to (para 4.35);

(b)   your CTC/WTC end on the day before your deadline day;

(c)   your HB (except in supported or temporary accommodation) and JSA(IB)/ESA(IR)/IS end two weeks later;

(d)   you aren't eligible for the transitional element or capital disregard.

Full MM: if you don't claim UC

4.34   In the full MM scheme, you can't get UC if you don't claim it. The other details are the same as in para 4.33(b)-(d).

4.31   C&P 10, 26(1); UCTP 8; NIC&P 10, 26(1); NIUCTP 10

4.32   UCTP 8, 46(3); NIUCTP 6, 47(3)

4.33   C&P 10, 26(1); UCTP 46; NIC&P 10, 26(1)

4.34   UCTP 46; NIUCTP 47

Examples: Managed migration to UC

All the examples fall within the full MM scheme (para 4.27).

1. UC claim made by the deadline day

James is a single person on JSA(IB) and HB. The DWP issues him a migration notice in February, giving him a deadline day of 14th May. He claims UC (as a single person) on 11th May.

- His UC starts on 11th May (para 4.31).
- The last day of his HB and JSA(IB) is 24th May.
- He is eligible for a UC transitional element if he would otherwise be worse off.

2. UC claim made after the deadline day but by the final deadline

Josie and Andrew are a couple on ESA(IR), CTC and HB. The DWP issues a migration notice in March, giving them a deadline day of 12th June. They claim UC (as a couple) on 24th June.

- Their UC starts on 12th June (para 4.32).
- The last day of their CTC is 11th June.
- The last day of their HB and ESA(IR) is 25th June.
- They are eligible for a UC transitional element if they would otherwise be worse off.

3. UC claim made after the final deadline

Alice is a single person on WTC, CTC and HB. The DWP issues her with a migration notice in January, giving her a deadline day of 7th April. She claims UC (as a single person) on 13th May.

- Her UC starts on 13th May (para 4.33).
- The last day of her CTC and WTC is 6th April.
- The last day of her HB is 20th April.
- She isn't eligible for a UC transitional element.

Backdating your UC

4.35   In natural and managed migration cases (except as in para 4.32), the DWP can backdate the start of your UC (and the end of your legacy benefits) for up to one month if you meet the conditions in para 3.36 and table 3.1.

Postdating your UC

4.36   In managed migration cases (except as in paras 4.32-33), the DWP can postdate the start of your UC (and the end of your legacy benefits) for up to one month. This is usually to make the dates fit better with your legacy payments.

4.35   C&P 26(2)(a),(b),(4); NIC&P 25(2),(a),(b),(4)

4.36   UCTP 58; NIUCTP 59

Becoming a couple or a single person

4.37   The rules in paras 4.31-34 apply if your claims for legacy benefits and UC are:

(a) as a single person in both cases;

(b) as a couple with the same partner in both cases (including, in the case of UC, a couple claiming as a single person: para 2.7).

4.38   But in any other situation (for example, you become a couple or a single person between getting legacy benefits and claiming UC):

(a) you aren't eligible for the transitional element (table 4.1) or capital disregard (para 4.55); but

(b) the rules in paras 4.31-34 are varied so that (in broad terms) if more than one deadline day or final deadline could apply to you, the earliest of them applies.

The transitional element

4.39   When you transfer to UC, the transitional element increases your UC if it would otherwise be lower than your legacy benefits. It is included in the UC calculation as described in para 9.4.

Who can get a transitional element

4.40   The rules for managed and natural migration are different:

(a) anyone who transfers to UC as part of managed migration may get a transitional element (para 4.41);

(b) severely disabled people who transfer to UC as part of natural migration may get a transitional element (paras 4.42-43);

(c) other people who transfer as part of natural migration can't get a transitional element.

These details and amounts are in the rest of this section.

The transitional element for managed migration

4.41   When you transfer to UC as part of managed migration, you can get a transitional element if:

(a) there was no gap between your legacy benefits and your UC. This applies to:

- ▪ full MM scheme cases as long as you claim by your final deadline (para 4.29), and
- ▪ in practice, all pilot MM scheme cases (para 4.24); and

(b) your claims for legacy benefits and for UC were:

- ▪ as single persons in both cases, or
- ▪ as a couple with the same partner in both cases (including, in the case of UC, a couple claiming as a single person: para 2.7).

4.37-38 UCTP 47, 56(4); NIUCTP 48, 57(4)

4.41   UCTP 48, 50; NIUCTP 49, 51

The transitional element for natural migration

4.42   When you transfer to UC as part of natural migration, you can get a transitional element if:

   (a)   you claimed UC on or after 27th January 2021;

   (b)   this was not because you became a couple with someone on UC;

   (c)   no more than one month before your UC began, you or your partner were entitled to JSA(IB), ESA(IR) or IS that included a severe disability premium (para 4.62); and

   (d)   you or your partner continued to meet the conditions for that premium until your UC began.

In the law this is called a 'transitional SDP element'.

4.43   The condition in para 4.42(c) isn't met if you were only on HB with a severe disability premium (paras 4.64-65); it has to be JSA(IB)/ESA(IR)/IS. But the condition is met if you are retrospectively awarded that premium in your JSA(IB)/ESA(IR)/IS or retrospectively awarded JSA(IB)/ESA(IR)/IS with that premium.

Amount of transitional element: first month

4.44   In your first UC assessment period, your transitional element:

   (a)   is calculated using your old and new entitlements in managed migration cases;

   (b)   is a fixed amount in natural migration cases.

Table 4.1 gives the details.

Amount of transitional element: following months

4.45   In your following UC assessment periods, your UC continues at the same amount (table 4.1) unless and until it reduces or ends (paras 4.46-48). The rules about this are the same as for both managed and natural migration cases.

UCTP sch 2 paras 1-4, 7, 8; SI 2021/4; NIUCTP sch 2 paras 1-4, 7, 8; NISR 2021/2

Table 4.1 **Amount of transitional element**

This table gives the amount you get in your first UC assessment period; for the following UC assessment periods see paras 4.45-48.

Calculation of managed migration cases

(Transitional element)

This applies to all claimants who qualify.

(a)   Your transitional element equals:

- your total legacy benefits (table 4.2);
- minus your indicative UC (table 4.3)

(b)   But if your deductible income exceeds your maximum UC (para 9.4), your transitional element equals:

- your total legacy benefits;
- plus the excess of your deductible income.

(c)   'Deductible income' means:

- 100% of your unearned income (after disregards);
- plus 63% of your earned income (after disregards and after a work allowance if you qualify for one: para 10.11).

Fixed amount for natural migration cases (transitional SDP element)

(Transitional SDP element)

This only applies if you used to get a severe disability premium (SDP) (paras 4.42-43).

(d)   Single people, couples claiming UC as a single person (para 2.7), and couples who got the single rate of SDP (para 4.62):

- receiving the LCWRA element (para 9.32)   £120.00
- not receiving the LCWRA element   £285.00

(e)   Joint claim couples (para 2.5) who got the double rate of SDP (para 4.62):

- Whether or not receiving the LCWRA element   £405.00

T4.1(a)-(c)   UCTP 55(1),(2); NIUCTP 56(1),(2)

T4.1(d)-(e)   UCTP sch 2 para 5; NIUCTP sch 2 para 5

Table 4.2 **Your total legacy benefits**

Your 'total legacy benefits' are used to work out your transitional element when you transfer to UC due to managed migration (table 4.1). In all cases:

- ■ use the following figures as at the day before your UC starts;
- ■ convert them to a monthly amount (as shown in brackets);
- ■ add them together to give your total legacy benefits.

(a) HB

- ■ Use the council's HB figure (x 52÷12), ignoring any adjustments for rent-free periods. Or the DWP can calculate this.
- ■ But exclude HB entirely if you live in supported or temporary accommodation (table 5.2).

(b) JSA(IB), ESA(IR) or IS

- ■ Use the DWP's figure (x 52÷12), and include any amount of JSA(IB)/ESA(IR) that is classified as being JSA(C)/ESA(C).

(c) CTC and/or WTC

- ■ Use HMRC's daily figure (x 365÷12).

(d) Benefit cap and sanctions

- ■ The benefit cap and its exceptions all apply (paras 9.75-79), but ensuring that it is not deducted twice (i.e. not from the HB figure in (a) and from the total).
- ■ Don't make deductions for sanctions etc (para 9.11(b)-(e)).

T4.2   UCTP 49, 53; NIUCTP 50, 54

Table 4.3 **Your indicative UC**

Your 'indicative UC' is used to work out your transitional element when you transfer to UC due to managed migration (table 4.1). In all cases:

- use the following figures as at the day before your UC starts;
- convert them to a monthly amount (as shown in brackets);
- use the ordinary rules (paras 9.4-10) to calculate your indicative UC.

(a) Standard allowance and elements

- Use the figures in table 9.2 for these (except as in (c) below).
- Don't include the coronavirus increase of £86.67.

(b) Children and young persons in your benefit unit

- If you were on CTC, include the same children/young persons as in your CTC.
- Otherwise, use the UC rules to decide who to include.

(c) Childcare costs element

- If you were on WTC, use the WTC childcare costs element (x 52÷12) for this.
- Otherwise, use the UC rules to decide this.

(d) Housing costs element

- If you were on HB, use the council's eligible rent including eligible services (x 52÷12), but ignore any adjustments for rent-free periods. Or the DWP can calculate this.
- Otherwise, use the UC rules to decide (only) service charges.

(e) Earned income

- If you were on CTC/WTC, use HMRC's annual figure (x 1÷12), then the DWP decides how much to deduct for tax and national insurance.
- If you were on JSA(IB)/ESA(IR)/IS (but not CTC/WTC), use the DWP's figure (x 52÷12).
- If you were only on HB, use the council's figure (x 52÷12).

(f) Unearned income and capital

- The DWP decides these using information about your legacy benefits from you.
- But if you were on CTC/WTC, any capital over £16,000 is disregarded (para 4.54).

(g) Benefit cap and sanctions

- The benefit cap and its exceptions all apply, apart from the grace period (paras 9.75-78).
- Don't make deductions for sanctions etc (para 9.11(b)-(e)).

T4.3   UCTP 49, 54; NIUCTP 50, 55

Reductions in transitional element

4.46   Your transitional element can reduce (para 4.47) but can't increase. If it reduces to nil, it can't be reinstated (except as described in para 4.52).

4.47   Each time you are awarded one of the following (chapter 9), or their amount increases, your transitional element reduces by the same amount:

   (a) the standard allowance;

   (b) the child element;

   (c) the disabled child addition;

   (d) the work capability elements;

   (e) the carer elements;

   (f) the housing costs element.

But if you are awarded the childcare costs element (para 9.42), or its amount increases, your transitional element doesn't reduce.

End of transitional element

4.48   Your transitional element ends when:

   (a) it reduces to nil (para 4.47); or

   (b) you become a couple or single person (para 4.49); or

   (c) your earned income reduces or ends as described in para 4.50; or

   (d) your UC ends, except as described in para 4.52.

Becoming a couple or a single person

4.49   Your transitional element and/or capital disregard (para 4.54) end if:

   (a) you have been getting UC as a single person (including a couple claiming as a single person: para 2.7) but become (or start claiming as) a couple; or

   (b) you have been getting UC as a couple (not a couple claiming as a single person) but become a single person or a couple with a different partner.

They end at the end of the assessment period in which (a) or (b) occurs.

Reductions in your earned income

4.50   Your transitional element and/or capital disregard end if your earned income:

   (a) was at or above the JSA or in certain cases the minimum income floor (paras 2.41-44) in your first UC assessment period; but

   (b) is lower than that (or nil) in any three consecutive assessment periods.

They end at the end of the third assessment period in (b).

4.46   UCTP 55(2),(3) sch 2 para 6; NIUCTP 56(2),(3) sch 2 para 6

4.47   UCTP 55(2)(b),(c),(4) sch 2 para 6; NIUCTP 56(2)(b),(c),(4) sch 2 para 6

4.48   UCTP 55(3), 56, 57 sch 2 para 6; NIUCTP 56(3), 57, 58 sch 2 para 6

4.49   UCTP 56(2)-(4), 57 sch 2 para 6; NIUCTP 57(2)-(4), 58 sch 2 para 6

4.50   UCTP 56(2) sch 2 para 6; NIUCTP 57(2) sch 2 para 6

End of UC

4.51   Your transitional element and/or capital disregard end when your UC ends. If you later go back on UC, they aren't reinstated unless para 4.52 applies.

Gaps in UC due to earned or unearned income

4.52   Your transitional element and/or capital disregard are reinstated if:

(a) you didn't qualify for UC in your first or a later assessment period because of the level of your earned income and/or unearned income; but

(b) you later qualify for UC after no more than three months without UC.

The amount of your UC transitional element is the same as if you had been on UC throughout.

4.53   This rule (para 4.52) can apply any number of times. It is particularly important for people whose income is not paid monthly (para 3.24).

The transitional capital disregard

4.54   The transitional capital disregard is for people with capital over £16,000 who transfer from CTC/WTC to UC.

Who can get a capital disregard

4.55   The conditions for getting the transitional capital disregard are as follows:

(a) your claim for UC is part of managed migration (para 4.22) and there is no gap between your legacy benefits and your UC. This applies to:

  ▪ full MM scheme cases so long as you claim by your final deadline (para 4.29), and

  ▪ in practice, all pilot MM scheme cases (para 4.24);

(b) on your 'migration day':

  ▪ you were on CTC or WTC or both, and

  ▪ you had capital over £16,000;

(c) your claims for legacy benefits and for UC must be:

  ▪ as a single person in both cases, or

  ▪ as a couple with the same partner in both cases (including, in the case of UC, a couple claiming as a single person: para 2.7).

Your 'migration day' is the day before your UC starts (paras 4.31-32).

4.51   UCTP 57(1) sch 2 para 6; NIUCTP 58(1) sch 2 para 6

4.52   UCTP 57(2),(3) sch 2 para 6; NIUCTP 58(2),(3) sch 2 para 6

4.55   UCTP 49, 51(1); NIUCTP 50, 52(1)

How the disregard affects your UC

4.56   The disregard applies to all your capital over £16,000. So:

(a) your capital doesn't stop you qualifying for UC (para 10.55); and

(b) only the first £16,000 of your capital counts as providing you with an assumed income (para 10.56).

You get this disregard in your actual UC (table 10.6(r)) whether or not you qualify for a transitional element. You also get it when your indicative UC is calculated (table 4.3(f)).

Duration of capital disregard

4.57   Your transitional capital disregard continues until:

(a) you become a couple or single person (para 4.49); or

(b) your earned income reduces or ends as described in para 4.50; or

(c) your UC ends, except as described in para 4.52; or

(d) your capital reduces below £16,000 (para 4.58); or

(e) you reach the 12 month time limit (para 4.59).

Changes in your capital

4.58   If your capital reduces to below £16,000:

(a) your transitional capital disregard ends, and can't be reinstated even if your capital changes again; but

(b) you can continue to get a transitional element if you qualify for it (para 4.39).

Apart from that, your transitional capital disregard continues despite changes in your capital.

The twelve month time limit

4.59   Your transitional capital disregard ends after you have received UC for 12 months. This means:

(a) 12 continuous assessment periods, or

(b) if you have breaks in your UC (for any reason), 12 assessment periods not counting the gaps.

But you can continue to get a transitional element if you qualify for it (para 4.39).

Severely disabled people

4.60   This section applies to severely disabled people. This means people who are entitled to a severe disability premium in their JSA(IB), ESA(IR) or IS (if you only get the premium in your HB, see paras 4.64-65).

4.56   UCTP 51(2); NIUCTP 52(2)

4.57   UCTP 51, 56, 57; NIUCTP 52, 57, 58

4.58   UCTP 51(3); NIUCTP 52(3)

4.59   UCTP 51(4); NIUCTP 52(4)

4.60   UCTP 4A, 63, sch 2; NIUCTP 2B, 64, sch 2

Severe disability premium

4.61 You are entitled to a severe disability premium if:

(a) you receive one or more of the following disability benefits:

- the daily living component of PIP, or
- the middle or highest care rate of the care component of DLA, or
- attendance allowance, or
- constant attendance allowance paid with an industrial injury or war disablement pension, or
- an armed forces independence payment; and

(b) you have no non-dependants living with you (paras 3.70-77) apart from non-dependants who receive any of the disability benefits in (a), or are (or were within the last 28 weeks) certified as severely sight impaired or blind; and

(c) no-one receives carer's allowance for caring for you.

4.62 The severe disability premium has two rates:

(a) single people get the single rate if you meet all the conditions in para 4.61:

(b) couples get the double rate if you both meet all the conditions

(c) couple get the single rate if:

- one of you meets all the conditions, and
- the other meets the first two conditions (para 4.61(a) and (b)) or is certified as severely sight impaired or blind.

In 2021-22 the rates are £67.30 and £134.60 per week. But UC has no equivalent so you are likely to need the transitional element when you transfer to UC (paras 4.63-65).

Transfers from JSA(IB)/ESA(IR)/IS to UC

4.63 If you transfer to UC and you were previously getting a severe disability premium in your JSA(IB), ESA(IR) or IS (with or without HB), you qualify for a transitional element whether your transfer was due to managed or natural migration (para 4.40).

Transfers from HB to UC

4.64 If you transfer to UC and were previously getting a severe disability premium in your HB but didn't qualify for JSA(IB)/ESA(IR)/IS:

(a) you qualify for a transitional element if your transfer was due to managed migration; but

(b) you don't qualify for a transitional element if it was due to natural migration.

4.61-62 UCTP 2(1) – 'severe disability premium'; NIUCTP 2(1)

4.63-64 UCTP 48-50, sch 2; NIUCTP 49-51, sch 2

4.65   The Court of Appeal has held that the DWP should not discriminate between natural and managed migration if you are severely disabled (R (TP, AR and SXC) v SSWP). If you are worse off due to natural migration, you can ask the DWP for a severe hardship payment (para 4.68) and, if this fails, appeal to a tribunal.

Previous UC claims

4.66   The rules in paras 4.60-64 have applied since 27th January 2021, and similar rules applied before 16th January 2019. But between those dates, if you were severely disabled you could claim legacy benefits or carry on getting UC if you were already on it, but you couldn't make a new claim for UC.

Discretionary help with migration losses

4.67   The two types of payment in this section have similar names but are legally separate.

Discretionary hardship payments from the DWP/DFC

4.68   The DWP/DFC can make discretionary hardship payments if:

(a)   your legacy benefits end as a result of you receiving a migration notice (para 4.28); and

(b)   you 'appear to be in hardship' as a result of them ending or as a result of the migration process.

4.69   The DWP/DFC used this discretion to pay the equivalent of a two-week run-on of JSA(IB), ESA(IR) or IS (para 4.8) before this became a legal requirement. It can now be used for severely disabled people who lose out due to natural migration (para 4.65) or for other individual cases of hardship.

Discretionary housing payments from the council

4.70   Your local council can make discretionary housing payments if:

(a)   you are entitled to a UC housing costs element or HB; and

(b)   you 'appear… to require some further financial assistance… in order to meet housing costs'.

4.71   This discretion is usually for people whose UC housing costs element is less than the rent due to their landlord (volume 2). It can be used to mitigate losses caused by migrating to UC and can also help in other situations.

4.65   UCTP 64; NIUCTP 65; R (TP, AR and SXC) v SSWP [2020] EWCA Civ 37 www.bailii.org/ew/cases/EWCA/Civ/2020/37.html

4.66   UCTP 4A; SI 2019/1152 regs 1(5), 7; SI 2013/983, art 5A(1); SI 2015 art 6(11); SI 2015/634 art 7(2);
             NIUCTP 2B; NISR 2019/152 regs 1(5), 6; NISR 2017/190, arts 8(1), 24(2)

4.68   UCTP 64; NIUCTP 65

4.70   The Discretionary Financial Assistance Regulations SI 2001 No 1167
             The Discretionary Financial Assistance Regulations (Northern Ireland) 2001 No 216

Chapter 5 **Housing costs**

- The housing costs UC and SMI can meet: see paras 5.1-6.
- Liability for housing costs: see paras 5.7-13.
- Occupying your home: see paras 5.14-17.
- Absences, moving home and two homes: see paras 5.18-34.

The housing costs UC and SMI can meet

5.1   When you claim UC, you can get UC towards your rent and service charges or support for mortgage interest (SMI) or both.

5.2   In each case you have to meet:

  (a) the payment condition – this says which housing costs can be met (paras 5.3-6);

  (b) the liability condition – this says you must have a legal obligation to make payments (paras 5.7-13); and

  (c) the occupation condition – this says you must occupy the accommodation as your home (paras 5.14-34).

UC's housing costs element

5.3   The housing costs element helps meet your rent and service charges if you are a renter or shared owner, or just your service charges if you are an owner-occupier (table 5.1). It is calculated and paid as part of your UC (paras 9.4, 12.1), but there are limits on the amount of rent and types of service charges that can be met (chapter 6).

Support for mortgage interest

5.4   SMI helps meet your mortgage interest or alternative finance payments if you are an owner occupier or shared owner. It is usually paid to your lender and is a loan that you are expected to pay back (chapter 8).

5.1   WRA 11; Welfare Reform and Work Act 2016, s18-19
      NIWRO 16; Welfare Reform and Work (Northern Ireland) Order 2016 No. 999, art 13-14

5.2   UC 25, 26; NIUC 26, 27

5.3   WRA 8(2); UC 23(1)(c), 25; NIWRO 13(2); NIUC 26

5.4   LMI sch 1 paras 2, 5; NILMI sch 1 paras 2, 5

Table 5.1 **The housing costs UC can meet**

Rent and service charge payments that can be included in UC

(a) Renters generally

- rent and service charges due under a tenancy, licence or permission to occupy;
- this includes houses, flats, rooms, bed and breakfasts, housing co-ops, Crown lettings, etc.

(b) Shared owners

- rent and service charges.

(c) Owners

- service charges.

(d) Houseboats, caravans and mobile homes

- rent and service charges (if you rent the accommodation); and
- mooring charges or site charges (whether you own or rent it).

(e) Hostels – except as in (h) or (i)

- rent and service charges.

(f) Charitable almshouses

- maintenance contributions if your landlord is a housing association that is a registered charity.

(g) Crofts and croft land in Scotland

- rent and service charges.

Rent and service charge payments that are excluded from UC

(h) Supported or temporary accommodation where you can get HB instead (table 5.2).

(i) Bail or probation hostels (also called 'approved premises').

(j) Care homes or private hospitals.

(k) Tents and similar moveable structures and their site.

(l) Owner occupier payments (chapter 8).

(m) Ground rent.

Note: Chapters 6 and 7 give further details about rent and service charges and explain how much you qualify for.

T5.1   UC 25(2), sch 1 paras 2, 3, 3A, 3B, 7-8; NIUC 26(2), sch 1 paras 2, 3, 4, 4A, 8-9

Supported or temporary accommodation

5.5   Table 5.2 gives all the types of supported or temporary accommodation. If you live in any of these, you can get HB towards your rent and service charges (not UC). So when you claim UC from the DWP, you need to claim HB from your local council at the same time.

5.6   The DWP says it follows the council's decision about whether your home is supported or temporary accommodation [www]. So if you disagree with the council's decision, you should ask the council to reconsider and/or appeal to a tribunal using the HB procedures (Volume 2 chapter 20).

Table 5.2 **Supported or temporary accommodation**

For supported accommodation see (a) to (e); for temporary accommodation (see (f)).

(a) Exempt accommodation

- ■ You rent from a not-for-profit landlord; and

- ■ you are provided with care, support or supervision by your landlord, or by someone else on your landlord's behalf.

(b) General supported accommodation

- ■ You rent from a not-for-profit landlord; and

- ■ you are provided with care, support or supervision by your landlord, or by someone else (this needn't be on your landlord's behalf); and

- ■ you were admitted to the accommodation to meet a need for this.

(c) Domestic violence refuges

- ■ You rent from a not-for-profit landlord or from a council that administers HB; and

- ■ the building you live in (or relevant part of it) is wholly or mainly used as non-permanent accommodation for people who have left their home as a result of domestic violence; and

- ■ the accommodation is provided to you for that reason.

(d) Local authority hostels

- ■ The building you live in is owned or managed by an authority which administers HB; and

- ■ it provides non-self-contained domestic accommodation with meals or adequate food-preparation facilities (and is not a care home or independent hospital); and

- ■ you are provided with care, support or supervision by your landlord, or by someone else (this needn't be on your landlord's behalf).

5.5-6   UC sch 1 paras 3(h),(i), 3A, 3B; NIUC sch 1 paras 3(e),(ea), 4, 4A

T5.2   UC sch 1 paras 3A, 3B; UCTP 5(2)(a), 6(8), 7(5)(a), 8(3), 14(3)
          NIUC sch 1 paras 4, 4A; NIUCTP 3(2)(a), 4(8), 5(5)(a), 6(3), 13(3)
          http://tinyurl.com/OG-Supported-Accom-2019
          HB Circular A8/2014 paras 36-44

(e) Resettlement accommodation

- You live in a hostel for homeless people; and

- the hostel received a resettlement grant under section 30 of the Jobseeker's Act 1995 in the past (these grants are no longer awarded).

(f) Temporary accommodation

- You rent from a council that administers HB or a registered housing association; and

- the accommodation was provided to you because you were homeless or to prevent you from becoming homeless.

Notes:

- A not-for-profit landlord means:
    - a registered or unregistered housing association,
    - a registered charity
    - a voluntary organisation, or
    - an English county council.

- Care, support or supervision has its ordinary English meaning: for case law about this, see volume 2.

- Domestic violence includes controlling or coercive behaviour, violence or psychological, physical, sexual, emotional, financial or other abuse, regardless of the gender or sexuality of the victim.

Liability for housing costs

5.7   To get UC or SMI towards your housing costs:

(a) you must be liable or treated as liable for them (paras 5.8-12);

(b) your liability must not be excluded (table 5.4).

What liability is

5.8   Liability for housing costs means having a legal obligation to pay them. This is normally expressed in a written letting or mortgage agreement. Further details for renters are in table 5.3.

Table 5.3 **Liability of renters**

(a) *Your letting agreement:* Although letting agreements are often in writing, an agreement by word of mouth can be sufficient to create a liability (R v Poole BC ex parte Ross).

(b) *Your landlord's circumstances:* To grant a letting and create a liability your landlord must have a sufficient legal interest in the dwelling (e.g. as an owner or tenant), but there can be exceptions (CH/2959/2006).

(c) *Your circumstances:* If you already have the right to occupy your home (e.g. as a joint owner) no-one can grant you a letting on it (e.g. another joint owner) so you cannot be liable.

(d) *If you are under 18 or unable to act:* If you have someone appointed to act for you they can enter a letting for you thus making you liable. If you do not and you are incapable of understanding an agreement you entered, the agreement may be void under Scottish law ([2011] UKHT 354 AAC) but not English and Welsh law (CH/2121/2006, ([2012] UKUT 12 AAC). If it is void, you are not liable.

(e) *Arrears, etc:* If you have arrears (even large arrears) or are paying less rent than your agreement says (whether or not your landlord has agreed to this), this does not by itself mean you are not liable ([2010] UKUT 43 AAC). But very large arrears would normally lead a landlord to end a letting, so they may suggest you are not liable (CH/1849/2007).

(f) *If your letting breaks your landlord's occupation agreement:* If by granting your letting your landlord has broken their own occupation agreement on your dwelling (e.g. because it says they must not rent it out), your own letting agreement is still valid so you are liable (Governors of Peabody Donation Fund v Higgins) until and unless your landlord's right to occupy is terminated.

(g) *If your landlord breaks the law:* If by granting your letting your landlord has committed a criminal offence (e.g. because a Housing Act prohibition order bans them from renting out your home), your letting agreement is unlikely to be valid and you are unlikely to be liable.

Who is liable for housing costs

5.9   You are liable for housing costs (and can get UC or SMI towards them) if:

(a) you are single and are solely liable; or

(b) you are a couple and one or both of you are liable; or

(c) you are single or a couple and are jointly liable with others (para 5.11).

Example: Liability for rent

Maggie has a tenancy of a rented house. Jack is her partner who lives with her. They claim UC.

■   Maggie and Jack can get UC towards their rent because one of them is liable (para 5.9).

T5.3   R v Poole BC ex parte Ross 05/05/95 QBD 28 HLR 351
        The Governors of Peabody Donation Fund v Higgins 20/06/83 CA [1983] 1 WLR 1091

5.9   UC 25(3); LMI 3(2)(b), sch 2 para 5(1); NIUC 26(3)

Who is treated as liable

5.10   You are treated as liable for housing costs (and can get UC or SMI towards them) if:

(a)   you are in a couple but claiming as a single person (para 2.7) and your partner is liable rather than you; or

(b)   a young person or child in your benefit unit is liable rather than you; or

(c)   someone else is liable but you have to make the payments (para 5.12); or

(d)   your landlord or mortgage lender waives the payments because you have carried out reasonable repairs or redecorations; or

(e)   you have a rent-free period allowed for in your letting agreement.

Example: Treated as liable for rent

Zubin has the tenancy of a rented flat. Gill is his adult daughter who lives with him and is on UC. Zubin goes abroad for a long visit and stops paying the rent. The landlord accepts rent from Gill.

■   Gill can get UC towards the rent because it is reasonable to treat her as liable for it (para 5.12).

Joint liability

5.11   If you are jointly renting or buying your home (e.g. with relatives or friends in a house share), you can get UC or SMI towards your share of the housing costs (paras 6.11, 8.10-11).

When someone else is liable but you are paying

5.12   You can get UC or SMI towards housing costs when:

(a)   the person who is liable for housing costs on your home isn't paying them;

(b)   you are paying them in order to continue living there;

(c)   it is reasonable to treat you as liable; and

(d)   it would be unreasonable to expect you to make other arrangements.

The person in (a) can be an individual, company or other body (R(H) 5/05).

Excluded liabilities

5.13   You can't get UC or SMI towards housing costs if liability is excluded. Table 5.4 gives all the types of excluded liability; further details for renters are in table 5.5.

5.10   UC 25(3)(a)(ii); LMI sch 2 para 5(2); NIUC 26(3)(a)(ii); NILMI sch 2 para 5(2)

5.10(a)-(b)   UC sch 2 para 1; LMI sch 2 para 5(1),(2)(a),(3); NIUC sch 2 para 1; NILMI sch 2 para 5(1),(2)(a)

5. 10(c)-(e)   UC sch 2 paras 2-4; LMI sch 2 paras 5(2)(b),(c), 7(4); NIUC sch 2 paras 2-4; NILMI sch 2 paras 5(2)(b),(c), 6(5)

5. 12   UC sch 2 para 2; LMI sch 2 para 5(2)(b); NIUC sch 2 para 2; NILMI sch 2 para 5(2)(b)

Table 5.4 **Excluded liabilities**

You can't get UC or SMI towards your housing costs in the following cases.

Rent

(a) Your landlord is a relative who lives with you.

(b) Your landlord is a company and you or a relative who lives with you are an owner or director of the company.

(c) Your landlord is a trustee of a trust and you or a relative who lives with you are a trustee or beneficiary of the trust.

Owner-occupier payments

(d) Your payments are due to someone who lives in your household.

Rent or owner-occupier payments

(e) Your liability is not commercial (table 5.5).

(f) Your liability was contrived in order to obtain UC/SMI towards housing costs or to increase the amount (table 5.5).

(g) Your liability was increased to recover arrears you owe on your current or former home (rather than across the board arrears).

Service charges

(h) The rules in (a) to (g) also apply to service charges.

Terminology

(i) 'Benefit unit': you, your partner and children/young persons (para 3.46).

(j) 'Relative': a member of your benefit unit, or a close relative of you or a member of your benefit unit. (This meaning only applies here but in the rest of this guide 'relative' means anyone related to you.)

(k) 'Close relative': a parent, parent-in-law, step-parent, daughter/son, daughter/son-in-law, step-daughter/son, sister, brother, or the partner of any of these.

(l) 'Lives with you': you share at least some essential living accommodation (CH/542/2006).

(m) 'Lives in your household': you live together as a unit (para 3.53).

T5.4　UC 2 definition: 'close relative', 25(3)(b), sch 2 paras 5-10; LMI sch 2 para 6
　　　NIUC 2, 26(3)(b), sch 2 paras 5-10; NILMI sch 2 para 6

Table 5.5 **Commerciality, contrivance and renters**

Commerciality

(a) *What makes a letting commercial:* The primary consideration is about what was agreed between you and your landlord rather than what in fact happens, and claiming towards your housing costs can be evidence that the agreement is commercial ([2020] UKUT 240 (AAC)). Not only the financial arrangements between you and your landlord but all the terms of your agreement should be taken into account (R v Sutton LBC ex parte Partridge). Each case must be considered on its individual facts and is a matter of judgment (R(H) 1/03). The arrangements between you should be 'arms length' (R v Sheffield HBRB ex part Smith). It is their true factual basis which matters.

(b) *Personal and religious considerations:* If your letting is in fact commercial, friendliness and kindness between you and your landlord does not make it non-commercial (R v Poole BC ex parte Ross, CH/4854/2003, [2009] UKUT 13 AAC). If your letting is non-commercial, the fact that it was drawn up in a way that meets your religious beliefs does not make it commercial (R(H) 8/04).

(c) *Lettings between family members:* A letting between family members may or may not be commercial. The family arrangement is not decisive by itself. If the letting enables a disabled family member to be cared for more easily, this is not decisive by itself. Each case depends on its individual circumstances (CH/296/2004, CH/1096/2008, CH/2491/2007).

(d) *If the circumstances of your letting change:* If your letting was commercial when it began, it can become non-commercial if there is an identifiable reason for this (CH/3497/2005).

Contrivance

(e) *What makes a letting contrived:* You must be liable for rent but the liability must have been contrived as a way of gaining UC. The word 'contrived' implies abuse of the UC scheme (CH/39/2007). There must be evidence of this (R v Solihull HBRB ex parte Simpson), and the circumstances and intentions of both you and your landlord should be taken into account (R v Sutton HBRB ex parte Keegan).

(f) *No liability vs contrived liability:* These are separate considerations and should not be confused (CSHB/718/2002). If your landlord is unlikely to evict you if you do not pay, this can be evidence that you are not liable (table 5.3(e)) or that your liability is contrived (Solihull case).

T5.5   R v Sutton LBC ex p Partridge 04/11/94 QBD 28 HLR 315; R v Sheffield HBRB ex p Smith 08/12/94 QBD 28 HLR 36;
        R (Ross) v Poole BC ex parte Ross 05/05/95 QBD 28 HLR 351; R (Simpson) v Solihull HBRB 03/12/93 QBD 26 HLR 370;
        R (Keegan) v Sutton HBRB 15/05/92 QBD 27 HLR 92; R (Baragrove Properties) v Manchester CC 15/03/91 QBD 23 HLR 337

(g) *Lettings between family members:* If your landlord is a relation of yours (e.g. your parent) this does not by itself mean your letting is contrived (Solihull case). But see tables 5.4(a) and 5.5(c) for other rules which may affect you.

(h) *Lettings to people on low incomes:* If you cannot afford your rent, this is not evidence that your letting is contrived (Solihull case). And there is no objection to landlords letting to people on low incomes in order to make a profit unless their charges and profits show abuse (CH/39/2007, R v Manchester CC ex parte Baragrove Properties).

Occupying your home

5.14   The general rule is that you can only get UC or SMI towards housing costs on accommodation in the UK which you normally occupy as your home (paras 5.15-17). But there are also rules about absences from home, moving home and getting UC/SMI on two homes (paras 5.18-34).

Types of accommodation

5.15   Your home can be:

(a) a dwelling, e.g. a house, flat, mobile home or houseboat; or

(b) part of a dwelling, e.g. a room in a hostel or in someone else's home.

This includes somewhere converted, such as when two flats have been knocked together to form a single home (R(H) 5/09; CH/1895/2008). It doesn't include business premises or somewhere used only for a holiday.

Your normal home

5.16   Whether you normally occupy accommodation as your home is decided in your and your benefit unit's particular circumstances (CH/2521/2002). It means more than paying housing costs or having the right to live there: it means being physically present – though exceptions can arise (R(H) 9/05). If you have more than one home (in the UK or abroad), only one can be your normal home. This is decided on the facts, including how much time you and your family spend in each of them.

Short-term accommodation

5.17   Your home can be somewhere short-term, e.g. if you move a lot or are staying in a hostel or refuge. But it must be a 'home' in the ordinary sense, and this doesn't normally include night shelters where you have no right to live during the day ([2013] UKUT 65 (AAC)).

5.14   UC 25(4), sch 3 para 1; LMI 3(2)(c), sch 3 para 12; NIUC 26(4), sch 3 para 1; NILMI sch 3 para 12

5.16   UC sch 3 para 1(1),(3); LMI sch 3 para 12(1),(2); NIUC sch 3 para 1(1),(3); NILMI sch 3 para 12(1),(2)

Absences from home

5.18   This section explains when you can get UC or SMI during an absence from home. If you are in a couple and your partner is absent, see also paras 3.58-59.

Temporary absences

5.19   You can get UC or SMI on your normal home during an absence if:

(a) your absence is temporary (para 5.20);

(b) it is not expected to exceed the time limit (para 5.21);

(c) it has not yet reached the time limit; and

(d) you remain liable for housing costs on your normal home.

Different rules apply when your home is being repaired (para 5.23) or you are in prison (paras 2.22-24), or you are absent abroad (paras 2.29-35).

Intending to return

5.20   Your absence is temporary if you intend to return to your normal home. This is decided by your own intentions rather than what a relative or official intends for you. But your return must be possible within the time limit. Wanting to return is not enough if your return is in fact impossible (CSHB/405/2005).

Time limits

5.21   The time limit for temporary absences from your normal home is:

(a) 12 months if your absence is due to a fear of violence (para 5.24); or

(b) six months if your absence is for any other reason.

For example, (b) applies if you are on holiday, working away from home, trying out a care home, going to care for (or be cared for by) a relative or friend, in hospital and so on.

5.22   The six month time limit also applies to absences from a temporary home you are staying in due to a fear of violence in your normal home (para 5.25).

Example: Going away for work

Robin rents a private flat in Cornwall and is on UC. He gets a live-in job in Berkshire that is expected to last for six months.

■   While he is away, Robin can get UC towards the rent on his flat for up to six months (para 5.21), and his earnings are included in the UC calculation.

5.18-19 UC sch 3 paras 1, 9(1),(3); LMI sch 3 paras 15(1),(4),18; NIUC sch 3 paras 1, 8(1),(3); NILMI sch 3 paras 15(1),(4) 18

5.20   UC sch 3 para 6(1)(c); LMI sch 3 para 15(1)(c); NIUC sch 3 para 5(1)(c); NILMI sch 3 para 15(1)(c)

5.21-22 UC sch 3 paras 6(4), 9(1),(3); LMI sch 3 paras 15(4), 18; NIUC sch 3 paras 5(4), 8(1),(3); NILMI sch 3 paras 15(4), 18

Repairs to your normal home

5.23 When you move somewhere temporary because of repairs to your normal home, you can get UC or SMI towards your housing costs on:

(a) your temporary home if:

■ you don't pay housing costs on your normal home (e.g. you live there with relatives or friends or own it outright), or

■ the housing costs on your normal home have stopped;

(b) your normal home in any other case.

Fear of violence

5.24 For UC/SMI purposes, you have a fear of violence if you fear violence towards yourself or a member of your benefit unit (para 3.46) either:

(a) in your normal home (whoever it would be from); or

(b) outside your normal home from a person who was your partner but is no longer.

No violence needs actually to have occurred so long as your fear of it is reasonable.

Temporary absence due to fear of violence

5.25 If you leave your normal home due to a fear of violence and intend to return to it, but it is unreasonable to expect you to do so straight away, you can get UC/SMI for up to 12 months towards housing costs on:

(a) your normal home; or

(b) the place you are staying; or

(c) both of these, if you are liable for housing costs on both.

5.26 But if one or both of the addresses are supported or temporary accommodation (table 5.2), you can get HB on one and UC/SMI on the other or HB on both for up to 52 weeks.

Example: Fear of violence

Jenny rents a council flat. Her former partner threatens her outside her home. Jenny goes to a refuge, and starts action to enable her to return to her flat.

■ Jenny can get UC towards the rent on both her flat and the refuge for up to 12 months (paras 5.21, 5.24, 5.26).

5.23   UC sch 3 para 3; LMI sch 3 para 13; NIUC sch 3 para 2; NILMI sch 3 para 13

5.24   UC sch 3 para 6(1); LMI sch 3 para 15(1); NIUC sch 3 para 6(1); NILMI sch 3 para 15(1)

5.25   UC sch 3 para 6(3); LMI sch 3 para 15(3); NIUC sch 3 para 5(3); NILMI sch 3 para 15(3)

5.26   UC sch 3 paras 6(2),(4), 9(3); LMI sch 3 para 15(2),(4); NIUC sch 3 paras 5(2),(4), 8(3); NILMI sch 3 para 15(2),(4)
        The Housing Benefit Regulations 2006 reg 7(6)(a)(i);

Moving home

5.27   When you move home your UC changes to take account of your new housing costs (for SMI see paras 8.23 and 8.35). The new amount of UC applies from the beginning of the assessment period containing the date of your move (table 11.1). But in some cases, you can get UC or SMI for up to a month before moving in (paras 5.28-30).

Waiting for adaptations for a disability

5.28   You can get UC or SMI towards housing costs on a new home for up to one month before moving in if:

  (a) you are liable for housing costs there;

  (b) you are waiting for it to be adapted to meet your disability needs or those of a member of your benefit unit (para 3.46);

  (c) you or the member of your benefit unit are getting:

   ■   the daily living component of PIP, or

   ■   the middle or highest rate of the care component of DLA, or

   ■   attendance allowance or an equivalent benefit (para 10.37); and

  (d) your delay in moving is necessary and reasonable.

The adaptations can include furnishing, carpeting and redecorating as well as changes to your new home's fabric or structure (R (Mahmoudi) v Lewisham LBC).

5.29   You can get UC or SMI towards housing costs on both your old and new home for up to one month before moving if:

  (a) you are liable for housing costs on both of them; and

  (b) you meet the other conditions in para 5.28.

Example: Waiting for adaptations

Wolfgang rents a bedsit and is offered the tenancy of a flat nearer work. He takes on the tenancy and moves in three weeks later after adaptations make it suitable for his wheelchair. He is on the daily living component of PIP.

   ■   Wolfgang can get UC towards both the bedsit and the flat (para 5.29). Because assessment periods are monthly, he gets UC on both rents for the whole of the assessment period in which he becomes liable for rent on the flat (table 11.1(a)).

5.28   UC sch 3 para 7; LMI sch 3 para 14; NIUC sch 3 para 6; NILMI sch 3 para 14

5.29   UC sch 3 para 5; LMI sch 3 para 16; NIUC sch 3 para 4; NILMI sch 3 para 16

Waiting to leave hospital or a care home

5.30   You can get UC or SMI towards your housing costs on a new home for up to one month before moving in if:

(a) you are liable for housing costs there; and

(b) you (or if you are a couple, both of you) are waiting to leave an NHS or independent hospital (or similar institution) or a care home.

You need to make your claim for UC promptly (para 3.30).

Two homes

5.31   You can get UC towards your housing costs on two homes when:

(a) you have a large family (para 5.33); or

(b) you are absent from your normal home due to fear of violence (para 5.25); or

(c)   you are waiting for adaptations for a disability (para 5.29).

You can get SMI on two homes in cases (b) and (c).

5.32   In any other case you can only get UC or SMI on one home (paras 5.16-17).

Large families

5.33   You can get UC towards your housing costs on two homes (with no time limit) if:

(a) you were housed in two rented homes by a social landlord (table 6.1) because of the number of children/young person; or

(b) you normally occupy them both with children/young persons.

No similar rule applies for private renters, owner occupiers or shared owners.

Calculating UC for two homes

5.34   When you qualify for UC towards your housing costs on two homes:

(a) both housing costs elements are included in the UC calculation (para 9.4); but

(b) deductions for earned income and housing cost contributions are only made once (paras 9.8, 9.63);

(c) the size criteria (para 6.15) apply to:

  ▪ the combined number of bedrooms in the case of large families (para 5.33), or

  ▪ each home separately in other cases (para 5.31(b) and (c)).

If you qualify for SMI on two homes, the two amounts are added together (para 8.20). For the benefit cap, see table 9.5.

5.30   UC sch 3 para 8; LMI sch 3 para 17; NIUC sch 3 para 7; NILMI sch 3 para 17

5.32   UC 25(4), sch 3 para 1; LMI 3(2)(c), sch 3 para 12; NIUC 26(4), sch 3 para 1; NILMI sch 3 para 12

5.33   UC sch 3 para 4; NIUC sch 3 para 3

5.34   UC sch 4 paras 17-19, 25(3),(4); LMI 10; NIUC sch 4 paras 16-18, 24(3),(4), NILMI 10
         R (Mahmoudi) v Lewisham CA (2014) www.bailii.org/ew/cases/EWCA/Civ/2014/284.html

Chapter 6 **Rent and service charges**

- ■ Introduction: see paras 6.1-6.
- ■ Social renters including under-occupation and high rents: see paras 6.7-22.
- ■ Service charges (for social renters and owner-occupiers): see paras 6.23-33.
- ■ Private renters including local housing allowances: see paras 6.34-55.

Introduction

6.1 This chapter applies to renters and shared owners. It explains how to work out your UC housing costs element, which is also called your eligible rent. The rules about this differ between social renters and private renters.

6.2 To qualify for a housing costs element you must meet the conditions in chapters 2 and 5 as well as this chapter. Chapter 9 explains how your housing costs element affects the amount of your UC, and how it can be reduced if you have one or more non-dependants.

Social renters

6.3 You are a social renter if you are liable to pay rent (with or without service charges) to a social landlord. This means all local authorities and most housing associations and housing trusts: see table 6.1.

Private renters

6.4 You are a private renter if you are liable to pay rent (with or without service charges) to a private landlord. This means anyone other than a social landlord, including an individual, a lettings agency, a company, a registered charity or a not-for-profit organisation.

Shared owners

6.5 If you are a shared owner (para 8.9) the rules for social renters apply if you have a social landlord, and the rules for private renters apply if you have a private landlord.

Discretionary housing payments

6.6 Your eligible rent can be lower than your actual rent (paras 6.15, 6.19, 6.36). In these cases you may be able to get a discretionary housing payment from your local council (para 4.70).

6.3   UC 2 definition: 'local authority', sch 4 paras 2, 30; NIUC 2, sch 4 paras 2, 29

6.4   UC sch 4 para 20; NIUC sch 4 para 19

Table 6.1 **Social landlords**

All the following are social landlords (in UC law 'a provider of social housing'). If you rent your home from any of them you are a social renter.

(a) Local authorities and public bodies:

- in England: county, district and parish councils, London boroughs, the City of London and the council of the Isles of Scilly;

- in Wales: county, county borough and community councils;

- in Scotland: the council that issues your council tax bill;

- in Northern Ireland: the Northern Ireland Housing Executive.

(b) Housing associations, trusts, etc:

- in England: registered providers of social housing (i.e. any landlord who is registered with the Regulator of Social Housing: but see note);

- in Wales and Scotland: registered social landlords, i.e. any landlord that is registered with the Scottish or Welsh Government;

- in Northern Ireland: a housing association registered with the DFC.

Note:

Registered providers of social housing can be profit making or non-profit making. You are a social renter if you rent:

- any housing from a non-profit making registered provider; or

- social housing from a profit making registered provider. This means housing let below a market rent (such as part of the Affordable Rent Programme) and shared ownership tenancies.

You are a private renter if you rent other housing from a profit making registered provider.

Social renters: eligible rent

6.7   Paragraphs 6.8-33 explain how to work out your eligible rent if you are a social renter (para 6.3). The rules are summarised in table 6.2.

6.8   The amount of your eligible rent depends on whether you are:

(a) a sole tenant – in other words, you are the only person liable for rent on your home; or

(b) a joint tenant with only your partner and/or a child or young person you are responsible for – in other words, you are all in the same benefit unit; or

(c) a joint tenant with at least one person who is neither your partner nor a child or young person you are responsible for – in other words, you are in different benefit units.

If (a) or (b) applies to you, see paras 6.9-10. If (c) applies to you, see paras 6.11-13.

Table 6.2 **Eligible rent: social renters**

Step 1: Rent and eligible service charges (paras 6.8-10)

Your eligible rent is the monthly total of your:

■ rent payments (before subtracting any discount: para 6.14); and

■ eligible service charge payments (if any).

But this is reduced if any of the following steps apply to you.

Step 2: Certain joint tenancies (paras 6.11-13)

If you are in a joint tenancy (for example a house-share) and at least one joint tenant is not in your benefit unit, the eligible rent is split between you and the other joint tenant(s).

Step 3: Reductions for under-occupation (paras 6.15-18)

If your home has more bedrooms than the UC rules say you are entitled to, your eligible rent is reduced by:

■ 14% if you have one extra bedroom;

■ 25% if you have two or more extra bedrooms.

But this does not apply if Step 2 applies to you.

Step 4: Reductions for high rents (paras 6.19-22)

If the amounts in Step 1 are unreasonably high, they can be referred to the rent officer, and this may mean your eligible rent is reduced. If this applies to you, this reduction is made before Step 2 or 3.

Eligible rent: the general rule

6.9   The general rule for social renters is that your eligible rent is the monthly total of:

(a) your rent payments; and

(b) your eligible service charge payments (if any).

See paras 6.23-33 for which service charges are eligible. For how to convert payments to a monthly figure, see para 9.59.

6.10   But your eligible rent is reduced if you are under-occupying (paras 6.15-18) and/or if your rent or service charge payments are unreasonably high (paras 6.19-22).

T6.2   UC sch 4 paras 3, 5, 6, 31, 32A, 34, 35; NIUC sch 4 paras 3, 5, 30, 33, 34

6.9   UC sch 4 paras 3, 5, 6, 32A, 34, 35; NIUC sch 4 paras 3, 5, 33, 34

Eligible rent: joint tenants not in the same benefit unit

6.11   If you have at least one joint tenant who is not in your benefit unit, the general rule in paras 6.9-10 applies to you, with two differences:

(a) your eligible rent is your share of the monthly total of rent and eligible service charge payments;

(b) the rules about under-occupation do not apply to you.

6.12   Your share is worked out as follows:

(a) start with the monthly total of your rent and eligible service charge payments;

(b) divide this by the total number of joint tenants (including yourself);

(c) multiply the result by the number of joint tenants (including yourself) who are in your benefit unit.

The last step is only needed in the kind of situation illustrated in example 4.

6.13   But if the above produces an unreasonable result, the DWP can agree to split the eligible rent in some other way, taking account of all the circumstances, including how many joint tenants there are and how you actually split your rent and service charges. See example 5.

Rent discounts

6.14   Some social landlords have a rent discount scheme which reduces your rent as a payment incentive (e.g. for prompt payment or online payment). If you get such a discount, and your landlord's scheme is approved by the DWP, the discount is not deducted from your eligible rent. For example, if your eligible rent is normally £800 but your rent is reduced by £25 for prompt payment, your eligible rent is still £800.

Examples: The amount of eligible rent

In all these examples, the tenants are social renters, the eligible rent for the dwelling (including eligible service charges) is £600 per month, they are not under-occupying, and the rent is not unreasonably high.

1. **A sole tenant**
   - The tenant's eligible rent is simply £600 per month.
2. **A couple who are the only joint tenants**
   - Their eligible rent is simply £600 per month.
3. **Three joint tenants who are not related**
   - Each one's eligible rent is £200 per month.
4. **Three joint tenants two of whom are a couple**
   - The couple's eligible rent is £400 per month (two-thirds of £600).
   - The single person's eligible rent is £200 per month (a third of £600).

6.11   UC sch 4 para 35(1),(2),(4); NIUC sch 4 para 34(1),(2),(4)

6.12   UC sch 4 paras 2 definition: 'listed persons', 35(4); NIUC sch 4 paras 2, 34(4)

6.13   UC sch 4 para 35(5); NIUC sch 4 para 34(5)

6.14   UC sch 4 para 32A

5. A different split of the eligible rent
- The couple in example 4 have one bedroom and have always paid half the rent. The same applies to the single person. The DWP agrees it is reasonable to split the eligible rent the same way.
- So the couple's eligible rent is £300 per month, and so is the single person's.

Social renters: under-occupation

6.15 Your eligible rent is reduced if you are under-occupying your home. You count as under-occupying if you have more bedrooms in your home than the UC rules say you qualify for. Other rooms (such as living rooms) are not taken into account.

Exceptions

6.16 The rules about under-occupation do not apply to you if:

(a) you have a joint tenant who is not in your benefit unit (para 6.11); or

(b) you are a shared owner (para 8.9).

Size of accommodation

6.17 You qualify for the number of bedrooms allowed by the 'size criteria' taking into account:

(a) the people in your benefit unit and any non-dependants you have; and

(b) your fostering, overnight care, disability and bereavement needs.

The details are in chapter 7.

The amount of the reduction

6.18 Your eligible rent is reduced by:

(a) 14% if you have one bedroom more than you are entitled to;

(b) 25% if you have two or more bedrooms more than you are entitled to.

See the following examples.

Examples: Reductions for under-occupation

1. One extra bedroom.
A couple are social renters who have two children under 10. They rent a three bedroom house and no-one else lives with them. The eligible rent for the dwelling is £1,000 per month.

They qualify for two bedrooms, one for themselves and one for the children. Because

---

6.15   UC sch 4 para 36(1); NIUC sch 4 para 35(1)

6.16   UC sch 4 paras 35(4), 36(5); NIUC sch 4 paras 34(4), 35(5)

6.17   UC sch 4 paras 8-12; NIUC sch 4 paras 7-11

6.18   UC sch 4 para 36(2)-(4); NIUC sch 4 para 36(2)-(4)

their home has one bedroom more than this, their eligible rent is reduced by 14% (£140) to £860 per month.

2. **Two extra bedrooms.**
    A single person is a social renter. She rents a three-bedroom house and no-one else lives with her. The eligible rent for the dwelling is £1,000 per month.

    She qualifies for one bedroom. Because her home has two bedrooms more than this, her eligible rent is reduced by 25% (£250) to £750 per month.

For further examples, see chapter 7.

Social renters: unreasonably high rents

6.19   Your eligible rent can be reduced (paras 6.20-22) if the DWP/DFC consider your rent or service charges are 'greater than it is reasonable to meet by way of the [UC] housing costs element'. For example, this could happen if your rent is higher than the LHA figure that would apply if you were a private renter but considering any special circumstances (ADM F3253).

Housing payment determinations in Great Britain

6.20   In Great Britain, the DWP asks the rent officer to make a housing payment determination (HPD). The rent officer:

(a) looks at the payments (rent and/or service charges) the DWP has asked them to consider;

(b) can ask the DWP or your landlord for further information about them;

(c) compares what you pay (or in the case of joint tenants what you pay between you) with what a landlord could reasonably be expected to obtain' on accommodation that matches yours (as far as possible) in terms of council area, number of bedrooms, landlord type (table 6.1(a) or (b)) and state of repair;

(d) tells the DWP what is a reasonable amount, or confirms what you are paying is reasonable;

(e) must agree that your rent payments (but necessarily your service charge payments) are reasonable if your home is in the Affordable Rent programme.

See para 6.53 for HPD redeterminations.

Reductions in Great Britain

6.21   if the rent officer decides your rent and/or service charge payments are unreasonably high, the DWP:

(a) uses the amount the rent officer says is reasonable (rather than the amount you actually pay) to work out your eligible rent; but

(b) can agree not to do this if it wouldn't be 'appropriate'.

And if the rules about joint tenants or under-occupying your home (paras 6.11-18) also apply to you, they apply after this rule (table 6.2).

6.19   UC sch 4 paras 3, 32(1),(2); NIUC sch 4 paras 3,31

6.20-21 UCROO 5, sch 2; C&P 40;

Reductions in Northern Ireland

6.22   In Northern Ireland, the DFC decides whether to reduce your eligible rent or service charges by comparing them with what a landlord could reasonably be expected to obtain (para 6.20(c)).

Service charges (social renters and owners)

6.23   This section is about service charges. It applies if:

(a) you are a social renter (para 6.3); or

(b) you are a shared owner (para 8.9) in a scheme run by a social landlord (para 6.5); or

(c) you are an owner-occupier (para 8.7); or

(d) you are only liable for service charges (para 5.3).

If you are a private renter, or shared owner in a scheme run by a private landlord, different rules apply: see paras 6.36-37.

6.24   For UC purposes:

(a) services means 'services or facilities for the use or benefit of persons occupying accommodation'; and

(b) 'service charge payments' means:

■   payments for all or part of the costs or charges relating to services or facilities, or

■   amounts which are fairly attributable to the costs or charges relating to available services or facilities.

6.25   Payments which meet the above definition are service charge payments whether they are:

(a) named in an agreement or not;

(b) paid in with the other payments you make on your home or separately;

(c) paid under the agreement under which you occupy your home or under a separate agreement.

Separating rent and service charges

6.26   When you claim UC or move home or your rent changes, you have to give the DWP one figure for your rent and another for the total of your eligible service charges (if any). Your landlord should tell you these or give them to the DWP for you, and the DWP normally accepts the landlord's figures [www]. But in the end it is the law that distinguishes rent from services, and between eligible and ineligible charges ([2009] UKUT 28 (AAC), CH/3528/2006).

6.22   UC sch 4 para 35(3),(4); NIUC sch 4 para 34(3),(4)

6.24   UC sch 1 para 7(1)(a),(b),(2); NIUC sch 1 para 8(1)(a),(b),(2)

6.25   UC sch 1 para 7(4); NIUC sch 1 para 8(4)

6.26   https://tinyurl.com/DWP-SC-Dec19

6.27   The following are examples of rent rather than service charges:

(a)   maintenance, repairs and insurance;

(b)   management costs;

(c)   council tax when the landlord is liable (para 15.17);

(d)   other normal overheads; and

(e)   associated administrative costs.

Which service charges are eligible for UC

6.28   A service charge is eligible for UC if it meets all the following conditions:

(a)   it is for an eligible kind of service, not an excluded kind (paras 6.29-30);

(b)   you have to pay it in order to occupy your home (para 6.31); and

(c)   the service and amount are reasonable (paras 6.32-33).

Eligible and excluded services

6.29   Table 6.3 lists the kinds of service charges which are eligible for UC, and those which are excluded from UC.

6.30   If a service charge is 'eligible', this means it is included in your eligible rent (if you are a social sector renter) or eligible housing costs (if you are an owner-occupier, shared owner, or only liable for service charges). If it is 'excluded', this means you can't get UC for it.

A condition of occupying your home

6.31   To be eligible for UC, a service charge must be one you have to pay in order to have the right to occupy your home (para 5.8). This does not need to have applied since you moved in so long as, when you agreed to pay it, the alternative was that you could lose your home.

Unreasonable kinds of service charges

6.32   A service charge can be excluded from UC if the services or facilities are of a kind which it is not 'reasonable to provide'. Although the rules about which service charges are eligible are already strict (table 6.3), this rule could, for example, apply to maintaining a luxury item such as a swimming pool (ADM para F2065).

6.28   UC sch 1 para 8(2)-(6); NIUC sch 1 para 9(2)-(6)

6.29   UC sch 1 paras 8(4),(6); NIUC sch 1 paras 9(4),(6)

6.31   UC sch 1 para 8(3); NIUC sch 1 para 9(3)

6.32   UC sch 1 para 8(5); NIUC sch 1 para 9(5)

Table 6.3 **Service charges**

Eligible service charges

Categories A to D are listed in the law as being eligible for UC.

Maintaining the general standard of accommodation (Category A)

- External window cleaning on upper floors.
- For owner-occupiers and shared owners only, separately identifiable payments for maintenance and/or repairs.

General upkeep of communal areas (Category B)

- Ongoing maintenance and/or cleaning of communal areas.
- Supply of water, fuel or other commodities to communal areas.

'Communal areas' include internal areas, external areas and areas for reasonable facilities such as laundry rooms and children's play areas. DWP guidance (ADM para F2072) says that ground maintenance (e.g. lawn mowing, litter removal and lighting for access areas) and tenant parking (excluding security costs) should be included.

Basic communal services (Category C)

- Provision of basic communal services.
- Ongoing maintenance, cleaning and/or repair in connection with basic communal services.

'Basic communal services' are those available to everyone in the accommodation, such as refuse collection, communal lifts, secure building access and/or TV/wireless aerials for receiving a free service. DWP guidance (ADM paras F2073-74) says that communal telephones (but not call costs) should be included, as should a fair proportion of the staff management and administration costs of providing communal services.

Accommodation-specific charges (Category D)

- Use of essential items in your own accommodation, such as furniture and domestic appliances.

Excluded service charges

The first two items are listed in the law as being excluded from UC. The others are excluded from UC because they do not fall within categories A to D, and are based on DWP guidance (ADM para F2077).

- Food of any kind.
- Medical or personal services of any kind, including personal care.
- Nursing care, emergency alarm systems or individual personal alarms.
- Equipment or adaptations relating to disability or infirmity.
- Counselling, support or intensive housing management.

T6.3   UC sch 1 para 8(4),(6); NIUC sch 1 para 9(4),(6)

- Fuel, water or sewerage charges for your own accommodation.

- Living expenses such as heating, lighting or hot water.

- Cleaning your own accommodation or having your laundry done.

- Gardening in your own garden.

- Recreational facilities or subscription/fee-based TV.

- Transport, permits, licences or maintenance of unadopted roads.

- Any other service or facility not included in categories A to D.

Special cases

The following are listed in the law as being excluded from UC, even if they are for items falling within categories A to D.

- Services or facilities that could be met by public funds (e.g. Supporting People) even if you do not yourself qualify for such help.

- Payments which result in an asset changing hands (e.g. if you pay for furniture but after a period it will become yours).

See also paras 6.31-33.

Example: Service charges for a leaseholder

Harry is on UC and his assessment periods begin on the 4th of each month. He owns the leasehold of his home and is liable to the freeholder for service charges that are eligible for UC (table 6.3). The freeholder charges these for financial years (1st April to 31st March). Each year, the freeholder issues an estimated bill in February (for the following year) and a final balance bill in May (for the preceding year).

Harry receives

(a) an estimated bill on the 10th February 2019 of £480 (for 2019-20) – this is averaged over the 12 months from 4th February 2019 as £40 per month;

(b) a final balance bill on 16th May 2019 of £60 (for 2018-19) – this is averaged over the 12 months from the 4th May 2019 as £5 per month;

(c) an estimated bill on 8th February 2020 of £516 (for 2020-21) – this is averaged over the 12 months from 4th February 2020 as £43 per month;

(d) a final balance bill on 9th May 2020 of £48 for (2019-20) this is averaged over the 12 months from 4th May 2020 as £4 per month.

So Harry's UC housing costs element is:

- £40 from 4th February 2019 (= (a) above)

- £45 from 4th May 2019 (= (a) + (b) above)

- £48 from 4th February 2020 (= (b) + (c) above)

- £47 from 4th May 2020 (= (c) + (d) above)

Note: This is the method the DWP is expected to use, as it is based on the method used in other DWP benefits (see e.g. DMG volume 13 para 78487).

Unreasonably high service charges

6.33   A service charge can be excluded from UC if the costs and charges relating to it are not of a 'reasonable amount'. But:

(a) if you are a social renter or shared owner, the service charge must be referred to the rent officer for a determination (paras 6.19-22). DWP guidance (ADM para F2068) confirms that this means the reasonable part of the amount for the service charge is eligible for UC (and only the unreasonable part is excluded);

(b) if you are an owner-occupier, DWP guidance (ADM para F2066) is that service charges should not be excluded from UC under this rule.

Private renters: eligible rent

6.34   Paragraphs 6.35-54 explain how to work out your eligible rent if you are a private renter (para 6.4).

6.35   The amount of your eligible rent depends on whether you are:

(a) a sole tenant – in other words you are the only person liable for rent on your home; or

(b) a joint tenant with only your partner and/or a child or young person you are responsible for – in other words, you are all in the same benefit unit; or

(c) a joint tenant with at least one person who is neither your partner nor a child or young person you are responsible for – in other words, you are in different benefit units.

If (a) or (b) applies to you, see paras 6.36-37. If (c) applies to you, see paras 6.38-40.

Eligible rent: the general rule

6.36   The general rule for private renters is that your eligible rent equals:

(a) your actual monthly rent (para 6.37); or

(b) if it is lower, the local housing allowance (LHA) figure which applies to you (para 6.43).

Actual monthly rent

6.37   Your actual monthly rent is the monthly total of your:

(a) rent payments; and

(b) service charge payments (if any).

See chapter 5 for which rent and service charge payments count. Unlike the rules for social renters, no service charges are excluded. For how to convert payments to a monthly figure, see para 9.59.

6.33   UC sch 1 para 8(5); NIUC sch 1 para 9(5)

6.36   UC sch 4 para 22; NIUC sch 4 para 21

6.37   UC sch 4 paras 3, 5, 6, 23, 24; NIUC sch 4 paras 3, 5, 22, 23

Eligible rent: joint tenants not in the same benefit unit

6.38   If you have at least one joint tenant who is not in your benefit unit, the actual monthly rent (para 6.37) is split between you and the other joint tenant(s). Your eligible rent equals:

(a)   your share of the actual monthly rent; or

(b)   if it is lower, the LHA figure which applies to you (para 7.18).

6.39   Your share is worked out as follows:

(a)   start with the actual monthly rent on your dwelling;

(b)   divide this by the total number of joint tenants (including yourself);

(c)   multiply the result by the number of joint tenants (including yourself) who are in your benefit unit.

The last step is only needed in the kind of situation illustrated in example 4.

Examples: Actual monthly rent and eligible rent

In all these examples the tenants are private renters.

1. A sole tenant

   ■   A sole tenant's actual monthly rent is £900.

   ■   If her LHA figure is £800, her eligible rent is £800.

2. A couple who are the only joint tenants

   ■   Their actual monthly rent is £700.

   ■   If their LHA figure is £800, their eligible rent is £700.

3. Three joint tenants who are not related

   ■   The actually monthly rent for their dwelling is £1,200.

   ■   So each one's share of it is £400 (⅓ of £1,200).

   ■   If the LHA figure (for each of them) is £350, each one's eligible rent is £350.

4. Three joint tenants, two of whom are a couple

   ■   The couple are claiming UC, but the single person is not.

   ■   The actual monthly rent for the dwelling is £1,200.

   ■   So the couple's share is £800 (⅔ of £1,200).

   ■   If their LHA figure is £1,000, their eligible rent is £800.

5. A different split of the actual monthly rent

   ■   The couple in example 4 have the use of three of the four bedrooms (they have children) and have always paid ¾ of the rent. The DWP agrees it is reasonable to split the actual monthly rent the same way.

   ■   So their share is now £900 (¾ of £1,200).

   ■   If their LHA figure is £1,000, their eligible rent is £900.

6.38   UC sch 4 para 24(1),(2),(4); NIUC sch 4 para 23(1),(2),(4)

6.39   UC sch 4 paras 2 definition: 'listed persons', 24(4); NIUC sch 4 paras 2, 23(4)

6.40 But if the above would produce an unreasonable result, the DWP can agree to split the actual monthly rent in some other way, taking account of all the circumstances including how many joint tenants there are and how you actually split your rent and eligible service charges. See example 5.

Legal terminology: 'core rent' and 'cap rent'

6.41 UC law and guidance uses these terms:

(a) 'core rent' means your actual monthly rent (or share of it);

(b) 'cap rent' means the LHA figure which applies to you.

Private renters: local housing allowances

6.42 LHAs are figures used in deciding your eligible rent (paras 6.36 and 6.38). They are set:

(a) in Great Britain by the rent officer, a government employee who is independent of the DWP; or

(b) in Northern Ireland by the Housing Executive (NIHE).

They are monthly figures that apply from April each year (para 6.51) and are published online in late January [www].

Which LHA figure applies to you?

6.43 The LHA figure that applies to you is the one for:

(a) the size of the accommodation you qualify for; and

(b) the area your home is in (also called a broad rental market area).

Size of accommodation

6.44 You qualify for the number of bedrooms allowed by the 'size criteria' taking into account:

(a) the people in your benefit unit and any non-dependants you have; and

(b) your fostering, overnight care, disability and bereavement needs.

The details are in table 7.1.

6.45 But for private renters (unlike social renters):

(a) the maximum number of bedrooms is always four; and

(b) there are further rules if you are single and aged under 35 (paras 6.46-47).

6.40   UC sch 4 para 24(5); NIUC sch 4 para 23(5)

6.42   UCRO0 4, sch 1; SI 2020/371; NIUCED 4, sch 1; NISR 2020/53
        https://lha-direct.voa.gov.uk/search.aspx
        www.nihe.gov.uk/Housing-Help/Local-Housing-Allowance/Current-LHA-rent-levels

6.43   UC sch 4 para 25(1),(2),(5); NIUC sch 4 para 24(1),(2),(5)

6.45-47 UC sch 4 paras 8, 12, 26, 29; NIUC sch 4 paras 7, 11, 25, 28

Single people under 35

6.46 You qualify for one-bedroom shared accommodation (rather than self-contained) if you are:

(a) a single person, or in a couple but claiming UC as a single person (para 2.7); and

(b) under 35 years old; and

(c) not in any of the excepted groups in table 6.4.

This rule does not amount to unlawful discrimination ([2020] UKUT 285 (AAC)).

Table 6.4 **Single people under 35: the UC excepted groups**

Single under-35-year-olds who fall in these excepted groups qualify for one-bedroom self-contained accommodation. Other single under-35-year-olds qualify for one-bedroom shared accommodation.

(a) You have one or more children or young persons in your benefit unit (paras 3.62 and 3.68).

(b) You are a foster parent or have a child placed with you for adoption (para 7.21).

(c) You have one or more non-dependants (paras 3.70-77).

(d) You are in receipt of:

■ the middle or highest rate of the care component of DLA, or

■ the daily living component of PIP, or

■ a benefit equivalent to attendance allowance (para 10.37).

(e) You were a 16/17-year-old care leaver (paras 2.11-12) and are now aged 18 or over but under 22.

(f) You are an ex-offender managed under a multi-agency (MAPPA) agreement because you pose a serious risk of harm to the public.

(g) You are aged 25 or over, and:

■ you have occupied one or more hostels for homeless people (para 6.47) for at least three months. This does not need to have been a continuous three months, and it does not need to have been recent; and

■ while you were there, you were offered and you accepted support with rehabilitation or resettlement within the community.

6.46   UC sch 4 paras 27, 28(1),(2); NIUC sch 4 paras 26, 27(1),(2)

T6.4   UC 2 definition: 'attendance allowance', sch 4 paras 28(3),(4), 29; NIUC 2, sch 4 paras 27(3),(4), 28

Hostels for homeless people

6.47   A hostel for homeless people (see table 6.4(g)) means a building that:

(a) provides non-self-contained domestic accommodation, together with meals or adequate food-preparation facilities;

(b) has the main purpose of providing accommodation together with care, support or supervision, in order to assist homeless people to be rehabilitated or resettled;

(c) is either:

■   managed or owned by a social landlord other than a local authority (table 6.1), or

■   run on a non-commercial basis, and wholly or partly funded by a government department or agency or local authority, or

■   managed by a registered charity or non-profit-making voluntary organisation;

(d) is not a care home (in Scotland a care home service) or independent hospital.

How LHA figures are set

6.48   From April 2021 all LHA figures remain the same as they were from April 2020, when they were set at the lower of:

(a) the rent at the 30th percentile (para 6.50);

(b) the national maximum (table 6.5).

In practice (b) is uncommon because the maximums were increased substantially from April 2020 due to coronavirus and remain the same from April 2021.

6.49   The rent officer or NIHE sets the LHA figures as described above and if necessary adjusts them to ensure that LHAs for small dwellings aren't higher than LHAs for large ones.

6.50   The rent at the 30th percentile means the highest rent within the bottom 30% of rents in the rent officer's data. This uses actual rents (including eligible service charges) payable during the year ending on the preceding 30th September, on accommodation which:

(a) is rented on an assured tenancy;

(b) is in a reasonable state of repair;

(c) is the correct size and in the correct area (para 6.43) or if necessary from comparable areas.

The rent officer excludes rents paid by people on UC or HB (this is to avoid the effect UC/HB could have on rent levels). The UC rules are slightly different from those used in HB (volume 2 chapter 11) but the LHA figures for UC and HB are usually the same.

6.47   UC 2 definition: 'local authority', sch 4 para 29(10); NIUC sch 4 para 28(6)

6.48   UCROO 4(1),(2), sch 1 para 2(2); SI 2020/1519 reg 4; NIUCED 4(1),(2), sch 1 para 2(2); NISR 2021/14 reg 4

6.49   UCROO 4(1), sch 1 para 5; NIUCED 4(1), sch 1 para 4

6.50   UCROO sch 1 para 3; NIUCED sch 1 para 3

Table 6.5 **LHA sizes of accommodation**

Size of accommodation	National monthly maximum
(a) one-bedroom shared accommodation	£1283.96
(b) one-bedroom self-contained accommodation	£1283.96
(c) two-bedroom dwellings	£1589.99
(d) three-bedroom dwellings	£1920.00
(e) four-bedroom dwellings	£2579.98

Notes:

■ This table only applies to private renters (para 6.42).

■ See chapter 7 for which size of accommodation applies to you.

■ Actual LHAs for (a) are usually lower than those for (b) (though the national maximums are the same).

Examples: LHAs and size of accommodation

All the following are private renters.

1. A single person aged 24

■ Unless she is in an excepted group (see table 6.4), she qualifies for the LHA for one-bedroom shared accommodation.

2. A single person aged 58

■ He qualifies for the LHA for one-bedroom self-contained accommodation.

3. A couple

■ They qualify for the LHA for one-bedroom self-contained accommodation.

4. A couple with a son aged 9 and a daughter aged 7

■ The couple qualify for the LHA for a two-bedroom dwelling.

5. The son in example 4 reaches the age of 10

■ Because the children are no longer expected to share a bedroom (table 7.1), the couple qualify for the LHA for a three-bedroom dwelling.

6. Three joint tenants who are not related

■ They are all under 35 and none of them is in an excepted group (table 6.4). So each one qualifies for the LHA for one-bedroom shared accommodation.

7. Two brothers who are joint tenants

■ They are in their 40s, and the daughter of one of them lives with him. So that brother qualifies for the LHA for a two-bedroom dwelling. The other brother qualifies for the LHA for one-bedroom self-contained accommodation.

For further examples about size of accommodation, see chapter 7.

T6.5   UCROO sch 1 para 2(2), SI 2020/371; NIUCED sch 1 para 2(2); NISR 2020/53

When LHA figures and changes take effect

6.51   This year's LHA figures haven't changed (para 6.48). In years when they do change, the new figures take effect:

(a)   on 6th April; or

(b)   if you are already on UC, from the first day of your assessment period ending on or after 6th April.

For example, if your assessment periods begin on the 7th of each month, (b) means your new LHA figure takes effect from 7th March.

6.52   Your LHA figure changes if:

(a)   you qualify for a different size of accommodation or move to a new area – this is a change of circumstances (table 11.1); or

(b)   the DWP used the wrong figure – this is an official error (paras 14.22-24); or

(c)   there was an error setting the LHA figure or areas (paras 6.53-55).

Rent officer redeterminations in Great Britain

6.53   In Great Britain, the rent officer can reconsider and if necessary correct:

(a)   any LHA figure or area (para 6.43); or

(b)   any housing payment determination (para 6.20).

This is called a redetermination and can be done with or without a request from the DWP. It also seems possible that you (or someone on your behalf) could request a redetermination, but the law doesn't say either way.

6.54   When a rent officer redetermination means a new figure applies to you:

(a)   if it is higher, the DWP's new decision takes effect from when its original decision took effect (or should have) – so you get arrears of UC back to then;

(b)   if it is lower, the DWP's new decision takes effect from the first day of the assessment period following the one in which the DWP receives the figure from the rent officer – so you haven't been overpaid UC.

Redeterminations in Northern Ireland

6.55   In Northern Ireland, the NIHE can correct any LHA figure or area, and the DFC can correct any rent determination it has made (para 6.22). The rules in para 6.54 apply in a similar way.

6.51   UCROO 4(3),(4); SI 2020/371; SI 2020/397; NIUCED 4(3),(4); NISR 2020/53; NISR 2020/61

6.52   D&A 19(2), 30, sch 1 paras 20, 21, 29; UCROO 6; NID&A 19(2), 30, sch 1 paras 20, 21, 29; NIUCED 5

6.53-54 D&A 19(2), 21, 30, 35(14)

6.55   NID&A 19(2), 21, 30, 35(14)

Chapter 7 **The size criteria**

- ■ The size criteria and your eligible rent: see paras 7.1-4.
- ■ The number of bedrooms you qualify for: see paras 7.5-7.
- ■ Which occupiers are included: see paras 7.8-18.
- ■ Qualifying for an additional bedroom: see paras 7.19-28.

The size criteria and eligible rent

7.1 This chapter explains how many bedrooms you qualify for in the calculation of your UC if you rent your home. The rules about this are known as the size criteria. Opponents of the rules say they are a 'bedroom tax'; supporters say they prevent a 'spare room subsidy'. The rules are not always the same as those used in HB (volume 2 chapter 11).

How the number of bedrooms affects your UC

7.2 If you rent your home, the housing costs element of your UC depends on the amount of your eligible rent (see paras 9.51-68). This in turn depends on how many bedrooms you qualify for, as follows:

(a) if you are a social renter:

- ■ the UC size criteria say how many bedrooms you qualify for (para 7.5 onwards),
- ■ your eligible rent is reduced if you have more bedrooms than you qualify for (paras 6.15-18),
- ■ whether a particular room is a bedroom can therefore be important (paras 7.6-7);

(b) if you are a private renter:

- ■ the UC size criteria say how many bedrooms you qualify for (para 7.5 onwards),
- ■ your eligible rent is limited to the local housing allowance figure which applies to you (paras 6.36-54),
- ■ whether a particular room is a bedroom is not relevant, because your LHA figure is based on how many bedrooms you qualify for, not how many there are in your home.

7.3 If you are a shared owner the rules in para 7.2(a) or (b) apply (depending on whether your shared ownership scheme is run by a social or private landlord), but only to your eligible rent, not to your owner-occupier payments (chapter 8). The size criteria do not apply if you are an owner occupier.

Case law about the size criteria

7.4 The European Court of Human rights: has decided that the size criteria unlawfully discriminate against women living in sanctuary schemes (A v UK), but the DWP may appeal to the European Grand Chamber about this. In other cases, there was found to be no unlawful discrimination against:

(a)   parents who care for a grown-up child who is disabled (JD v UK)

(b)   separated parents with shared care of a child (R (Cotton and others) v SSWP);

(c)   gypsy travellers ([2019] UKUT 43 (AAC)).

And another case resulted in changes to the law so that the rules about additional bedrooms (paras 7.22-28) don't discriminate between adults and children (R (Daly and others) v SSWP).

The number of bedrooms you qualify for

7.5   Table 7.1 shows how to work out the number of bedrooms you qualify for. But there are further rules:

(a)   for all renters who have a joint tenant who isn't in your benefit unit (para 7.18);

(b)   for all renters who have had a bereavement (paras 11.27-28);

(c)   for private renters only who are single and under 35 (para 6.46).

And for private renters only, the maximum number of bedrooms is always four.

Table 7.1 **The UC size criteria**

The size criteria are based on the occupiers of your home (paras 7.8-18).

General rules

One bedroom is allowed for each of the following occupiers of your home:

■   yourself, or yourself and your partner if you are claiming UC as a couple;

■   each young person aged 16 or over;

■   each non-dependant aged 16 or over;

■   two children under 16 of the same sex;

■   two children under 10 of the same or opposite sex;

■   any other child aged under 16.

Children are expected to share bedrooms in whatever way results in the smallest number of bedrooms. See examples 5 and 6.

Additional bedrooms

One or more additional bedrooms can be allowed for:

■   a foster parent or if you are waiting to adopt (para 7.21);

■   a person who requires overnight care (paras 7.22-24);

■   a disabled person who can't share a bedroom (paras 7.25-28).

7.4   JD and A v United Kingdom [2019] ECHR 753 https://www.bailii.org/eu/cases/ECHR/2019/753.html
         R (Cotton and others) v SSWP [2014] EWHC Admin 3437 https://www.bailii.org/ew/cases/EWHC/Admin/2014/3437.html
         R (Daly and others) v SSWP [2016] UKSC Civ 58 https://www.bailii.org/uk/cases/UKSC/2016/58.html

7.5   UC sch 4 para 26; NIUC sch 4 para 25

T7.1   WRA 40 definition: 'child'; UC sch 4 paras 10, 12; NIWRO 46; NIUC sch 4 paras 9, 11

What counts as a bedroom

7.6   Whether a particular room in your home is a bedroom (rather than a living room, storage room, etc) can be important if you are a social renter (para 7.2). Neither UC law nor DWP guidance (ADM paras F3110-38) define what a bedroom is (but see para 7.7). In practice, the DWP is likely to follow your landlord's description of whether a room is a bedroom (for example in your letting agreement), but you can ask the DWP to reconsider this and appeal to a tribunal if you disagree (chapter 14).

7.7   There have been a number of court and Upper Tribunal decisions about what is a bedroom, and these are summarised in table 7.2.

Examples: How many bedrooms you qualify for

1. A single person who is the only occupier

She qualifies for one bedroom. If she is a private renter under 35, see para 6.46 for whether she qualifies for shared or self-contained accommodation.

2. A couple who are the only occupiers

They qualify for one bedroom.

3. A single person with three children

He has sons aged 15 and 8 and a daughter aged 13. The sons are expected to share a bedroom. So the household qualifies for three bedrooms.

4. The older son in example 3 reaches 16

Now none of the children are expected to share a bedroom. So the household qualifies for four bedrooms.

5. A couple with four children

They have daughters aged 13 and 4 and sons aged 14 and 8. The children are expected to share bedrooms in the way that results in the smallest number of bedrooms (the daughters sharing, and also the sons). The household qualifies for three bedrooms.

6. The couple in example 5 have a baby

The couple now qualify for four bedrooms. No way of sharing bedrooms can result in a lower number.

7. A single person with two non-dependants

The household qualifies for three bedrooms. This is the case even if the non-dependants are a couple: see para 7.14.

Examples including additional bedrooms are later in this chapter.

Table 7.2 **What counts as a bedroom: case law**

Assessing the room.

The Court of Session has held that whether a room is a bedroom is determined by 'an objective assessment of the property as vacant which is not related to the residents or what their actual use or needs might be' (SSWP v Glasgow CC and Another). In the same way, the Court of Appeal has held that the assessment should be 'carried out… in respect of a nominally vacant house' and that 'the characteristics of the particular individuals are irrelevant' (SSWP v Hockley).

The term 'bedroom'.

The term 'bedroom' has its ordinary or familiar English meaning ([2014] UKUT 525 (AAC)). The landlord's designation of the room or its description in the building's plans can be of use in borderline cases rather than being conclusive ([2014] UKUT 525 (AAC); [2018] UKUT 180 (AAC)). And a room can stop counting as a bedroom if exceptional circumstances relating to physical or mental disability mean it is now used as a living room ([2015] UKUT 282 (AAC)).

Practical factors.

Factors to be considered include '(a) size, configuration and overall dimensions, (b) access, (c) natural and electronic lighting, (d) ventilation, and (e) privacy' taking account of the adults and children referred to in the regulations (paras 7.8-16), and the relationship of the room to the other rooms in the house ([2014] UKUT 525 (AAC), [2018] UKUT 180 (AAC)). So long as the room is accessible, it is not a requirement that the door opens all the way ([2020] UKUT 247 (AAC)). It should be possible to get into bed from within the room, and there should be somewhere to put clothes and a glass of water, for example a bedside cabinet with drawers ([2016] UKUT 164 (AAC); [2017] UKUT 443 (AAC)).

Overcrowding and unfitness.

The overcrowding rules differ from the size criteria, taking into account living rooms as well as bedrooms, but they can sound 'warning bells' that a room with very small dimensions may not be a bedroom ([2014] UKUT 525 (AAC); [2016] UKUT 164 (AAC); [2017] UKUT 443 (AAC)). A room contaminated with asbestos cannot be counted as a bedroom ([2018] UKUT 287 (AAC)).

T7.2   SSWP v Glasgow CC and Another [2017] CSIH 35 https://www.bailii.org/scot/cases/ScotCS/2017/[2017]CSIH35.html
        SSWP v Hockley [2019] EWCA Civ 1080 https://www.bailii.org/ew/cases/EWCA/Civ/2019/1080.html

Which occupiers are included

7.8 The following occupiers of your home are taken into account in deciding how many bedrooms you qualify for:

(a) the people in your benefit unit (paras 7.10-13); and

(b) non-dependants (paras 7.14-16).

In the law these are called the members of your 'extended benefit unit'. See also paras 11.27-28 for the 'bereavement run-on' which can mean you continue to qualify for a bedroom for up to three months for a member of your extended benefit unit who has died.

7.9 The DWP decides which occupiers to include, not (for example) the rent officer. Decisions about this are appealable to a tribunal: [2010] UKUT 79 AAC.

People in your benefit unit

7.10 Your benefit unit is yourself, your partner if you are claiming UC as a couple, and any children or young persons you are responsible for. For more on who is in your benefit unit, see paras 3.46-69. Table 7.1 shows how many bedrooms you qualify for.

7.11 A child or young person is included as an occupier even if the 'two child limit' means they are not included in your maximum UC (paras 9.4 and 9.17). But a child or young person who spends time in more than one home (for example with each parent) can only be included as an occupier in one of these (para 3.67).

If you or your partner are temporarily absent

7.12 If you and/or your partner are temporarily absent, you are included as an occupier during:

(a) an absence from Great Britain which meets the conditions in paras 2.32-35; or

(b) the first six months that you are a prisoner if you meet the conditions in para 2.24.

If a child or young person is temporarily absent

7.13 A child or young person who is temporarily absent is included as an occupier during:

(a) any period they are included in your benefit unit (para 3.69);

(b) the first six months they are in local authority care (para 3.68); or

(c) the first six months they are a prisoner (para 2.22).

But (b) and (c) only apply if they were included in your benefit unit immediately before their absence, and you then qualified for the housing costs element in your award of UC.

7.8 UC sch 4 para 9(1); NIUC sch 4 para 8(1)

7.10 UC sch 4 para 10(1)(a),(b),(d)-(f); NIUC sch 4 para 9(1)(a),(b),(d)-(f)

7.12 UC sch 4 para 11(1),(3); NIUC sch 4 para 10(1),(3)

7.13 UC sch 4 para 11(1),(2); NIUC sch 4 para 10(1),(2)

Non-dependants

7.14   Non-dependants are normally adult sons, daughters or other relatives or friends who live with you on a non-commercial basis. For more on who is a non-dependant, see paras 3.70-77. If you have one or more non-dependants the rules are as follows:

(a) you are allowed one bedroom for each non-dependant over 16 (table 7.1). This means two bedrooms for two non-dependants over 16 even if they are a couple;

(b) one bedroom is allowed for each young person over 16 who is the responsibility of a non-dependant (rather than of you or your partner) – because they also count as a non-dependant (para 3.73);

(c) a child under 16 who is the responsibility of a non-dependant is taken into account as a child in the normal way (table 7.1) (DWP, Freedom of Information request, 5103 of 2016 [www]).

If a non-dependant is temporarily absent

7.15   A non-dependant who is temporarily absent is included as an occupier during:

(a) an absence from Great Britain which meets the conditions in paras 2.32-35; or

(b) the first six months that they are a prisoner if they meet the conditions in para 2.24; or

(c) the first six months in any other circumstances so long as their absence is not expected to exceed six months. (For example they could be away studying.)

But these only apply if they were your non-dependant or included in your benefit unit (e.g. as a child or young person) immediately before their absence, and you then qualified for the housing costs element in your UC.

Non-dependants in the armed forces

7.16   A non-dependant who is temporarily absent is included as an occupier if they are:

(a) your or your partner's son, daughter, step-son, or step-daughter; and

(b) a member of the armed forces who is away on operations (para 2.31).

There is no time limit to this rule so long as they intend to return. But it only applies if they were your non-dependant or included in your benefit unit (para 7.10) immediately before their absence (whether or not you then qualified for the housing costs element in your UC).

Other people in your home

7.17   Bedrooms are not allowed for anyone other than those described above (paras 7.8-16). For example they are not allowed for:

(a) your partner if you are in a couple but claiming UC as a single person (para 2.7);

(b) your husbands and wives in a polygamous marriage, other than the one you are claiming UC with (para 3.61);

(c) lodgers of yours;

7.14   WRA 40 definition: 'child'; UC sch 4 para 10(1)(c); NIWRO 46; NIUC sch 4 para 9(1)(c)
        https://tinyurl.com/DWP-FOI-5103-2016

7.15   UC sch 4 para 11(1),(4),(5)(a)-(c),(6); NIUC sch 4 para 10(1),(4),(5)(a)-(c),(6)

7.16   UC sch 4 paras 2 definition: 'member of the armed forces', 11(1),(4),(5)(d); NIUC sch 4 paras 2, 10(1),(4),(5)(d)

(d) separate tenants of your landlord (if your accommodation is rented out in separate lettings);

(e) a resident landlord/landlady;

(f) joint tenants who are not in your benefit unit (para 7.18);

(g) non-dependants of any of the above (but see para 3.77 for non-dependants of joint tenants);

(h) children and young persons for whom any of the above are responsible;

(i) children for whom a non-dependant of yours is responsible (but see para 7.14);

(j) foster children (but see para 7.21 for when an additional bedroom is allowed for a foster parent).

Joint tenants not in the same benefit unit

7.18 The following rules apply if you are in a joint tenancy (for example a house share) and at least one joint tenant is not in your benefit unit:

(a) if you are a private renter, the size criteria apply separately to each single joint tenant or joint tenant couple, so you each have your own LHA figure (para 6.38);

(b) if you are a social renter, the size criteria do not apply to you at all (para 6.16).

Additional bedrooms

7.19 You may qualify for an additional bedroom for an occupier of your home who:

(a) is a foster parent or has a child placed with them for adoption (see para 7.21); or

(b) requires overnight care from a non-resident carer (see paras 7.22-24); or

(c) can't share a bedroom due to their disability (see paras 7.25-28).

7.20 You could qualify for one additional bedroom under each of (a) and (b), and two under (c) (one for you/your partner and one for a child). But if you are a private renter, the maximum number of bedrooms (under the general rules in table 7.1 and these rules) is always four.

Fostering/kinship and pre-adoption

7.21 You qualify for an additional bedroom if you, or your partner if you are claiming UC as a couple:

(a) are a foster parent (in Scotland a kinship carer) and:

- have a child placed with you, or
- are waiting for placement or between placements, but this only applies for up to 12 months in each period in which you don't have a placement; or

(b) have a child placed with you for adoption (unless you are the child's close relative: see table 5.4(k).

Only one additional bedroom is allowed, even if you have more than one child placed with you. But if any child requires overnight care, see paras 7.23-24.

7.19   UC sch 4 paras 12(9), 26; NIUC sch 4 paras 11, 25

7.21   UC 2 definition: 'foster parent', 89(3)(a), sch 4 para 12(1)(b),(4),(5),(9); NIUC 2, 88(3)(a), sch 4 para 11(1)(b),(4),(5),(9)

Example: A foster parent

A couple are foster parents. They have two sons of their own aged 13 and 11, and two foster daughters aged 12 and 9.

The couple qualify for one bedroom for themselves, and one for their two sons. Although they do not qualify for a bedroom for the foster daughters under the general rules (table 7.1), they qualify for one additional bedroom as foster parents. So they qualify for three bedrooms in all.

People who require overnight care

7.22   You qualify for an additional bedroom if an occupier of your home (para 7.23):

(a) is in receipt of:

- the daily living component of personal independence payment, or

- the middle or highest rate of the care component of disability living allowance, or

- constant attendance allowance or armed forces independence payment paid as part of an industrial injury or war disablement pension; and

(b) is provided with overnight care on a regular basis (para 7.24) by one or more people who stay in your home and are engaged for this purpose, but who do not live with you.

Only one additional bedroom is allowed, even if more than one occupier meets these conditions.

7.23   For this rule, the occupiers of your home are:

(a) the people in your benefit unit (you, your partner, children and young persons: paras 7.10-13); and

(b) non-dependants (paras 7.14-16); and

(c) any child placed with you or your partner as a foster child (or child in kinship care) or prior to adoption (para 7.21).

7.24   It is not necessary for an actual bedroom to be available for your overnight carer(s). And the care does not have to be every night or on the majority of nights; but must be provided regularly –which means 'habitually, customarily or commonly', not just 'on occasion' or 'when needed': [2014] UKUT 325 (AAC).

Example: A person who requires overnight care

A husband and wife live alone. The husband receives the daily living component of personal independence payment, and a rota of carers stay every night of the week to care for him. At the weekend his wife provides overnight care for him.

The couple qualify for one bedroom under the general rules (table 7.1), and one additional bedroom because the carers provide regular overnight care. So they qualify for two bedrooms in all.

7.22-23 UC sch 4 para 12(A1),(3),(9); NIUC sch 4 para 11(A1),(3),(9)

Disabled people who can't share a bedroom

7.25   You qualify for an additional bedroom for:

(a)   you and your partner if you meet the conditions in para 7.26;

(b)   a child under 16 in your home who meets the conditions in para 7.27.

You can qualify under (a) or (b) or both.

7.26   You and your partner meet the conditions if:

(a)   you are a joint claim couple (para 2.5); and

(b)   one or both of you is in receipt of:

- the daily living component of personal independence payment, or
- the middle or highest rate of the care component of disability living allowance; or
- the higher rate of attendance allowance; and

(c)   due to your or your partner's disability, you are 'not reasonably able to share a bedroom' with each other.

7.27   A child under 16 meets the conditions if he or she:

(a)   is the responsibility of:

- you, or your partner if you are a joint claim couple (paras 3.65-69 and 7.13), or
- a non-dependant who is an occupier of your home; and

(b)   is in receipt of the middle or highest rate of the care component of disability living allowance; and

(c)   due to his or her disability, is 'not reasonably able to share a room with another child'.

But an additional bedroom is only allowed if this is needed to ensure the child has their own bedroom. (Young persons aren't included because they qualify for their own bedroom under the general rules in table 7.1.)

7.28   DWP guidance (ADM para F5135) gives examples of a child who 'disrupts the sleep of and may pose a risk to' or 'would significantly disturb the sleep of' another child; but this does not suggest that these are the only two situations in which an additional bedroom can be allowed.

Examples: Disabled people who can't share a bedroom

1.   A couple live alone. One partner is disabled.

Under the general rules (table 7.1) they qualify for one bedroom. An additional bedroom is needed and allowed, so they qualify for two bedrooms.

2.   A couple have one child aged 14 who is disabled.

Under the general rules they qualify for two bedrooms. No additional bedroom is needed or allowed.

7.25-27 UC sch 4 paras 1(2) definition: 'joint renter, 12(1)(c),(d),(6),(6A),(8),(9); NIUC sch 4 paras 1(2),11(1)(c),(d),(6),(6A),(8),(9)

3. A single person has two children aged 12 and 10. One child is disabled.

    Under the general rules they qualify for two bedrooms. An additional bedroom is needed and allowed, so they qualify for three bedrooms.

4. A couple have two children aged eight and six. One partner in the couple is disabled and one child is disabled.

    Under the general rules they qualify for two bedrooms. Two additional bedrooms are needed or allowed, so they qualify for four bedrooms.

Chapter 8 **Support for mortgage interest**

- Who can get SMI: see paras 8.1-17.
- The amount of your SMI: see paras 8.18-26.
- Claims, payments, repayments and appeals: see paras 8.27-37.
- SMI for people on other benefits: see paras 8.38-44.

Who can get SMI

8.1   Support for mortgage interest (SMI) can help you meet your mortgage interest or related payments. It is paid as a DWP loan and is secured on your home.

8.2   You can get SMI if you are an owner-occupier or shared owner. Table 8.1 summarises who qualifies.

Table 8.1 **Who can get SMI**

You can get SMI if you meet the following conditions.

   (a) The payments for your accommodation are owner-occupier payments (para 8.4).

   (b) You are liable to make the payments (paras 5.7-13).

   (c) You occupy the accommodation as your home (paras 5.14-34).

   (d) You have claimed UC (paras 3.2-11).

   (e) You don't have any earned income (para 8.12).

   (f) You qualify for UC or would do except that your unearned income is too high (para 8.19).

   (g) You complete a qualifying period (para 8.14).

   (h) You consent to the DWP's loan offer and to a charge on your home (para 8.30).

Note:

You can also get SMI if you have claimed SPC, JSA(IB), ESA(IR) or IS (paras 8.39-44).

8.1   Welfare Reform and Work Act 2016, s18; The Welfare Reform and Work (Northern Ireland) Order 2016, No 999, art 13

8.2   Welfare Reform and Work Act 2016, s18(1),(8); LMI 3(2), 5(2);
The Welfare Reform and Work (Northern Ireland) Order 2016, No 999, art 13(1),(8); NILMI 3(2), 5(2)

T8.1   LMI 3(1)-(2),(4), 5; NILMI 3(1),(2),(4), 5

8.3　　　SMI is legally separate from UC and other benefits. In Great Britain the law is made under sections 18-21 of the Welfare Reform and Work Act 2016, and is in the Loans for Mortgage Interest Regulations 2017 (SI 2017/725). DWP guidance is in ADM memo 8/18 [www]. In Northern Ireland the law is made under articles 13-16 of the Welfare Reform and Work (Northern Ireland) Order 2016 and the Loans for Mortgage Interest Regulations (Northern Ireland) 2017 (NISR 2017/176).

Owner-occupier payments

8.4　　　'Owner occupier payments' are:

(a)　interest on a mortgage or loan secured on your home (para 8.5); and

(b)　payments under an alternative finance arrangement (para 8.6).

Capital repayments are never included in SMI. But the limitations that apply when you are on other benefits (paras 8.40-42) don't apply when you are on UC.

Mortgages and other loans

8.5　　　You can get SMI towards any mortgage or other loan that is secured on your home. In the case of a loan, this applies even if it was taken out to purchase items other than your home (e.g. a car loan, a loan for home improvements or a loan to pay service charges). If there is more than one mortgage/loan secured on your home, these are added together (up to the capital limit: para 8.20).

Alternative finance arrangements

8.6　　　You can get SMI towards any 'alternative finance arrangement' that is recognised by UK law and was undertaken to purchase your home (either full ownership or shared ownership). Alternative finance arrangements are defined in Part 10A of the Income Tax Act 2007 (as amended). They are usually designed for religious purposes but can be used by anyone. Although they are structured to avoid the payment or receipt of interest, the lender's return is equivalent to the finance costs of borrowing. Many different types of product are recognised by UK law: the most common examples are in table 8.2.

Table 8.2 **Examples of alternative finance arrangements**

Purchase and resale (Murabaha)

The finance provider buys the home and immediately re-sells it to the home owner at an agreed higher price, payable either in instalments or in one lump sum at a later date.

Diminishing shared ownership (Musharaka)

This is a partnership contract used to purchase a property. The bank and a customer usually both acquire beneficial interests in the asset. The home owner may pay a fee for

---

8.3　　　https://tinyurl.com/ADMmemo8-18

8.4　　　LMI sch 1 para 5; NILMI sch 1 para 5

8.5　　　LMI 2(1) definition: 'relevant accommodation', sch 1 para 5(1)(a),(2); NILMI 2(1), sch 1 para 5(1)(a),(2)

8.6　　　LMI sch 1 para 5(1)(b),(3),(4); NILMI sch 1 para 5(1)(b),(3),(4)

the use of the asset, while also making payments in stages to gradually acquire an increasing share in, and ultimately all, the ownership of the home.

Profit share agency (Mudaraba/Wakala)

The customer deposits money with a finance institution (usually a bank) and either allows the bank to use it or appoints them as their agent to invest it. Any profits made are shared by the bank and the customer as agreed. The customer may pay a fee to the bank for its services.

Investment bonds (Sukuk)

These are similar to corporate bonds or a collective investment scheme. The finance institution provides the money to the customer to acquire the home in return for a share certificate in the ownership of the property. The property is used and managed by the home owner on behalf of the certificate holders.

Owner occupiers

8.7   If you are an owner occupier, you can get:

(a) SMI towards your owner occupier payments; and

(b) UC towards your eligible service charges (if any): see para 6.23.

There is a qualifying period for both of these (paras 8.14-17). No deduction is made from either of them for non-dependants (para 9.62).

Shared owners

8.8   If you are a shared owner, you can get:

(a) SMI towards your owner occupier payments; and

(b) UC towards your eligible rent including eligible service charges (chapter 6).

There is a qualifying period for owner occupier payments (paras 8.14-17) but not for eligible rent or service charges. Deductions can be made from your eligible rent for non-dependants (para 9.63) but not from your owner-occupier payments.

8.9   In England and Wales 'shared owner' means you own a percentage of the value of your home (typically 25%, 50% or 75%) on a shared ownership lease. In Scotland it means you jointly own your home with your landlord and have the right to purchase their share. In each case, you usually pay rent as well, but this is not part of the definition ([2020] UKUT 28 (AAC)).

8.7   LMI 3(2), sch 1 para 5; UC 25(2)(c), 26(3), sch 1 para 7, sch 5 para 3(3); NILMI 3(2), sch 1 para 5; NIUC 26(2)(c), 27(3), sch 1 para 8, sch 5 para 3(3)

8.8   LMI 3(3), sch 1 para 5; UC 25(2)(a),(c), 26(2),(4), sch 1 para 7, sch 5 para 3(3); NILMI 3(3), sch 1 para 5;
NIUC 26(2)(a),(c), 27(2),(4), sch 1 para 8, sch 5 para 3(3)

8.9   UC 26(6); NIUC 27(6)

Joint owner-occupiers and joint shared owners

8.10   If you are a joint owner or joint shared owner with your partner, paras 8.7-8 apply in the ordinary way.

8.11   But if you are a joint owner or joint shared owner with someone who is not in your benefit unit, you can only get SMI/UC towards a share of your housing costs. The share is decided:

(a)   in the case of SMI, 'by reference to the appropriate proportion of the payments'; and

(b)   in the case of UC, as described in paras 6.11-13 or 6.38-40.

In practice the shares in (a) and (b) are normally the same.

Earned income

8.12   You can't get SMI if you have earned income, and:

(a)   if you're an owner-occupier, you can't get UC towards service charges (para 6.23); but

(b)   if you're a shared owner, you can get UC towards rent and service charges (chapter 6).

The same applies if you are a couple and either of you has earned income (even if you are claiming UC as a single person).

8.13   There are no exceptions to the rule in para 8.12. It applies to any kind of earned income you or your partner have (paras 10.2 and 10.7), irrespective of the nature of the work, its duration or the level of earnings. Working for only one day, or for just one hour during your assessment period disqualifies you.

Examples: Support for mortgage interest

1. An owner occupier

Anna owns her home and has a mortgage on it. She is on UC and has no other income.

Once she completes her qualifying period, she can get loan payments from the DWP towards her mortgage interest.

2. A shared owner couple

Kevin and Lucy are buying their home in a shared ownership scheme. They are on UC and have no other income.

Once they complete their qualifying period, they get loan payments from the DWP towards their mortgage interest. And both during and after their qualifying period, they can get UC towards their eligible rent and service charges.

3. Earned income

Kevin gets a job with low earnings and he and Lucy continue to qualify for UC.

Because they now have earned income, their loan payments stop. But they continue to get UC towards their eligible rent and service charges.

8.10   LMI 3(3); NILMI 3(3)

8.11   LMI 3(3); NILMI 3(3)

8.12-13 LMI 3(4); UC sch 5 paras 1(3), 4; NILMI 3(4); NIUC sch 5 para 4

The SMI qualifying period

8.14   The SMI qualifying period is nine consecutive UC assessment periods (nine months), during which you must be getting UC.

8.15   If you have already begun a qualifying period, it continues to run when you:

(a)   transfer from JSA(IB), ESA(IR) or IS to UC with no gap between them longer than one month; or

(b)   become a couple or single person while you are on UC (paras 3.5-7).

And if you are already getting SMI in these cases, your SMI continues without a new qualifying period.

8.16   But if there is a break in your UC at any time, you have to start a new qualifying period to get SMI.

SMI and UC during the qualifying period

8.17   During the qualifying period:

(a)   if you are an owner occupier, you can't get SMI, and can't get UC towards service charges;

(b)   if you are a shared owner, you can't get SMI, but can get UC towards rent and service charges.

The amount of your SMI

Calculating your monthly SMI

8.18   Your monthly SMI is calculated as follows:

(a)   start with:

- the capital you owe on your mortgage, loan or alternative finance agreement (paras 8.5-6), or

- your share of it if you are a joint owner or joint shared owner (para 8.10), or

- if lower, the capital limit (para 8.20);

(b)   multiply by the standard rate of interest (para 8.25);

(c)   divide by 12 to give a monthly figure;

(d)   if you have a mortgage or loan protection policy, subtract the monthly amount you receive.

Because the calculation uses a standard rate of interest, your SMI is unlikely to match what you actually pay.

8.14   LMI 2(1) definition: 'qualifying period', 8(1)(b); NILMI 2(1), 8(1)(b)

8.15   LMI 21; NILMI 21

8.16   LMI 9(1)-(2), (3)(a); NILMI 9(1)-(2),(3)(a)

8.17   LMI 8(1)(b); UC 25(2), 26(2),(3), sch 5 para 5; NILMI 8(1)(b); NIUC 26(2), 27(2),(3), sch 5 para 5

8.18   LMI 11(1), 12(1); NILMI 11(1), 12(1)

Example: Calculating SMI

1. Monthly SMI

Marcia is an unemployed home owner who qualifies for UC.

She purchased her home for £140,000 with a £120,000 repayment mortgage from her bank. The term of the loan is 25 years. At the time of her claim she has repaid £20,000 of the outstanding capital. The interest rate currently charged by her bank on her mortgage is 4.00%. Her current mortgage payments are £640.12 per month (including capital and interest).

She has completed her initial qualifying period (para 8.14) and qualifies for SMI. On the date she completes her qualifying period the standard rate of interest is 2.61%.

Marcia's loan payments are calculated as follows:

Total outstanding capital (£120,000 – £20,000)	£100,000
Standard rate of interest	2.61%
Annual amount of SMI (2.61% x £100,000)	£2,610
Monthly amount of SMI (£2,610 divided by 12)	£217.50

2. Adjusting SMI for unearned income

Curtis owns his home and has a mortgage on it. He has been on UC for over nine months and gets UC of £409.89 per month and SMI of £50 per month.

He starts to receive unearned income of £430 per month from an annuity. His UC stops because his unearned income exceeds his maximum UC (para 9.4) by £20.11 per month.

Curtis's SMI is reduced by the £20.11 per month 'excess' income, so he now gets SMI of £29.89 per month (para 8.19).

Adjusting your SMI if you have unearned income

8.19   If you have unearned income, this is first subtracted from your UC (para 9.8). Then, the remainder of your unearned income (if any) is subtracted from your SMI.

The capital limit

8.20   The capital limit is £200,000 except when it is increased as described in paras 8.21-22. If you qualify for SMI on two homes (para 5.31), the capital limit (and the increase) applies separately to each of them.

8.19   LMI 2(1) definition: 'applicable amount', 11(1) step 4, 12(1) step 4; UC sch 5; NILMI 2(1), 11(1), 12(1); NIUC sch 5

8.20   LMI 11(1),(2), 12(1),(2); NILMI 11(1)(2), 12(1),(2)

Increasing the capital limit for disability adaptations

8.21 The capital limit is increased if:

(a) you, your partner, or a child or young person you are responsible for is getting:

- the daily living component of PIP, or
- the middle or highest rate of the care component of DLA, or
- attendance allowance or equivalent benefit (para 10.37); and

(b) you have a mortgage, loan or alternative finance arrangement (paras 8.5-6) which was to pay for adaptations that were necessary to meet that person's disablement needs; and

(c) as a result, the total capital you owe is greater than £200,000.

8.22 In this case, the £200,000 limit applies to capital you owe for anything other than the adaptations. The capital you owe for adaptations is added, even if this takes the total above £200,000.

Changes in the capital you owe

8.23 Once you are entitled to SMI, its amount is recalculated when the amount of capital you owe changes. This applies whether the capital you owe increases (e.g. because you have taken out a new mortgage/loan or alternative finance arrangement) or decreases (e.g. because you have made a capital repayment).

8.24 But the change in your SMI doesn't take effect until the first anniversary date on or after the change in the capital you owe. 'Anniversary dates' are counted from the first day you were entitled to SMI in your UC or JSA(IB), EAS(IR)/IS (paras 8.39-44).

The standard rate of interest

8.25 A standard rate of interest is used to calculate your SMI (para 8.18). This is the average mortgage rate published by the Bank of England. On 6th April 2021 it was 2.61%.

8.26 The standard rate of interest only changes when the Bank of England publishes an average mortgage rate that differs from it by 0.5% or more. This new standard rate applies in the calculation of SMI from the date six weeks later. At least seven days before that, the DWP must publish the new standard rate online [www], along with the date it will apply from.

8.21   LMI 2(1): 'disabled person', 11(3), sch 3 para 14(3); NILMI 2(1), 11(3), sch 3 para 14(3)

8.22   LMI 11(3); NILMI 11(3)

8.23-24 LMI 11(4)-(5), 12(4)-(5); NILMI 11(4)-(5), 12(4)-(5)

8.25   LMI 13(2),(3),(7); NILMI 13(2),(3),(7)

8.26   LMI 13(4)-(6); NILMI 13(4)-(6) www.gov.uk/support-for-mortgage-interest/what-youll-get

Claims, payments, repayments and appeals

How to get SMI

8.27 To get SMI you need to tell the DWP that you are liable for owner-occupier payments. You should do this when you claim UC, and/or when the amount of capital you owe changes.

The DWP's offer of SMI

8.28 The DWP should send an offer of SMI to you, of if you are a couple to both of you. This contains:

   (a)   a summary of the terms and conditions relating to the loan payments;

   (b)   the fact that there will be a charge (in Scotland, a standard security) on your property (para 8.29); and

   (c)   details of where to get further information and independent legal and financial advice.

The charge on your home

8.29 If you accept the DWP's offer, the charge (or standard security) on your property will be registered with the Land Registry. You must 'execute' (sign) the relevant documentation about this. If you are a couple who are joint owners (or joint shared owners) both of you must do this (even if you are claiming UC as a single person).

Accepting or refusing the offer

8.30 If you accept the DWP's offer, you are awarded SMI once your qualifying period is complete (para 8.14). If you refuse it or don't reply to it, you can't get SMI, but:

   (a)   if you are an owner-occupier, you can get UC towards service charges (para 6.23); or

   (b)   if you are a shared owner, you can get UC towards rent and service charges (chapter 6).

If you later change your mind the DWP should send you a new offer.

How the DWP pays your SMI

8.31 The DWP pays your SMI to your lender (the provider of your mortgage, loan or alternative finance agreement), who must use the payments in the following order:

   (a)   towards your current interest;

   (b)   towards your arrears of interest;

   (c)   towards the capital amount you owe;

   (d)   towards any other debts you owe the lender.

The DWP doesn't charge the lender for this service. But if your lender isn't approved or chooses not to receive payments, the DWP pays you.

8.27   LMI 2(1) 'claimant', 'joint claimant', 'single claimant', 'qualifying benefit', 3(1),(2); NILMI 2(1), 3(1),(2)

8.28   LMI 5, 6; NILMI 5, 6

8.29   LMI 5(2); NILMI 5(2)

8.30   LMI 4, 5(1), 8(1)(b); UC 26(2)-(5); LMI 4, 5(1), 8(1)(b); NIUC 27(2)-(5)

8.31   LMI 17, sch 4 paras 4, 5; SI 2020/666; NILMI 17, sch 4 paras 4, 5; NISR 2020/125

8.32   The DWP makes the payments monthly in arrears. The payment dates don't necessarily match the dates your UC is paid.

Duration of SMI payments

8.33   SMI payments begin when your qualifying period is completed (para 8.14) and continue for as long as you meet the conditions (table 8.1).

Moves

8.34   If you move home you can transfer the SMI you owe to your new home, so long as:

(a) you inform the DWP in advance of your plans;

(b) your solicitors write to the DWP agreeing to transfer the charge on your old home to your new home; and

(c) the purchase of your new home is completed within 12 weeks of the sale of your old home.

The DWP can agree to pay your solicitor's costs in transferring the charge, and add this to the SMI you owe.

Repayments

8.35   Except as described in para 8.34, the SMI you owe becomes payable (with interest) when:

(a) your home is sold, transferred or disposed of (other than to your partner); or

(b) you die (or in the case of a couple, the last of you who owns your home dies).

But you (or your estate) can't normally be made to repay more than the value of your home.

Interest on SMI

8.36   The DWP charges monthly compound interest on the SMI you have received. The interest rate is set for each half year beginning 1st January and 1st July. The DWP uses the most recent weighted average interest rate on conventional gilts published by the Office for Budget Responsibility [www]. On 6th April 2021, the rate was 0.3%. Interest ceases when you die (or in the case of a couple, the last of you who owns your home dies), or in any other case when the the SMI you owe is repaid.

Early repayments

8.37   You can choose to make early repayments at any time, so long as each repayment (other than the final one) is at least £100. If you ask for a 'completion statement', the DWP tells you the balance you owe. The statement is valid for 30 days, during which you aren't charged any interest. If you don't pay the full balance during that period, your repayments and interest resume.

8.32   LMI 7; NILMI 7

8.33   LMI 8(1)(b), 9(1)-(3); NILMI 8(1)(b), 9(1)-(3)

8.34   LMI 16A

8.35   LMI 16; NILMI 16

8.36   LMI 15; NILMI 15 https://obr.uk

8.37   LMI 16(8),(9); NILMI 16(6),(7)

Appeals

8.38   Appeals about your entitlement to loan payments and their amount are dealt with in the same way as UC (chapter 14). You can't appeal about when and how payments are made, but you can ask the DWP to reconsider this.

SMI if you are on SPC, JSA(IB), ESA(IR) or IS

8.39   You can get SMI if you are on SPC, JSA(IB), ESA(IR) or IS. Paras 8.39-44 give the main differences that apply in these cases. If you transfer from these benefits to UC, see para 8.15.

The payments SMI can meet

8.40   If you are on SPC, JSA(IB), ESA(IR) or IS (rather than UC), you can only get SMI towards interest on a mortgage or loan you took out:

(a)   to purchase your home or increase your equity in it; or

(b)   to pay for qualifying repairs and improvements (table 8.3); or

(c)   to pay off either of the above.

In the case of SPC only, you can also get SMI payments under an alternative finance arrangement.

SMI restrictions for new or increased mortgages or loans

8.41   The SMI restrictions in para 8.42 only apply to new or increased mortgages or loans that you took out while:

(a)   you or someone in your family were on SPC, JSA(IB), ESA(IR) or IS; or

(b)   you were in a gap of up to 26 weeks between periods in which (a) applied.

And the restrictions only apply while you are currently on SPC, JSA(IB), ESA(IR) or IS. They never apply while you are UC.

8.38   SSA 8(3)(bc): 'relevant benefit', 28(3)(k), 39(1A); NISSO 9(3)(bc), 28(3)(k), 39(1A)

8.39   LMI 3(2); NILMI 3(2)

8.40   LMI sch 1 paras 1, 2(1)-(4); NILMI sch 1 paras 1, 2(1)-(4)

8.41   LMI sch 1 para 3(1)-(4); NILMI sch 1 para 3(1)-(4)

Table 8.3 **Qualifying repairs and improvements**

If you are on SPC, JSA(IB), ESA(IR) or IS, you can get SMI towards a loan that you took out for any of the following. (If you are on UC, see instead para 8.5.)

Measures to provide

(a) a bath, shower, wash basin, sink or lavatory, and necessary associated plumbing, including the provision of hot water not connected to a central heating system;

(b) ventilation and natural lighting;

(c) drainage facilities;

(d) facilities for preparing and cooking food;

(e) insulation;

(f) electrical lighting and sockets;

(g) storage facilities for fuel or refuse.

Repairs

(h) to an existing heating system;

(i) of unsafe electrical defects.

Other improvements

(j) damp proofing measures;

(k) measures to make your home better suited to the needs of a disabled person;

(l) measures needed to provide separate sleeping accommodation for two children/young persons of opposite sexes who are aged 10 or over but under 20.

8.42   When the restrictions apply (para 8.41), you can only get SMI on the new mortgage/loan or increased part of the mortgage/loan if:

(a) it was for a new home better suiting the needs of a disabled person; or

(b) it was for a new home needed to provide separate sleeping accommodation for two children/young persons of opposite sexes aged 10 or over but under 20; or

(c) it replaced any of the mortgages/loans in para 8.40 – but in this case your SMI is limited to the SMI you got on the mortgage/loan; or

(d) it was taken out while you were on HB – but in this case your SMI is limited to the amount of your HB plus any housing costs you were getting in your SPC, JSA(IB), ESA(IR) or IS.

Even when your SMI is limited as in (c) or (d), it increases when the standard rate of interest increases (para 8.26).

T8.3   LMI sch 1 para 2(5); NILMI sch 1 para 2(5)

8.42   LMI sch 1 para 3(5)-(9); NILMI sch 1 para 3(5)-(9)

Income, capital and non-dependants

8.43   If you are on SPC, JSA(IB), ESA(IR) or IS (rather than UC):

(a) having earned income doesn't by itself stop you getting SMI, but it reduces your SMI in the same way as unearned income (para 8.19);

(b) the capital limit is usually £100,000 instead of £200,000 (para 8.20), but apart from that the adjustment for disability adaptations applies in the same way (para 8.21);

(c) if you have one or more non-dependants (para 3.70), deductions are made from your SMI – these depend on your and your non-dependant's circumstances and there are several exceptions: the rules are the same as in SPC (volume 2 chapter 22).

Qualifying period and SMI run-on

8.44   The other main differences from UC are as follows:

(a) if you are on SPC, there is no qualifying period;

(b) if you are on JSA(IB), ESA(IR) or IS, the qualifying period is 39 consecutive weeks, but after gaps in that benefit of no more than 52 weeks you don't have to complete a fresh qualifying period;

(c) if you are on JSA(IB), ESA(IR) or IS (not UC or SPC), you qualify for a 'run on' of four extra weeks of SMI when you start employment or self-employment, so long as it is for at least 30 hours per week and is expected to last at least five weeks.

8.43   LMI 2(1): 'Modified Rules', 3(4), 11(1) – step 4,(2), 14, sch 1 paras 1-3; NILMI 2(1), 3(4), 11(1),(2), 14, sch 1 paras 1-3

8.44   LMI 2(1): 'qualifying period', 8(1)(b),(c), 9(4)-(6); NILMI 2(1), 8(1)(b),(c), 9(4)-(6)

Chapter 9 **Calculating UC**

- The amount of your UC: see paras 9.1-11.
- The standard allowance, child element and two child limit: see paras 9.12-28.
- The work capability, carer and child costs elements: see paras 9.29-50.
- The housing costs element: see paras 9.51-61.
- Housing cost contributions from non-dependants: see paras 9.62-68.
- The benefit cap: see paras 9.69-79.
- Hardship payments if a sanction applies to you: see paras 9.80-88.

The amount of your UC

9.1   This chapter explains how your UC is calculated and how your housing costs are taken into account.

9.2   Your UC is assessed for each monthly assessment period of your award. For how monthly assessments can affect your UC, see paras 3.23-27, 3.38-42, 10.22 and 10.24.

The calculation

9.3   The following steps (paras 9.4-11) give the calculation of UC. Table 9.1 summarises the rules.

Your maximum UC

9.4   Your 'maximum UC' is the total of:

(a) a standard allowance for your basic living needs, or for both of you if you are a joint claim couple (para 9.14);

(b) additional amounts (called 'elements') for children and young persons, work capability, carers and childcare costs (paras 9.15-50);

(c) a housing costs element towards your rent and/or service charges (paras 9.51-61);

(d) a transitional element if you have migrated from legacy benefits to UC (paras 4.39-53).

See chapter 8 for help with your owner-occupier housing costs.

Your income and capital

9.5   The amount of UC you qualify for depends on your income and capital. If you are in a couple, your partner's income and capital are included with yours. This is done even if you are in a couple but claiming UC as a single person (para 2.7).

9.4   WRA 1(3), 8(2); NIWRO 6(3), 13(2)

9.5   WRA 5; UC 3(3), 18(2), 22(3); NIWRO 10; NIUC 3(2), 18(2), 23(3)

Table 9.1 **Amount of UC**

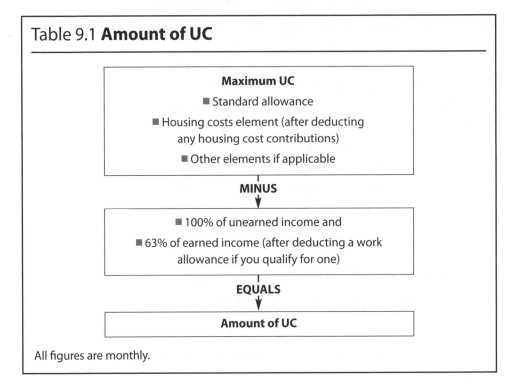

Maximum UC
- Standard allowance
- Housing costs element (after deducting any housing cost contributions)
- Other elements if applicable

MINUS
- 100% of unearned income and
- 63% of earned income (after deducting a work allowance if you qualify for one)

EQUALS

Amount of UC

All figures are monthly.

Capital and the capital limit

9.6 If your capital is over £16,000 you do not qualify for UC. See chapter 10 for how your (and your partner's) capital is assessed and which kinds of capital are counted or ignored.

Income and the amount of UC

9.7 If you have no income, you qualify for maximum UC (para 9.4).

9.8 If you have income, you qualify for maximum UC minus:

   (a) the whole of your unearned income; and

   (b) 63% of your earned income (after a work allowance has been deducted if you qualify for one).

See chapter 10 for how your (and your partner's) income is assessed, the work allowance, and which kinds of income are counted or ignored.

Minimum UC

9.9 If you qualify for at least one penny a month you are awarded UC.

T9.1   WRA 5(1)(b),(2)(b), 8(1),(3),(4); UC 22(1), (3); NIWRO 10(1)(b),(2)(b), 13(1),(3),(4); NIUC 23(1), (3)

9.6   WRA 5(1)(a),(2)(a); UC 18(1); NIWRO 10(1)(a),(2)(a); NIUC 18(1)

9.7   WRA 5(1)(b),(2)(b), 8(1)(a); NIWRO 10(1)(b),(2)(b), 13(1)(a)

9.8   WRA 5(1)(b),(2)(b), 8(1),(3),(4); UC 22(1),(3); NIWRO 10(1)(b),(2)(b), 13(1),(3),(4); NIUC 23(1),(3)

9.9   UC 17; NIUC 17

Rounding

9.10   Amounts used in the calculation of UC are rounded to the nearest penny, with halfpennies being rounded upwards.

Other calculation rules

9.11   Your UC can be reduced if:

(a) the 'benefit cap' applies to you (paras 9.69-79);

(b) a sanction applies to you (paras 9.80-88);

(c) an advance of UC is recovered (paras 12.25 and 12.29);

(d) part of your UC is paid to a third party (paras 12.37-59);

(e) an overpayment is recovered (paras 13.10 and 13.21).

Examples: Amount of UC

All figures are monthly and show the standard allowances after the coronavirus increase ends (para 9.14). None of the claimants have capital.

1. Single renter aged 23, no income

His eligible rent is £400.

Maximum UC

■ standard allowance	£257.33
■ housing costs element (eligible rent)	£400.00
■ total	£657.33
Amount of UC	£657.33

2. Couple over 25, renters, two children aged 5 and 7, unearned income only

Their eligible rent is £1250. Their unearned income is £300 maintenance received by one partner.

Maximum UC

■ standard allowance	£509.91
■ two child elements (£282.50 + £237.08)	£519.58
■ housing costs element (eligible rent)	£1250.00
■ total	£2279.49
Income deduction	
■ unearned income £300 x 100%	– £300.00
Amount of UC	£1979.49

9.10   UC 6(1); NIUC 7(1)

3. Couple over 25, renters, no children, earned income only

Their eligible rent is £1300. Their earned income is £2500.

Maximum UC

- standard allowance   £509.91
- housing costs element (eligible rent)   £1300.00
- total   £1809.91

Income deduction

- earned income £2500 x 63%   – £1575.00

Amount of UC   £234.91

(They don't qualify for a work allowance: see paras 10.11-12 and the examples there.)

Allowances and elements

9.12   This section explains which UC allowances and elements you qualify for. The ones you qualify for are added together to give your maximum UC (para 9.4).

9.13   Table 9.2 summarises the allowances and elements that have fixed amounts. The housing costs element (paras 9.51-68) and transitional element vary (paras 4.39-53).

Standard allowance

9.14   Everyone qualifies for a standard allowance (table 9.2). You get:

(a) the single rate if you are a single person, or in a couple but claiming UC as a single person (para 2.7). A lower figure applies if you are under 25;

(b) the couple rate if you are a joint claim couple (para 2.5). A lower figure applies if you are both under 25.

The monthly coronavirus increase of £86.67 equals £20 per week. It is added to whichever standard allowance applies to you, but only in assessment periods beginning on or before 6th September 2021.

Child element

9.15   You qualify for a child element for each child or young person in your benefit unit (paras 3.62-69):

(a) if at least one child/young person was born before 6th April 2017, you get

- the higher rate for one child/young person, and
- the lower rate for each of the others;

(b) otherwise you get the lower rate for each child/young person.

But if you have any children who were born on or after 6th April 2017, you may be affected by the two child limit (para 9.17).

9.14   WRA 9; UC 36(1), (3); SI 2021/313 reg 2; NIWRO 14; NIUC 38(1), (3); NISR 2021/67 reg 2

9.15   WRA 10; UC 24(1), 36(1); UCTP 43; NIWRO 15; NIUC 25(1), 38(1)

Disabled child addition

9.16   You qualify for the disabled child addition for each child or young person who meets one of the following conditions:

(a) you get the higher rate for each child/young person who is:

   ■ entitled to the highest rate of the care component of DLA, or

   ■ entitled to the enhanced rate of the daily living component of PIP, or

   ■ certified as blind or severely sight-impaired by a consultant ophthalmologist;

(b) you get the lower rate for each child/young person who is entitled to DLA or PIP but does not meet the conditions in (a).

You get a disabled child addition for every child/young person who meets these conditions, even if the number of your child elements is affected by the two child limit.

Table 9.2 **UC allowances and elements (2021-22)**	
	Monthly amount
Standard allowance	
■ single under 25	£257.33
■ single aged 25 or over	£324.84
■ couple both under 25	£403.93
■ couple at least one aged 25 or over	£509.91
■ coronavirus increase	£86.67
Child element	
■ higher rate	£282.50
■ lower rate	£237.08
Disabled child addition	
■ higher rate	£402.12
■ lower rate	£128.89
Work capability elements	
■ LCW element	£128.89
■ LCWRA element	£343.63
Carer element	£163.73
Childcare costs element	
■ maximum for one child	£646.35
■ maximum for two or more children	£1108.04

9.16   WRA 10; UC 2 definition: 'blind', 24(2), 36(1); NIWRO 15; NIUC 2, 25(2), 38(1)

T9.2   UC 36(1); SI 2021/313 reg 2; NIUC 38(1); NISR 2021/67 reg 2

The two child limit

9.17   The 'two child limit' applies to both children and young persons. It only affects you if:

(a) you have more than two children/young persons in your benefit unit (paras 3.62-69); and

(b) at least one of them was born on or after 6th April 2017 (when the two child limit was first introduced).

The Court of Appeal decided that the two child limit doesn't amount to unlawful discrimination (SC and Others v SSWP).

How the two child limit works

9.18   If you have one child/young person you get one child element. Or if you have two you get two child elements.

9.19   But if you have three or more, you get a child element for:

(a) each child/young person who has full protection (para 9.20); and

(b) the oldest two other children/young persons (decided by their date of birth, or time of birth for twins, etc); and

(c) any other child/young person who:

- has third child protection (para 9.21), or

- was born before 6th April 2017 (para 9.22).

These rules are applied in the order (a),(b),(c) – this is illustrated in the examples.

Full protection

9.20   'Full protection' can apply to any child/young person (whether your first, second, third, etc). The qualifying conditions relate to:

(a) adoption (para 9.23); and

(b) non-parental care (para 9.24).

Third child protection

9.21   'Third child protection' can only apply to your third or subsequent child/young person (counting only those that don't have full protection). The qualifying conditions relate to:

(a) multiple births (twins etc) (para 9.25); or

(b) non-consensual conception (para 9.26).

9.17   SC and Others v SSWP [2019] EWCA Civ 615 http://www.bailii.org/ew/cases/EWCA/Civ/2019/615.html

9.18   UC 24(1); NIUC 25(1)

9.19   UC 24A, 24B; NIUC 25A, 25B

9.20   UC 24A(1)(za); NIUC 25A(1)(za)

9.21   UC 24A(1)(b); NIUC 25A(1)(b); [2018] EWHC 864 (Admin)
        http://www.bailii.org/ew/cases/EWHC/Admin/2018/864.html

Born before 6th April 2017

9.22 You get a child element for every child/young person who was born before 6th April 2017, and this continues for as long as they continue to be children/young persons (paras 3.63-64). But the law only refers to third and subsequent children/young persons, because the oldest two get a child element under the ordinary rule (para 9.19).

Examples: The two child limit

The examples use 'child' to include both children and young persons. Except when stated, none of them qualify for full protection or third child protection (paras 9.20-21).

1. Three children all born before 6th April 2017

A single person has three children, all born before 6th April 2017. She gets three child elements as follows.

- First child   Yes (oldest two)
- Second child   Yes (oldest two)
- Third child   Yes (born before 6.4.17)

2. Three children, two born before 6th April 2017

A couple have three children, two born before 6th April 2017. They get two child elements as follows.

- First child   Yes (oldest two)
- Second child   Yes (oldest two)
- Third child   No (not born before 6.4.17)

3. Three children, all born on or after 6th April 2017

A single person has three children, all born on or after 6th April 2017. He gets two child elements as follows.

- First child   Yes (oldest two)
- Second child   Yes (oldest two)
- Third child   No (not born before 6.4.17)

4. Three children, younger two are twins

A couple have three children, all born on or after 6th April 2017. The younger two are twins. They get three child elements as follows.

- First child   Yes (oldest two)
- Second child (older twin)   Yes (oldest two)
- Third child (younger twin)   Yes (third-child protection)

9.22   UC 24A(1)(b),(3); NIUC 25A(1)(b),(3)

5. Three children, older two are twins

A couple have three children, all born on or after 6th April 2017. The older two are twins. They get two child elements as follows.

- First child (older twin)   Yes (oldest two)
- Second child (younger twin)   Yes (oldest two)
- Third child   No (no third-child protection)

6. Five children, two adopted

A single person has two adopted children, and three other children born after 6th April 2017. He gets four child elements as follows.

- Adopted child   Yes (full protection)
- Adopted child   Yes (full protection)
- First other child   Yes (oldest other two)
- Second other child   Yes (oldest other two)
- Third other child   No (no third-child protection)

7. Adopted child and twins

A couple have one adopted child, and three other children born after 6th April 2017. The youngest two are twins. They get four child elements as follows.

- Adopted child   Yes (full protection)
- First other child   Yes (oldest other two)
- Second other child (older twin)   Yes (oldest other two)
- Third other child (younger twin)   Yes (third-child protection)

Adoption

9.23   A child/young person has full protection (para 9.20) if he or she:

(a) is adopted by you or your partner; or

(b) is placed for adoption with you or your partner.

But this doesn't apply if you or your partner are their parent or step-parent (except as in para 9.28). And it doesn't apply to adoptions arranged directly from outside the British Isles.

Non-parental care

9.24   A child/young person has full protection (para 9.20) if he or she:

(a) is looked after by you or your partner under formal arrangements made (now or before they reached 16) by social services or a court, or confirmed by you or your partner being entitled to guardian's allowance for them; or

---

9.23   UC sch 12 paras 1, 3, 6; NIUC sch 12 paras 1, 3, 6

9.24   UC sch 12 paras 1, 4; NIUC sch 12 paras 1, 4

(b) is looked after by you or your partner under informal arrangements (made by you or your partner) if they would otherwise be likely to enter local authority care (in practice a social worker will be asked to confirm this); or

(c) is a child whose parent is also a child (under 16) and in your benefit unit (paras 3.62-69) – for example, if you have a 15-year-old daughter with a baby, this means the baby.

But (a) and (b) don't apply if you or your partner are their parent or step-parent.

Multiple births (twins, etc)

9.25 A child/young person has third-child protection (para 9.21) if he or she was born to you or your partner and:

(a) is the second-born of twins, both of whom are in your benefit unit (paras 3.62-69); or

(b) is the second-born or later-born of triplets or a larger multiple birth, counting only those in your benefit unit.

Non-consensual conception

9.26 A child/young person has third-child protection (para 9.21) if he or she was born to you or your partner as a result of non-consensual intercourse with a person who doesn't (or doesn't now) live with you, for example due to rape or controlling or coercive behaviour.

9.27 Because this is an extremely sensitive issue, the DWP accepts evidence:

(a) from a third party it has approved for this purpose, normally a health professional, registered social worker or specialist charity; or

(b) that the person has been convicted of a relevant offence; or

(c) that the Criminal Injuries Compensation Board has made a relevant award to you; or

(d) from yourself, if you wish to provide this.

Step parents

9.28 The protections in paras 9.23 and 9.25-27 continue if:

(a) you are a step-parent of a child/young person; and

(b) you were previously getting UC as a couple with their parent or adoptive parent; and

(c) you have remained on UC since then with no break longer than six months.

The same applies if you were getting CTC, JSA(IB) or IS within the six months before your UC began.

9.25   UC sch 12 paras 1, 2, 6; NIUC sch 12 paras 1, 2, 6

9.26-27 UC sch 12 paras 1, 5, 6; UCTP 42; NIUC sch 12 paras 1, 5, 6; NIUCTP 43

9.28   UC 2 definition: 'step-parent', sch 12 paras 1, 6; UCTP 41; NIUC 2, sch 12 paras 1, 6; NIUCTP 42

Work capability elements

9.29   There are two work capability elements:

(a) the LCW element which is only for old cases (para 9.31); and

(b) the LCWRA element, which is for both current and old cases (para 9.32).

The amounts are in table 9.2.

9.30   You can only get one of these elements as follows:

(a) if you meet the conditions for both elements, you get the LCWRA element;

(b) if you are a joint claim couple, only one of you has to meet the conditions;

(c) if you meet the conditions for a carer element see table 9.3.

If you start or stop qualifying for an element, see paras 11.24-25.

LCW element

9.31   You qualify for an LCW element if:

(a) you have limited capability for work (LCW) (paras 2.47-48); and

(b) you meet the earnings condition (para 9.33); and

(c) you have had LCW or LCWRA since before 3rd April 2017; and

(d) you made your UC claim:

   ▪ before 3rd April 2017, or

   ▪ when you were on ESA, SDA, IB or IS, if you claimed that benefit before 3rd April 2017.

LCWRA element

9.32   You qualify for an LCWRA element if:

(a) you have limited capability for work and work-related activity (LCWRA) (paras 2.47-48); and

(b) you meet the earnings condition (para 9.33); and

(c) either:

   ▪ you complete a waiting period (para 9.34), or

   ▪ you are swapping from an LCW element to an LCWRA element, or

   ▪ you are terminally ill (para 9.37), or

   ▪ you qualify for an LCWRA element because you were on ESA, SDA, IB or IS when you made your UC claim (para 9.38).

Earnings condition

9.33   If you have earnings above the 16-hour threshold, which is currently £617 per month (para 2.45), you can't get an LCW or LCWRA element unless:

(a) you are on PIP, DLA, attendance allowance or an equivalent benefit (para 10.37); or

(b) you have one of the medical conditions in table 2.5.

9.29-32 WRA 12; UC 27, 36(1); SI 2017/204 sch 2 paras 8-15; NIWRO 17; UC 28, 38(1); SI 2017/146 sch 2 paras 1-5

9.33   UC 41(2),(3); NIUC 42(2),(3)

The LCWRA waiting period

9.34   The LCWRA waiting period is three months beginning with:

(a)   the day you first provide medical evidence; or

(b)   the day you request an LCWRA element in the situations in para 9.33(a) or (b).

Your LCWRA element is then awarded from the beginning of the assessment period following the one in which the three months end.

UC during the waiting period

9.35   During the waiting period you don't get an LCWRA element. But if the amount of your income means you would qualify for UC with the LCWRA element and wouldn't qualify without it, you are awarded UC of one penny a month. This is so that you can count as being on UC.

Breaks in your UC

9.36   If you have a break in your UC of no more than six months:

(a)   you don't have to complete a new waiting period when you reclaim; but

(b)   if your waiting period was incomplete, it continues to run during the break, and after it if necessary.

You only have to start a new waiting period after a break in your UC of more than six months.

Examples: The LCWRA waiting period

1. A new UC claim

John is awarded UC from 26th July, so his assessment periods begin on the 26th of each month. On 19th August, he provides medical evidence and the DWP agrees he qualifies for an LCWRA element.

- His waiting period runs from 19th August to 18th November (three months)
- He is awarded the LCWRA element from 26th November (the first day of his assessment period).

2. A break in UC

Helen is on UC, and her assessment periods begin on the 5th of each month. On 21st September she provides medical evidence and the DWP agrees she qualifies for an LCWRA element. Then her UC stops from the 5th October to 4th February.

- Her waiting period runs from 21st September to 20th December (three months)
- She is awarded the LCWRA element from 5th February.

9.34-36 UC 28; UCTP 19, 20, 20A; NIUC 29; UCTP 19-21

People who are terminally ill

9.37   Being terminally ill means suffering from a progressive disease which is likely to lead to death within six months. No matter how long it takes you to inform the DWP about this, you are awarded the LCWRA element back to when you became terminally ill (para 11.24).

If you are on ESA, SDA, IB or IS when you claimed UC

9.38   ESA assesses capability for work in the same way as UC but uses different terminology. If you were on ESA when you claimed UC:

(a) the ESA 'work-related activity component' converts into an LCW element in your UC;

(b) the ESA 'support component' converts into an LCWRA element in your UC;

(c) if you were in the 13-week 'assessment phase' for the ESA support component, time spent in it counts towards the waiting period for the LCWRA element (which in this case is 13 weeks, not three months).

Similar rules apply if you were on SDA, IB, or IS for disability or incapacity when you claimed UC.

Carer element

9.39   You qualify for the carer element if:

(a) you are the carer of a severely disabled person (they could be someone in your household, including your partner, or someone outside it) and;

(b) you don't receive any earned income for caring for them; and

(c) either

   ■ you get carer's allowance for this; or

   ■ you meet the conditions for carer's allowance, or you would do except that your earnings are too high. The main condition is that you are regularly and substantially caring for them for at least 35 hours per week.

The amount is in table 9.2. If you are claiming UC as a couple and you each meet the above conditions in relation to a different severely disabled person, you get two carer elements (one each). Further rules are in paras 9.40-41.

Shared care

9.40   Only one person can count as the carer for each severely disabled person. This applies to carer's allowance as well as the carer element. If two or more people meet the conditions for carer's allowance and/or the carer element, you choose who is to count as the carer, or if you do not the DWP chooses. So unless you agree to change who counts as the carer, you can't get the carer element if your partner or anyone else gets carer's allowance or the carer element for the severely disabled person.

9.37   UC 2 definition: 'terminally ill', schs 8, 9; SI 2020/289 reg 3; UC 2, schs 8, 9; NISR 2020/33 reg 3

9.38   UC 40(1); UCTP 19, 20, 20A, 21-27; NIUC 41(1); UCTP 19-28

9.39   WRA 12; UC 29(1)-(3), 30, 36(1); NIWRO 17; NIUC 30(1)-(3), 31, 38(1)

9.40   UC 29(1),(3); NIUC 30(1),(3)

Carer element and work capability elements

9.41   If you are a single person (or claiming UC as a single person) you cannot get a carer element and an LCWRA or LCW element at the same time. You get the element which is worth most. If you are claiming UC as a couple there are limits to getting these at the same time. You get the element (or combination of elements) that is worth most but without making you better off than two single people. Table 9.3 gives the rules about this.

Table 9.3 **Carer element and LCW/LCWRA elements**

This table explains which element(s) you get if you meet the conditions for both an LCW/LCWRA element and a carer element (paras 9.29-40).

Single people who meet the LCWRA condition	■ You get the LCWRA element (but not the carer element).
Single people who meet the LCW condition	■ You get the carer element (but not the LCW element).

Couples who meet the LCWRA condition	■ You get the LCWRA element.
	
	 ■ You also get one carer element (never two), but only if:
	
	   ■ both of you meet the LCWRA condition and one or both of you meet the carer condition, or
	
	   ■ one of you meets the LCWRA condition and the other one meets the carer condition.

Couples who meet the LCW condition	■ You get two carer elements (but no LCW element) if both of you meet the carer condition. ■ You get one carer element if one of you meets the carer condition. You also get the LCW element, but only if the other one meets the LCW condition.

Childcare costs element

9.42   You qualify for the childcare costs element if you meet:

(a) the work condition (paras 9.43-44); and

(b) the childcare costs condition (paras 9.45-48).

The amount is 85% of your childcare costs up to a fixed limit (paras 9.49-50).

9.41   UC 29(4); NIUC 30(4)

T9.3   UC 29(4); NIUC 30(4)

9.42   WRA 12; UC 31; NIWRO 17; NIUC 32

The work condition

9.43   If you are a single person you meet the work condition if you:

(a) are in paid work (para 10.8); or

(b) have an offer to start paid work in your current or next assessment period; or

(c) ceased paid work in your current or previous assessment period; or

(d) are receiving statutory sick, maternity, paternity or adoption pay or maternity allowance.

9.44   If you are in a couple (even if you are claiming UC as a single person):

(a) both of you must meet the work condition in para 9.43; or

(b) one of you must meet the work condition and the other one must be unable to provide childcare because they:

■   have limited capability for work or for work and work-related activity (para 2.47); or

■   meet the conditions for carer's allowance (whether or not they have claimed it), or would do so except that their earnings are too high (see para 9.39), or

■   are temporarily absent from your household (see para 3.58).

The childcare costs condition

9.45   You meet the childcare costs condition if you or your partner (if you are claiming UC as a couple) pay childcare charges for a child or young person you are responsible for. This means:

(a) a child under 16; or

(b) a young person aged 16, but only in the period before the first Monday in September following their 16th birthday.

This applies even if the number of your child elements is affected by the two child limit.

9.46   Childcare charges only count for these purposes if they are to enable you to:

(a) continue in paid work; or

(b) take up paid work, in the situation in para 9.43(b); or

(c) maintain arrangements you had before you left paid work, in the situations in para 9.43(c) and (d).

9.47   In order to count for these purposes, the childcare charges must be paid to:

(a) a registered childminder, childcare agency or equivalent (including an approved childcare provider outside Great Britain); or

(b) an out-of-school-hours (or pre-school age) scheme provided by a school as part of its school activities.

9.48   Childcare provided by the child's 'close relative' (table 5.4(k)) in the child's home, or by the child's foster parent, is not included.

9.43   UC 31(1)(a),(2); NIUC 33(1)(a),(2)

9.44   UC 3(6), 32(1)(b),(2); NIUC 3(5), 33(1)(b),(2)

9.45   UC 33(1)(a), 35(9); NIUC 34(1)(a), 37(6)

9.46   UC 33(1)(b); NIUC 34(1)(b)

9.47-48 UC 35; NIUC 37

The amount of the childcare element

9.49   The amount of your childcare element is:

(a)   85% of the monthly childcare charges you pay (para 9.50); or

(b)   the maximum amount in table 9.2 (if that is lower than the 85%).

But any amount of your childcare charges is ignored which: the DWP considers excessive for the extent of your or your partner's paid work; or is met by an employer or any other person; or is met by government payments in connection with any work-related activity or training you are undertaking.

9.50   Childcare changes are taken into account in a particular assessment period if you (or your partner):

(a)   report them to the DWP within that assessment period or the next one (or later in special circumstances: table 11.1); and

(b)   paid them:

  ■   in that assessment period, for childcare provided in that assessment period or in the preceding month – in this case, the whole amount is taken into account, or

  ■   in either of the two preceding months, for childcare provided in that assessment period – in this case, only the amount attributable to that assessment period is taken into account (calculated on a daily basis).

The High Court has decided that childcare payments you are liable for (but haven't yet paid) in the periods in (b) should also be taken into account (R (Salvato) v SSWP).

Example: Childcare element and amount of UC

Kate is 29 and has a child of 7. She works and pays a registered childminder £500 a month. Her eligible rent is £800 a month and she has no non-dependants. She has no capital, and her earnings (after deducting the work allowance) are £1500 a month. The standard allowance is shown after the coronavirus increase ends (para 9.14).

Maximum UC

■ Standard allowance	£324.84
■ Child element (higher rate)	£282.50
■ Childcare element (85% of £500)	£425.00
■ Housing costs element (eligible rent)	£800.00
■ Total	£1832.34

Amount of UC

■ Maximum UC	£1832.34
■ Earned income deduction (63% of £1500)	– £945.00
■ Monthly amount of UC	£887.34

9.49   UC 34, 36(1); NIUC 35, 38(1)

9.50   UC 33(1)(za); NIUC 34(1)(a)
             R (Salvato) v SSWP [2021] EWHC 102 (Admin) www.bailii.org/ew/cases/EWHC/Admin/2021/102.htm

The housing costs element

9.51   You qualify for a housing costs element if you are liable to pay rent and/or service charges on your home (chapter 5). You or your landlord need to give the DWP details of these (para 3.27).

9.52   Your housing costs element is added to the standard allowance and other elements you qualify for to give the amount of your maximum UC (para 9.4).

Renters

9.53   If you are a renter your housing costs element equals:

   (a)   your monthly eligible rent (paras 6.9 and 6.36);

   (b)   minus any housing cost contributions expected from non-dependants living with you (paras 9.62-68).

9.54   If the housing cost contributions are greater than (or equal to) your monthly eligible rent, your housing costs element is nil. No part of the housing cost contributions is ever deducted from your standard allowance or from other elements you qualify for.

Shared owners

9.55   If you are a shared owner your housing costs element equals your monthly eligible rent minus any housing cost contributions (paras 9.53-54). See chapter 8 for help with your mortgage interest, etc.

Owner-occupiers

9.56   If you are an owner-occupier your housing costs element equals only your eligible service charges (para 6.23). Unlike the rules for renters, there is no deduction for housing cost contributions. See chapter 8 for help with your mortgage interest, etc.

9.57   But if you are an owner-occupier you do not qualify for a housing costs element if you have any kind of earned income (paras 10.7-8). If you are in a couple (even if you are claiming UC as a single person) you do not qualify if either of you has earned income.

If you only pay service charges

9.58   If you only pay service charges your housing costs element equals only your eligible service charges (para 6.23). There is no deduction for housing cost contributions.

9.51   WRA 11(1),(2); UC 25; NIWRO 16(1),(2); NIUC 26

9.53   UC 26(1),(2), sch 4 paras 13,14(2), 22, 23; NIUC 27(1),(2), sch 4 paras 12, 13(2), 21,22

9.54   UC sch 4 para 14(3); NIUC sch 4 para 13(3)

9.55   UC 26(1),(4)-(6), sch 5 para 4(3); NIUC 27(1),(4)-(6), sch 5 para 4(3)

9.56   UC 26(1),(3), sch 5 para 9; NIUC 27(1),(3), sch 5 para 9

9.57   UC sch 5 para 4(1),(2); NIUC sch 5 para 4(1),(2)

9.58   UC 26(1),(3), sch 5 para 9; NIUC 27(1),(3), sch 5 para 9

Converting rent and service charges to a monthly figure

9.59   Because UC is a monthly benefit, rent or service charge payments which are not monthly are converted to a monthly figure:

(a)   multiply weekly payments by 52 then divide by 12;

(b)   multiply two-weekly payments by 26 then divide by 12;

(c)   multiply four-weekly payments by 13 then divide by 12;

(d)   multiply three-monthly payments by 4 then divide by 12;

(e)   divide annual payments by 12.

9.60   These rules apply to rent and service charges in all cases. They do not apply to SMI for mortgage interest etc (chapter 8). The law gives no specific rule for daily rent payments. But these usually occur only in the types of accommodation where UC cannot be paid towards housing costs (table 5.2).

Rent-free and service charge-free periods

9.61   If you have rent-free or service charge-free periods (periods during which rent or service charges are not payable), first calculate the annual figure as follows:

(a)   if your payments are weekly, subtract the number of rent-free weeks from 52, and multiply your weekly payment by the result;

(b)   if your payments are two-weekly, subtract the number of rent-free two-weeks from 26, and multiply your two-weekly payment by the result;

(c)   if your payments are four-weekly, subtract the number of rent-free four-weeks from 13, and multiply your four-weekly payment by the result;

(d)   in any other case, add together all the payments you are liable to make over a 12 month period.

Then divide the result by 12.

Housing cost contributions

9.62   This section describes the housing cost contributions which are deducted from your eligible rent to obtain your housing costs element. This applies if you are a renter or a shared owner, but not if you are an owner-occupier (paras 9.53-57).

Housing cost contributions and non-dependants

9.63   One housing cost contribution is deducted from your eligible rent for each non-dependant you have. If two non-dependants are a couple, this means two deductions (not one between them).

9.59   UC sch 4 para 7(1),(2), sch 5 para 13(1),(3); NIUC sch 4 para 6(1),(2), sch 5 para 13(1),(3)

9.61   UC sch 4 para 7(2)(d),(3),(3A),(4), sch 5 para 13(4),(4A),(5); NIUC sch 4 para 6(2)(d),(3),(4),(5), sch 5 para 13(4),(5),(6)

9.63   UC sch 4 para 13; NIUC sch 4 para 12

9.64   A non-dependant is usually an adult son, daughter, other relative or friend who lives with you on a non-commercial basis: for the details see paras 3.70-77. A housing cost contribution can be described as the amount they are expected to contribute towards your housing costs.

The amount of the contribution

9.65   In 2021-22 the monthly amount of the housing cost contribution is £75.53. This figure applies to each non-dependant, no matter what income they have. But see paras 9.67-68 for when no contribution applies at all.

9.66   The UC contribution of £75.53 per month contrasts with the HB figures which vary with the non-dependant's income and can be up to £445 (monthly equivalent).

When no contribution applies

9.67   No housing cost contribution applies for any of the non-dependants in your home if:

(a)   you are a single person (or claiming UC as a single person) and you are in any of the groups in table 9.4(a)-(e); or

(b)   you are a couple and at least one of you is in any of the groups in table 9.4(a)-(e).

9.68   No housing cost contribution applies for any particular non-dependant in your home who is in any of the groups in table 9.4(f)-(o).

Table 9.4 **No housing cost contributions**

Your circumstances

No housing cost contributions apply for any non-dependants in your home if you or your partner are:

(a)   on the daily living component of PIP;

(b)   on the middle or highest rate of the care component of DLA;

(c)   on attendance allowance or an equivalent benefit (para 10.37);

(d)   entitled to (a), (b) or (c) but not receiving it because of being in hospital; or

(e)   certified as severely sight-impaired or blind by an ophthalmologist or have regained your sight in the last 28 weeks).

9.65   UC sch 4 para 14(1); NIUC sch 4 para 13(1)

9.67   UC sch 4 para 15(1); NIUC sch 4 para 14(1)

T9.4   UC 2 definition: 'blind', sch 4 para 15(2); NIUC 2, sch 4 para 14(2)

9.68   UC sch 4 para 16(1); NIUC sch 4 para 15(1)

T9.4   UC sch 4 paras 2 definition: 'member of the armed forces', 16(2); NIUC sch 4 paras 2, 15(2)

Non dependant's circumstances

No housing cost contribution applies for any non-dependant who is:

(f) under 21;

(g) on SPC;

(h) responsible for a child under five years old;

(i) your son, daughter, step-son or step-daughter (or your partner's if you are claiming UC as a couple) and is a member of the armed forces away on operations;

(j) on the daily living component of PIP;

(k) on the middle or highest rate of the care component of DLA;

(l) on attendance allowance or an equivalent benefit (para 10.37);

(m) entitled to (j), (k) or (l) but not receiving it because of being in hospital;

(n) on carer's allowance; or

(o) a prisoner (para 2.22).

Note: There is no housing cost contribution for someone who doesn't 'normally live' with you, even if they may eventually return (paras 3.71-72).

Examples: Housing cost contributions

All figures are monthly. No-one in these examples (except the younger son in example 2) is in any of the groups in table 9.4.

1. One non-dependant

Ewan's eligible rent is £600. He has one non-dependant, his daughter aged 30.

- Eligible rent   £600.00
- Housing cost contribution   – £75.53
- Housing costs element   £524.47

2. Two non-dependants

Rosie's eligible rent is £950. She has two non-dependants, her sons aged 20 and 24.

- Eligible rent   £950.00
- Housing cost contribution (older son only)   – £75.53
- Housing costs element   £874.47

3. Two non-dependants who are a couple

Hazel's eligible rent is £700. She has two non-dependants, her son and daughter-in-law.

- Eligible rent   £700.00
- Two housing cost contributions (2 x £75.53)   – £151.06
- Housing costs element   £548.94

The UC benefit cap

9.69   This section describes how the 'benefit cap' can reduce your UC so that the total of your UC and other welfare benefits does not exceed a fixed monthly figure. Exceptions are given in paras 9.73-79. If your UC is reduced because of the benefit cap, you may be able to get a discretionary housing payment from your local council or (in Northern Ireland) welfare supplementary payments (volume 1 chapter 23). The Supreme Court has held that the benefit cap does not discriminate unlawfully: R (SG and others) v SSWP; R (DA and others) v SSWP; R (DS and others) v SSWP.

The amount of the benefit cap

9.70   The monthly amount of the benefit cap is as follows:

(a) if you are a single person (or claiming UC as a single person) and are not responsible for any children or young persons:

■   £1284.17 in Greater London,

■   £1116.67 elsewhere;

(b) if you are a single person and are responsible for at least one child or young person, or a joint claim couple (with or without children/young persons):

■   £1916.67 in Greater London,

■   £1666.67 elsewhere.

Greater London means the London boroughs and the City of London.

The amount of the UC reduction

9.71   Table 9.5 shows how the amount of the reduction (if any) is calculated.

9.72   The calculation in table 9.5 takes account of the welfare benefits shown there, using the amounts before any reductions for sanctions, recoveries of overpayments and administrative penalties, or payments to third parties. But the following are not included:

(a) any amount of a welfare benefit you do not receive because of the rules about overlapping benefits;

(b) any ESA you are disqualified from receiving.

Benefits other than UC are calculated and converted to a monthly figure as described in para 10.33. Your partner's benefits are included if you are in a couple (even if you are claiming UC as a single person). But if you become a couple while you are on UC, and your new partner is on HB but not UC, their benefits are not included during the assessment period in which you become a couple.

9.69   R (SG and others) v SSWP UKSC (2015) www.bailii.org/uk/cases/UKSC/2015/16.html;
        R (DA and others) v SSWP [2019] UKSC 21 www.bailii.org/uk/cases/UKSC/Civ/2019/21.html

9.70   UC 80A; NIUC 80A

9.72   UC 78(2), 80; UCTP 9; NIUC 78, 80

Table 9.5 **Calculating UC benefit cap reductions**

For each assessment period of one month:

(a) Add together your and your partner's entitlement to all the following welfare benefits in that month (para 9.72):

- universal credit
- child benefit
- JSA or ESA (except the two-week run on: para 4.8)
- maternity allowance
- bereavement allowance (but not bereavement support payments).

(b) If you qualify for the UC childcare costs element in that month (para 9.42), subtract its full amount (para 9.49) from the above total. (Otherwise skip this step.)

(c) If the result exceeds the monthly benefit cap (para 9.70) your UC for that month is reduced by the amount of this excess.

Notes:

- For supported or temporary accommodation (table 5.2) the benefit cap doesn't include your HB.

- For other accommodation, the benefit cap includes the UC housing costs element on your home (or both homes if you qualify on two: para 5.31).

- The benefit cap doesn't include SMI (chapter 8).

- Step (b) 'protects' the childcare costs element from the UC benefit cap (even if the amount of your UC is less than your childcare costs element). It is described in a more complicated way in the law, but this table gives the correct result.

Benefit cap exceptions

9.73   Table 9.6 and paras 9.74-79 give the situations in which the benefit cap does not apply.

Earned income above the 16-hour threshold

9.74   The benefit cap does not apply to you in any assessment period in which you have earned income at or above the 16-hour threshold, which is currently £617 per month (para 2.45). This applies whether you are a single person or in a couple (regardless of your age). And if you are in a couple, your partner's earned income is included (even if you are claiming UC as a single person). (If you are paid four-weekly, the way earned income is assessed may change: para 3.24(b).)

The grace period after a reduction in earned income

9.75   The benefit cap does not apply to you during a 'grace period'. You qualify for a grace period if you had earned income at or above the 16-hour threshold (para 9.74) in each of the 12 months before your grace period begins and:

(a) your earned income reduces below the 16-hour threshold (or ends) while you are on UC; or

(b) you or your partner (even if you are claiming UC as a single person) ceased paid work (para 10.8) before your entitlement to UC began.

The rules in these cases are in paras 9.76-78.

9.76   If your earned income reduces below the 16-hour threshold (or ends) while you are on UC (para 9.75):

(a) your grace period starts on the first day of the assessment period in which that happens;

(b) it lasts for nine months (in other words, nine assessment periods).

9.77   If you or your partner ceased paid work before your entitlement to UC began (para 9.75):

(a) your grace period starts on the day after you or your partner ceased paid work (if this applies to both you and your partner, use the most recent of these days);

(b) it lasts nine months – but the benefit cap does not apply to you until the assessment period following the one in which the grace period ends.

9.78   If your entitlement to UC ends before the end of the nine months, your grace period ends when your UC ends.

Receiving certain benefits

9.79   The benefit cap does not apply to you in any assessment period in which you (or your partner if you are claiming UC as a couple) receive one of the benefits in table 9.6.

Examples: The UC benefit cap and the grace period

1. A reduction in earned income

A single person has been on UC for over 12 months. She has had earned income at or above the 16-hour threshold throughout that time, so no benefit cap has applied to her (para 9.74). Her assessment periods start on the 23rd of each month. She loses her job on 31st March.

Her grace period (para 9.76) begins on 23rd March and lasts nine months until 22nd December. The benefit cap applies to her from 23rd December.

2. Losing paid work then claiming UC

A single person has been working for many years with earned income at or above the 16-

---

9.75   WRA 40 definition: 'claimant'; UC 78(2), 82(1)(b),(2)-(4); NIWRO 46; NIUC 78(2), 82(1)(b),(2)-(4)

9.76   UC 82(2)(a); NIUC 82(2)(a)

9.77   UC 82(2)(b); NIUC 82(2)(b)

9.78   UC 82(2); NIUC 82(2)

9.79   UC 83; NIUC 83

hour threshold. He loses paid work on 15th January. When he claims UC a few weeks later, he is awarded it from 26th February. So his assessment periods begin on the 26th of each month.

His grace period (para 9.77) begins on 16th January and lasts nine months until 15th October. The benefit cap applies to him from the first day of his next assessment period, which is 26th October.

Table 9.6 **The UC benefit cap: excepted groups**

(a) You have earned income equal to or above the 16-hour threshold (para 9.74).

(b) You are in a 'grace period' after your income dropped below the 16-hour threshold (paras 9.75-78).

(c) You qualify for:

- the LCWRA element in your UC (para 9.32), or

- the support component in your ESA, or

- the carer element in your UC (para 9.39).

(d) You are in receipt of:

- personal independence payment,

- disability living allowance,

- carer's allowance,

- guardian's allowance,

- attendance allowance or equivalent benefit (para 10.37),

- industrial injuries benefit,

- a war widow's, widower's, or surviving civil partner's pension,

- a war disablement pension,

- a payment under the Armed Forces and Reserve Forces compensation scheme, or

- a payment from a foreign government similar to any of the last three items;

or are entitled to any of these, but not receiving it because of being in hospital or a care home.

(e) You are responsible for a child or young person who is in receipt of:

- disability living allowance,

- personal independence payment, or

- carer's allowance (young persons only);

or is entitled to any of these, but not receiving it because of being in hospital or a care home.

Note: If you are claiming UC as a couple, references to 'you' also include your partner.

T9.6   UC 82,83; NIUC 82,83

Hardship payments

9.80　　This section summarises the hardship payments you may be able to get if your UC is reduced due to a sanction.

Sanctions

9.81　　In broad terms, a sanction can apply to you if:

(a) you fail to apply for a vacancy, take up an offer of work or meet another work-related requirement when you are on UC (para 2.38); or

(b) you lost work or pay voluntarily or for no good reason before claiming UC; or

(c) a sanction is transferred from your JSA or ESA to your UC.

There are detailed rules about how long a sanction lasts. The longest possible period is 26 weeks if you are aged 18 or over, or 4 weeks if you are aged 16 or 17 (ADM memo 9/19).

9.82　　The monthly amount of the sanction equals:

(a) the whole of your standard allowance (table 9.2) if you are aged 18 or over; but

(b) 40% of that if you are aged 16 or 17, or don't have to carry out any work-related requirement or only have to carry out a work-focused interview (table 2.4); but

(c) nil if you have limited capacity for work and work-related activity (para 2.47).

This is deducted from your UC at a daily rate for each day a sanction applies to you. The daily rate is the monthly amount multiplied by 12 then divided by 365. If you are claiming UC as a couple, half the daily rate applies for each one of you a sanction applies to.

Who qualifies for a hardship payment

9.83　　The DWP must award you a hardship payment if:

(a) you are aged 18 or over; and

(b) your sanction equals the whole of your standard allowance (para 9.82(a)); and

(c) you make an application (para 9.84); and

(d) you have met any work-related requirements applying to you during the seven days before your application is made; and

(e) the DWP accepts that you are 'in hardship' (para 9.85).

See paras 9.86-87 for the period and amount.

Applying for a hardship payment

9.84　　You can apply for a hardship payment on a form provided for this purpose or in any other manner accepted by the DWP. If you are claiming UC as a couple, either of you may apply. You must provide the information and evidence which is required, and accept that the hardship payment is recoverable (para 9.88). A separate hardship application is needed for each period (para 9.86).

9.81　　WRA 26, 27; UC 100-113, sch 11; NIWRO 31, 32; NIUC 98-110, sch 11

9.82　　UC 90, 91, 111; NIUC 89, 90, 108

9.83　　WRA 28, UC 116(1); NIWRO 33, NIUC 111(1)

9.84　　UC 116(1)(c)-(e); NIUC 111(1)(c)-(e)

What 'in hardship' means

9.85 You are accepted as being in hardship only if you (or you and your partner if you are claiming UC as a couple):

(a) cannot meet your 'most basic and essential needs' for accommodation, heating, food and/or hygiene, or those of a child or young person you are responsible for; and

(b) cannot do so solely because of the sanction; and

(c) have made 'every effort' to:

- access alternative support to meet or partially meet these needs, and

- stop incurring expenditure which does not relate to them.

The period of the hardship payment

9.86 Each hardship payment covers the period:

(a) from the date you applied (or if later, the date you provided the information and evidence required);

(b) to the day before your next normal monthly payment of UC is due (or if that is seven days or less, to the day before the next but one payment is due).

The amount of the hardship payment

9.87 The amount of your hardship payment is calculated as follows:

(a) start with the amount of UC you lost (as a result of the sanction) in the assessment period before the one in which you made your application;

(b) multiply this by 60%;

(c) multiply the result by 12;

(d) then divide by 365;

(e) then multiply by the number of days your hardship payment covers (para 9.86).

For sanctions lasting longer than a couple of months or so, the effect of this roundabout calculation is approximately the same as if your sanction was 40% of your standard allowance.

Repaying hardship payments

9.88 Hardship payments are recoverable, and the DWP usually recovers them at the 25% rate used for overpayments (table 13.2(a)). This means you are expected to repay them by receiving less UC in the future. But you do not have to repay them during any assessment period in which your earnings (including your partner's if you are claiming UC as a couple) are at least the national minimum wage for your expected hours of work. And once you have had this level of earnings for 26 weeks since a sanction last applied to you, they stop being recoverable altogether.

9.85   UC 116(2),(3); NIUC 116(2),(3)

9.86   UC 117; NIUC 112

9.87   UC 118; NIUC 113

9.88   UC 119; NIUC 114

Chapter 10 **Income and capital for UC**

- General rules about income and capital: see paras 10.1-6.
- Earned income and the work allowance: see paras 10.7-15.
- Employed earnings: see paras 10.16-22.
- Self-employed earnings: see paras 10.23-30.
- Unearned income: see paras 10.31-52.
- Capital: see paras 10.53-72.
- Notional income and capital: see paras 10.73-89.

General rules

10.1 This chapter explains how your income and capital are assessed for UC purposes. It describes which kinds of income and capital are counted and which are 'disregarded' (which means ignored). If you have capital over £16,000 you cannot get UC: see para 10.55. Otherwise your income (including assumed income from capital) affects how much UC you get (paras 10.9 and 10.32). For the UC calculations, see paras 9.3-10.

Whose income and capital are taken into account

10.2 The assessment of your UC takes into account:

  (a) your income and capital if you are a single person;

  (b) your and your partner's income and capital if you are in a couple.

Your partner's income and capital are included with yours even if you are claiming UC as a single person (para 2.8). In this chapter, 'your' income and capital includes the income and capital of your partner.

10.3 When members of a polygamous marriage count as a couple or single person (paras 3.60-61), only the income and capital of that particular couple or single person are included (not the income and capital of others in the polygamous marriage).

Distinguishing capital from income

10.4 The UC regulations do not provide a definition of income or capital, but the distinction is usually straightforward. For example:

  (a) capital includes savings, investments and property, but some capital is disregarded;

  (b) income includes earnings, maintenance and benefits, but some income is disregarded.

The rest of this chapter gives the rules for all of these.

10.1   WRA s3, 5; UC 18(1); NIWRO 8, 10, NIUC 18(1)

10.2-3   UC 18, 22(1),(3); NIUC 18, 23(1),(3)

10.5   A particular payment you receive might be capital (for example an inheritance) or income (for example earnings). This depends on 'the true characteristics of the payment in the hands of the recipient', not what the payment is called by the person paying it: Minter v Hull City Council.

10.6   However, a payment of income can turn into capital. For example, if you receive wages, benefits etc monthly, what you have not spent by the end of the month becomes part of your capital: CH/1561/2005.

Earned income

10.7   Your earned income means your income from one or more of the following:

(a)   employment (paras 10.16-22);

(b)   self-employment (paras 10.23-30); and

(c)   any other paid work (para 10.8).

It can also include notional earnings (paras 10.74 onwards), but not rent you receive (paras 10.51 and 10.71-72). For DWP guidance see ADM chapter H3.

10.8   'Paid work' means work for which payment is made or expected. It includes employment and self-employment. It also includes being paid for a one-off job even if you are neither employed nor self-employed. It doesn't include work which is for a charitable or voluntary organisation or as a volunteer, and for which only expenses are paid or expected.

Why earned income is assessed

10.9   Your earned income is taken into account as follows:

(a)   if you qualify for a work allowance (paras 10.11-12):

- first the work allowance is deducted from your monthly earned income,

- then your 'maximum UC' is reduced by 63% of the remainder (paras 9.7-8);

(b)   if you don't qualify for a work allowance:

- your maximum UC is reduced by 63% of your monthly earned income;

(c)   but if you have earned income (no matter how much or how little) you can't get SMI towards mortgage interest etc (para 8.12).

10.10   The UC reduction of 63% of earned income is more generous than the reduction in JSA, ESA and IS, which is 100%. This is designed to encourage people to take up employment or become self-employed or increase their earnings.

10.5   Minter v Hull CC 13/10/11 CA (2011) www.bailii.org/ew/cases/EWCA/Civ/2011/1155.html

10.7   UC 52; NIUC 51

10.8   UC 2 definition: 'paid work', 52(a)(iii); NIUC 2 definition: 'paid work', 51(a)(iii)

10.9   UC 22(1),(3); NIUC 23(1),(3)

The work allowance

10.11   You qualify for a work allowance if you or your partner:

(a) are responsible for at least one child or young person (paras 3.62-69); and/or

(b) have limited capability for work or for work and work-related activity (paras 9.31-32).

The UC work allowance is deducted from your monthly earned income (from employment, self-employment, etc: paras 10.7-8). It can be described as the monthly amount you are allowed to 'keep' before your earned income affects the amount of your UC.

10.12   The amounts of the work allowance are in table 10.1. These apply whether you are single or in a couple. If you are in a couple they apply to your combined earnings (even if you are claiming UC as a single person: para 2.7). The higher amount applies where your UC does not include a housing costs element.

Table 10.1 **The UC work allowance (2021-22)**

Monthly amounts for single people/couples with children/young persons or with limited capability for work (paras 10.11-12).

(a)	Renters in supported or temporary accommodation (table 5.2)	£515
(b)	Other renters	£293
(c)	Shared owners	£293
(d)	Owner occupiers	£515
(e)	People with service charges only	£293
(f)	People with no housing costs	£515

Example: Earned income, work allowance and housing costs element

Penny is single, over 25 and has one child. Her monthly eligible rent is £400. Her monthly earned income is £1,000. Deducting her work allowance of £293 gives £707. Her standard allowance is shown after the coronavirus increase ends (para 9.14).
Maximum UC:

■	standard allowance	£324.84
■	child element (higher rate)	£282.50
■	housing costs element (eligible rent)	£400.00
■	total	£1007.34
	Deduction for earned income: £707 x 63%	– £445.41
	Amount of UC	£561.93

10.11   UC 22(1)(b),(3); NIUC 23(1)(b),(3)

10.12   UC 22(2); NIUC 23(2)

T10.1   UC 22; UCTP 5A; NIUC 23; NIUCTP 3A

The six-month earnings review period

10.13   Earnings review periods (para 10.14) are for people who have claimed UC but whose earnings are too high to qualify for UC (ADM memo 10/20). During this period, the DWP:

(a) keeps your earnings under review to see if you qualify for UC; and

(b) awards you UC (and treats you as having made a claim) when and if you do qualify; but

(c) carries forward your 'surplus earnings' in some cases (para 10.15).

10.14   The DWP may treat you as making a new claim in each of the five monthly assessment periods after:

(a) you make a claim for UC that is unsuccessful because your earnings are too high; or

(b) you are getting UC and it stops because your earnings are too high.

Each month starts on the same day as your assessment periods would have had your initial claim been successful or your UC had continued (para 3.38). The process is repeated if you go on and off UC because your earnings are too high.

Surplus earnings

10.15   'Surplus earnings' only apply during an earnings review period that follows a break in UC, not one that follows an unsuccessful new claim (para 10.14). They are calculated and carried forward as explained in table 10.2. They never apply to recent victims of domestic violence (table 2.4(l)) and in practice are uncommon unless you are paid at long intervals or your earnings vary a great deal.

Table 10.2 **Surplus earnings**

This table explains how to assess surplus earnings during the six-month review period that follows a break in your UC because your earnings were too high (para 10.15).

(a) Calculate surplus earnings in final assessment period of old award

- Start with your monthly earned income (without deducting any work allowance).
- Deduct your 'nil UC threshold' (see below).
- Deduct a further £2,500 (this allowance reduces to £300 in April 2022).
- Any remaining earnings are your 'surplus earnings'.

(b) Carry forward surplus earnings to next month

- Add your surplus earnings to your earned income (if any) in the next month, and deduct a work allowance if you qualify for one.
- Calculate UC using the resultant amount (paras 9.4-11) to see whether you now qualify.
- If you do qualify, you are awarded UC (and you no longer have surplus earnings).
- If you don't, repeat steps (a) and (b) until the end of the six-month review period.

10.13-15   UC 54A; C&P 32A; NIUC 54; NIC&P 31A

T10.2   UC 54A; NIUC 54 For £2500 allowance see SSWP determination: https://tinyurl.com/SoSDetermination

> ### (c) The nil UC threshold
>
> - Start with your maximum UC (para 9.4).
> - Deduct unearned income (if any).
> - Multiply the result by 158.73% (the inverse of 63%).
> - This gives your nil UC threshold (in other words, the amount of earned income used to exactly reduce your UC to nil).

Example: The six-month earnings review period

Bob claims UC on 24th September and qualifies for a standard allowance of £324.84 plus housing costs of £575.16, totalling £900. His earnings vary depending on how much commission he gets. He doesn't qualify for a work allowance.

- In the month commencing 24th September, Bob's net earnings are £1500. 63% of this is £945.00 so he doesn't qualify for UC.
- In the month commencing 24th October, his net earnings are £1200. 63% of this is £756. He qualifies for UC of £900 – £756 = £144, and is awarded this (without having to make a new claim) because he is within the six-month earnings review period that began on 24th September (paras 10.13-14).
- In the months commencing 24th November, December and January, his net earnings are between £1500 and £1800 each month so he doesn't qualify for UC.
- In the month commencing 24th February, his net earnings are £800. 63% of this is £504. He qualifies for UC of £900 – £504 = £396. He is awarded this (without having to make a new claim) because he is within the six-month earnings review period that began on 24th November (para 10.14).
- Bob's earnings haven't been high enough for surplus earnings to affect him (table 10.2).

Employed earnings

What are employed earnings

10.16   Your 'employed earnings' are your earnings from employment 'under a contract of service' (an employment contract) or 'in an office'. People employed in an office include directors of limited companies, local authority councillors and clergy. Employed earnings include payments under the job retention scheme introduced due to coronavirus.

The amount of your employed earnings

10.17   The amount of your employed earnings in an assessment period is:

(a) all the earnings you receive in that period which are subject to income tax (for exceptions see paras 10.15, 10.18-20); and

---

10.16   UC 52(a)(i), 55(1); NIUC 51(a)(i), 55(1)

10.17   UC 55(1),(2),(4),(5); NIUC 55(1),(2),(4),(6)

(b) repayments and refunds of income tax and national insurance in that period; and

(c) any statutory sick, maternity, paternity, adoption or parental bereavement pay you receive in that period;

(d) minus amounts for your income tax, national insurance, pension contributions and payroll giving in that period (para 10.21).

See also paras 10.11-12 for the work allowance.

Excluded earnings

10.18   Employee benefits, such as free use of your employer's facilities, are not included in your earnings whether you pay tax on them or not.

Expenses paid by your employer

10.19   If your employer pays you expenses, these are:

(a) included in your earnings if they are taxable (for example if your employer pays your travel costs between your home and workplace);

(b) not included if they are not taxable (for example if your employer pays your travel costs between workplaces).

Expenses if you are in a service user group

10.20   Expenses you are paid that arise from your participation as a service user are not included in your earnings and are disregarded. This applies if you are a member of the service user group (or the carer of a service user group member), for a body which has a statutory duty to provide health, social care or social housing services or for the DWP in relation to social security, child support or certain employment-training initiatives.

Deductions from employed earnings

10.21   The following are deducted from your employed earnings:

(a) tax and national insurance contributions you pay in the assessment period;

(b) tax-deductible pension contributions you make in that period; and

(c) amounts you donate in that period under a PAYE 'payroll giving' scheme approved for tax purposes.

Information used to assess employed earnings

10.22   In most cases, the DWP uses information from HMRC to assess your employed earnings. This is because PAYE law requires most employers to provide details of employees' earnings to HMRC using its Real Time Information system. In most cases, the DWP counts you as receiving the earnings when it gets this information (paras 3.23-24). But the DWP makes its own decision if this information is likely to be unreliable, or your employer fails to provide it, or you disagree with it. It can also adjust its decision if an employer reports your earnings late

---

10.18   UC 55(2); NIUC 55(2)

10.19   UC 55(3)(a); NIUC 55(3)(a)

10.20   UC 53(2), 55(3)(b); NIUC 52(2), 55(3)(b)

10.21   UC 53(1), 55(4A),(5); NIUC 52(1), 55(5),(6)

([2017] UKUT 347 (AAC)). If these arrangements are not in place for some reason, you should report your employed earnings to the DWP each month. The DWP should tell you when you have to do this. If you fail to follow the reporting instructions, the DWP can make an estimate or suspend your UC (para 11.31). If your earnings change, see also paras 11.19-20.

Self-employed earnings

What are self-employed earnings

10.23 Your 'self-employed earnings' are your earnings from any kind of business which is a 'trade, profession or vocation' where you are not employed by someone else. This applies whether you are a sole trader or in a partnership, and includes payments from the self-employed income support scheme introduced due to coronavirus. For DWP guidance see ADM chapter H4.

The amount of your self-employed earnings

10.24 The amount of your self-employed earnings in an assessment period is your business income in that period (para 10.25) minus:

(a) your allowable business expenses in that period (paras 10.26-28), and

(b) payments you make to HMRC for your income tax and national insurance and/or tax relievable pension contributions made in that period (para 10.29), and

(c) certain unused losses (para 10.29).

But if this gives a low figure, you can be counted as having a higher amount of earnings: see paras 10.78-81. See also paras 10.11-12 for the work allowance.

Business income

10.25 Your business income is all the income actually received in relation to your business, including:

(a) money payments (cash, credit transfers, cheques, etc);

(b) payments in kind (this means in goods, not money);

(c) repayments and refunds of income tax, national insurance and VAT; and

(d) the value of assets you sell or stop using for your business (if you earlier claimed them as an allowable expense).

Money owed to you (for example if someone hasn't paid you yet) is not included. Nor are loans or capital payments into your business.

10.22   AA 159D; UC 54, 61; NIAA 159D; NIUC 53, 62

10.23   UC 52(a)(ii), 57(1); NIUC 51(a)(ii), 57(1)

10.24   UC 57(2); NIUC 57(2)

10.25   UC 57(4)-(5); NIUC 57(3)-(4)

Allowable business expenses

10.26   Your business expenses in the assessment period are allowable only if they are:

(a) 'wholly and exclusively incurred' for the purposes of your business; and

(b) not 'incurred unreasonably' (i.e. they should be reasonably appropriate, necessary and not excessive); and

(c) not excluded expenses (para 10.28).

If you pay VAT, you may include this as an allowable business expense. Money you owe (for example if you haven't paid a bill yet) is not allowable. For DWP guidance see ADM paras H4197-4275.

Expenses for mixed purposes

10.27   If you have expenses which are partly for business and partly for private purposes, the identifiable business part is allowable if it meets the conditions in para 10.26. This is done by making a calculation of your business and personal use. But in some situations you can use flat rate allowances instead (and must do this if you use a car for business purposes): see table 10.3.

Excluded expenses

10.28   The following expenses are not allowable:

(a) any expenditure on non-depreciating assets (including property, shares or assets held for investment);

(b) losses relating to periods before 11th April 2018 (para 10.29);

(c) any business entertainment;

(d) capital repayments on any loan.

The first £41 per month of interest you pay on business loans is allowable, but anything beyond that is not.

Deductions from self-employed earnings

10.29   The following are deducted from your self-employed earnings:

(a) income tax and class 2 and/or 4 national insurance contributions you pay to HMRC in the assessment period in respect of your trade, profession or vocation; and

(b) tax-deductible pension contributions you make in that period (unless these have already been deducted from any employed earnings you have: para 10.21); and

(c) 'unused losses'. These are self-employed business losses you incurred during your current UC award, or during a previous UC award, so long as the gap between awards was no longer than six months, or during such a gap. But in each case losses from before 11th April 2018 are not deducted.

10.26   UC 58(1),(2); NIUC 59(1),(2)

10.27   UC 58(1)(b),(4), 59(1); NIUC 59(1)(b),(5), 60(1)

10.28   UC 58(3),(3A); NIUC 59(3),(4)

10.29   UC 53(1), 57(2), 57A; NIUC 52(1), 57(2), 58

Table 10.3 **Self-employed expenses: flat rate allowances and adjustments**

If you use a car for your business you can only claim the flat rate allowance in (a) as a business expense; you can't claim any actual expenses for buying or using it. Otherwise, (a) (for other types of vehicle) and (b) and (c) are options; you can choose to use them or can make a calculation of actual business use (para 10.27). All amounts are monthly.

(a) Allowance for business use of a motor vehicle

If you use a motor vehicle for both business and personal purposes, the flat rate allowance for business use depends on your business mileage in the month. It is:

- for a motorcycle, 24p per mile;
- for a car, van or other motor vehicle:
    - 45p per mile for the first 833 miles, plus
    - 25p per mile after that.

(b) Allowance for business use of your home

If you use your home for business purposes, the flat rate allowance for business use depends on the number of hours you spend there on 'income-generating activities' in the month. It is:

- £10 for at least 25 (but not more than 50) hours;
- £18 for more than 50 (but not more than 100) hours;
- £26 for more than 100 hours.

(c) Adjustment for personal use of business premises

This applies to premises you mainly use for business purposes but which you (or you and anyone else) also occupy for personal use. (For example, if your business is running a care home and you live there or stay there.) The flat rate amount is deducted from the total allowable expenses on the premises in the month. It is:

- £350 if one person (you) occupies the premises;
- £500 if two people (including you) do so;
- £650 if three or more people (including you) do so.

T10.3   UC 53(1), 59(2)-(4); NIUC 52(1), 60(2)-(4)

Information used to assess self-employed earnings

10.30   You should report your self-employed earnings to the DWP each month. The DWP usually expects you to do this between seven days before and 14 days after the end of each assessment period (para 3.38), giving information on:

(a) the business income you actually receive during that assessment period;

(b) the allowable expenses you actually pay out during that assessment period; and

(c) the tax, national insurance and pension contributions you actually pay out during that assessment period.

If you fail to follow the reporting instructions, the DWP can make an estimate or suspend your UC (para 11.31). See also paras 11.19-20.

Example: Assessing self-employed earnings

Lesley is a self-employed plumber who provides the following information for a particular month. She used her van wholly for business purposes and all her expenses are allowable. So her self-employed earnings are as shown below.

Income received		£1,492
Use of van	£314	
Buying in stock for use in trade	£170	
Payment to sub-contractor	£80	
Telephone, postage, stationery	£76	
Advertising, subscriptions	£42	
Use of home (table 10.3(b))	£18	
Tax/NI paid to HMRC	£68	
Total allowable expenses		£768
Self-employed earnings		£724

Unearned income

10.31   Only certain kinds of income count as your 'unearned income'. These are summarised in table 10.4 and further details are in paras 10.34-52. All other kinds of unearned income are disregarded: for some examples see para 10.36.

Why unearned income is assessed

10.32   Your 'maximum UC' is reduced by the whole amount of your unearned income (paras 9.7-8). Unearned income can also affect the amount of SMI towards mortgage interest etc (para 8.19).

10.30   UC 54, 61(1); NIUC 53, 62(1)

10.31   UC 66; NIUC 66

Converting unearned income to a monthly figure

10.33   To convert unearned income to a monthly figure:

(a) multiply weekly payments by 52 then divide by 12;

(b) multiply four-weekly payments by 13 then divide by 12;

(c) multiply three-monthly payments by four then divide by 12;

(d) divide annual payments by 12.

If your unearned income fluctuates, the monthly amount is calculated over any identifiable cycle, or if there isn't one, over three months or whatever period would give a more accurate result. For student income see table 10.5.

Table 10.4 **What counts as unearned income in UC**

(a) Retirement pension income (para 10.34)

(b) The following social security benefits (para 10.35):
- JSA(C);
- ESA(C);
- carer's allowance;
- bereavement allowance (but not bereavement support payments);
- maternity allowance;
- widow's pension;
- widowed mother's allowance;
- widowed partner's allowance;
- industrial injuries benefit;
- severe disablement allowance.

(c) Payments from a foreign government analogous to any of the above.

(d) Maintenance from your current or former spouse or civil partner (para 10.38).

(e) Student income (para 10.39).

(f) Training allowances (para 10.44).

(g) Sports Council awards (para 10.45).

(h) Some insurance payments (para 10.47).

(i) Income from an annuity (para 10.48).

(j) Income from a trust (paras 10.63-64).

(k) Assumed income from capital (para 10.56).

(l) Capital treated as income (para 10.60).

(m) Some kinds of rental income and other taxable income (paras 10.50-51 and 10.71-72).

In many cases there are further rules and/or disregards. See the paras shown above, and for notional unearned income see para 10.82.

10.33   UC 73; NIUC 73

T10.4   UC 66(1)(a)-(m); UCTP 25; NIUC 66(1)(a)-(m); NIUCTP 26

Example: Unearned income and amount of UC

Chris and Terry are in their 30s and have one child aged 3. Chris has JSA(C) of £74.70 a week, which is £323.70 a month. Terry has maintenance of £300 a month. So their monthly unearned income is £623.70. (Child benefit is disregarded.) They have no earnings or capital, and their eligible rent is £400. Their standard allowance is shown after the coronavirus increase ends (para 9.14).

Maximum UC:

■	standard allowance	£509.91
■	child element (lower rate)	£237.08
■	housing costs element (eligible rent)	£400.00
■	total	£1,146.99
	Deduction for unearned income	– £623.70
	Amount of UC	£523.29

Retirement pension income

10.34   Retirement pension income counts in full as unearned income. This means any kind of state, occupational or personal retirement pension, including any increase for a partner (but for SPC see para 10.36). Periodic payments from the Payment Protection Fund, and foreign state retirement pension, also count in full as unearned income. See also para 10.82.

Social security benefits

10.35   Table 10.4(b) lists the social security benefits which count as unearned income. They count in full, except for any amount you do not receive because of the rules about overlapping benefits.

Benefits which are disregarded

10.36   Unearned income that is not identified in the UC regulations is disregarded in your UC assessment. Examples of disregarded benefits and other payments are:

(a) PIP, DLA, attendance allowance and equivalent benefits (para 10.37);

(b) child benefit and guardian's allowance;

(c) HB, JSA(IB), ESA(IR), IS, SPC, CTC and WTC;

(d) war pensions;

(e) fostering and kinship care payments and local authority cash benefits;

(f) bereavement support payments;

(g) carers allowance supplement paid to a carer in Scotland.

Statutory sick, maternity, paternity and adoption pay count as employed earnings (para 10.17).

10.34   UC 66(1)(a),(da),(la),(2), 67; NIUC 66(1)(a),(da),(la),(2), 67

10.35   UC 66(1)(b); NIUC 66(1)(b)

10.36   UC 66; NIUC 66

Benefits equivalent to attendance allowance

10.37   The following benefits are equivalent to attendance allowance:

(a) increases in industrial injuries benefit for constant attendance or exceptionally severe disablement;

(b) increases in a war disablement pension for attendance, constant attendance or exceptionally severe disablement;

(c) armed forces independence payments;

(d) payments for attendance under the Personal Injuries (Civilians) scheme; or

(e) adult disability payment and child disability payment in Scotland.

Maintenance

10.38   Payments for your or your partner's maintenance (under an agreement or court order) count in full as unearned income, but only if they are paid by your current or former husband, wife or civil partner. All other maintenance (e.g. for a child) is disregarded.

Student income

10.39   If you are in full-time advanced education (para 2.16), student grants and loans count as your unearned income (paras 10.40-43 and table 10.5). If you are in non-advanced education, education maintenance allowances and all other student grants and loans are disregarded. But for training allowances see para 10.44.

Student loans

10.40   You are counted as having income from a student loan if you receive the loan under a government scheme, or you could obtain one by taking reasonable steps to do so. The amount you are counted as receiving is:

(a) the maximum amount of student loan you could obtain by taking reasonable steps to do so (including increases for extra weeks); but

(b) 30% of that maximum amount in the case of a postgraduate master's degree loan; or

(c) nil in the case of a student support loan.

This applies even if your actual loan has been reduced because you, your partner, your parent or anyone else is expected to contribute to it, or because you have a grant.

Student grants

10.41   You are counted as having income from a student grant if you receive any kind of educational grant or award from government or any other sources.

10.37   UC 2 definitions: 'attendance allowance', 'war disablement pension'; NIUC 2

10.38   UC 66(1)(d); NIUC 66(1)(d)

10.39   UC 66(1)(e), 68(1),(6); NIUC 66(1)(e), 68(1),(6)

10.40   UC 68(2),(5),(7), 69; NIUC 68(2),(5),(7), 69

10.41   UC 68(3),(4),(7); NIUC 68(3),(4),(7)

10.42 If you have income from both a grant and a student loan (paras 10.40-41), only the following parts of the grant (if you receive them) are counted:

(a) amounts for the maintenance of your partner, child, young person, non-dependant or anyone other than yourself; and

(b) amounts specified in the grant as being towards your rent payments (but only if they are rent payments which can be met by UC: table 5.1).

The rest of your grant (or all of it if you don't receive either of the above) is disregarded.

10.43 If you have income from a grant but not from a student loan (paras 10.40-41), the whole of your grant is counted except for any amounts included in it for:

(a) tuition or examination fees;

(b) any kind of disability you have;

(c) term-time residential study away from your educational establishment;

(d) maintaining a home whose costs are not included in your housing costs element and which is not your term-time address;

(e) the maintenance of anyone not included in your or anyone else's UC award;

(f) books and equipment;

(g) travel expenses as a result of your attendance on the course;

(h) childcare costs.

Training allowances

10.44 Training allowances count as unearned income only if:

(a) they are paid under a government work programme training scheme; and

(b) they are for your living expenses (para 10.46) or are instead of UC.

Sports Council awards

10.45 Sports Council awards count as unearned income only if they are for your living expenses (para 10.46).

'Living expenses'

10.46 For the above purpose (paras 10.44-45) living expenses mean the cost of food, ordinary clothing or footwear, household fuel, rent, council tax or other housing costs, for yourself, your partner and any child or young person you are responsible for.

10.42   UC 68(3), sch 1 para 2; NIUC 68(3), sch 1 para 2

10.43   UC 70; NIUC 70

10.44   UC 66(1)(f); NIUC 66(1)(f)

10.45   UC 66(1)(g); NIUC 66(1)(g)

10.46   UC 66(2); NIUC 66(2)

Table 10.5 **The monthly amount of student income**

Your income from a student loan and/or grant (paras 10.39-43) is calculated as follows:

- it is averaged over the number of monthly assessment periods described below;
- then £110 is disregarded in each of those assessment periods.

(a) One year or shorter courses

Average student income:

- from the assessment period in which the course starts;
- to the assessment period before the one in which the course ends.

(b) Two year or longer courses with long vacations

For each year, average student income:

- from the assessment period in which:
  - the course starts (first year), or
  - the previous long vacation ends (other years);
- to the assessment period before the one in which:
  - the following long vacation starts, or
  - the course ends (final year).

(c) Two year or longer courses without long vacations

For each year, average student income:

- from the assessment period in which:
  - the course starts (first year), or
  - the year starts (other years);
- to the assessment period before the one in which:
  - the next year starts, or
  - the course ends (final year).

'Long vacation'

This means the longest vacation in any year, but if it is less than one month you do not count as having long vacations.

Insurance payments

10.47   Insurance payments count as your unearned income only if they are paid under a policy you took out to insure yourself against losing income due to illness, accident or redundancy.

Annuities, trusts, personal injury and compensation

10.48   For the rules about income and capital relating to these, see paras 10.63-67.

T10.5   UC 68(1),(7), 71; NIUC 68(1),(7), 71

10.47   UC 66(1)(h); NIUC 66(1)(h)

Other taxable income

10.49   Other income you have counts as unearned income if it is taxable under Part 5 of the Income Tax (Trading and Other Income) Act 2005, and is not earned income (paras 10.7-30).

10.50   For example, this can include royalties, copyright, patent and similar payments, unless these are part of your self-employed (or employed) earnings.

Rent received from a lodger/sub-tenant in your home

10.51   Because income from a boarder or sub-tenant is not defined as income for UC purposes it is not taken into account as your unearned income (ADM para H5112). But if you are self-employed and renting out rooms as part of your business then this income is taken into account as part of your self-employed earnings. See paras 10.71-72 if you receive rent on property other than your home.

Other unearned income

10.52   The following also count as unearned income:

(a)   assumed income from capital (para 10.56);

(b)   some instalments or regular payments of capital (para 10.60); and

(c)   notional unearned income (para 10.82).

Capital

10.53   All of your capital is taken into account unless it is disregarded. Table 10.6 lists all the kinds of disregarded capital. See paras 10.4-6 for how to distinguish capital from income. For DWP guidance on capital see ADM chapters H1 and H2.

10.54   For example your capital includes:

(a)   savings (in cash or in a savings account etc);

(b)   investments (shares etc);

(c)   property (unless it is disregarded: table 10.6); and

(d)   lump sum payments you receive (for example an inheritance).

It can also include notional capital (paras 10.83-88).

Why capital is assessed

10.55   Your capital (apart from disregarded capital) is taken into account as follows:

(a)   if it is more than £16,000 you are not entitled to UC; otherwise

(b)   the first £6,000 is ignored;

(c)   the remainder up to £16,000 is counted as providing you with an assumed amount of income (para 10.56).

10.49   UC 66(1)(m); NIUC 66(1)(m)

10.51   UC 66; NIUC 66

10.53   UC 46(1); NIUC 46(1)

10.54   UC 72(1); NIUC 72(1)

10.55   UC 72(1); NIUC 72(1)

Assumed income from capital

10.56   The assumed income from your capital is calculated as follows:

(a) from the total amount of your capital (apart from disregarded capital) deduct £6,000;

(b) then divide the remainder by 250;

(c) each £250 (or part of £250) in excess of the £6,000 is treated as producing a monthly income of £4.35;

(d) this gives the monthly amount of your assumed income from capital. It is counted as your unearned income (paras 10.31-32). The law calls it the 'yield' from your capital.

The kinds of capital disregarded in (a) and in para 10.55 are described throughout this chapter. They are the same for both these purposes except in relation to certain annuities and trusts (paras 10.63-64).

Example: Assumed income from capital

Valda has capital, assessed under the rules in this chapter, of £12,085.93.

- The first £6,000 is ignored, leaving £6,085.93.
- Dividing £6,085.93 by £250 (rounded up) gives 25.
- 25 x £4.35 = £108.75.
- Valda's assumed monthly income from capital is £108.75.

Table 10.6 **Disregarded capital**

Your home and other premises

In (a) to (e) only one dwelling can be a person's home at any one time. In (a) to (c) there is no time limit.

(a) Your home.

(b) The home of a 'close relative' (table 5.4(k)) who is over 66 or has limited capability for work or for work and work-related activity (paras 2.47-49).

(c) The home of your partner if:

- your relationship has not ended; but
- you live apart (para 3.52), for example, one of you is in residential care.

(d) A home you intend to occupy if:

- you acquired it within the past six months*; or
- you are taking steps to obtain possession of it, and first sought legal advice about this or began proceedings within the past six months*; or

---

10.56   UC 66(1)(k), 72; NIUC 66(1)(k), 72

T10.6(a)-(q) UC sch 10 paras 1 to 17 respectively, also para 1(2) for (a) to (e); NIUC sch 10 paras 1 to 19

- you are carrying out essential repairs or alterations to make it fit for occupation, and began doing so within the past six months*.

(e) Your former home if you ceased to occupy it because your relationship with your partner has ended, and:

- they are a lone parent and live in it as their home (in this case there is no time limit); or

- you ceased to occupy it within the past six months*.

(f) A home or any other premises you are taking reasonable steps to dispose of, and began doing so within the past six months*.

Business assets

(g) Any assets wholly or mainly used for a business you are carrying on (para 10.23).

(h) Any assets which were wholly or mainly used for a business you ceased within the past six months* if:

- you are taking reasonable steps to dispose of them; or

- you ceased business because of 'incapacity' and reasonably expect to begin again when you recover.

Money in a life insurance, pension or funeral plan scheme

(i) The value of a life insurance policy.

(j) The value of an occupational or personal pension scheme.

(k) The value of a funeral plan contract, if its only purpose is to provide a funeral.

Money held for particular purposes

(l) Money deposited with a housing association as a condition of occupying your home.

(m) Money you received within the past six months*, and which you intend to use to buy a home, if:

- it is the proceeds of the sale of your former home; or

- it is a grant made to you for the sole purpose of buying a home; or

- it was deposited with a housing association.

You should be actively seeking to meet this intention and it must be reasonably likely to be achieved ([2020] UKUT 247 (AAC)).

(n) Money you received under an insurance policy within the past six months* because of loss or damage to your home or personal possessions.

(o) Money you received within the past six months* which:

- is for making essential repairs or alterations to your home or former home: and

- was given to you (as a grant, loan, gift or otherwise) on condition that it is so used.

Benefits and other amounts

(p) A social fund payment you received within the past 12 months.

(q) A payment you received from a local authority within the past 12 months, if it was paid:

- by social services to avoid taking a child into care or to a child or young person who is leaving or has left care; or

- to meet anyone's welfare needs relating to old age or disability (for example a community care or direct care payment) apart from any living expenses described in para 10.46.

(r) A payment of arrears or compensation for late payment of UC or any UK social security benefit that doesn't count as income for UC (e.g. para 10.36(a)-(c)). This disregard lasts for 12 months. It is extended until the end of your current UC award (when this is longer) if the payment:

- was £5,000, or more; and

- was made because of an official error or error of law (para 14.22); and

- was made while you were on UC, or SPC, JSA(IB), ESA(IR), IS, HB, CTC or WTC if your UC began within one month of them ending.

(s) Any payment made to you as a holder of the Victoria Cross or George Cross. There is no time limit.

(t) The additional amount (£2,500 or £3,500) awarded in the first month of bereavement support payments. This disregard lasts for 12 months.

(u) An early years assistance awarded in Scotland within the past 12 months.

(v) In Northern Ireland an ex-gratia payment made by the Secretary of State to members of families of the disappeared for up to 52 weeks from the date of the payment, or without time limit, a payment under Victims and Survivors Order 2006.

Personal possessions

(w) Your personal possessions. This means any physical assets other than land, property or business assets: R(H) 7/08.

Extending the six-month disregards

* The DWP can extend any of the six-month disregards in this table if it is reasonable to do so in the circumstances.

Note: See paras 10.65-67 for further disregards relating to personal injury, compensation and independent living payments; and paras 4.54-59 for the transitional capital disregard.

T10.6(r)   UC sch 10 para 18; UCTP 10A, sch 2 para 7; SI 2019/1152 reg 3(8); NIUC sch 10 para 18; NIUCTP 8A, sch 2 para 7; NISR 2019/152 reg 2(10)

T10.6(s-u)   UC sch 10 paras 19-21 respectively; NIUC sch 10 paras 19-21

T10.6(w)   UC 46(2); NIUC 46(2)

T10.6(*)   UC 48(2); NIUC 48(2)

Valuing capital

10.57   Each item of your capital is calculated as follows:

(a) start with its current market or surrender value;

(b) then disregard 10% if selling it would involve costs;

(c) then disregard any debt or charge secured on it.

Jointly held capital

10.58   If you own a capital item jointly with one or more other people, you are assumed to own it in equal shares unless you provide evidence that it should be divided in some other way.

Capital you hold for someone else

10.59   If you hold someone else's capital for them, it does not count as yours. For example, you might be looking after your child's savings for them, or someone you are caring for may have put your name on a joint bank account with them so you can deal with their money for them. It is up to you to provide evidence that the money is not yours, but you do not need to be a formally documented trustee for them ([2010] UKUT 437 (AAC)).

Instalments and regular payments

10.60   Instalments of capital count as capital, except when an instalment would take your capital over £16,000, in which case it counts as unearned income. Other regular payments count as unearned income – for example annuities (para 10.64).

Capital held in a foreign currency

10.61   If you hold capital in a currency other than sterling, any charge or commission for converting it to sterling is disregarded from it.

Capital outside the UK

10.62   The following rules apply if you possess capital in a country outside the UK:

(a) if there is no prohibition in that country against bringing the money to the UK, its market value is the market value in that country;

(b) if there is such a prohibition, its market value is the amount it would raise if it was sold to a willing buyer in the UK.

The rules in paras 10.57-58 and 10.61 then apply.

10.57   UC 49(1); NIUC 49(1)

10.58   UC 47; NIUC 47

10.60   UC 46(1)(a),(3),(4), 66(1)(l); NIUC 46(1)(a),(3), (4), 66(1)(l)

10.61   UC 49(3); NIUC 49(3)

10.62   UC 49(2); NIUC 49(2)

Annuities and trusts

10.63   An annuity is an investment made with an insurance company which in return pays you a regular amount – for your retirement or for other purposes. A trust is a way of holding capital so that the trustees control it on behalf of one or more beneficiaries. The following annuities and trusts are disregarded in calculating your capital (for all UC purposes):

(a)   retirement annuities (table 10.6(j));

(b)   annuities and trusts that hold personal injury payments (para 10.65); and

(c)   certain government funded trusts (para 10.67).

Income you receive from (a) counts as retirement pension income (para 10.34). Income you receive from (b) or (c) is disregarded (paras 10.65-67).

10.64   For all other annuities and trusts:

(a)   their capital value is included when deciding whether your total capital is over £16,000 – and if it is over £16,000 you don't qualify for UC (para 10.55), but if it isn't over £16,000, steps (b) to (d) apply;

(b)   payments of income you receive from the annuity or trust count as your unearned income;

(c)   if you do receive payments of income, the capital value of the annuity or trust is disregarded when calculating your assumed income from capital (para 10.56);

(d)   if you don't receive payments of income, the capital value of the annuity or trust is included when calculating your assumed income from capital.

Personal injury payments

10.65   A personal injury payment means money which was awarded to you, or which you (or someone on your behalf) agreed to, as a consequence of a personal injury you had. Personal injury payments are disregarded in calculating your capital if they:

(a)   are held in a trust (other capital in the trust deriving from them is also disregarded);

(b)   are administered by a court on your behalf, or can only be used under a court's direction; or

(c)   were paid to you within the past 12 months. This may allow time for them to be placed in a trust so that (a) then applies.

10.66   Personal injury payments are disregarded in calculating your unearned income if they are:

(a)   income paid to you from a trust whose capital value is disregarded under para 10.65(a) or (b); or

(b)   regular payments to you under an agreement or court order; or

(c)   payments to you from an annuity which was purchased using a personal injury payment.

10.63   UC 66(1)(i),(j), 67(l), 75; NIUC 66(1)(i),(j), 67(l), 75

10.64   UC 72(2); NIUC 72(2)

10.65-66   UC 75; NIUC 75

Compensation and independent living payments

10.67   Payments from government established or approved schemes and trusts are disregarded in the calculation of both your capital and your income, if the payment:

(a) compensates or supports you after having been diagnosed with variant Creutzfeldt-Jacob disease; or

(b) compensates or supports you after having been infected with contaminated blood products (examples include the former Macfarlane Trust, Eileen Trust, MFET Ltd and the Scottish Infected Blood Support Scheme); or

(c) compensates you because you were interned or suffered forced labour, injury, property loss or loss of a child in the Second World War; or

(d) compensates or supports you because of the bombings in London on 7th July 2005 or Manchester on 22nd May 2017, or the terrorist attacks in London on 22nd March 2017 or 3rd June 2017; or

(e) supports you, if you have a disability, to live independently in your home (for example Independent Living Fund payments from your council or ILF Scotland).

Also disregarded are payments made to people affected by the Grenfell Tower fire; by the National Emergencies Trust; the Child Migrants Trust and the new style ESA special payments. If you are the parent, partner, son or daughter of a person in (a) or (b), payments from the trust or scheme to you, or passed on to you by that person (as a payment or inheritance), are disregarded in most circumstances.

Actual income from capital

10.68   'Actual income from capital' means:

(a) interest (on a savings account etc);

(b) dividends (on shares etc);

(c) rent (on property you rent out); and

(d) any other 'actual income derived from' your capital.

Paras 10.69-72 give the rules about this.

Income from disregarded capital

10.69   If the capital is disregarded in the assessment of UC (table 10.6), actual income you receive on it counts as your income. It is usually unearned income (para 10.49). But if you are self-employed, income you receive on your business assets is included in your self-employed earnings (para 10.25). For rent see para 10.71.

Income from counted capital

10.70   If the capital is counted in the assessment of UC (para 10.53), actual income you receive on it counts as your capital from the day it is due. For example this applies to interest you receive on (and leave in) a savings account. For rent see para 10.72.

10.67   UC 76; NIUC 76

10.68   UC 72(3); NIUC 72(3)

10.70   UC 72(3); NIUC 72(3)

Rent received on disregarded property

10.71   The rule in para 10.69 means that if you receive rent on a property which is disregarded (table 10.6 (b) to (f)), the rent counts as your income. Since it is the taxable amount which is taken into account (para 10.49) the expenses you incur on the property are deducted. For rent from a lodger in your home, see para 10.51.

Rent received on counted property

10.72   The rule in para 10.70 means that if you receive rent on a property which is not disregarded, the rent counts as your capital from the day it is due. But your capital goes down when you pay for expenses you incur on that property. See the example. (If you receive rent from a property business different rules apply: see paras 10.16, 10.23 and 10.87.)

Example: Rent received on a counted property

Leroy owns a house he does not live in. He rents the rooms there to separate tenants through an agency. The house does not fall within any of the capital disregards, and because he has a large mortgage its capital value is not over £16,000 (see para 10.57).

Leroy's income from the rent is taken into account as capital (para 10.72). Each month he receives rent of £900 from which he pays £800 for agency fees, council tax, utility bills and his mortgage. This means his capital goes up by £100 a month.

Notional income and capital

10.73   This section explains when you are counted as having income or capital you do not in fact have. This is called 'notional' income or capital.

Notional earnings: trade disputes

10.74   You are counted as having notional earnings if you withdraw your labour as part of a trade dispute (go on strike). In this case, the amount of your notional earnings is what you would receive if you hadn't done so. This rule doesn't apply if your earnings are lower for other reasons, for example if you are paid less during school holidays or aren't paid for absences, in which case your reduced income is taken into account.

Notional earnings: deprivation

10.75   You are counted as having notional earnings if:

  (a) you have deprived yourself of earnings, or your employer has arranged for this; and

  (b) the purpose of this was to make you entitled to UC or to more UC. This is assumed to apply to you if you actually became entitled to UC or more UC, and this was a foreseeable and intended consequence of what you or your employer did.

In this case, the amount of your notional earnings is the amount you have deprived yourself of.

10.71   UC 66(1)(m); NIUC 66(1)(m)

10.72   UC 72(3); NIUC 72(3)

10.74   UC 2 definition: 'trade dispute', 56; NIUC 2, 56

10.75   UC 52(b), 60(1),(2); NIUC 51(b), 61(1),(2)

Notional earnings: paid less than the going rate

10.76   You are counted as having notional earnings if:

(a) you provide services (para 10.77) to a person who pays nothing for them, or less than what would be paid for comparable services locally; and

(b) that person has the means to pay for them, or pay more for them; and

(c) you are not engaged to provide the services:

- by a charitable or voluntary organisation and the DWP is satisfied that it is reasonable to provide the services free of charge or at less than the local rate, or

- as a service user (para 10.20), or

- under a government training or employment programme.

In this case, the amount of your notional earnings is what would be reasonable for the provision of the services.

Notional earnings: gainful self-employment

10.77   The rules about self-employed notional earnings and the minimum income floor are in paras 10.78-81. The DWP has suspended these rules due to coronavirus for the period 13th March 2020 to 31st July 2021 (both dates included). In practice the suspension applies to all UC cases, whether you have coronavirus or not, and the DWP has said it will use its discretion to disapply it after that in the case of people affected by coronavirus [www].

10.78   As and when these rules apply (para 10.77), you are counted as having notional earnings if:

(a) you are in 'gainful self-employment'. This means your business is your main employment and is 'organised, developed, regular and carried on in the expectation of profit'; and

(b) you are required to carry out all the work requirements in para 2.38; and

(c) your own monthly earnings are below your own minimum income floor (para 2.43); and

(d) your combined monthly earnings (if you are in a couple) are below your combined minimum income floors; and

(e) you are not in a UC start-up period (para 10.81); and

(f) you are not in the first 12 months since you transferred to UC (as part of natural or managed migration: chapter 4).

In (c) and (d), monthly earnings mean earnings (including surplus earnings: para 10.15) from this and any other employment or self-employment (after deductions for tax and national insurance). For DWP guidance see ADM paras H4020-57.

10.76   UC 52(b), 60(3),(4); NIUC 51(b), 61(3),(4)

10.77   SI 2020/371 regs 2(1)(a)-(d),(2),10(2A) SI 2021/313 reg 3; NISR 2020/53 regs 2(1)(a)-(d),(2),10(2A); NISR 2021/67 reg 3
          Budget Red Book 2021 para 2.22 https://tinyurl.com/Red-Book-2021-MIF

10.78-80 UC 62, 64; NIUC 63, 65
          Parkin v SSWP [2019] EWHC 2356 (Admin) http://www.bailii.org/ew/cases/EWHC/Admin/2019/2356.html

10.79 In this case, the amount of your notional earnings is:

(a) the difference between:

- your own monthly earnings, and

- your own monthly minimum income floor (para 2.43); or

(b) if it is lower (and you are in a couple), the difference between:

- your combined monthly earnings, and

- your combined monthly minimum income floors.

10.80 The overall effect is that the total of your actual and notional earnings is at least as much as your minimum income floor (or your combined minimum income floors if you are in a couple). The High Court has held that this rule is not unlawful (Parkin v SSWP).

The UC start-up period

10.81 You qualify for a UC start-up period if:

(a) you have not had a start-up period for that trade, profession or vocation at any time before; and

(b) you are taking active steps to increase your earnings from it up to your minimum income floor (para 2.43); and

(c) you have not begun a UC start-up period:

- within the past five years, or

- (at any time) for a similar business.

The start-up period lasts for 12 months starting from the beginning of the assessment period in which the DWP agrees you are in gainful self-employment (para 10.78(a)). But it can be brought to an early end if you stop being in gainful self-employment or stop taking steps to increase your earnings.

Notional unearned income: available on application

10.82 You are counted as having notional unearned income equal to any amount which:

(a) would be available to you if you applied for it; but

(b) you haven't applied for.

This rule can apply to any kind of unearned income (table 10.4) except UK social security benefits. For example, it can apply to personal or occupational pension schemes. If you are over 60 and not on PIP, the DWP can require your pension holder to provide information relevant to this.

10.81   UC 63; NIUC 64; C&P 41; NIC&P 38

10.82   UC 66(1), 74; NIUC 66(1), 74

Notional capital: deprivation

10.83   You are counted as having notional capital if:

(a) you have deprived yourself of capital; and

(b) the purpose of this was to make you entitled to UC or to more UC.

In this case, the amount of your notional capital is the amount you have deprived yourself of. See paras 10.84-86 for further details.

Notional capital: exceptions

10.84   The rule in para 10.83 does not apply when you spend capital to:

(a) pay off or reduce any debt you owe; or

(b) buy goods or services if this is reasonable in your circumstances.

What deprivation means

10.85   In deciding whether you have deprived yourself of capital, 'the test is one of purpose', and you can only have deprived yourself if obtaining UC formed 'a positive part' of your planning: [2011] UKUT 500 (AAC). If it is clear that you did not (or could not) appreciate what you were doing, or the consequences of it, you cannot count as having deprived yourself: R(H) 1/06. For further examples of how deprivation has been interpreted, see volume 2 chapter 13. For DWP guidance see ADM paras H1795-1846.

How notional capital reduces

10.86   If you are counted as having notional capital (para 10.83), the amount reduces as follows (whether you are on UC or not):

(a) if your notional capital is more than £16,000, it reduces each month by the amount of UC you would qualify for (if any) in that month without the notional capital;

(b) if your notional capital is more than £6,000 (but not more than £16,000), it reduces each month by the assumed amount of income it produces (para 10.56).

Notional capital and earnings: companies

10.87   You are counted as having notional capital and earnings from a company if:

(a) your relationship to the company is analogous to that of a sole owner or partner; and

(b) the company carries on a trade or a property business; and

(c) the company is not an intermediary or managed service company paying you taxable earnings (under Chapter 8 or 9 of Part 2 of the Income Tax (Earnings and Pensions) Act 2003).

10.83   UC 50(1); NIUC 50(1)

10.84   UC 50(2); NIUC 50(2)

10.86   UC 50(3); NIUC 50(3)

10.87   UC 77(1),(5),(6); NIUC 77(1),(5),(6)

10.88   In this case, you are counted as having notional capital equal to the value of the company or your share in it. But the value of company assets used wholly and exclusively for trade purposes is disregarded, and your actual holding in the company is also disregarded. For DWP guidance, see ADM paras H1874-82.

10.89   And you are counted as having notional earnings equal to the income of the company or your share of it. This is calculated using the rules for self-employed earnings (paras 10.24-30). If it is your main employment the rules about notional earnings from self-employment apply (paras 10.78-80), but you do not qualify for a UC start-up period (para 10.81).

10.88   UC 77(2),(3)(a); NIUC 77(2),(3)(a)

10.89   UC 77(3)(b),(c),(4); NIUC 77(3)(b),(c),(4)

Chapter 11 **UC changes**

- Changes of circumstances: see paras 11.1-10.
- When changes of circumstances take effect: see paras 11.11-29.
- Suspending, restoring and terminating UC: see paras 11.30-41.

Changes of circumstances

11.1   This section explains how your UC changes when there is a change in your or someone else's circumstances. It applies when:

(a) you or someone else report a change; or

(b) the DWP becomes aware of a change without it being reported.

The duty to report changes

11.2   You have a duty to report any change of circumstances which you might reasonably be expected to know could affect:

(a) your continuing entitlement to UC;

(b) the amount of UC awarded; or

(c) the payment of UC.

These are sometimes called 'relevant changes'.

11.3   This duty applies:

(a) to you if you are a single person, or in a couple but getting UC as a single person;

(b) to both of you if you are getting UC as a couple;

(c) to someone acting on your behalf (paras 3.8-10) or receiving UC on your behalf (para 12.6);

(d) to your landlord if part of your UC is paid to them (paras 12.30, 12.37 and 12.48);

(e) to a third party if part of your UC is paid to them (para 12.55).

11.1   D&A 23, sch 1 paras 21, 29; NID&A 23, sch 1 paras 21, 29

11.2   C&P 38(1),(4), D&A 36(9); NIC&P 37(1),(4), NID&A 36(9)

11.3   C&P 38(1),(4),(7),(8), 41; NIC&P 37(1),(4),(7),(8), 38

Kinds of change you should report

11.4   The DWP should explain the kinds of change you need to tell it about. These include moving home, changes in your rent, income or capital and other changes relating to you, your benefit unit, non-dependants, or someone you are caring for.

Kinds of change your landlord should report

11.5   If part of your UC is paid to your landlord, they should report changes that affect how much UC they receive, and whether UC should be paid to them. This includes changes in your rent or when you move home.

How to tell the DWP about changes

11.6   You should normally be able to tell the DWP about changes via your online account if you have one (para 3.13). If you are told not to use that method, you should be given a contact point you can telephone or write to about changes. In Great Britain you may also be able to report births and deaths by using the Tell Us Once service through the local register office or DWP Bereavement Service.

Reporting changes promptly

11.7   You should tell the DWP promptly about changes. If you delay reporting a change that increases your UC, you may get less UC than you could have done (table 11.1(b)).

Information and evidence

11.8   The DWP can ask you (or another person in para 11.3) for information and evidence about a change of circumstances. The rules are the same as when you made a claim (paras 3.19-20). If you fail to provide this the DWP could suspend payments of your UC (para 11.31).

Decisions about changes

11.9   The DWP makes a decision about:

(a) how the change affects your UC; and

(b) (if it does) when the change takes effect.

This is called a 'supersession' or (in a few cases) a 'revision'. These terms are explained in table 14.1, but you don't have to use them when you contact the DWP.

Notices and appeals

11.10   The DWP normally sends you a notice about its decision (para 14.5), and if you disagree you can ask for a reconsideration and appeal (paras 14.9 and 14.31). However, some changes don't automatically require a notice, mainly changes in earned income, and in these cases you can request a notice (e.g. in order to appeal: para 14.37).

11.6   C&P 2 definition: 'appropriate office', 38(5), 39, sch 2; NIC&P 2, 37(5), sch 1
         www.gov.uk/after-a-death/organisations-you-need-to-contact-and-tell-us-once

11.8   C&P 38(2),(3); D&A 33(2),(3); NIC&P 37(2),(3) NID&A 33(2),(3)

11.9   SSA 9-10; D&A sch 1 paras 20, 21, 29; NISSO 10-11; NID&A sch 1 paras 20, 21, 29

11.10   SSA 8, 10; NISSO 9, 11; D&A 7; NID&A 7

When changes of circumstances take effect

11.11   This section explains when changes in circumstances take effect (alter your UC). Table 11.1 summarises the rules.

The general rule

11.12   The general rule is that your UC changes from the first day of the assessment period in which the change of circumstances takes place. But there are exceptions for changes that are reported late (paras 11.13-15) and further details in some cases (paras 11.16-29).

Table 11.1 **When changes of circumstances take effect**

Type of change	When it takes effect
Changes increasing your UC	
(a) Reported to the DWP, or made by the DWP, within the time limit (the end of the assessment period or in some cases later: para 11.15)	The first day of the assessment period (para 3.38) in which the change takes (or took) place
(b) Reported or made outside the time limit	The first day of the assessment period in which the change is reported, or the DWP first takes action to make it (if this is earlier)
Changes reducing or ending your UC	
(c) All cases	The first day of the assessment period in which the change takes (or took) place

---

Examples: Changes of circumstances

1. Starting to pay for childcare costs

Abigail is working and getting UC. Her assessment periods begin on the 26th of each month. She starts paying a childminder to look after her son on 6th June and qualifies for more UC because she is entitled to a childcare costs element.

■ If she reports this to the DWP by 25th June, she is within the time limit and her UC increases from 26th May.

■ If she reports this between 26th June and 25th July and doesn't have special circumstances for her delay, her UC increases from 26th June.

11.12   D&A sch 1 para 20; NID&A sch 1 para 20

T11.1   D&A sch 1 paras 20, 21, 29; NID&A sch 1 paras 20, 21, 29

2. An increase in capital

Barney is unemployed and getting UC. His assessment periods begin on the 26th of each month. His capital increases on 6th June and he qualifies for less UC.

- Whenever he reports this to the DWP, his UC reduces from 26th May.
- If the increase in his capital is so great that he no longer qualifies for UC, his UC ends on 25th May.

3. Size of accommodation needed

Desmond is getting UC and his assessment periods begin on the 21st of each month. His daughter moves out on 1st October and he qualifies for less UC because he is no longer entitled to a bedroom for her.

- Whenever he reports this to the DWP, his UC reduces from 21st September.

Time limit for getting your arrears

11.13   When a change increases your UC you may not be paid all your arrears unless you (or someone else) report the change within the time limit (para 11.14).

Time limit for advantageous changes

11.14   A change is reported within the time limit if:

(a) you report it to the DWP by the end of the assessment period in which it takes place; or

(b) you report it up to 12 months later than (a), and the DWP agrees to a request from you to extend the time limit (para 11.15); or

(c) the DWP takes action to make the change by the end of the assessment period in which it takes place.

Extending the time limit

11.15   The DWP extends the time limit for reporting a change by up to 12 months (para 11.14(b)) if:

(a) there are special circumstances why you couldn't report the change earlier; and

(b) it is reasonable to allow you extra time – the longer you take the more compelling your reasons have to be.

Para 14.21 gives examples of special circumstances that are likely to be accepted.

Rent increases

11.16   Chapter 6 explains how your rent and/or service charges affect your UC. If you report increases within the time limit, your UC increases from the first assessment period in which your payments change (table 11.1). If the DWP delays your increase to a later assessment period (and you didn't delay reporting the increase) you should ask for a reconsideration and (if that fails) appeal (chapter 14).

11.13   D&A sch 1 para 20; NID&A sch 1 para 20

11.14-15   D&A 36; NID&A 36

11.16   UC sch 4 paras 3, 6; D&A sch 1 paras 20, 21, 29; NID&A sch 1 paras 20, 21, 29; NIUC sch 4 paras 3, 5

11.17   You should tell the DWP when your rent or service charges change, and the DWP normally asks you in early April each year to update your housing costs on your online account. When part of your UC is paid to your landlord, both of you have a duty to tell the DWP about changes (paras 11.4-5), though in practice the DWP expects you to do this rather than leave it to your landlord (paras 12.35-36). If you delay reporting a rent increase you could lose UC (table 11.1(b)).

Examples: Rent increases

1. Monthly rent due in advance

Clodagh is getting UC and her assessment periods begin on the 5th of each month. Her rent is due monthly in advance and her payments increase on 1st July (covering the month of 1st to 31st July).

- So long as she reports this on or before 4th July, she is within the time limit and her UC increases from 5th June.

2. Weekly rent due in arrears

Elvira is getting UC and her assessment periods begin on the 19th of each month. Her rent is due weekly in arrears and her payments increase on Saturday 24th July (covering the week of 18th to 24th July).

- So long as she reports this on or before 18th August, she is within the time limit and her UC increases from 19th July.

Changes in earnings

11.18   The DWP expects:

(a)   HMRC to pass on the details your employer reports about your employed earnings (para 10.22); and/or

(b)   you to report your self-employed earnings (para 10.30).

If you or HMRC do this within the time limit, your UC changes from the first day of the assessment period in which your employed earnings change (table 11.1).

11.19   But the DWP can:

(a)   estimate your earnings in an assessment period in which you (or your employer) don't report them;

(b)   allow extra time for you (or your employer) to report your earnings in an assessment period in which they reduce – and in this case you don't have to meet the conditions in para 11.15;

(c)   disregard your earnings in an assessment period in which you stop work – but you can't insist on the DWP doing this ([2015] UKUT 696 (AAC)).

11.18   D&A sch 1 paras 20, 21, 29; NID&A sch 1 paras 20, 21, 29

11.19   D&A sch 1 para 22; UC 54; NID&A sch 1 para 22; NIUC 53

11.20 Whenever you stop getting UC because your earnings increase, you get a six-month review period during which the DWP should award you UC if your earnings reduce again (para 10.13).

Changes in DWP benefits

11.21 You shouldn't need to tell the DWP (because it knows already) when your entitlement to any DWP benefit starts, stops or changes. This also applies to changes in your partner's, child's or young person's entitlement to a DWP benefit.

11.22 In these cases, your UC changes:

(a) from the first day of your assessment period in which the DWP benefit changes; or

(b) from when your UC began, if this is later.

11.23 If this means your UC increases from a date in the past, you are awarded arrears back to then. But if it means your UC reduces or ends from a date in the past, you have been overpaid back to then.

Changes in capability for work

11.24 When you start qualifying for an LCWRA element (para 9.32) your UC changes as described in table 11.1. But if this is because:

(a) the DWP has received new evidence from a health care professional etc; or

(b) the DWP has changed its mind about the need for you to be assessed (para 2.48); or

(c) you have told the DWP you or your partner are terminally ill (para 9.37);

your UC increases (to include the LCWRA element) from the first day of your assessment period in which you began to meet the LCWRA condition (or from when your UC began, if this is later). This rule means you are awarded arrears of UC back to then.

11.25 When you stop qualifying for an LCWRA or LCW element (para 9.31), your UC changes as described in table 11.1. But if you couldn't reasonably have been expected to know that you no longer qualify (or that you should report this to the DWP), your UC reduces (to remove the LCWRA/LCW element) from the first day of your assessment period in which the DWP makes its decision about this. This rule means you haven't been overpaid UC.

Reaching pension age

11.26 Your UC continues until the end of the assessment period in which:

(a) you reach 66, if you are single; or

(b) the younger of you reaches 66, if you are a couple.

You can claim SPC and/or HB up to four months/17 weeks earlier, and these then start on the exact day you (or your partner) reach 66. So, you usually get SPC/HB at the same time as UC for up to a month. This doesn't count as an overpayment and you don't have to repay it.

11.21-23 D&A 12, 21, sch1 para 31; NID&A 12, 21, sch 1 para 31

11.24 D&A sch 1 paras 23-25, 28, 30; NID&A sch 1 paras 23-25, 28, 30

11.25 D&A 5(2)(c), 23(2), 26(1),(3), 35(9), sch 1 para 28; NID&A 5(2)(c), 23(2), 26(1),(3), 35(9), sch 1 para 28

11.26 UCTP 5(2)(c), 6(8A); D&A sch 1 para 26; NIUCTP 3(2)(c), 4(8A); NID&A sch 1 para 26

Bereavement run-on

11.27 The bereavement run-on delays the impact of a death on your UC. You qualify for a bereavement run-on if one of the following has died:

(a) your partner if you were claiming UC as a couple;

(b) a child or young person you were responsible for;

(c) a person you were caring for, if you qualified for the UC carer element for caring for them (para 9.39); or

(d) a non-dependant.

11.28 In these cases, your maximum UC (para 9.4) is calculated as though the person had not died during:

(a) the assessment period containing the date of the death; and

(b) the next two assessment periods.

But changes in your financial and other circumstances are taken into account in the normal way. The examples illustrate how bereavement run-on works.

Examples: Bereavement run-on

1. Death of a partner

A homeowner couple are on UC and their assessment periods start on the 13th of each month. Their maximum UC includes the LCWRA element for one of them (para 9.32).

The partner who qualifies for the LCWRA element dies on 3rd June.

■ Because of the bereavement run-on, the surviving partner continues to qualify for the LCWRA element up to and including 12th August. But the surviving partner's new financial circumstances are taken into account from 13th May.

2. Death of a non-dependant

A single person renting a housing association flat is on UC and his assessment periods begin on the last day of each month. His mother lives with him (she is his non-dependant) so he qualifies for two-bedroom accommodation in calculating his housing costs element (para 7.8) but his mother is expected to make a housing cost contribution (para 9.63). His mother dies on 3rd June.

■ Because of the bereavement run-on, he continues to qualify for two-bedroom accommodation until 31st August, and a housing cost contribution continues to be deducted until then.

11.27-28 UC 37; NIUC 39

Other changes

11.29 Other changes alter your UC as described in table 11.1 – for example, changes in unearned income, capital and your household details. But the following have special rules:

(a) becoming a couple or a single person (paras 3.5-6);

(b) changes resulting from a reconsideration (para 14.9);

(c) amendments to the regulations and up-ratings (para 14.26);

(d) new case law (para 14.27).

Suspending, restoring and terminating UC

11.30 This section explains how the DWP can suspend, restore or terminate your UC. The general rules about this are in paras 11.31-37, and the rules for appeals cases are in paras 11.38-41.

Suspending UC

11.31 Suspending UC means that all or part of your UC payments is stopped for the time being. The DWP has told its decision-makers that they should always take account of whether hardship will result before doing this (ADM para A4317).

11.32 The DWP can suspend all or part of your UC when:

(a) it doubts whether you meet the conditions of entitlement for UC;

(b) it is considering whether to change a decision about your UC (paras 11.1 and 14.9);

(c) it considers there may be an overpayment of UC; or

(d) you don't appear to live at your last notified address.

The DWP can do this straightaway or first ask for information or evidence (para 11.33).

Information and evidence

11.33 When the DWP requires information or evidence, it must notify you of what it requires and how long you have to provide it. It must allow you at least 14 days and can allow longer. The DWP can then suspend all or part of your UC if you don't:

(a) provide the information or evidence within the time allowed; or

(b) satisfy the DWP within that time that it doesn't exist or is impossible to obtain.

Restoring UC

11.34 The DWP must restore payments of your UC when it is satisfied that:

(a) UC is properly payable;

(b) there are no outstanding matters to be resolved; and

(c) you have provided any information or evidence it required, or it doesn't exist or is impossible to obtain.

11.32   SSA 22; D&A 44(1),(2)(a); NISSO 22, NID&A 43(1),(2)(a)

11.33   SSA 22; D&A 45; NISSO 22, NID&A 44

11.34   D&A 46(a),(b); NID&A 45(a),(b)

11.35   Restoring UC means paying the UC that was suspended. The payments should be of the same amount as before; but the rules in paras 11.11-29 apply if there has been a change of circumstances or a decision was wrong.

Terminating UC

11.36   The DWP must terminate your UC if:

(a) it suspended payments of your UC in full;

(b) it required you to provide information or evidence;

(c) more than one month has passed since it required this; and

(d) you haven't provided the information or evidence or satisfied the DWP that it doesn't exist or is impossible to obtain.

The DWP can extend the time limit of one month if this is reasonable (ADM para A4338).

11.37   Terminating UC means you don't get any more payments and your entitlement ends. The DWP can only terminate UC on the date it was suspended from ([2020] UKUT 71 (AAC)). If your UC should have stopped from an earlier date the rules in paras 11.11-29 apply. The DWP should notify you when it terminates your UC.

Suspending and restoring UC in appeals cases

11.38   The DWP can suspend all or part of your UC when an appeal is pending against:

(a) a decision of a First-tier Tribunal, Upper Tribunal or court in your own case; or

(b) a decision of an Upper Tribunal or court in another person's case, and it appears to the DWP that the outcome of the appeal could mean your UC should be changed.

11.39   An appeal counts as 'pending' if:

(a)   the DWP has requested a statement of reasons from the First-tier Tribunal and is waiting for this; or

(b) the DWP is waiting for a decision from the Upper Tribunal or court; or

(c) the DWP has received the statement of reasons or decision and:

■   is considering whether to apply for permission to appeal, or

■   has applied for permission to appeal and is waiting for a decision on this, or

■   has received permission to appeal and is considering whether to appeal; or

(d) the DWP has made an appeal and it hasn't yet been decided; or

(e) you or the other person (para 11.38) have made an appeal and it hasn't yet been decided.

In cases (a) to (d) the DWP should keep you informed of its plans.

11.36   SSA 23; D&A 47; NISSO 23, NID&A 46

11.38   SSA 21; D&A 44(1),(2)(b),(c); NISSO 21, NID&A 43(1),(2)(b),(c)

11.39   SSA 21(3); D&A 44(3)-(5); NISSO 21(3), NID&A 43(3)-(5)

11.40   The DWP must restore payments of your UC when:

(a) it runs out of time to request a statement of reasons, apply for permission to appeal, or appeal; or

(b) it withdraws an application for permission to appeal, or an appeal; or

(c) it is refused permission to appeal and can't take any further steps to obtain it.

But if the DWP needs information or evidence, the rules in paras 11.33-37 apply.

Changing decisions about suspending, restoring or terminating UC

11.41   You can ask the DWP to reconsider a decision about suspending, restoring or terminating your UC (para 14.9). You can then appeal to a tribunal about a decision to terminate your UC or to alter it when it is restored, but not about a decision to suspend your UC or to restore it without altering it (table 14.3).

11.40   D&A 46(c),(d); NID&A 45(c),(d)

Chapter 12 **UC payments**

- How and when your UC is paid: see paras 12.1-12.
- Help with budgeting and payments: see paras 12.13-18.
- Advance payments: see paras 12.19-29.
- Payments to landlords towards rent and rent arrears: see paras 12.30-54.
- Payments to third parties towards debts: see paras 12.55-59.

Getting your UC

How UC is paid

12.1   The general rule is that your UC is paid into a bank, building society or other account. This means the account you told the DWP about (para 3.21).

12.2   If you can't use a bank or similar account, the DWP can agree to pay you through its payment exception service (ADM B1006). This allows you to collect your UC using a single payment card at an outlet displaying the Single Payment logo [www].

Payment to couples

12.3   If you are a couple, your UC can be paid into an account in one name or joint names. If you can't agree about this, the DWP makes the decision.

12.4   The DWP can also change which of you it makes the payment to, or in exceptional circumstances split the payments between you, if this is in your interests (para 12.7).

Payments to an appointee or attorney

12.5   If you are unable to act, you may have an appointee, attorney or similar person acting for you (paras 3.8-11). Your UC can be paid into their account, or a joint account if you have one with them.

Payments to someone on your behalf

12.6   The DWP can pay all or part of your UC to someone on your behalf if this is necessary to protect your interests (para 12.7). For this rule, you don't have to be unable to act and they don't have to be an appointee, attorney, etc. For example, your UC could be paid to a relative or carer if they are managing your UC on your behalf. This rule is also used for rent payments to landlords (para 12.37).

12.1   C&P 46(1)(a); NIC&P 41(1)

12.2   www.gov.uk/payment-exception-service

12.3   C&P 46(1)(a),(b), 47(4),(5); NIC&P 41(1), 42(4),(5)

12.4   C&P 47(6); NIC&P 42(6)

12.5   C&P 46(1)(a),(c),(d), 57; NIC&P 41(1), 52

12.6   C&P 58(1); NIC&P 53(1)

'Your interests'

12.7   In this chapter, 'your interests' means:

(a)   your own interests;

(b)   your partner's interests if you are a couple (even if you are claiming UC as a single person: para 2.7);

(c)   the interests of a child or young person you or your partner are responsible for (para 3.62);

(d)   the interests of a person you get a UC carer element for (para 9.39).

When UC is paid

12.8   Your UC is paid as follows:

(a)   in England and Wales you are paid monthly unless the DWP agrees to twice-monthly payments (para 12.9);

(b)   in Scotland, once you have received your first monthly payment you can choose between monthly and twice-monthly payments thereafter;

(c)   in Northern Ireland, you are paid twice-monthly unless you choose to be paid monthly.

If you are paid twice-monthly, you get half your UC on the normal pay day and the other half 15 days later (para 12.14(a)).

12.9   The DWP can agree to pay your UC:

(a)   twice-monthly in England and Wales if you are having problems budgeting and there is risk of financial harm to you or your family;

(b)   four times a month throughout the UK in exceptional circumstances.

See para 12.14(a) for DWP guidance.

Payment date

12.10   Monthly payments of UC are made in arrears. They should be made within seven days after the end of the assessment period they are for, or as soon as possible after that.

Payments if you die

12.11   If you die, the DWP can pay or distribute your UC to your personal representatives, legatees, next of kin or creditors. If the person is under 16, the DWP makes the payment to someone over 16 who will use it for their well-being. A written application for these payments has to be made within 12 months after your death, or later if the DWP agrees.

12.7   C&P 47(6), 58(1); NIC&P 42(6), 53(1)

12.8(a)   C&P 47(1); NIC&P 42(1)

12.8(b)   SSI 2017/227

12.8(c)   NIC&P 42(1)

12.10   C&P 45, 47(1),(2); NIC&P 40, 42(1),(2)

12.11   C&P 56; NIC&P 51

Payments due more than a year ago

12.12 You lose the right to any payment of UC that you haven't received within 12 months after it became due. This rule has been confirmed (CDLA/2807/2003), but the period can be extended if you have continuous good cause from a date within the 12 months to when you write requesting the payment (R(S) 2/63).

Help with budgeting and payments

12.13 Monthly UC payments need to be budgeted in the same way as monthly wages from employment. Not everyone finds this easy, and the DWP offers help with budgeting and payments (paras 12.15-17) either when you claim UC or during your UC award. If the DWP doesn't offer this you can request it, or someone on your behalf (paras 3.8-11) or your landlord can (paras 12.34-36).

How UC is paid

12.14 DWP guidance on budgeting and payment includes:

(a) *UC operational guidance: Money guidance and alternative payment arrangements* [www];

(b) *Guidance: Alternative Payment Arrangements* [www].

For other guidance to landlords see para 12.31.

Budgeting support

12.15 Citizens Advice and Citizens Advice Scotland are DWP partner organisations and provide help with claiming UC, money advice and alternative payment arrangements (the 'Help to Claim' service). The DWP is allowed to share information with one of these partners if it is used to provide 'advice, assistance or support' to you.

Alternative payment arrangements

12.16 The DWP can provide the following alternative payment arrangements:

(a) changing who UC is paid to if you are a couple (para 12.4);

(b) paying UC to someone on your behalf (paras 12.5-6);

(c) increasing the frequency of UC payments (para 12.9);

(d) making an advance payment when you are waiting for your UC or if you have one-off expenses (paras 12.19-29);

(e) paying part of your UC to your landlord towards rent or rent arrears (paras 12.30-54);

(f) paying part of your UC to a third party towards debts (paras 12.55-58).

If you are having current difficulties, the DWP says paying part of your UC to your landlord takes priority amongst these.

12.12   C&P 55; NIC&P 50

12.14(a)   House of Commons, Deposited Papers, 29th October 2020 https://tinyurl.com/OG-money-guide-Oct-2020

12.14(b)   https://tinyurl.com/UC-APA

12.15   The Social Security (Information-sharing in relation to Welfare Services etc) Regulations 2012, No 1483, regs 2 –
           'universal support initiative', 5(1)(h), 10(1)(e), 16(d), 17(3)(c)

12.17 Table 12.1 lists the factors the DWP takes into account when it is considering alternative payment arrangements. The DWP should tell you when it is considering starting, changing or stopping these so that you can give your views.

Table 12.1 **Alternative payment arrangements**

The DWP takes these factors into account when it considers whether to make payments to your landlord towards your rent (para 12.37) as well as other alternative payment arrangements (para 12.16). See also paras 12.30-36.

Tier 1 factors

These indicate you have a 'highly likely/probable' need for alternative payment arrangements.

- (a) you have drug, alcohol or other addiction problems, e.g. gambling.
- (b) You have learning difficulties, e.g. with literacy and/or numeracy.
- (c) You have severe or multiple debt problems.
- (d) You are in supported or temporary accommodation.
- (e) You are homeless.
- (f) You are a victim of domestic violence or abuse.
- (g) You have a mental health condition.
- (h) You are currently in rent arrears, e.g. under threat of eviction or repossession.
- (i) You are aged 16 or 17 or a care leaver.
- (j) You have multiple and complex needs.

Tier 2 factors

These indicate you have a 'less likely/possible' need for alternative payment arrangements.

- (k) Payments are being made from your UC to a third party, e.g. for fines, utility arrears.
- (l) You are a refugee or asylum seeker.
- (m) You have a history of rent arrears.
- (n) You were previously homeless or in supported accommodation.
- (o) You have a physical or mental disability.
- (p) You have just left prison or hospital.
- (q) You are recently bereaved.
- (r) You have problems using English.
- (s) You are ex-services.
- (t) You are not in education, employment or training.

DWP Alternative Payment Arrangements, Annex A, 13th May 2020 (see footnote 12.14)

Discretionary housing payments

12.18   You may be able to get a discretionary housing payment from your local council towards your rent [www]. The council can grant these to people on UC with a housing costs element as well as those on HB. These are discretionary so you shouldn't rely on getting a payment. For further details see volume 2 chapter 23.

Advance payments

12.19   You may be able to get:

(a)   a UC advance while you are waiting for a payment of your UC (paras 12.22-25);

(b)   a budgeting advance if you have one-off expenses while you are on UC (paras 12.26-29).

In the law these are called 'payments on account'.

12.20   The DWP provides guidance on advances [www]. You can apply online, or call the UC helpline or speak to your work coach. You will be expected to explain why you are applying.

12.21   If the DWP agrees to pay you an advance, it must notify you that it will be repayable (paras 12.25 and 12.29), and if you are a couple it must also notify your partner. You can't appeal about an advance, but you can ask the DWP to reconsider (para 14.9).

Who can get a UC advance

12.22   The DWP can pay you a UC advance if you are in financial need (para 12.23). It can provide:

(a)   new claim advances for people waiting for their first UC payment,

(b)   benefit transfer advances for people transferring to UC from legacy benefits, and

(c)   change of circumstances advances for people whose circumstances change in a way that increases their UC;

12.23   You are in financial need if there is a serious risk of damage to your health or safety or your partner's, or that of a child or young person you are responsible for. DWP guidance (para 12.20) says this includes when you can't afford to pay your rent or buy food.

12.24   The DWP decides the amount of a UC advance. The guidance (para 12.20) says that if you are making a new UC claim it can pay up to 100% of your estimated UC; and that it aims to make the payment within five working days, or on the same day if you are in immediate need.

12.25   A UC advance is repayable. The DWP can recover it in the same way as an overpayment (para 13.36) and usually does this by making deductions from your future payments of UC. You have 24 months to complete the repayment [www], but in exceptional circumstances you can ask for your repayments to be delayed for up to three months.

12.18   https://www.gov.uk/government/publications/discretionary-housing-payments-guidance-manual

12.20   https://www.gov.uk/guidance/universal-credit-advances

12.21   POA 8, 17; D&A sch 3 para 14; NIPOA 8, 17; NID&A sch 3 para 11

12.22   POA 4, 5, 6; NIPOA 4, 5, 6

12.23   POA 7; NIPOA 7

12.25   POA 10; NIPOA 10 Budget Red Book 2021, para 2.23 https://tinyurl.com/Red-Book-2021-MIF

Who can get a budgeting advance

12.26   A budgeting advance can be towards:

(a) you or your partner getting employment or self-employment; or

(b) 'intermittent' expenses, e.g. furniture, household equipment, clothing and footwear.

The DWP says it also considers rent and removal expenses when you move home; home improvements, maintenance and security; and funeral expenses.

12.27   The DWP can pay you a budgeting advance if:

(a) you are on UC; and

(b) during the past six months, you haven't earned more than £2,600 if you are a single person or £3,600 if you are a couple; and

(c) you have repaid any previous budgeting advances and are likely to repay this one; and

(d) you have been getting UC, JSA(IB), ESA(IR), IS or SPC for a continuous period of at least six months. (The DWP says it also includes HB in this list.)

But (d) doesn't apply when the expenses necessarily relate to getting or keeping employment or self-employment, for example up-front childcare or travel costs (if you have a job offer) when you can't get help with these from the DWP's Flexible Support Fund.

Table 12.2 **Maximum amount of budgeting advance**

Your circumstances	Maximum amount of budgeting advance
Single and not responsible for a child or young person	£348
A couple and not responsible for a child or young person	£464
Responsible for a child or young person	£812

12.28   The DWP decides the amount of the budgeting advance. This can't be below £100 or above the maximum in table 12.2. The amount you can get is reduced pound for pound by any capital you have above £1,000 (excluding disregarded capital: table 10.6). If this would reduce the amount to below £100, you can't get a budgeting advance.

12.29   A budgeting advance is repayable. The DWP can recover it in the same way as an overpayment (para 13.36) and usually does this by making deductions from your future payments of UC. by making deductions from your future payments of UC. You have 24 months to complete the repayment, but this can be extended in exceptional circumstances.

12.26   POA 11, 12; NIPOA 11, 12

12.27   POA 12, 13, 14; NIPOA 12, 13, 14

T12.2   POA 15; NIPOA 15

12.28   POA 15, 16; NIPOA 15, 16

12.29   POA 17; NIPOA 17

Table 12.3 **Payments to a landlord**

Payments towards your rent, including service charges

These are paid calendar monthly.

(a) In England and Wales, your UC housing costs element (or possibly more) can be paid to your landlord if this is in your interests: paras 12.43-44.

(b) In Scotland and Northern Ireland, you can choose to have your UC housing costs element paid to your landlord: paras 12.45-47.

Payments towards rent arrears

These are paid four-weekly.

(c) Throughout the UK, part of your UC standard allowance can be paid to your landlord if you have rent arrears: paras 12.53-54.

Note: The payments are sometimes called 'deductions' because the amount paid to your landlord is deducted from your UC. If the DWP is making both payments, the different payment intervals can cause landlords difficulties (para 12.48 and see the example towards the end of this chapter).

Payments to landlords

12.30 If you are a renter or a shared owner, part of your UC can be paid to your landlord. This section gives general information about this, and table 12.3 gives a summary. The next sections give the detailed rules about payments towards your:

(a) rent (paras 12.37-47); and

(b) rent arrears (paras 12.48-54).

If your landlord has an agent to collect the rent, payments can be made to them, and in this chapter references to a 'landlord' include an agent.

12.31 The DWP guidance in para 12.14 includes payments to landlords. The following are mainly for landlords:

(a) *UC and rented housing: guide for landlords*; and

(b) *Alternative payment arrangements*.

Requests by you or your landlord

12.32 You can ask the DWP to make payments to your landlord towards rent and/or rent arrears, or your landlord can, or the DWP can do this without your request. Payments can be made whether you have a social or a private landlord (paras 12.34-36).

12.31   https://tinyurl.com/UC-landlord-guide
         https://tinyurl.com/UC-APA

T12.3   C&P 58(1), sch 6 para 7; NIC&P 53(1), sch 5 para 7

12.32   C&P 58(1), sch 6 para 7; NIC&P 53(1), sch 5 para 7

Conditions for making landlord payments

12.33　　The DWP will only make payments to your landlord if:

(a) you or your landlord request it; and

(b) either you have rent arrears that meet the conditions for payment under those grounds (paras 12.38, 12.48) or at least one of the factors in table 12.1 applies to you.

How you can request landlord payments

12.34　　You can request payments be made to your landlord for rent and/or rent arrears through your UC journal or you can call the UC helpline (0800 328 5644) or speak to your work coach.

Requests for information and payments by a social landlord

12.35　　If you rent your home from a social landlord (table 6.1) the DWP can tell them if you have made a claim for UC or (if you get UC) when your next payment is due, whether it is your first and the amount of your housing costs element (but no more). Social landlords can sign up to be a DWP 'trusted partner' [www] and most do. Being a trusted partner means the DWP accepts your landlord's notice that you meet the criteria for landlord payment (para 12.33) (on trust that they will only request it if you do). Trusted partners can use the DWP landlord portal to request information and/or payment and to verify any rent details you have given. But the DWP doesn't accept rent changes notified through the portal on your behalf following a recent unsuccessful scheme to pilot it (para 11.17).

Requests for information and payments by other landlords

12.36　　Any landlord or managing agent (including a social landlord who is not a trusted partner) can request payments using the online service tool [www]. Data protection law does not allow the DWP to share information about you with your landlord unless you are present and/or give your 'explicit consent'. But a landlord who has requested payments can call the UC helpline (para 12.34) to track their application if they can answer some basic security questions about you (see DWP landlord guide: para 12.31).

Payments to your landlord towards rent

When payments are made in England and Wales

12.37　　In England and Wales, the DWP can pay part or all of your UC to your landlord towards your rent (including service charges) if this is necessary to protect your interests or those of a family member or someone you are caring for (para 12.7). The DWP calls these 'managed payment to landlord'. They are paid to your landlord (or agent: para 12.30) calendar monthly, to match the calendar monthly payment of your UC.

12.35　The Social Security (Information-sharing in relation to Welfare Services etc.) Regulations 2012, No 1483, regs 2 – 'social landlord', 5(1)(g),(h),(3A), 10(1)(e); Landlord Portal and Trusted Partner Scheme (Dec 2020) https://tinyurl.com/TrustedLL

12.36　https://directpayment.universal-credit.service.gov.uk

12.37　C&P 58(1)

Requests and disputes in England and Wales

12.38   You can request payments to your landlord or your landlord can (paras 12.32-36). The DWP says (para 12.31(a)) it is likely to make payments if:

(a) you have at least two months' rent arrears; or

(b) you have repeatedly underpaid your rent and have at least one month's rent arrears.

Except where your landlord is a trusted partner (para 12.35) the DWP requires evidence of your arrears. If your landlord provides this and you disagree with the amount, the DWP should give you the opportunity to dispute it (ADM D2026-28).

12.39   DWP guidance also says (ADM D2021-23) that:

(a) payments are likely if:

■ you have a history of persistent misspending, and

■ you are threatened with eviction or repossession of your home, and

■ you have no other suitable means of dealing with the debt;

(b) payments are not usually made if:

■ you agree to clear the debt, or

■ there is evidence that you're determined to do so, or

■ paying your landlord isn't in your interests.

When (a) applies, payments to your landlord are 'the first priority' over other alternative payment arrangements, 'in order to safeguard your home'. And if the DWP agrees to more frequent UC payments (para 12.9) or to split payments between you and your partner (para 12.4), it 'automatically' makes payments to your landlord.

12.40   If your HB was previously paid to your landlord, the DWP says (para 12.14(a)) you 'must be offered' payments of UC to your landlord whether or not you have rent arrears, 'providing [you] continue to meet the Tier 1 and Tier 2 factors' in table 12.1. These factors also apply in other UC cases.

12.41   The DWP should tell you and your landlord who it decides to pay, and when it changes who it pays. The importance of this was emphasised in relation to HB in R(H) 1/08 and R(H) 2/08.

12.42   You can't appeal about whether part or all of your UC should be paid to your landlord towards your rent, or about how much the payment should be. But you can ask the DWP to reconsider (para 14.9), use the formal complaints procedure (para 14.64) and in some cases you may be able to apply for a judicial review.

Amounts in England and Wales

12.43   The DWP has discretion about how much to pay your landlord towards your rent. The amount should reflect your interests (para 12.37) or those of a family member or person you are caring for (para 12.7). For example, if your UC is reduced because of a sanction (para 9.81) and you have limited money for food and basic living needs, the amount paid to your landlord could be small or nil. Or if you have other income as well as UC, it could be high.

12.42   D&A sch 3 para 1(n); NID&A sch 3 para 1(n)

12.44   In practice the DWP usually limits payments to the amount of your housing costs element (para 9.51). But the law allows 'part or all' of your UC to be paid to your landlord towards your rent (and this is different from payments towards rent arrears: paras 12.53-54). So in appropriate cases, the DWP could pay more. For example, if your rent is higher than your housing costs element (because of limitations on eligible rent, non-dependants, ineligible services, etc) the DWP could pay your landlord up to the full amount of your rent. Also, if your UC is lower than your housing costs element (because of the level of your income etc) the DWP could pay the whole of your UC to your landlord. For appeals, see para 12.41.

Payments in Scotland and Northern Ireland

12.45   In Scotland, you can choose to have your UC housing costs element paid to your landlord: you don't have to give a reason.

12.46   In Northern Ireland, your UC housing costs element is always paid to your landlord unless you choose to have it paid to you.

12.47   In Scotland and Northern Ireland paras 12.37-44 apply if you have chosen to have your housing costs element paid to you, and/or to questions about whether the DWP can pay more than the housing costs element to your landlord.

Payments to your landlord towards rent arrears

When payments are made

12.48   The DWP can pay part of your UC to your landlord towards your arrears of rent (including service charges) if:

   (a)   the rent arrears relate to your current home (para 5.16); and

   (b)   your earned income, if you have any, isn't above the UC work allowance (para 12.50); and

   (c)   either:

         ■   you are getting a UC housing costs element on your home, or

         ■   your home is exempt accommodation (table 5.2(a)) and you are getting HB there.

The DWP calls these 'third party payments'. Unlike other payments, these are paid to your landlord or agent (para 12.30) four-weekly, but with the monthly amount being paid in only 12 of the 13 four-week cycles that occur over the year (table 12.3 and see the example towards the end of this chapter).

12.49   The arrears can be of rent and/or service charges, whether these are eligible for UC or HB or ineligible. And this applies whether or not your rent/services are or were being met by UC or HB.

12.43-44   C&P 58(1); NIC&P 53(1)

12.46   Welfare Reform and Work Act 2016 s18-21; NIWRO arts 13-16; SI 2017/725; NISR 2017/176

12.48   C&P 60, sch 6 paras 2, 7; NIC&P 55, sch 5 paras 2, 7

12.49   C&P sch 6 para 7(3),(8); NIC&P sch 5 para 7(3),(8)

12.50   Payments to your landlord towards rent arrears:

(a) can only begin if your earned income was below the UC work allowance (table 10.1), or you had no earned income, in your previous assessment period;

(b) must stop if you had earned income above the work allowance in your previous three assessment periods.

If you are a couple, this rule applies to your combined earned income.

Requests and disputes

12.51   You can request payments to your landlord or your landlord can (paras 12.32-36), and in either case the DWP needs evidence of arrears. If your landlord provides this and you disagree with the amount, the DWP should give you the opportunity to dispute it (ADM D2026-28). The DWP should tell you and your landlord when it starts, changes or ends making payments to your landlord.

12.52   You can appeal about whether part of your UC should be paid to your landlord towards rent arrears, and about how much the payments should be.

Amounts

12.53   The DWP decides how much to pay your landlord towards rent arrears. This is based on your UC standard allowance (para 9.14) and whether any other payments to third parties are being made from your UC (paras 12.55-59).

12.54   First, the amount is calculated on a calendar monthly basis:

(a) it must be at least 10% of your standard allowance, regardless of any other third party payments being made from your UC; and

(b) it can be up to 20% of your standard allowance, so long as this doesn't make the total third party payments from your UC more than 25% (para 12.58) [www].

Then it is converted to a four-weekly basis for payments to take place (para 12.48).

Example: Payments to a landlord

Luke is a single tenant aged 42. He is on UC and qualifies for a standard allowance of £324.84 and a housing costs element of £800.00, totalling £1124.84.

Luke has problems budgeting his rent, and also has rent arrears. The DWP decides to pay his landlord:

▪ the housing costs element towards rent	£800.00
▪ 20% of the standard allowance towards rent arrears	£64.97
▪ Total	£864.97

12.50   C&P sch 6 para 7(6),(7); NIC&P sch 5 para 7(6),(7)

12.52   SSA 12; NISSO 13

12.54   C&P sch 6 paras 4, 7(5); NIC&P sch 5 paras 4, 7(5)
          Budget Red Book 2021 para 2.23 https://tinyurl.com/Red-Book-2021-MIF

So in each assessment period until the DWP reviews this (for example, when Luke's arrears are reduced):

- Luke gets   £259.87
- his landlord gets   £864.97
- Total   £1124.84

But the actual payments to his landlord are split between monthly amounts towards the rent (£800) and four-weekly amounts towards the rent arrears (£64.97) (paid in 12 out of 13 four-weekly cycles: para 12.48).

Payments to third parties towards other debts

When payments are made

12.55   The DWP can pay part of your UC to a third party towards debts you owe them, if the debt is for:

(a)   owner-occupier payments that aren't met by SMI (chapter 8), for example because they built up when you weren't on UC;

(b)   fuel and/or water charges on your home;

(c)   council tax and rates on your home;

(d)   child maintenance;

(e)   a court fine or compensation order;

(f)   a refugee integration loan; and

(g)   certain qualifying loans made to you by a credit union or similar mutual organisation.

The DWP calls these 'third party payments', and says they are only used when 'other avenues of recovery have been exhausted'.

12.56   The limits on your earned income are the same as for rent arrears payments (paras 12.53-54). Requests and disputes are also dealt with in a similar way (paras 12.51-52).

Amounts

12.57   For each debt, the DWP can pay up to 5% of your UC standard allowance (para 9.14). In the case of fuel, it can also agree to pay your ongoing charges.

12.55   C&P 60, sch 6 paras 1, 3(2), 6-12; NIC&P 55, sch 5 paras 1, 6-12

12.57-58   C&P sch 6 paras 3, 4, 5; NIC&P sch 5 paras 3, 4, 5

12.58   The total amount deducted from your UC towards rent arrears (para 12.48) and other third party debts (para 12.55) is limited as follows:

(a) the DWP can't pay towards more than three debts at any one time – when necessary, priority is given to rent arrears and owner-occupier payments, then fuel and water;

(b) DWP policy sets the maximum at 25% of your UC standard allowance (but the law allows up to 40% except as described for rent arrears in para 12.54(a);

(c) the payments from your UC must leave you with at least 1p of your UC.

These limits don't apply to sanctions (para 9.81) or the recovery of overpayments (para 13.36).

12.59   Table 12.4 gives the overall priority for all deductions that can be made from UC.

Table 12.4 **Deductions from UC: priority order**

General deductions

(a) Fraud penalties

(b) Sanctions

(c) Repayment of advances

Third party debts and other deductions

(d) Owner housing costs arrears

(e) Rent and service charge arrears at the minimum rate (para 12.54(a))

(f) Fuel costs arrears

(g) Council tax and rates arrears

(h) Court fines and compensation orders

(i) Water charges arrears

(j) Child maintenance

(k) Repayment of social fund loans

(l) Repayment of DWP/tax credit/HB overpayments and civil penalties

(m) Refugee integration loans or credit union loans

(n) Rent and service charge arrears above the minimum rate (para 12.54(b))

Note:

This table is a summary. DWP guidance gives further details [www].

T12.4   C&P sch 6 para 5; NIC&P sch 5 para 5
         DWP Operational Guidance, House of Commons Deposited Papers 29th October 2020
         https://tinyurl.com/OG-Deductions-Priority-2020

Chapter 13 **UC overpayments**

- ■ What is an overpayment: see paras 13.1-9.
- ■ Recoverability: see paras 13.10-14.
- ■ The amount of an overpayment: see paras 13.15-21.
- ■ Who overpayments can be recovered from: see paras 13.22-35.
- ■ Methods of recovery: see paras 13.36-51.
- ■ Fraud and penalties: see paras 13.52-63.

What is an overpayment

13.1   If you are paid more UC than you are entitled to, this is an overpayment. It is also an overpayment if more UC is paid for you to someone else (e.g. your landlord) than you were entitled to.

13.2   Overpayments usually arise when a decision about your UC was wrong. This could be due to:

(a) claimant error – you or your partner gave the DWP the wrong information, failed to give relevant information or were late telling the DWP about a change in your circumstances;

(b) landlord or third-party error – your landlord, employer or someone else gave the DWP the wrong information or failed to give relevant information;

(c) official error – the DWP made a mistake or was late acting on information;

(d) no-one's fault – you have received a benefit or other income for a period in the past.

13.3   Overpayments can also arise when a decision about your UC was correct but there was a payment hiccup – for example the DWP made the same payment twice.

Decisions and notices

13.4   For all UC overpayments the DWP should make the following decisions and send you a notice about them (paras 13.5-7):

(a) an entitlement decision (except for the overpayments in para 13.3); and

(b) an overpayment decision.

Entitlement notices

13.5   An entitlement notice gives the new details about your UC entitlement (para 14.5). It corrects the original wrong decision. Or if the overpayment stretches back over two or more original decisions, it should correct each one. Corrections are also called 'revisions' and 'supersessions' (table 14.1).

13.1-3   AA 71ZB(1)(a),(3),(5); NIAA 69ZB(1)(a),(3),(5)

13.6   The DWP advises that the entitlement decision should clearly revise or supersede the original decision, or each of the original decisions (ADM D1032-33). If there is an appeal the tribunal will expect evidence of this (R (IS) 2/96). Failure to do this means the overpayment decision has no force or effect (ADM D1035).

Overpayment notices

13.7   An overpayment notice should give:

(a) the overpayment period;

(b) the amount that is recoverable; and

(c) who it is recoverable from.

If an overpayment is recoverable from more than one person (para 13.27), the notice should name both and be sent to both (CH/3622/2005; R(H) 6/06).

Reconsiderations and appeals

13.8   You can ask the DWP to reconsider any matter relating to an overpayment (para 14.9), for example:

(a) whether you have been overpaid;

(b) the amount of the overpayment;

(c) whether the overpayment is recoverable;

(d)   who it should be recovered from;

(e) the method of recovery.

13.9   You can appeal to a tribunal (para 14.31) about:

(a) whether you have been overpaid and/or the amount of the overpayment, so long as your appeal is based on:

  ■ the DWP's entitlement decision (para 13.5) – if you are successful this reduces the overpayment, or

  ■ the amount that can or should be deducted under the rules about diminishing notional capital or moving home (paras 13.17-19 and 13.30); or

(b) who an overpayment should be recovered from (para 13.22); or

(c) the method of recovery (para 13.36).

But you can't appeal to a tribunal about whether an overpayment is recoverable (para 13.10) or the method of recovery (para 13.36). And you can't appeal about the cause of an overpayment because this is irrelevant to the matters in (a) and (b): [2018] UKUT 332 (AAC).

13.6   AA 71ZB(3); NIAA 69ZB(3)

13.9   D&A sch 3; NID&A sch 3

Recoverability

13.10   All overpayments of UC are recoverable (so long as they have been properly decided: para 13.6). This is the case even if they were due to official error ([2018] UKUT 323 (AAC) [www]) or no-one's fault.

13.11   The DWP recovers overpayments when it can but has discretion not to do so (paras 13.12-14). Guidance on these and related matters is in the DWP's Benefit Overpayment Recovery Guide (BORG) [www].

Discretion not to recover

13.12   The DWP can waive recovery of an overpayment (not go ahead with it). It considers this (BORG para 8.3) when recovery would be:

(a)   detrimental to you or your family's health or welfare; or

(b)   not in the public interest.

13.13   You can write asking the DWP to waive recovery. If your reasons are financial, you should give full details of your household income and expenditure. If they are health-related, you should say how recovery would be detrimental and include supporting evidence from a medical practitioner or hospital.

13.14   If you are unable to repay an overpayment, the DWP has a range of hardship options including temporary suspension of recovery or writing off the overpayment (BORG para 5.4).

The amount of an overpayment

13.15   The amount of an overpayment for a particular period is:

(a)   the amount that was actually paid for that period;

(b)   minus the amount you were entitled to for that period.

13.16   But there are special rules relating to:

(a)   capital (para 13.17);

(b)   the award of another DWP benefit (paras 13.20);

(c)   moving home (para 13.30).

Diminishing capital

13.17   An overpayment is recalculated if:

(a)   it occurred because of an error about your capital (no matter who caused the error); and

(b)   the overpayment period is over three months.

13.10   LP v SSWP (UC) [2018] UKUT 332 (AAC)
          www.bailii.org/uk/cases/UKUT/AAC/2018/332.html

13.11   https://tinyurl.com/DWPBORG

13.12   AA 71ZB(1)(a); NIAA 69ZB(1)(a)

13.15   AA 71ZB(1); NIAA 69ZB(1); D&A 21, 35; NID&A 21, 35.

13.17-19 OPR 7; NIOPR 7

13.18   At the end of the first three months of the overpayment period:

(a)   the DWP treats your capital as reduced by the amount overpaid during those three months; and

(b)   this reduced capital figure is used to calculate the overpayment after that.

At the end of each subsequent three months of the overpayment, the DWP repeats (a) and (b).

13.19   This rule reduces the overpayment in some cases. It reflects the fact that if you had received less UC (due to the capital being taken into account) you might have used some of it to meet your living and housing costs.

Example: Diminishing capital

Richie is getting UC of £1,000 per month based on having no income or capital. The DWP later finds he had undeclared capital of £18,000 throughout his time on UC.

His overpayment is calculated as follows:

■   For the first three months he doesn't qualify for UC (para 10.55). So, his overpayment is £1,000 per month. For three months this is £3,000

■   His capital is then treated as reduced by £3,000 to £15,000. This gives him an assumed income of £156.60 (para 10.56) which reduces his UC entitlement to £843.40 per month.

■   For the second three months his overpayment is (£1,000 − £843.40 =) £156.60 per month. For three months this is £469.80.

■   His capital is then treated as reduced by £469.80 to £14,530.20, and his UC entitlement is recalculated. This procedure is repeated at the end of each complete three months of his overpayment period.

The award of another DWP benefit

13.20   Your UC can be adjusted if:

(a)   you are awarded another DWP benefit for a past period; and

(b)   this reduces your entitlement to UC for that period (because the other benefit counts as income for UC purposes).

In this case, the DWP can treat part of the UC you were paid as having been for the other benefit. This rule prevents an overpayment arising.

Example: The award of another DWP benefit

Lyra is getting UC of £600 per month. Later she is awarded industrial injuries disablement benefit (IIDB) of £36.58 per week for the entire period she has been on UC, and this is taken into account as income of £158.51 per month (table 10.4 and para 10.33).

The DWP decides to treat £158.51 per month of the UC she has been paid as though it was IIDB. So, she does not get her IIDB arrears but she has not been overpaid.

13.20   AA 71ZF; NIAA 69ZF; OPR 6; NIOPR 6

Other amounts treated as overpayments

13.21   The DWP can recover the following in the same way as it recovers UC overpayments:

(a) UC hardship payments (para 9.88) and UC payments on account (para 12.25) if you are no longer on UC;

(b) penalties and court costs relating to overpayments (paras 13.52-63);

(c) overpayments of most other DWP benefits (a full list is in BORG appendix 1).

Who overpayments can be recovered from

The general rule

13.22   Unless any of the other rules in this section apply, an overpayment is recoverable from you (the claimant).

13.23   For example, this applies to overpayments relating to your income or capital, or your personal, family or household details. But for overpayments towards housing costs, rent arrears or other debts, see paras 13.28-35.

Couples

13.24   When you are claiming UC as a couple (para 2.4) and an overpayment was paid to one or both of you, it is recoverable from you or your partner. If you separate, the DWP says the amount you owe is split equally between you (BORG para 2.22).

Appointees, attorneys etc

13.25   When an overpayment was paid to an appointee, attorney or someone else on your behalf (paras 12.5-6) it is recoverable from you or them.

Landlords and agents

13.26   The rules about recovering overpayments from landlords are in paras 13.28-35 and table 13.1. In this chapter, we use 'landlord' to mean either your landlord or your landlord's agent – whichever of them collects your rent.

Overpayments recoverable from more than one person

13.27   When an overpayment is recoverable from more than one person (e.g. you or your landlord in paras 13.29 and 13.33), the DWP can choose which of them to recover from. Changes in their circumstances or the relationship between them may alter the action taken to recover it (BORG 2.22).

13.21   AA 71ZG, 71ZH; NIAA 69ZG, 69ZH; OPR 3; NIOPR 3

13.22   AA 71ZB(2), OPR 4; NIAA 69ZB(2), NIOPR 4

13.24   AA 71ZB(6); NIAA 69ZB(6)

13.25   OPR 4(2),(3); NIOPR 4(2),(3)

13.26   OPR 4(3); NIOPR 4(3)

Overpayments towards housing costs

13.28   The following rules (paras 13.29-33) are about overpayments of amounts the DWP pays you or your landlord towards your rent (para 12.37). They apply to overpaid rent payments and the DWP treats them as applying to overpaid service charge payments (para 6.23).

Housing costs overpaid due to a move

13.29   An overpayment of UC for housing costs that results from you moving home is recoverable:

(a) from you if it was paid to you (not from your landlord);

(b) from you or your landlord if it was paid to your landlord.

13.30   However, if the housing costs were payable to you on both homes, or to the same landlord on both homes, the DWP can treat the overpayment on the old home as having been correctly paid on the new home. So, an overpayment only remains if the new housing costs are lower than the old ones.

Example: Moving home

Lynda and Saeed are getting UC which includes a housing element of £880 per month towards their rent. The whole of this £880 is paid to their landlord. They move to a cheaper home rented from the same landlord and their housing element is now £800 per month. The DWP delays acting on this.

The DWP decides to treat what they were paid for their old home as having been paid for their new home (para 13.30). This means they have only been overpaid £80 per month. The DWP can recover this from them or their landlord.

Housing costs overpaid due to misrepresentation

13.31   An overpayment of UC for housing costs that was caused by misrepresentation (other than one resulting from a move) is recoverable:

(a) from you if you caused the overpayment (not from your landlord, even if it was paid to them);

(b) from your landlord if they caused the overpayment (not from you, even if it was paid to you).

13.32   A person has 'caused' an overpayment if it occurred because they misrepresented or failed to disclose a material fact (whether fraudulently or not). The DWP gives extensive advice on this (ADM D1133 onwards) and says that a landlord should only be regarded as having caused an overpayment if they had a legal duty to disclose a fact in question (ADM D1170).

13.28   OPR 2(1) def of 'housing costs', 4(4); NIOPR 2(1), 4(4)

13.29   OPR 4(5); NIOPR 4(5)

13.30   OPR 9; NIOPR 9

13.31-32   OPR 4(6); NIOPR 4(6)

Housing costs overpaid for other reasons

13.33   Any other overpayment of UC for housing costs is recoverable:

(a)   from you if it was paid to you (not from your landlord);

(b)   from you or your landlord if it was paid to them. But if your landlord was paid more than your housing costs, the excess is recoverable only from them.

Overpayments towards rent arrears and other debts

13.34   This rule applies to overpayments of amounts the DWP pays:

(a)   your landlord towards rent arrears (para 12.48); or

(b)   a third party towards other debts (para 12.55).

13.35   in this case, an overpayment is recoverable from you (not from the landlord or third party). But if the landlord or third party was paid more than the amount calculated in paras 12.54 and/or 12.58, the excess is recoverable from them.

Methods of recovery

13.36   The DWP can recover overpaid UC by any lawful method, but usually uses one of the methods in this section. Table 13.1 summarises the methods for overpayments that are recoverable from you (see (a) to (e)) or from your landlord (see (f)-(i)), and how they affect your rent or rent arrears.

Table 13.1 **Overpaid UC: recovery methods and rent arrears**

Overpayments that are recoverable from you

Recovery methods

(a)   Deductions from your UC when it is payable to you (para 13.37)

(b)   Deductions from your UC when it is is payable to your landlord (para 13.40)

(c)   Deductions from your other benefits (para 13.43)

(d)   Deductions from your earnings (para 13.44)

(e)   Sending you a bill, making payment arrangements and court action (para 13.49)

Effect on your rent or rent arrears

- Method (b) creates rent arrears (if you don't pay the shortfall in your rent)
- Methods (a) and (c) to (e) don't create rent arrears

13.33   OPR 4(7)-(8); NIOPR 4(7)-(8)

13.34-35   OPR 4(2); NIOPR 4(2)

13.36   AA 71ZB(7); NIAA 69ZB(7)

Overpayments that are recoverable from your landlord

Recovery methods

(f)   Deductions from your UC when it is payable to your landlord (para 13.40)

(g)   Deductions from another (blameless) tenant's UC that is payable to your landlord (para 13.47)

(h)   Deductions from your landlord's own UC or other benefits (para 13.48)

(i)   Sending your landlord a bill, making payment arrangements and court action (para 13.49)

Effect on your rent or rent arrears

■   Method (f) creates rent arrears (if you don't pay the shortfall in your rent) unless your landlord has committed an offence (para 13.42)

■   Methods (g) to (i) don't create rent arrears unless your tenancy agreement expressly allows recovered overpayments to be charged as additional rent

Note

■   In this table a landlord includes an agent (para 13.26).

Deductions from your UC when it is payable to you

13.37   The DWP can make deductions from UC that is payable to you:

(a)   when an overpayment is recoverable from you;

(b)   but not when an overpayment is recoverable from your landlord.

13.38   When an overpayment is recoverable from you the DWP:

(a)   can make limited deductions (para 13.39) from current payments of UC, including payments that were suspended and then restored (para 11.40);

(b)   doesn't make deductions from arrears of UC when these are 'for a specific reason and are earmarked for a specific purpose or expenditure' (BORG para 5.50) such as rent or childcare costs;

(c)   can make unlimited deductions from other arrears of UC (up to the whole amount).

13.39   Deductions from current payments of your UC:

(a)   must not exceed the maximum rate in table 13.2;

(b)   can be lower if the maximum rate would cause your family hardship;

(c)   must not reduce your UC to below 1p.

13.37-39   AA 71ZC(1),(2)(b), 71ZF; NIAA s 69ZC(1),(2)(b), 69ZF; OPR 10, 11; NIOPR 10, 11

Table 13.2 **Recovery of overpayments: maximum deductions from UC (2021-22)**

(a) Fraud cases and earned income cases: 25% of UC standard allowance
(cases in paras 13.52-63 and cases in which your UC was reduced for earned income, para 9.8(b))

single person under 25	£64.33
single person aged 25 or over	£81.21
couple both under 25	£100.98
couple at least one aged 25 or over	£127.48

(b) All other cases: 15% of UC standard allowance

single person under 25	£38.60
single person aged 25 or over	£48.73
couple both under 25	£60.59
couple at least one aged 25 or over	£76.49

Notes

■ This table gives the figures after the coronavirus increase ends (para 9.14) [www].

■ 'Single person' here includes a couple claiming as a single person (para 2.7).

■ The DWP must consider your personal circumstances rather than automatically deducting the maximum figures (R (Blundell and Others) v SSWP).

■ The 25% maximum rate also applies to recovery of advance payments (paras 12.25, 12.29).

Deductions from your UC when it is payable to your landlord

13.40   The DWP can make deductions from the part of your UC that is payable to your landlord:

(a) when an overpayment is recoverable from you; or

(b) when an overpayment is recoverable from your landlord.

In these cases, the DWP can make unlimited deductions (up to the whole amount).

13.41   Except as described in para 13.42, the deductions leave you with more rent to pay. They put you in rent arrears if you don't make up the shortfall in your rent.

T13.2   OPR 11(2)-(4); NIOPR 11(2)-(4)
           R (Blundell and Others) v SSWP [2021] EWHC 608 (Admin) www.bailii.org/ew/cases/EWHC/Admin/2021/608.html

13.40   AA 71ZC(1),(2)(b), 71ZF; NIAA s 69ZC(1),(2)(b), 69ZF; OPR 10, 11; NIOPR 10, 11

13.42   But if your landlord has been found guilty of an offence relating to the overpayment or has agreed to pay a penalty as an alternative to prosecution, the landlord:

(a) must treat you as having paid the amounts that were deducted; and

(b) can't put you into rent arrears for those amounts.

The DWP must notify both you and your landlord when this rule applies and explain (a) and (b) in each notification.

Deductions from your other benefits

13.43   When an overpayment is recoverable from you, the DWP can make deductions from any of the following benefits from you are getting:

(a) PIP, DLA, AA;

(b) JSA, ESA, SDA;

(c) retirement pension, SPC;

(d) maternity allowance, child's special allowance, guardian's allowance;

(e) widow's pension, widowed mother's allowance, widowed parent's allowance, bereavement pension;

(f) invalid care allowance;

(g) industrial injuries benefit including any amounts for constant attendance, severe disablement or reduced earnings.

Deductions from your earnings

13.44   When an overpayment is recoverable from you, the DWP can require your employer to make deductions from your earnings (without the need for a court order). This is sometimes called making a 'direct earnings attachment' (DEA). The DWP says this method of recovery is useful for people who no longer get benefits and won't come to a voluntary agreement to make payments [www].

13.45   The DWP should send a notice to both you and your employer before deductions are made. The employer should tell the DWP if they are not in fact your employer or if they think they are exempt from the deduction arrangement because they are a new business or a micro-business. This should be done within ten days of the day after the notice was sent.

13.46   Your employer calculates the amount (which can include £1.00 towards administration), informs you of the amount and pays it to the DWP. The employer must also keep records of the amounts deducted and of people for whom such deductions have been made. You must tell the DWP within seven days if you leave the employment or when you become employed or re-employed. Your employer should also tell the DWP if you are no longer employed by them. It is a criminal offence to fail to make or pay deductions or to provide information. Guidance for employers is available online [www].

13.42   AA 71ZC(3), OPR 15; NIAA 69ZC(3), NIOP 15

13.43   AA 71ZC(1), 71ZF; NIAA s69ZC(1), 69ZF; OPR 11; NIOPR 11

13.44-46 AA 71ZD; NIAA 69ZD; OPR part 6, sch 2; NIOPR part 6, sch
              DWP Direct Earnings Attachment: an employers' guide (Dec 2020) https://tinyurl.com/EarningsAttachment

Deductions from a 'blameless' tenant's UC payments

13.47 When an overpayment is recoverable from your landlord, the DWP can recover it by making deductions from payments to that landlord of another tenant's UC. In this guide we call this recovery from a 'blameless' tenant because the tenant had nothing to do with the overpayment. In these cases, the blameless tenant's obligation to the landlord is treated by the law as paid off and the landlord cannot in law put the 'blameless' tenant into rent arrears because of this deduction.

Deductions from your landlord's own benefits

13.48 When an overpayment is recoverable from your landlord, the DWP can recover it from the landlord's personal entitlement to UC or to any of the benefits in para 13.43. This is in practice rare.

Recovery through the courts

13.49 UC overpayments are recoverable through the county court in England and Wales and through the sheriff court in Scotland. The DWP tries to recover court costs when there is a court judgment in its favour. It can add these to the recoverable overpayment and recover them by any method by which overpaid UC can be recovered.

Time limits on recovery

13.50 In England, Wales and Northern Ireland the DWP/DFC can't use the courts to enforce a recovery (para 13.49) more than six years from the date you were first notified of the decision (para 14.7) but this does not stop the DWP/DFC from recovering the overpayment by other means (such as deductions from your future UC payments: para 13.37). In Scotland the time limit for recovery through the courts is five years from the date you were notified or 20 years by any method.

Bankruptcy etc

13.51 An overpayment can't be recovered if:

(a) the DWP made the overpayment decision (para 13.7) before you were granted a bankruptcy order (unless the overpayment was due to fraud); or

(b) the overpayment was included in a debt relief order (DRO) in England and Wales or a sequestration order in Scotland.

While the order is in force and after it ends, the DWP can't recover the overpayment by any method (including by making deductions from your UC or other benefits): SSWP v Payne and Cooper; Re Nortel Companies [www].

13.47 AA 71ZC(2)(c),(4); NIAA 69ZC(2)(c),(4); OPR 15; NIOPR 15

13.48 AA 71ZC(1),(2)(a); NIAA 69ZC(1),(2)(a)

13.49 AA 71ZE; NIAA 69ZE

13.50 Limitation Act 1980 s9, 38(11) (as amended by WRA 108);
Prescription and Limitation (Scotland) Act 1973 s6, 7 sch 1 para 1(b);
Limitation (Northern Ireland) Order 1989 arts 2(11), 6 (as amended by NIWRO 111)

13.51 SSWP v Payne & Cooper 14/12/11 UKSC [2011] UKSC 60 www.bailii.org/uk/cases/UKSC/2011/60.html
Re Nortel Companies 24/07/13 UKSC [2013] UKSC 52 www.bailii.org/uk/cases/UKSC/2013/52.html

Fraud and penalties

13.52　　The DWP's Counter Fraud and Compliance Directorate in Great Britain and the DFC's single Fraud Investigation Service in Northern Ireland are responsible for investigating fraud and related offences across all social security benefits, tax credits and HB – but not CTR, which is the responsibility of local authorities. Prosecutions are conducted by the Crown Prosecution Service in England and Wales, the Procurator Fiscal in Scotland and the Public Prosecution Service in Northern Ireland but in some cases you may be offered the chance of paying a penalty rather than face prosecution (paras 13.58-63).

Fraud offences by the claimant

13.53　　You (the claimant) can be prosecuted under one of the social security fraud offences if you:

(a) make a false statement; or

(b) produce, provide or supply any document or that is false in a material particular,

with the view to receiving UC (or other DWP benefit). You also commit an offence if you fail to promptly report a change of circumstances that you have a duty to notify (para 11.2) with the knowledge that it affects your award.

13.54　　If you are convicted in the magistrates' court you are liable for an unlimited fine or up to three months in prison (or both), or up to six months in prison (and/or a fine) if the offence involved dishonesty. If you are convicted in the crown court for dishonestly making a false statement or failing to report a change the maximum sentence is seven years in prison (and/or a fine). You are dishonest if you knew you were not telling the truth.

13.55　　If you are convicted for fraud or agree to pay a penalty (paras 13.58-61) the DWP can reduce your UC (or other benefits) for a fixed period.

Fraud offences by the landlord

13.56　　If you are a landlord/agent you can be prosecuted for fraud (paras 13.53-54) if you assist the claimant by providing false information, etc. You also commit an offence if you (the landlord/agent) receive UC on behalf of one (or more) of your tenants (paras 12.37-47) and you dishonestly (or knowingly) fail to report a change of circumstances promptly that you could reasonably be expected to know affects the claimant's entitlement to UC. You also commit this offence if you dishonestly cause the payee not to report the change (for example, if the landlord withholds relevant information from his/her agent so that the agent continues to be paid).

13.52　　AA 111A, 112, 115A, 115C, 115D; NIAA 105A, 106, 109A

13.53　　AA 111A, 112; NIAA 105A, 106

13.54　　AA 111A(3), 112(2); NIAA 105A(3), 106(2)

13.55　　The Social Security (Loss of Benefit) Regulations 2001 No 4022
　　　　　The Social Security (Loss of Benefit) Regulations (Northern Ireland) 2002 No 79

13.56　　AA 111A(1C)-(1E), 112(1C),(1D); NIAA 105A(1C)-(1E), 106(1C),(1D)

13.57   If the landlord is a company, the company is liable for any offence (para 13.56) committed as well as any director, manager, secretary or officer of the company who consented to the act or omission from which the offence arose. If a landlord/agent is convicted of an offence or agrees to a pay a penalty (para 13.58) the DWP may decide that it is not in the claimant's interests to pay housing costs to them, or if the claimant is on HB in supported or temporary accommodation (table 5.2) the council may stop paying HB to the landlord.

Administrative penalties

13.58   The DWP may offer you the chance to pay an 'administrative penalty' rather than face prosecution, if:

(a)   a UC overpayment was caused by an 'act or omission' on your part; and

(b)   there are grounds for bringing a prosecution against you for an offence relating to that overpayment.

The DWP decides whether to offer an administrative penalty and calculates the amount [www]. You do not have to agree to a penalty. You can opt for the possibility of prosecution instead.

13.59   The DWP's offer of a penalty must be in writing, explain that it is a way of avoiding prosecution, and give other information – including the fact that you can change your mind within 14 days (including the date of the agreement), and that the penalty will be repaid if you successfully challenge it by asking for a reconsideration or appeal. The DWP does not normally offer a penalty (but prosecutes instead) if an overpayment is substantial or there are other aggravating factors (such as you being in a position of trust).

13.60   The amount of the penalty is 50% of the recoverable overpayment. This is subject to a minimum of £350 and a maximum of £5,000 where your act or omission causing the overpayment occurred wholly on or after 1st April 2015. The maximum penalty where the relevant act or omission occurred before that date is £2,000. In Northern Ireland the maximum penalty is £2,000.

13.61   The DWP may also make an offer of a penalty where your act or omission could have resulted in an overpayment and it thinks there are grounds for bringing a prosecution for a related offence. In these cases, the penalty is the fixed amount of £350.

13.57   AA 115; NIAA 109

13.58   AA 115A(1)-(1A); NIAA 109A(1)-(1A)
          DWP Penalties policy: in respect of social security fraud and error (14 August 2017)
          https://tinyurl.com/DWP-penalty-policy

13.59   AA 115A(5)-(6); NIAA 109A(5)-(6)

13.60   AA 115A(3)(a)-(b); art 1(3) of SI 2015/202; NIAA 109A(3)(a)-(b)

13.61   AA 115A(3A); NIAA 109A(3A)

Civil penalties

13.62   In Great Britain the DWP may impose a civil penalty of £50 on you if you:

(a) negligently make an incorrect statement or representation or negligently give incorrect information or evidence relating to a claim or award and fail to take reasonable steps to correct the error; or

(b) without reasonable excuse, fail to provide required information or evidence relating to a claim or award or fail to tell the DWP about a relevant change of circumstance; and

(c) in any of these circumstances this results in the DWP making an overpayment; but

(d) you have not been charged with an offence or cautioned.

The DWP's staff guidance on civil penalties (and when to impose them) is set out in ADM D1271-1302 [www].

13.63   The amount of the civil penalty is added to the amount of the recoverable overpayment. If you have been successfully prosecuted for fraud or offered an administrative penalty or caution, the DWP cannot issue you with a civil penalty for the same offence.

13.62   AA 115C-115D; SI 2012/1990; NISR 1997/514; NISR 2016/63
        DWP ADM Ch D1; https://tinyurl.com/ADM-D1

Chapter 14 **UC decisions and appeals**

- Decision rights: see paras 14.1-3.
- Decisions, notices and reasons: see paras 14.4-8.
- Reconsiderations: see paras 14.9-16.
- When reconsidered decisions take effect: see paras 14.17-30.
- Appeals to a tribunal: see paras 14.31-46.
- Tribunal hearings and decisions: see paras 14.47-59.
- Further appeals and complaints: see paras 14.60-65.

Decision rights

14.1   This chapter explains the rights that go with UC decisions. The main rights are:

(a) getting the reasons for a decision;

(b) asking the DWP to reconsider;

(c) appealing to a tribunal; and

(d) making a further appeal.

Who has decision rights?

14.2   These rights belong to:

(a) you (the claimant) or either of you if you are claiming UC as a couple (para 2.5);

(b) an attorney or appointee who is acting for you (paras 3.8-10), including someone managing your UC after your death;

(c) a landlord/agent about whether UC should be paid to them towards rent arrears (para 12.48) or whether an overpayment is recoverable from them (para 13.33);

(d) a representative acting for you or for a landlord/agent (para 14.35).

Time limits

14.3   Many of the rights in this chapter have a time limit of one month from the date a decision is issued (or corrected: para 14.25). The date of issue is usually taken to mean the day the notice becomes available to view on your online account (para 3.13), or the day it is posted or handed to you. 'One month' means a calendar month counted as follows:

(a) if the date of issue is 17th January, the month runs up to and includes 17th February;

(b) if the date of the issue is 31st January, the month runs up to and includes 28th February (29th February in leap years).

14.2   SSA 12(2),(4); D&A 49(a),(b),(d); NISSO 13(2),(4); NID&A 48(a),(b),(e)

14.3   D&A 3, 4; FTPR 12; UTPR 12(1),(2); C&P 3, sch 2; NID&A 3, 4; NIC&P 3, sch 1; NIDAR99 31(1), 32, 58(1)

For appeals, this means 5pm on the last day, or if that isn't a working day, 5pm on the next working day. For reconsiderations, the DWP always accepts requests on the next day (ADM A3049). For both, up to 13 months can be allowed in special circumstances (paras 14.20, 14.40).

Decisions, notices and reasons

Decisions

14.4   The DWP makes a decision about your UC:

(a) when you claim (para 3.17);

(b) when your circumstances change (para 11.9);

(c) when your UC is overpaid (para 13.4); and

(d) when you ask for a reconsideration (para 14.14).

For a summary of how decisions are made, see paras 1.31-37.

Decision notices

14.5   The DWP sends you a decision notice about each decision it makes. (The law requires this for appealable decisions and in practice the DWP does it in all cases.) The notice tells you:

(a) what the decision is;

(b) the reasons for it (in most cases); and

(c) your rights to a written statement, to request a reconsideration and to appeal.

14.6   Notices are normally sent to your online account but can alternatively be sent by post or given to you by telephone or in person (paras 3.13-14).

14.7   The DWP also notifies:

(a) your partner if you are claiming UC as a couple. It does this even if the notice is about sanctions or fraud, but has said it intends to protect sensitive information about your health and similar matters;

(b) your landlord etc if it decides to pay UC to them (para 12.37). It normally does this by post, saying how much they will receive but not what your personal and financial details are.

Getting a written statement of reasons

14.8   If the reasons for a decision aren't in the decision notice, you can ask the DWP for a written statement of reasons within one month of the notice's date of issue. The DWP provides this within 14 days of your request or as soon as practicable after that. In this case, your time limit for getting arrears of UC is extended: para 14.19(b).

14.4   SSA 8(1)(a),(3)(aa), 9(1), 10(1); D&A 5, 8, 9, 22-24; NISSO 9(1)(a),(3)(aa), 10(1), 11(1); NID&A 5, 8-9, 22-24

14.5   SSA 8, 10, 12(6), D&A 7(1),(3), 51; NISSO 9, 11, 13(6), NID&A 7(1),(3), 51

14.6   D&A 3, 4; C&P 2 definition: 'electronic communication' 3, sch 2; NID&A 3, 4; NIC&P 2, 3, sch 1

14.7   SSA 12(2),(4); D&A 2 definition: 'claimant', 49(a),(b),(d); NISSO 13(2),(4); NID&A 2, 48(a),(b),(e)

14.8   D&A 5(1), 7(1),(3)(b),(4); NID&A 5(1), 7(1),(3)(b),(4)

Reconsiderations

14.9   You (or another person in para 14.2) can ask the DWP to reconsider any UC decision it has made. This is usually because you think the DWP has got the facts wrong or applied the law incorrectly. Reconsiderations can be about:

(a) whether you qualify for UC;

(b) the amount of your UC and how it is calculated;

(c) when your UC begins, changes or ends;

(d) whether you have been overpaid; or

(e) any other matter (unlike appeals there are no exceptions).

The DWP can also reconsider a decision without a request, for example because a case is being checked or there are new regulations or new case law (paras 14.26-27).

14.10   A reconsideration is also called a 'revision' (the legal term), a 'mandatory revision' (because you can't miss this out if you want to go to a tribunal) or, if your request is outside the time limit (paras 14.20-21) an 'anytime revision' or 'anytime review'.

When to request a reconsideration

14.11   You can request a reconsideration at any time. But you could be worse off if you don't stick to the time limit, because you could get a substantially lower payment of arrears (table 14.2).

How to request a reconsideration

14.12   Requests for a reconsideration should normally be in writing or by telephone, and it is advisable for you to keep a copy or a written record. The DWP says [www] it accepts requests made:

(a) in its appeal form CRMR1 (in Northern Ireland form MR2 (NI)) [www];

(b) in a letter;

(c) via your online account;

(d) by telephone; or

(e) in person.

The contact details should be in your decision notice.

Information and evidence

14.13   When you request a reconsideration, you should provide any new information or evidence you have. If the DWP needs further information or evidence, it should request this, and must take it into account if you provide it within one month.

14.9   SSA 9(1), D&A 5, 9; NISSO 10(1), D&A 5, 9

14.10   SSA 9(1), 12(3A); D&A 5, 7-9; NISSO 10(1), 13(3A); NID&A 5, 7-9

14.11   D&A 5, 9(b), 21, 24, 35(2),(4); NID&A 5, 9(b), 21, 24, 35(2),(4)

14.12   SSA 9(1); D&A 2 definition: 'appropriate office' 3, 4, 5; NISSO 10(1); NID&A 3-5
https://tinyurl.com/Form-CRMR1
https://tinyurl.com/Form-MR2-NI

14.13   D&A 20(2)(3), 33(2),(3); C&P 38(2),(3),(4); NID&A 20(2)(3), 33(2),(3); NIC&P 37(2),(3),(4)

Reconsideration decisions

14.14   The DWP makes a decision about whether your UC should change, and if so, how and when. This is also called a 'revision' or a 'supersession'. These terms are explained in table 14.1, but you don't have to use them when you contact the DWP.

14.15   The law doesn't set a time limit for dealing with reconsiderations, but the DWP normally does this reasonably quickly unless they are complex.

Reconsideration notices

14.16   The DWP sends you a decision notice telling you:

(a) whether it has altered your UC;

(b) if it has, what it has altered and when this takes effect; and

(c) your rights (para 14.1).

Table 14.1 **Decisions, revisions and supersessions**

Decisions: The DWP makes decisions:

(a) when you claim UC (chapter 3);

(b) when you report a change of circumstances, or the DWP is aware of a change without you reporting it (para 11.1); and

(c) when you ask for a decision to be changed because you think it is wrong, or the DWP realises it is wrong without you asking (para 14.9).

The kinds of decision in (b) and (c) are also called revisions and supersessions. Asking for a decision to be changed is often called 'requesting a reconsideration'.

Revisions: A revision is a decision which alters your UC from the same date (in most cases) as the decision it is altering. Revisions are mainly used when a wrong decision is changed. If a revised decision is advantageous to you it usually has a time limit (paras 11.14-15, 14.18-21).

Supersessions: A supersession is a decision which alters your UC from a date later than the decision it is altering. Supersessions are mainly used for changes of circumstances, and sometimes when a wrong decision is changed. If a superseding decision is advantageous to you it often has a time limit (paras 11.14-15 and 14.18-21). A 'closed period supersession' is used when a change of circumstances took place in the past and it has already come to an end. It means your UC is altered, but only for that past fixed period (CH/2595/2003).

14.14   SSA 9, 10; D&A 5, 8, 20(1), 22, 32, 33(1); NISSO 10, 11; NID&A 5, 8, 20(1), 22, 32, 33(1)

T14.2   SSA 10(5); D&A 21, 24, 35(2),(4); NISSO 11(5); NID&A 21, 24, 35(2),(4)

When reconsidered decisions take effect

14.17   The DWP can reconsider any decision if you request it, or it can do so on its own initiative (e.g. because it notices an error). When the DWP changes a decision it has reconsidered, the new decision takes effect (alters your UC) from the date in table 14.2.

Table 14.2 **When reconsidered decisions take effect**

Type of reconsideration	When it takes effect
Decisions increasing or reinstating your UC	
(a) Reconsiderations requested or made within the time limit (one month, or in some cases up to 13 months: para 14.19)	The date the original decision took effect (or should have)
(b) All cases correcting an official error at any time (para 14.22)	The date the original decision took effect (or should have)
(c) Other cases	The first day of the assessment period in which the reconsideration is requested, or the DWP first takes action to make it (if this is earlier)
Decisions reducing or ending your UC	
(d) All cases	The date the original decision took effect (or should have)

Notes:

■   This table applies to wrongly made decisions; for the equivalent rule for a change of circumstance see table 11.1.

■   For rent officer redeterminations, see para 6.53.

■   In the law, (a), (b) and (d) are revisions and (c) is a supersession (table 14.1).

Examples: When reconsiderations take effect

1. Capital that should be disregarded

Eva has been getting UC since 9th January and her assessment periods begin on the 9th of each month. She realises that she forgot to tell the DWP that some of her capital comes from an insurance payment in December for flood damage to her home. She asks the DWP to increase her UC and the DWP agrees (table 14.2).

■   If she requests the change on (or before) 8th February, she is within the time limit and her UC increases from 9th January.

■   If she requests the change on 15th February and doesn't have special circumstances for her delay, her UC increases from 9th February.

14.17   SSA 10(5),(6); D&A 21, 34; NISSO 11(5),(6); NID&A 21, 34

2. Undeclared earnings

Frank has been getting UC since 9th January and his assessment periods begin on the 9th of each month. The DWP discovers he has been working since before he claimed UC and reduces his UC (table 14.2).

■　Whenever the DWP makes the change, his UC decreases from 9th January.

3. An official error

Gertrude claimed UC on 9th January. She is a full-time student with a low income. Although she told the DWP when she claimed that she was a foster parent and had a foster child placed with her, the DWP said she wasn't entitled to UC. She asks the DWP to change this decision and the DWP agrees because of official error (para 14.22).

■　Whenever she requests the change, she is awarded UC from 9th January.

Time limit for getting your arrears

14.18　If a wrong decision is changed so that it increases or reinstates your UC you may not be paid all your arrears unless the reconsideration was requested (or made by the DWP) within the time limit. But this rule doesn't apply if the wrong decision was due to an official error (para 14.22) – including if the DWP made an error of law (para 14.63) – or a change of circumstance where a separate but similar rule applies instead (paras 11.14-15).

14.19　Your request is within the time limit if:

(a) you make it within one month of being notified (para 14.3) of the original decision; or

(b) you ask for a written statement of reasons (para 14.8) within that month, and you make your reconsideration request within 14 days of:

■　the end of that month, or

■　the DWP providing the written statement (if later); or

(c) you make your reconsideration request up to 12 months later than (a) or (b), you ask the DWP to extend the time limit, and the DWP agrees (para 14.20); or

(d) the DWP first takes action to make the change within one month of the decision being issued.

Extending the time limit

14.20　The DWP extends the reconsideration time limit by up to 12 months (para 14.19(c)) if:

(a) there are special circumstances why you couldn't request a reconsideration earlier (para 14.21); and

(b) it is reasonable to allow you extra time – the longer you take the more compelling your reasons need to be.

14.19　D&A 2 definition: 'date of notification', 5(1), 6, 38(4); NID&A 2, 5(1), 6, 38(4)

14.20　D&A 6(1)-(6); NID&A 6(1)-(6)
　　　　Explanatory Memorandum to SI 2017/1015 paras 7.28-30 – www.legislation.gov.uk/uksi/2017/1015/memorandum/contents

14.21 The law doesn't define 'special circumstances'. The DWP interprets this broadly, and usually accepts delays unless there is an exceptional reason not to. The following are some examples of what can be included (ADM A3055):

(a) a death or serious illness;

(b) not being in the UK;

(c) normal postal services being adversely affected;

(d) learning or language difficulties;

(e) difficulty getting evidence or information to support the application; and

(f) ignorance or misunderstanding of the law or time limits.

Official errors

14.22 In the case of official errors (paras 14.23-24), there is no time limit for changes. So your reconsideration request can be made at any time, and (if you are successful) you get arrears of UC back to the date of the original decision took effect or should have taken effect (table 14.2(b)).

14.23 There is an official error when:

(a) the DWP, HMRC or someone acting for them (e.g. a contractor) makes an error; and

(b) neither you nor anyone else (e.g. your landlord) materially contributed to it.

The error could be getting the facts wrong (which you or someone else provided information or evidence about), getting the law or case law wrong (but for changes in the law or case law see paras 14.26-27), or making an accidental error (para 14.25).

14.24 There is also an official error when the DWP uses the wrong figure for any of the following (or uses a figure when none should apply), even if you or someone else did contribute to it:

(a) a local housing allowance (para 6.42),

(b) a housing payment determination (para 6.20),

(c) the benefit cap (para 9.69),

(d) a sanction (para 9.81), or

(e) a penalty (para 13.58).

Accidental errors

14.25 There is an accidental error when the DWP fails to record, or to put into action, its true intentions (e.g. by mis-entering data on a computer) (ADM A3042). The DWP can correct an accidental error at any time. Any resulting change in your UC takes effect from the date the original decision took effect (or should have).

14.22 D&A 6(7); NID&A 6(7)

14.23 D&A 2 definition: 'official error', 9, 12, 14, 19; NID&A 2, 9, 12, 14, 19

14.24 D&A 2 definitions: 'official error', 'designated authority'; NID&A 2

14.25 D&A 8, 9, 21; NID&A 8, 9, 21

14.25 D&A 38; NID&A 38

Amendments to regulations and up-ratings

14.26   When an amendment to regulations affects your UC, it takes effect on the first day of your assessment period that begins on or after the date the amendment comes into force. For UC figures that are up-rated in April, this means 6th April; for other amendments, the date is given in the amending regulations.

New case law

14.27   When new case law (in another person's appeal) affects your UC, it takes effect from the date the Upper Tribunal, the Northern Ireland Commissioners or the court gives its judgment in that case (but see para 14.28).

Stayed decisions

14.28   The DWP can 'stay' (put on pause) a decision about your UC if it depends on the outcome of a test case being appealed to the Upper Tribunal, the Northern Ireland Commissioners or a court. This means that:

(a) for the time being, the DWP makes its decision in your case based on the least favourable outcome of the test case (even if that means you don't get any UC), and explains in the decision notice that the decision has been stayed;

(b) when the judgment is given in the test case, the DWP alters its decision in your case in line with the test case, and this takes effect on the date the original decision in your case took effect (or should have).

After a reconsideration

14.29   If your reconsideration request is unsuccessful or only partly successful, you can:

(a) appeal to a tribunal (paras 14.31-32); or

(b) request another reconsideration (para 14.9).

Usually, (a) is advisable, but (b) can be useful if you have new facts, evidence or arguments.

14.30   However if your reconsideration was unsuccessful because:

(a) it was outside the time limit (paras 14.19-20); and

(b) it was not about official error (para 14.22);

you can't appeal to a tribunal (CSJSA/513/2016 and DWP memo ADM 08/19). You can ask for another reconsideration, or you may be able to apply for judicial review (para 14.62).

Appeals to a tribunal

First-tier Tribunal/Appeal Tribunal

14.31   When a UC decision is appealable (para 14.32), you (or another person in para 14.2) can appeal about it to:

14.26   D&A 23(1), sch 1 paras 32-33; NID&A 23(1), sch 1 paras 32-33

14.27   SSA 27; D&A 35(5); NISSO 27; NID&A 35(5)

14.29   SSA 27; D&A 35(5); NISSO 27; NID&A 35(5)

(a)   a First-tier Tribunal in Great Britain; or

(b)   an Appeal Tribunal in Northern Ireland.

These tribunals are independent of the DWP. You can only appeal to them after asking the DWP to reconsider (para 14.9). Useful information about appeals is in ADM chapter A5.

Which decisions are appealable

14.32   All UC decisions are appealable to a tribunal except the non-appealable decisions summarised in table 14.3. If a decision is non-appealable, you can ask the DWP to reconsider it (para 14.9), make a complaint (para 14.64), or you may be able to apply for judicial review (para 14.62).

Table 14.3 **Non-appealable UC decisions**

(a)   Who can claim on your behalf if you are unable to act (paras 3.8-10).

(b)   What information or evidence the DWP can require (paras 3.19-29).

(c)   The amount of an LHA figure (para 6.42) or housing payment determination (para 6.20) – but the rent officer can redetermine these (para 6.53).

(d)   Whether UC amounts should be affected by your age (e.g. para 9.14) or by up-ratings (para 1.22).

(e)   Who counts as the carer of a severely disabled person where care is shared (para 9.40).

(f)   Whether the DWP should suspend or restore your UC (paras 11.31-35).

(g)   How and when your UC is paid (i.e. any matter in paras 12.1-12).

(h)   UC advances and budgeting advances (paras 12.19-24, 12.26-28) – but you can appeal about deductions from future UC (paras 12.25, 12.29).

(i)   Whether (and/or how much) UC should be paid to your landlord towards your rent (paras 12.37-47) – but you can appeal about payments towards rent arrears (paras 12.48-54).

(j)   Whether an overpayment of UC is recoverable and/or the method of recovery (see paras 13.8-9 for further details).

(k)   Appeals in which the reconsideration was refused because it was outside the time limit and was not about official error (para 14.30).

(l)   Whether the DWP should stay a UC decision or appeal (paras 14.28, 14.46).

(m) Whether a tribunal should correct or set aside a decision it has made (paras 14.58-59).

Appeal terminology

14.33   When you appeal to a tribunal the following terms are often used:

(a) 'appellant' – you (the person making the appeal);

(b) 'respondent' – the DWP (the maker of the decision you have appealed), also anyone else who has a right of appeal in your case (e.g. your landlord in some overpayment cases: para 14.2);

(c) 'party' – any of the above.

How to appeal

14.34   You can appeal using form SSCS1 in Great Britain or NOA1(SS) in Northern Ireland. These forms are available from many advice agencies or online [www]. Or you can appeal by letter or email. In each case you need to meet the appeal requirements (para 14.37).

Representatives

14.35   If you wish, you can ask a representative to appeal (or act in any other way) for you. They could be an advice worker, a solicitor or a friend or family member. Once you have informed the DWP and tribunal in writing about this, your representative can do anything you could do in relation to your appeal (except for signing a witness statement). The DWP and the tribunal should accept this until you or the representative inform them in writing to the contrary.

Where to send your appeal

14.36   In Great Britain you send your appeal to Her Majesty's Courts and Tribunals Service (HMCTS) which sends a copy to the DWP. In Northern Ireland you send it to the DFC which forwards it to the Appeals Service (TAS(NI)). The addresses are:

(a) in England and Wales, HMCTS, SSCS Appeals Centre, PO Box 1203, Bradford BD1 9WP;

(b) in Scotland, HMCTS, SSCS Appeals Centre, PO Box 27080, Glasgow G2 9HQ;

(c) in Northern Ireland, The Appeals Service (NI), PO Box 2202, Belfast, BT1 9YJ.

Appeal requirements

14.37   Your appeal should:

(a) be written in English or Welsh, and signed by you or your representative;

(b) say what decision you are appealing about and why you consider it is wrong (this is called your submission: para 14.38);

(c) give your name and address, and those of your representative if you have one;

14.33   FTPR 1(3) definitions: 'appellant', 'respondent', 'party'; NISSO 14(4), 15(3)(a),(b); NIDAR99 1(2) definitions: 'claimant', 'party to proceedings'

14.34   FTPR 13(1), 22(2)(d); NIDAR99 33
         https://tinyurl.com/Form-SSCS1
         https://tinyurl.com/Form-NOA1SS

14.35   FTPR 11(2),(5); NIDAR99 49(8)

14.36   FTPR 22(2)(d); NIDAR99 33(1)(b)

14.37   FTPR 22(3),(4); NIDAR99 33(1)(c),(d)

(d) say which address you want documents about your appeal to be sent to;

(e) give the name and address of any respondent other than the DWP (para 14.33);

(f) enclose a copy of the DWP's reconsideration notice (para 14.16);

(g) enclose copies of any statement of reasons (para 14.8) and other relevant documents;

(h) be within the appeal time limit (paras 14.39-40);

(i) say whether you want to attend a hearing or have the appeal decided on the papers (para 14.49);

(j) in the case of a hearing, say which dates you won't be available over the next six months, and whether you have particular needs (e.g. for a signer, interpreter or wheelchair access).

Your submission

14.38   Your submission should say which part of the DWP's decision you disagree with, why you think it is wrong, and what you think it should be. You shouldn't lose out by not using precise legal terms and references, so long as what you say is clear (ADM A5428).

Time limit for appeals

14.39   You are within the appeal time limit in Great Britain if:

(a) your appeal reaches the tribunal within one month of the reconsideration notice being issued (para 14.16); or

(b) your appeal reaches the tribunal up to 12 months later than (a), you ask the tribunal to extend the time limit, and the tribunal also agrees (para 14.40).

In Northern Ireland these time limits relate to when the appeal reaches the DFC.

Extending the time limit

14.40   The tribunal extends the appeal time limit by up to 12 months (para 14.39) if:

(a) neither the DWP nor any other party to the appeal objects; or

(b) they do object, but the tribunal considers the appeal should go ahead. In this case, the tribunal first asks for your comments on the objection.

14.41   If you have one of the following special circumstances, the DWP is unlikely to object to your appeal going ahead (ADM A5081):

(a) you were unable to deal with the reconsideration notice or make an appeal because of illness; mental or physical disability or learning difficulty;

(b) you had difficulty obtaining an appeal form or getting a representative;

(c) you didn't receive the reconsideration notice;

(d) you made your appeal earlier, but it didn't reach the tribunal;

(e) you were wrongly advised by the DWP or an advice worker or a solicitor;

(f) (in some cases) you have a very strong case or there is a lot of money involved.

14.39   FTPR 22(2)(d),(6)(a),(8); NIDAR99 31(a), 32

14.40   FTPR 22(8); NIDAR99 32(4)-(8)

The DWP's response to your appeal

14.42   After receiving your appeal (para 14.36), the DWP sends a written response to the tribunal within 28 days, or longer if the tribunal agrees. It also sends a copy to you or your representative, and to any other party to the appeal.

14.43   However if the DWP decides it wholly agrees with your appeal, it changes its UC decision in your favour, sends you a decision notice and awards any arrears of UC (in which case your appeal lapses). Or if the DWP only partly agrees with your appeal, it tells the tribunal this in its written response (ADM A5160-61).

14.44   The DWP must deal with your appeal in one of the ways in paras 14.42-43 or 14.46. In particular, it has no power to lapse your appeal in other circumstances.

Further submissions

14.45   After receiving the copy of the DWP's response, you can make a further written submission or provide further evidence to the tribunal within one month, or longer if the tribunal agrees, HMCTS/TAS(NI) sends a copy of this to the DWP and to any other party to the appeal.

Stayed appeals

14.46   The DWP can 'stay' (put on pause) your appeal if it depends on the outcome of a test case being appealed to the Upper Tribunal, the Northern Ireland Commissioners or a court. This means that:

(a)   for the time being, your appeal doesn't go ahead; or

(b)   when the judgment is given in the test case:

   ■   the DWP alters its decision in your case in line with the test case, and this takes effect on the date the original decision in your case took effect (or should have),

   ■   the rules about whether your appeal goes ahead or 'lapses' are the same as in para 14.43.

Tribunal hearings and decisions

14.47   The tribunal that deals with your appeal normally consists of just one judge, or a judge plus a medically or financially qualified person in appropriate cases. The tribunal's role is inquisitorial, not adversarial, so it can look afresh at your whole case, not just the part you have appealed.

14.42   FTPR 24(1)(c),(5)

14.43   D&A 52; NID&A 51

14.44   D&A 52(1); NIDAR99 51(1)

14.45   FTPR 24(6),(7)

14.46   FTPR 53; NIDAR99 52

14.47   TCEA 3(3), 4(3), sch 2 para 2(2); NISSO 8; NIDAR99 36

Directions

14.48   The tribunal can issue directions to the parties about the conduct of the appeal at any time (see table 14.4 for examples). You or any party can ask the tribunal for directions or the tribunal can make them without a request. And if you fail to comply with a direction, the tribunal could strike out your appeal (so that it doesn't go ahead).

Table 14.4 **Directions a tribunal can give**

A tribunal can give directions about any UC appeal. For example (ADM A5428) it can:

(a) Set, extend or shorten any time limit.

(b) Allow or require the provision or amendment of documents, information, evidence or submissions.

(c) Hold a hearing (or not: para 14.49) and decide how it is run.

(d) Deal with preliminary matters in advance of a hearing.

(e) Adjourn or postpone a hearing.

(f) Join appeals so that they are dealt with together.

(g) Treat one appeal as a lead case and 'stay' other similar cases until the lead case is decided (para 14.46).

(h) Transfer proceedings to another court or tribunal in certain circumstances.

Note: The law has been temporarily amended during the coronavirus outbreak to make it easier for tribunals in Great Britain to:

■   hold video or audio recorded hearings;

■   deal with urgent appeals without a hearing; or

■   close hearings to the public.

How appeals are dealt with

14.49   Every appeal is considered at a hearing unless you, the DWP, any other party and the tribunal itself all agree that it can be decided on the papers. Research shows that you have a better chance of success if you attend (along with your representative if you have one).

Hearings

14.50   Hearings take place at venues throughout the UK [www]. They are theoretically open to the public, but in practice it is rare for any member of the public to attend. You should get at least 14 days' notice of the date, time and venue of your hearing. Before and during the hearing you have the rights in paras 14.51-52 and so do the DWP and any other party.

14.48   FTPR 5, 6, 8; NIDAR99 38

T14.4   FTPR 5, 5A, 30A; SI 2020/416; NIDAR99 38

14.49   FTPR 27(1);

14.50   FTPR 28, 29(1),(2); NIDAR99 49(2),(3)
          http://sscs.venues.tribunals.gov.uk/Venues/venues.htm
          https://www.communities-ni.gov.uk/topics/appeals-service-and-appealing-decisions

Before the hearing

14.51   Before the hearing takes place, you can write requesting the tribunal:

   (a)   to issue directions (table 14.4);

   (b)   to postpone the hearing (e.g. if you need time to obtain more evidence);

   (c)   to withdraw (end) your appeal (or withdraw any part of it).

At the hearing

14.52   When the hearing takes place, you have the right:

   (a)   to attend;

   (b)   to have a representative with you (para 14.35);

   (c)   to have a friend or relative with you (for support, or to help you put your case if you don't have a representative);

   (d)   to put your case;

   (e)   to question the DWP and any other party about their case;

   (f)   to ask for the hearing to be adjourned (e.g. if you need to obtain further evidence);

   (g   to withdraw your appeal if the tribunal gives you permission to do so.

Tribunal decisions

14.53   The tribunal reaches a decision once it has considered all the evidence. In reaching its decision the tribunal should:

   (a)   consider the relevant law including any applicable case law;

   (b)   identify the relevant facts based on the available evidence; and

   (c)   where the facts are in doubt or dispute, establish them (if necessary, on the balance of probability); and

   (d)   apply the law to the relevant facts to arrive at a reasoned decision.

Tribunal's decision notices

14.54   The tribunal should write to you as soon as practicable after making its decision, saying:

   (a)   what its decision is (e.g. whether your UC should change, and if so, how and when);

   (b)   how to get a statement of reasons (para 14.56); and

   (c)   how and when to make a further appeal (para 14.60).

If you attend a hearing, you may be told the decision on the day.

14.51   FTPR 5(3)(h), 6(2),(3), 17

14.52   FTPR 11(5),(7), 17(1)-(3), 28; NIDAR99 49(7),(8),(11)

14.53   TECA 22, 23, sch 5

14.54   FTPR 33(1),(2); NIDAR99 53(2),(3)

When tribunal decisions take effect

14.55   If the tribunal changes your UC, its decision notice either gives the new amounts and dates they take effect or clearly instructs the DWP how to work these out (ADM A5501). The DWP should action this as soon as practicable unless it knows that a further appeal is pending (para 14.60).

Statement of reasons

14.56   You can get a statement of reasons by asking the clerk at the hearing, or by applying to the tribunal up to one month after receiving its decision notice (this can be extended if the tribunal agrees). The statement gives the tribunal's findings of fact as well as its reasons for its decision. It is necessary to have this if you want to make a further appeal (para 14.60).

Record of proceedings

14.57   You can get a copy of the record of proceedings by applying to the tribunal up to six months after receiving its decision notice. This means six months after the last activity in relation to the decision such as a correction, or from the date the statement of reasons was issued ([2015] UKUT 509 (AAC)). The record gives a summary of the evidence and submissions received by the tribunal. It isn't necessary to have this if you want to make a further appeal, but it is often useful.

Changes to tribunal decisions

14.58   A tribunal decision can be changed if:
- (a) the tribunal (after a request from you, the DWP or another party, or without a request):
   - corrects an accidental error (an error that fails to record what the tribunal intended), or
   - sets the decision aside (para 14.59); or
- (b) you, the DWP or another party make a further appeal (para 14.60); or
- (c) the DWP alters the decision because:
   - your or someone else's circumstances change (para 11.1), or
   - new factual evidence shows the decision was wrong.

The time limit for any request in (a) is one month.

14.55   FTPR 5(3)(I); D&A 44(1)-(4); NID&A 43(1)-(4)

14.56   FTPR 34(2)-(4); NIDAR99 53(4), 54

14.45   Practice Statement: Record of Proceedings in Social Security and Child Support Cases in the Social Entitlement Chamber, 3 November 2008
          https://tinyurl.com/Practice-Statement-Nov-08; NIDAR99 55

14.58   TCEA 9; FTPR 36, 37, 38; D&A 23(1)(a), 31(a); NID&A 23(1)(a), 31(a); NIDAR99 56, 57

Setting aside

14.59   'Setting aside' a tribunal decision means it is cancelled and the appeal starts again (with a new hearing or a new consideration of the papers). The tribunal can set a decision aside if it is in the interests of justice to do so; and

(a)   a document was not sent to, or was not received at any appropriate time by, the tribunal or any party; or

(b)   any party or representative was not present at a hearing; or

(c)   there has been some other procedural irregularity.

Further appeals

Upper Tribunal/Northern Ireland Commissioners

14.60   You can write asking for permission to make a further appeal:

(a)   to the Upper Tribunal in Great Britain (against a decision of the First-tier Tribunal);

(b)   to the Northern Ireland Commissioners in Northern Ireland (against the decision of an Appeal Tribunal).

The DWP or another party can also do this. In all cases the further appeal has to be on the grounds that there was an error of law (not that you just disagree about the facts), and you may well need help from a lawyer or advice worker at this stage. See para 14.63 for the meaning of error of law.

14.61   To begin with, you send your further appeal to the First-tier Tribunal or Appeal Tribunal. They then decide:

(a)   to reconsider and alter their own decision; or

(b)   to give you permission to appeal, in which case you send your further appeal to the Upper Tribunal or Northern Ireland Commissioners; or

(c)   to refuse permission, in which case you can apply directly to the Upper Tribunal or Northern Ireland Commissioners for permission to appeal.

In all cases, you should use form UT1 in Great Britain or form OSSC1 in Northern Ireland [www]. And in each case the time limit is normally one month (which the tribunal can extend in limited circumstances).

14.59   FTPR 37; NIDAR99 57

14.60   FTPR 38(2),(3),(6); NISSO 14, 15; NIDAR99 58

14.61   TCEA 10; FTPR 39(1),(2),(4), 40(2); UTPR 21(4)(a)-(e), 22, 23(2)(a),(4); NIDAR99 58
https://tinyurl.com/Form-UT1
https://tinyurl.com/OSSC1
https://tinyurl.com/OSSC1-guidance

The appeal courts and judicial review

14.62   Depending on the situation you may be able to:

(a) Appeal to the Court of Appeal against a decision of the Upper Tribunal or Northern Ireland Commissioners on a point of law of wide-ranging significance. You must apply to the Upper Tribunal for permission to appeal within three months of the date of its decision or, if permission is refused, to the Court of Appeal within 21 days after that (seven days if it is for a judicial review) [www].

(b) Apply for judicial review of a decision you can't appeal (para 14.32) or a decision of the Upper tribunal. For decisions you can't appeal you should apply for permission to proceed to the High Court (Court of Session in Scotland), within 21 days of the decision [www].

In these cases, you will almost certainly need to get professional legal advice and representation.

What is an error of law?

14.63   An appeal to the Upper Tribunal can only be made on an error of law. An error of law is where the First-tier Tribunal did one or more of the following:

(a) failed to apply the correct law;

(b) wrongly interpreted the relevant Acts or regulations;

(c) followed a procedure that breached the rules of natural justice;

(d) took irrelevant matters into account, or did not consider relevant matters, or did both of these things;

(e) did not give adequate reasons in the full statement of reasons;

(f) gave a decision which was not supported by the evidence;

(g) decided the facts in such a way that no tribunal properly instructed as to the law, and acting judicially, could have reached that decision.

These are examples, not an exhaustive list (R(IS) 11/99).

14.62   TCEA 13, 14A-14C; UTPR 44(2),(3), ; SI 2008 No. 2834
        https://www.justice.gov.uk/courts/procedure-rules/civil/rules/part52#52.7
        https://www.justice.gov.uk/courts/procedure-rules/civil/rules/part52#52.9
        https://www.justice.gov.uk/courts/procedure-rules/civil/rules/part52#52.12

Complaints

Making a complaint

14.64   If you want to make a complaint, rather than an appeal, you should first contact the DWP office you are dealing with, explain the matter and give them the opportunity to put things right. It is probably best to do this in writing so that you have a record of the action you have taken. If this is unsuccessful the DWP has a formal complaints procedure that may provide a remedy for your problem [www]. If you remain dissatisfied, you can escalate your complaint by asking the Independent Case Examiner to look at it (this is a free and independent complaint resolution and examination service provided by the DWP) [www]. If you're still dissatisfied, you can ask your MP [www] to send your complaint to the Parliamentary and Health Service Ombudsman (this is also a free and independent service) [www].

The response to your complaint

14.65   The DWP says that if it gets something wrong it will act quickly to put it right. This might include any of the following: an apology; an explanation; putting things right, or a special payment if something the DWP has done (or not done) has caused injustice or hardship (see DWP (2012) *Financial Redress for Maladministration*) [www].

14.64   www.gov.uk/government/organisations/department-for-work-pensions/about/complaints-procedure
         www.gov.uk/government/organisations/independent-case-examiner
         www.parliament.uk/mps-lords-and-offices/mps/
         www.ombudsman.org.uk/

14.65   www.gov.uk/government/publications/compensation-for-poor-service-a-guide-for-dwp-staff

Chapter 15 **Council tax**

- What is council tax and who is liable to pay it: see paras 15.1-21.
- Reducing your council tax bill: see paras 15.22-30.
- Claims, changes and appeals: see paras 15.31-36.

What is council tax

15.1 Council tax is a tax on dwellings that helps to pay for local services. It applies in England, Scotland and Wales.

15.2 Local councils send out the bills for council tax. In most cases:

(a) one or more residents of a dwelling are liable for council tax there, but in some cases the owner/landlord is liable instead;

(b) the amount of your bill depends on which valuation band your dwelling is in and whether you qualify for any reduction.

This chapter gives the details and the exceptions.

Council tax bands

15.3 The amount of council tax depends on what valuation band a dwelling is in:

(a) in England and Scotland there are eight bands, from A to H;

(b) in Wales there are nine, from A to I.

You can find out which band your home is in online [www]. The amounts for each band are always in proportion to band D (table 15.1).

Dwellings

15.4 There is one council tax bill per dwelling. A 'dwelling' is a single residential property, for example a house, a flat, a mooring with a houseboat or a pitch with a mobile home. (The last two are 'hereditaments', but we use 'dwellings' for all of them in this guide.)

Your home

15.5 Your 'home' is the dwelling where you live or mostly live. The law calls this your 'sole or main residence'.

15.2   LGFA 1

15.3   LGFA 5(1),(2) www.gov.uk/council-tax-bands www.saa.gov.uk

15.4   LGFA 3, 4, 7

15.5-6 LGFA 6(1)(2)(a)-(e),(3),(5) definition: 'resident'

Table 15.1 **Council tax bands**

Band	Proportion: England and Wales	Proportion: Scotland
A	6/9 of band D (67%)	240/360 of band D (67%)
B	7/9 of band D (78%)	280/360 of band D (78%)
C	8/9 of band D (89%)	320/360 of band D (89%)
D	–	–
E	11/9 of band D (122%)	473/360 of band D (131%)
F	13/9 of band D (144%)	585/360 of band D (163%)
G	15/9 of band D (167%)	705/360 of band D (196%)
H	18/9 of band D (200%)	882/360 of band D (245%)
I (Wales only)	21/9 of band D (233%)	

Percentages are rounded.

Residents and occupiers

15.6   The people living in a dwelling are either:

(a) 'residents' – over 18-year-olds who live there as their sole or main residence, including householders, lodgers and non-dependants (paras 15.7-9); or

(b) other occupiers – under 18-year-olds and people with no sole or main residence or whose sole or main residence is elsewhere.

Only residents can be liable for council tax (para 15.10) but both residents and other occupiers can affect whether you qualify for a reduction (para 15.22).

Householders

15.7   We use 'householders' (not a legal term) for residents of a dwelling who own or rent it. You can be a sole householder, householder couple, or joint householder (paras 15.14-16).

Lodgers

15.8   A lodger is someone over 18 who pays a commercial rent to you (or your partner) to live in part of your home.

Non-dependants

15.9   A non-dependant is someone over 18 who:

(a) lives in your home – for example a son, daughter, other relative or friend; but

(b) isn't your partner, young person (para 3.64), joint householder or lodger.

T15.1   LGFA 5(1),(2), 36(1)

Who is liable for council tax

15.10   This section explains when the residents of a dwelling are liable for council tax (paras 15.11-16) and when the owner/landlord is liable instead (paras 15.17-21).

When the residents are liable

15.11   The general rule is that liability for council tax falls on the resident(s) of a dwelling. If there is more than one, it falls on the resident(s) with the highest legal interest which is the first of the following:

(a) the freehold owner;

(b) the leasehold owner;

(c) the tenant;

(d) the licensee;

(e) any other resident(s).

15.12   If you are a couple who reside together and you are liable as in para 15.11, your partner is also liable, even when they have a lesser interest.

'FTS/SMI'

15.13   The rules in paras 15.14-16 refer to people who are full-time students (FTS) or severely mentally impaired (SMI) or as described in table 15.4(a),(b).

Sole householders

15.14   If you are a single person (para 3.47) and own or rent your home just in your name:

(a) you are liable for council tax on your home; but

(b) when you are FTS/SMI, your home is exempt from council tax unless other adults live with you (table 15.3(a)).

Householder couples

15.15   If you are a couple (para 3.49) and own or rent your home either in one name or in both your names:

(a) you are both jointly liable for council tax on your home; but

(b) when one of you is FTS/SMI, only the other is liable; or

(c) when both of you are FTS/SMI, your home is exempt from council tax unless other adults live with you (table 15.3(a)).

15.11   LGFA 6(1)(2)(a)-(e)

15.12   LGFA 9(1),(2)

15.13   LGFA 6(4), sch 1 paras 2, 4

15.14   LGFA 6(1),(2)(a)-(e)

15.15   LGFA 6(3),(4), 9(1),(2)

Joint householders

15.16   If you are single or a couple and own or rent your home with one or more others (e.g. relatives or friends in a house-share):

(a) you are all jointly liable for council tax on your home; but

(b) when one or more of you is FTS/SMI, only the other(s) are liable; or

(c) when all of you are FTS/SMI, your home is exempt unless other adults live with you (table 15.3(a)).

When the owner is liable not the residents

15.17   Non-resident owners are liable if there are no residents in the dwelling (para 15.21). Additionally, in the classes of dwelling in table 15.2, the owner/landlord is liable for the council tax, not the resident(s). This is the case even if all the occupiers are FTS/SMI or under 18, because the council tax exemptions in table 15.3 don't apply.

Table 15.2 **Owner liable not residents**

(a) A house in multiple occupation (para 15.18).

(b) A bail/probation hostel or hostel providing personal care (para 15.20(a),(b)).

(c) A care home or independent hospital.

(d) A dwelling occupied by a minister of religion.

(e) A dwelling occupied by a religious community (table 15.4(l)).

(f) A second home occupied only by live-in staff and their families.

(g) A dwelling provided to asylum seekers by the Home Office.

(h) An empty dwelling (para 15.21).

Note:

■   If you live in an HMO or hostel, your rent usually includes an amount towards the landlord's council tax.

15.16   LGFA 6(3),(4)

15.17   LGFA 8, CT(LO) 2

T15.2(a)-(g) LGFA 8(1)-(3); CT(LO) 2, Classes A to F

T15.2(a)   CT(LO) 2, Class C substituted by SI 1993/151, amended by SI 1995/620 reg 2

T15.2(b),(c) CT(LO) 2, Class A as substituted by SI 2003/3125, amended by SI 2015/643

T15.2(d)   CT(LO) 2, Class E amended by SI 1995/620 reg 3

T15.2(e)   CT(LO) 2, Class B

T15.2(f)   CT(LO) 2, Class D

T15.2(g)   CT(LO) 2, Class F added by SI 2000/537

T15.2(h)   LGFA 6(1),(2)(f)

Houses in multiple occupation

15.18   A house in multiple occupation (HMO) is a building that:

(a) has been constructed or adapted for occupation by more than one household; or

(b) is inhabited by one or more people each of whom:

- is a tenant of or has a licence to occupy only part of the dwelling, or

- has a licence to occupy but is not solely or jointly liable to pay rent for the whole dwelling.

The adaptation in (a) can be adding locks to rooms, converting the use of a room, etc, depending on the details of the individual case (CTGM 8.3.5).

15.19   The most familiar example of an HMO is a house where the landlord lets out rooms separately and there is a shared bathroom/WC, kitchen and/or living room. But any dwelling that meets the conditions in para 15.18 is an HMO for council tax purposes, even if it doesn't count as an HMO for Housing Act licensing or other purposes.

Hostels

15.20   A hostel is:

(a) a bail or probation hostel ('approved premises');

(b) a building or part of a building used solely or mainly for residential accommodation that is provided in non-self-contained units, together with personal care for people who are elderly, disabled, have a past or present alcohol or drug dependence or a past or present mental disorder; or

(c) a dwelling (including a night shelter) that provides non self-contained accommodation:

- for people with no fixed abode or settled way of life; and

- where the individual lettings are licences rather than tenancies.

Empty dwellings

15.21   A dwelling with no occupiers is exempt from the council tax in some cases (table 15.3). Otherwise, the landlord/owner:

(a) qualifies for a 50% discount for the first six months that the dwelling is empty (this six months continues to run even when the dwelling changes hands); but

(b) in England and Wales, may be liable for up to four times the normal amount of council tax if it is empty for longer periods.

National rules prevent the increases in (b) in certain cases, but otherwise local councils decide whether and when to apply them and must publish their rules about this.

15.18   Table 15.2 Class C as amended by SI 1993/151 and SI 1995/620

15.20   LGFA sch 1 paras 7, 10; in DDO 6 definition: 'hostel' as substituted by SI 2003/3121 art 4

15.21   LGFA 11(2), 11A, 11B, as amended by the Rating (Property in Common Occupation) and Council Tax (Empty Dwellings) Act 2018, s2

Reducing your council tax bill

15.22   You can get help with council tax if you qualify for:

(a) an exemption (para 15.23);

(b) a disability reduction (para 15.24);

(c) a discount (para 15.26); and/or

(d) a council tax rebate (chapter 16).

Your council may also offer discounts for prompt payment or for payment by one of its preferred methods.

Council tax exemptions

15.23   When a dwelling is exempt, no one has to pay council tax on it. Your council tax bill should show you have a nothing to pay. Table 15.3 lists all the classes of exempt dwelling.

Table 15.3 **Council tax exempt dwellings**

(a) A dwelling whose only occupiers are any combination of:
- full time students (table 15.4(a)),
- people who are severely mentally impaired (table 15.4(b)),
- in Wales, young care leavers (table 15.4(d)), or
- under 18-year-olds.

(b) An unoccupied dwelling left empty by a student or someone who became a student within six weeks after leaving.

(c) A hall of residence predominantly for students.

(d) An unoccupied dwelling whose owner/renter (the last person liable for council tax):
- resides elsewhere to receive personal care,
- resides elsewhere to provide personal care,
- is in hospital or long-term care,
- has died within the last six months, or
- is detained in prison or hospital.

15.22   LGFA 4, 11, 13, 13A

15.23   LGFA 4(1)-(4)

T15.3(a) CT(ED) Class N substituted by SI 1993/150,
              amended by SI 1995/619, SI 2004/2865; Class U substituted by SI 1999/536; Class S added by SI 1995/619

T15.3(b) CT(ED) Class K substituted by SI 1993/150

T15.3(c) CT(ED) Class M amended by SI 1993/150 and SI 1994/539

T15.3(d) CT(ED) Class I substituted by SI 2003/3121; Classes D, E, F and J amended/substituted by SI 1994/539

(e) An unoccupied dwelling that is owned by a charity and was in use by the charity within the last six months.

(f) In Wales, an unoccupied dwelling that has been vacant:

- for less than six months, or

- for less than 12 months and which requires major repairs or structural changes to make it habitable.

(g) An unoccupied dwelling awaiting occupation by a minister of religion.

(h) An unoccupied dwelling whose owner/renter (the person who would now be liable for council tax) is bankrupt.

(i) An unoccupied dwelling that has been repossessed by a mortgage lender.

(j) An unoccupied dwelling whose occupation is prohibited by law or by a planning restriction.

(k) UK armed forces accommodation owned by the Secretary of State for Defence.

(l) Visiting forces accommodation.

(m) A dwelling where the liable resident has diplomatic immunity.

(n) An empty houseboat mooring or mobile home pitch.

(o) An unoccupied annex or dwelling, that can't be let separately due to a planning restriction.

(p) An annex or self-contained part of a property occupied by a dependant relative who is over 65, or severely mentally impaired (table 15.4(b)), or substantially and permanently disabled.

Notes:

- None of the exemptions apply to HMOs, hostels or any dwelling where the owner is liable, not the residents (table 15.2).

- Items (a)-(l) also apply in Scotland but the exact conditions may differ in some cases. Certain other categories of dwelling are also exempt, including sheltered housing for elderly or disabled residents if it is owned by a housing association.

T15.3(e) CT(ED) Class B, amended by SI 1994/539

T15.3(f) CT(ED) Classes A and C abolished in England by SI 2012/2965

T15.3(g) CT(ED) Class H

T15.3(h) CT(ED) Class Q added by SI 1993/150, amended by SI 1994/539

T15.3(i) CT(ED) Class L

T15.3(j) CT(ED) Class G substituted by SI 2006/2318

T15.3(k) CT(ED) Class O amended by SI 1992/2941

T15.3(l) CT(ED) Class P added by SI 1992/2941

T15.3(m) CT(ED) Class V added by SI 1997/656, definition – 'dependent relative' in class amended by SI 1998/291

T15.3(n) CT(ED) Class R added by SI 1994/539

T15.3(o) CT(ED) Class T added SI 1995/619

T15.3(p) CT(ED) Class W added by SI1997/656, definition – dependent relative in class amended by SI 1998/291

Council tax disability reductions

15.24   When you qualify for a disability reduction:

(a) your council tax is reduced to the amount for the next band down – for example, for homes in band D the bill is reduced to the amount for band C;

(b) if your home is in band A (the lowest band) your bill is reduced by one sixth.

Who gets a disability reduction

15.25   You qualify for a disability reduction if:

(a) you are disabled, or at least one disabled adult or child has their home with you; and

(b) your home provides:

  ■ an additional kitchen or bathroom for the disabled person's use; or

  ■ an additional room (not a kitchen, bathroom or toilet) used predominantly to meet their special needs; or

  ■ sufficient floor space to use a wheelchair if they need one; and

(c) this is of major importance to the disabled person's well-being, taking account of the nature and extent of their disability; and

(d) you make a written application for it (see also para 15.34).

Your home doesn't need to have been specifically adapted. For example, it could be that the disabled person has to have a separate bedroom or a bedroom downstairs.

Council tax discounts

15.26   When you qualify for a discount, your council tax is reduced by 25% ('single occupancy' discount) or 50% ('empty dwelling' discount) (but see para 15.21).

Who gets a discount

15.27   Discounts depend on how many adults there are in your home (this means people over 18) and how many of them are 'disregarded persons' (table 15.4).

15.28   When you are the only adult in your home, you qualify for:

(a) a 25% discount; or

(b) a 50% discount if you are a disregarded person (table 15.4)

15.29   When there are two adults in your home (including you), you qualify for :

(a) a 25% discount if one of you is a disregarded person; or

(b) a 50% discount if you both are.

15.30   When there are three or more adults in your home, you qualify for:

(a) a 25% discount if all but one of you are disregarded persons; or

(b) a 50% discount if you all are.

15.24   LGFA 13(1),(4),(6),(7); CT(RD) 4 as amended by SI 1999/1004

15.25   CT(RD) 3(1),(3)

15.26   LGFA 11(1)-(3), 11A(1)-(4)

15.27-30   LGFA 11(1)-(3)

Examples: Council tax discounts

1. Single person with discount

June owns her home and is the only person who lives there.

- She qualifies for a 25% discount – because she is the only adult there.

2. Couple with no discount

Jane and John are a couple. They rent their home and are the only people who live there.

- They don't qualify for a discount – because there are two adults and neither are disregarded persons.

3. Couple with discount

Geoff and Gina are a couple. They rent their home and Geoff is severely mentally impaired.

- They qualify for a 25% discount – because there are two adults and one is a disregarded person (table 15.4(b)).

4. Single person plus non-householder

Geri rents her home. Her father lives with her and is on the guarantee credit of SPC.

- Geri can't get a discount – because there are two adults, and neither are disregarded.

- But she can get second adult rebate – because her father is a non-dependant with a low income (para 17.19).

Table 15.4 **Council tax disregarded persons**

The following 'disregarded persons' affect discounts (paras 15.27-30), non-dependant contributions in main CTR (table 17.2) and second adult rebate (paras 17.18-23). Definitions (a) and (b) also apply for exemptions (table 15.3).

(a) Full-time students

Anyone who:

- is on a one-year or longer UK or EU course at level 3 or above (A levels, degrees etc) and is expected to study at least 21 hours per week, for at least 24 weeks per year; or

- is under 20 and is on a three-month or longer UK or EU course and is expected to study for at least 12 hours per week during term times; or

- is studying to be included for the first time in the nursing register; or

- is a foreign language assistant registered with the British Council; or

- is under 20 and left one of these courses during May to October – this applies until 31st October in the year they leave.

T15.4(a)-(m) LGFA 11(5), sch 1

T15.4(a)   LGFA sch 1 paras 4, 5; DDO 4, sch 1 paras 2-7; DDR 3 Class C; SI 1993/149; SI 1994/543; SI 2006/3396 art 2(2)(b)

(b) People who are severely mentally impaired

Anyone who has a medical certificate confirming they have a severe impairment of intelligence and social functioning, and receives (or would receive but for being over 66):

- the daily living component of PIP; or
- the middle or highest rate of the care component of DLA; or
- attendance allowance or an equivalent benefit (para 10.37); or
- JSA(IB) or IS on the grounds of incapacity for work; or
- IB or SDA; or
- in England and Wales, the LCW or LCWRA element of UC; or
- in Scotland, UC or ESA.

(c) Under 20-year olds for whom child benefit is payable

Anyone aged under 20 for whom child benefit child benefit could be paid. For details see 'young person' (para 3.64.)

(d) Care leavers under 25/26 (Wales and Scotland only)

Anyone who:

- is under 25 (Wales) or 26 (Scotland); and
- was in local authority care at any time after the age of 16, but has since left care; and
- in Wales only, was in care between the ages of 14 and 16 for one or more periods totalling at least three months (but ignoring any short-term placements intended to last less than four weeks).

(e) Youth trainees under 25

Anyone under 25 who is undertaking government funded youth training.

(f) Apprentices

Anyone who is studying for an accredited qualification as part of their employment and is paid no more than £195 per week.

(g) Carers

Any carer who provides care for at least 35 hours per week to someone in your home, if the person they care for gets or could get:

- the daily living component of PIP (in Scotland it must be the enhanced rate); or
- the middle or highest rate of the care component of DLA (in Scotland it must be the highest rate); or

---

T15.4(b)   LGFA sch 1 para 2; DDO 3; SI 1994/543; SI 2013/388 sch para 12; SI 2013/591 sch para 5; SI 2013/630 reg 55

T15.4(c)   LGFA sch 1 para 3

T15.4(d)   See Appendix 4

T15.4(e)   LGFA sch 1 para 4(1); DDO 4, sch 1 para 8; SI 2006/3396 art 2(2)(c)

T15.4(f)   LGFA sch 1 para 4(1); DDO 4, sch 1 para 1; SI 2006/3396 art 2(2)(a)

T15.4(g)   LGFA sch 1 para 9(1)(b),(g); DDR 2; sch paras 3, 4; SI 1994/540; SI 1996/637; SI 2013/388 sch para 3; SI 2013/591 sch para 6; SI 2013/725

- attendance allowance (in Scotland it must be the higher rate) or an equivalent benefit (para 10.37).

For example, the carer can be a relative or friend of the person they care for; but not their partner/spouse, nor (in the case of a child/young person under 18) their parent.

(h) Live-in care workers

Any carer who:

- provides care to someone in your home; and
- was introduced by a local council, government department or charity; and
- is paid no more than £44 per week.

(i) Night shelter and homeless hostel residents

Anyone who, on any day has his/her sole or main residence under a licence agreement in a resettlement/homeless hostel or night shelter (para 15.20(c)) that mainly provides non-self-contained accommodation.

(j) Care home and hospital residents

Anyone whose sole or main residence is an NHS hospital, independent hospital or care home, or hostel that provides personal care for people who require it due to old age, disability, mental disorder or past or present alcohol or drug dependence (para 15.20(b)).

(k) Prisoners, bail hostel residents and hospital detainees

For details about who is a prisoner or hospital detainee see paras 2.22 and 2.27.

(l) Members of religious communities

Any member who is maintained by the community and has no money of their own (apart from an occupational pension).

(m) Non-British partners of students

Any spouse or civil partner who is not permitted to work or claim benefits.

(n) Diplomats etc

Anyone who has diplomatic immunity or is a member of visiting forces, and in some cases their spouse, civil partner or dependants.

Note:

- Details for Wales and Scotland may differ in some cases.

T15.4(h)   LGFA sch 1 para 9(1),(2)(a)-(g); DDR 2; sch paras 1, 2; SI 2006/3395 reg 4

T15.4(i)   LGFA sch 1 para 10

T15.4(j)   LGFA sch 1 paras 6, 7; DDO 6(b) definition: 'hostel' as substituted by SI 2003/3121 art 4

T15.4(k)   LGFA sch 1 paras 1, 7; DDO 2, 6(a) definition: 'hostel' as substituted by SI 2003/3121 art 4

T15.4(l)   LGFA sch 1 para 11; DDR 3 Class B

T15.4(m)   LGFA sch 1 para 11; DDR 3 Class A, Class E; SI 1995/620 reg 4

T15.4(n)   LGFA sch 1 para 11; DDR 3 Class A, Class D, Class F; SI 1992/2942 reg 2; SI 1995/620 reg 4; SI 1997/657

Claims, awards and appeals

Claims and awards

15.31   The council uses information you provide, or that it already holds, to decide:

(a) who is liable for council tax; and

(b) who qualifies for exemptions, disability reductions or discounts.

When your liability increases, you have 21 days to inform the council, otherwise you can incur a penalty. When it reduces there is no time limit (para 15.34) but the longer you leave it, the more difficult it may be to provide any evidence the council needs.

Changes to your council tax bill

15.32   When your circumstances change, your council tax starts, changes or ends on the exact day. For example, when you move:

(a) your council tax on the new home starts on the day of your move;

(b) your council tax on the old home ends on the day before (or later in some cases if you leave it empty).

Reconsiderations and appeals

15.33   You can ask the council to reconsider a decision it has made about any of the matters in para 15.31. After that you can appeal to the Valuation Tribunal in England, Wales or Scotland. You normally have two months to do this.

15.34   When there has been a mistake about whether or when you are liable for council tax, or qualify for an exemption or discount, there is no time limit on how far back the council can go. If you make an appeal the Limitation Act 1980 sets a six-year time limit from the date on which 'the cause of action accrued' but the Valuation Tribunal has interpreted this phrase fairly widely (CTGM 10.3.7(b)-(c)). For example, your council must take reasonable steps to find out if you qualify for a discount or an exemption and the tribunal may decide the time limit starts from the date they do this. But if your appeal relates to a disability reduction the time limit runs back from the date you first apply for it (Arca v Carlisle CC).

15.35   A dispute about liability, a discount etc (para 15.34) is not a defence against the council getting a liability order in the magistrate's court for unpaid council tax. This is because only the Valuation Tribunal can decide these disputes (Lone v LB Hounslow (2019)).

15.36   The time limits and procedures to appeal about a council tax rebate are different and vary between England and Wales (paras 18.6-10) and Scotland (paras 18.23-25).

15.31   CT(A&E) 11, 16; CT(RD) 5

15.32   LGFA 2

15.33   LGFA 15, 16

15.34   CT(A&E) 8, 14; Arca v Carlisle [2013] RA 248

15.35   Lone v LB Hounslow [2019] EWCA Civ 2206 www.bailii.org/ew/cases/EWCA/Civ/2019/2206.html

Chapter 16 **Council tax rebates**

- Who can get CTR: see paras 16.1-12.
- Local CTR/CTR classes: see paras 16.13-19.
- Discretionary CTR: see paras 16.20-23.
- Exclusions from CTR: see paras 16.24-31.
- CTR claims and changes: see paras 16.32-46.

Who can get CTR

16.1 Council tax rebates (CTR) apply in England, Scotland and Wales. This chapter and chapter 17 describe the different kinds of council tax rebate you can get and these are summarised in table 16.1. The law calls them 'council tax reductions' and some councils in England call them council tax support.

Table 16.1 **Kinds of CTR**

(a) Main CTR

Main CTR has national rules that apply in England for pension age claims, and in Wales and Scotland for all claims. It is for when you have a low income, and if you have a non-dependant they may be expected to contribute (paras 17.4-17).

(b) Second adult rebate

SAR has national rules that apply in England for pension age claims and in Scotland for all claims. It is for when you have a non-dependant who stops you getting a discount (para 15.26) but has a low income (paras 17.18-25).

(c) Local CTR /CTR classes

Councils in England must have a local CTR scheme for working age claims, and this is made up of CTR classes (para 16.11). Councils can also have CTR classes for pension age claims in England and all claims in Wales (paras 16.7-9). Local CTR classes have local rules (para 16.13).

(d) Discretionary CTR

Discretionary CTR applies in England and Wales. Councils can award it whether or not you qualify for any of the above (para 16.20).

Residents

16.2   To get any of the kinds of CTR you must be a resident who is liable for council tax (para 15.6). If you are jointly liable with one or more others (apart from just your partner in a couple) the figures used in the main CTR and SAR calculations are shared between you (paras 17.16, 17.25).

Non-dependants

16.3   Non-dependants are usually adult sons, daughters, other relatives or friends who live with you (para 15.9). They can't get CTR themselves but may affect your CTR (para 17.6).

Working age and pension age

16.4   Working age means under 66 and pension age means 66 or over. Table 16.2 shows whether you can get working age or pension age CTR.

Table 16.2 **Pension age or working age CTR**

Single person

(a)	Over 66	Pension age CTR
(b)	Under 66	Working age CTR

Couple

(c)	Both over 66	Pension age CTR
(d)	Both under 66	Working age CTR
(e)	Mixed ages (one over, one under 66):	
	▪ Applicant is over 66	Pension age CTR
	▪ Applicant is under 66	Working age CTR

National variations

16.5   Paras 16.6-12 summarise the CTR variations between Scotland, Wales and England. The most notable is that:

(a) CTR for all ages in Scotland and Wales and for pension age claims in England have mainly national rules; but

(b) CTR for working age claims in England has mainly local rules.

16.2   LGFA sch 1A para 2(2)(a),(b); CTP sch 1 paras 1(1), 2(a), 3(a), 4(1)(a); CTR 13(a), 14(a), 15(1)(a), 16(a), 17(a), 18(1)(a)

16.3   LGFA sch 1A para 2(2)(c); CTP 9; CTR 9

16.4   Pensions Act 1995, sch 4 para 1(6); CTP 2(1) definitions: 'pensioner', pensionable age, 'qualifying age for state pension credit'; CTR 2(1)

T16.2   CTP 3, sch 1 para 2(f), 3(f), 4(e), sch 8 paras 3, 4(1); CTR 3, 13(f), 14(g), 15(1)(e), 16(f), 17(g), 18(1)(e), 109(1)

16.5   LGFA sch 1A para 2(1),(3),(8),(9); CTP 11(1), 14(1), sch 1 paras 1-4

CTR in Scotland

16.6   Every council in Scotland operates the national CTR rules. The council:

(a)   must have main CTR and SAR for both pension age and working age claims (chapter 17);

(b)   must include the alternative main CTR calculation for dwellings in bands E to H (para 17.17); and

(c)   must fully disregard war pensions (table 17.3(j)).

Discretionary CTR doesn't apply.

CTR in Wales

16.7   Every council in Wales must have a CTR scheme. This scheme:

(a)   must include main CTR for both pension age and working age claims (chapter 17);

(b)   may lengthen the backdating period (para 16.42) and/or the period of extended CTR (para 17.36);

(c)   may increase the disregard for war pensions (table 17.3(j)); and

(d)   may have additional CTR classes that supplement main CTR (para 16.8).

The council must also provide for discretionary CTR.

16.8   CTR classes must follow the rules in paras 16.13-16. They are in practice uncommon. Those that exist are like SAR or council tax discounts, where a flat rate is awarded to people who meet the conditions set by the council.

Pension age CTR in England

16.9   Every council in England must have a CTR scheme for pension age claims, made up of CTR classes. This scheme:

(a)   must include main CTR (para 17.4) – this counts as two classes (class A for claimants without excess income and class B for those with excess income);

(b)   must include SAR (para 17.18) – this counts as one class (class C);

(c)   may increase the disregard for war pensions (table 17.3(j)); and

(d)   may have additional CTR classes that supplement main CTR and/or SAR (para 16.10).

The council must also provide for discretionary CTR.

16.10   CTR classes must follow the rules in paras 16.13-16. They are in practice rare.

16.6   LGFA 80(1),(2); CTS 12, 14(1), 14A(1), sch 4 paras 12, 19; CTS66+ 12, 14(1), 14A(1), sch 3 paras 1-2

16.7   LGFA 13(1)(b),(c),(4),(5), sch 1B paras 2(1), 3, 4; CTPW 14, 21-24, 32, 33, 34(4),(5)

16.8   LGFA 13A(1)(b),(4),(5), sch 1B paras 3-5; CTPW 3-10, 12, 14-18, 27-29

16.9   LGFA sch 1A para 2(1)-(4),(8),(9); CTP 11(1), 14(1), sch 1 paras 1-4

16.10   LGFA 13A(2), sch 1A paras 2, 3, 5; SI 2017/1305, reg 2

Working age CTR in England

16.11   Every council in England must have a CTR scheme for working age claimants made up of CTR classes. This scheme:

(a)   must include one or more CTR classes giving the council's primary rules for working age CTR – this is sometimes called 'local CTR' (para 16.12);

(b)   may increase the disregard for war pensions (table 17.3(j)); and

(c)   may have additional CTR classes that supplement local CTR (para 16.12).

The council must also provide for discretionary CTR.

16.12   All CTR classes must follow the rules in paras 16.13-16. For examples of local CTR, see paras 16.17-19.

Example: Working age CTR in England

Joyce is a care leaver aged 23. She has lost her job and claims UC and CTR. The DWP awards her UC. Her local council has two CTR classes that apply to her:

- a reduced form of main CTR based on 80% of the council tax (para 16.17) – the council calls this class D;

- a flat rate 25% reduction for care leavers under 25 (para 16.19) – the council calls this class G;

and people who qualify for both get whichever is the most.

Joyce's CTR claim covers both classes, and she is awarded the council's class D.

Local CTR/CTR classes

16.13   When councils set CTR classes, there are requirements (in paras 16.14-16) about:

(a)   basing classes on financial need;

(b)   following national rules; and

(c)   setting and changing classes.

Those requirements apply to the CTR classes that make up working age CTR in England (local CTR) and all other CTR classes in England and Wales.

Financial need

16.14   CTR classes must be based on financial need, not on other factors such as length of residence (R (Winder) v Sandwell MBC). This means your or your family's:

(a)   own financial circumstances; or

(b)   membership of a group that is generally at higher risk of being in financial need than the wider population, such as people with disabilities, carers, young care leavers and others.

16.11   LGFA 13A((1)(a),(c),(2),(3), sch 1A para 2(1)-(4)

16.12   LGFA 13A(2), sch 1A paras 2, 3, 5; SI 2017/1305, reg 2

16.13   LGFA sch 1A paras 2(1),(3),(5)-(7),(9), 3(1)-(3), 5; SI 2017/1305, reg 2; CTP 11-15, sch 1 paras 1-5

16.14   LGFA 13A(2), sch 1B para 3(4)-(7)
          R (Winder) v Sandwell MBC [2014] www.bailii.org/ew/cases/EWHC/Admin/2014/2617.html

Following national rules

16.15   And all local CTR classes must follow the national CTR rules about:

(a)   what is a 'working age' claim;

(b)   who is included in your household;

(c)   which migrants and recent arrivals are excluded;

(d)   certain minimum standards relating to claims, decision notices and appeals.

Setting and changing CTR classes

16.16   All CTR classes apply and can be changed from 1st April each year. Councils must:

(a)   consult with local residents about classes and changes to them – this must be done in a 'meaningful way' (R (Moseley) v Haringey LBC);

(b)   include transitional rules when changes to schemes end or reduce your entitlement; and

(c)   publish details of their classes and how you can apply (which most councils do on their website).

Any changes in CTR classes must be confirmed by 11th March (in Wales, 31st January) in time for the new financial year starting on 1st April.

Local CTR: classes based on national CTR

16.17   Some councils have CTR classes for working age claims that adopt the national CTR rules in full (the 'default scheme'). Many more have variations on national CTR that do one or more of the following:

(a)   reduce the amount of council tax that can be met by CTR (this is often the only variation);

(b)   set a minimum award;

(c)   reduce the upper capital limit;

(d)   increase or restructure the non-dependant contributions and the income bands;

(e)   vary the assessment of different kinds of income;

(f)   increase the excess income taper above 20%;

(g)   limit or remove entitlement to backdated CTR;

(h)   limit or remove entitlement to SAR; or

(i)   set their own rates for some or all of the allowances, premiums and components in the calculation of the applicable amount.

These schemes have the advantages of sensitivity to changes in income and being similar to other benefits, but the disadvantages of requiring frequent changes in the award.

16.15   LGFA sch 1A para 2(9); CTP 3-15, sch 7, sch 8
          R (Moseley) v Haringey LBC [2014] www.bailii.org/uk/cases/UKSC/2014/56.html

16.16   LGFA sch 1A paras 3(1),(3),(5), 5(1)-(6); SI 2017/1305 reg 2

16.17   LGFA 13A(2), sch 1A para 2(2),(4)

Local CTR: classes based on income bands

16.18   Some councils have CTR classes for working age claims that are based on income bands. Usually your CTR equals a high percentage of your council tax if you are in the lowest income band, and the percentage reduces for higher income bands. These classes have the advantage of simplicity and less frequent changes in your CTR, but the disadvantages of sudden jumps from one amount of CTR to another (or to nil) when your income crosses between bands.

Local CTR: other kinds of classes

16.19   CTR classes can also be designed in other ways. For example, some councils have CTR classes that are like SAR or council tax discounts, where a flat rate is awarded to people who meet conditions set by the council.

Discretionary CTR

16.20   Discretionary CTR applies in England and Wales, not Scotland. Councils can award it based on the individual merits of your claim or on the basis of your membership of a group at risk of financial need.

16.21   If you are awarded discretionary CTR you can get:

(a)   additional CTR to top up your main CTR, SAR or local CTR; or

(b)   some CTR even when you don't qualify for these (for example, if your income is too high or you are excluded: para 16.24).

These could reduce the amount of council tax you have to pay to a lower figure or to nil.

16.22   The council must tell you how to request discretionary CTR. It can also treat any claim for group based CTR (para 16.14(b)) as a request for discretionary CTR. You can appeal almost any decision about discretionary CTR to a tribunal (para 18.14) (SC v East Riding of Yorkshire Council [2014]).

16.23   During 2020-21 and 2021-22 the 'Covid-19 hardship fund' from MHCLG is providing English councils with grant funding to support local CTR schemes. There is a 'strong expectation' that councils will use it for discretionary CTR to reduce the annual council tax bill by a further £150 (or to nil if it is less) for any working age claimant who qualifies for local CTR. MHCLG guidance advises councils that claimants shouldn't be required to make a separate claim or be affected by coronavirus to qualify [www].

16.18   LGFA 13A(2), sch 1A para 2(2),(4)

16.19   LGFA 13A(2),(3), sch 1A para 2(1)-(4)

16.20   LGFA 13A(1)(c),(6),(7)

16.21   LGFA 13A(1)(c),(6), sch 1A para 2(2),(4)

16.22   LGFA 13A(1)(c),(6),(7); CTP sch 7 para 9(2)
            SC v East Riding of Yorkshire Council [2014] EW Misc B46 (UT) www.bailii.org/ew/cases/cases/Misc/B46.html

16.23   MHCLG Council Tax Covid-19 Hardship Fund: Local Authority Guidance
            https://tinyurl.com/DCTR-Covid-19
            2021/22: House of Commons Debates 25 November 2020, Volume 684, Col 836

Exclusions from CTR

16.24   You may be excluded from:

(a) main CTR and SAR if you are absent from home (paras 16.25-29);

(b) main CTR and SAR if you are a migrant (para 16.30);

(c) main CTR (not SAR) if you are a full-time student (para 16.31);

(d) main CTR (not SAR) if you have capital over £16,000 (paras 17.5, 17.32).

In the case of local CTR/CTR classes, councils must apply exclusion (b) to working age and pension age claims and (d) to pension age claims. They can choose whether to apply any of the other exclusions. None of the exclusions apply to discretionary CTR.

Absences from home

16.25   You are excluded from main CTR and SAR while you (the claimant) are absent from your home unless you meet one of the conditions in paras 16.26-29.

Temporary absences within Great Britain

16.26   You can get CTR during an absence within Great Britain:

(a) for up to 52 weeks if it is due to you receiving medically approved treatment or convalescence or to accompany a family member who is; or

(b) for up to 52 weeks if you are a hospital patient or it is due to domestic violence, studying, attending training or imprisonment; or

(c) for up to 13 weeks if you are in a care home for a trial period; or

(d) for up to 13 weeks for any other absence.

Temporary absences outside Great Britain

16.27   In England, you can get CTR during an absence outside Great Britain:

(a) for up to 26 weeks if it is due to your employment as a mariner, offshore worker, Crown servant or in the armed forces;

(b) for up to 26 weeks if it is due to receiving or providing care or to domestic violence; or

(c) for up to eight weeks if it is due to a death in your family; or

(d) for up to four weeks in any other case.

The details are the same as HB (volume 2 chapter 3).

16.28   In Scotland, the rules are the same as in para 16.27 except that (a) applies without time limit and also includes aircraft workers; (b), (c) and (d) have time limits of six, two and one month(s); and (d) only applies if you haven't had more than two absences outside Great Britain in the past 12 months.

16.24   LGFA sch 1A para 2(9); CTP 11-13; sch 1 paras 2(b),(d), 3(b),(d), 4(1)(b),(d), 5; CTR 13-24, 75(1),(2)

16.25   CTP 12(2),(6),(7), sch 1 paras 2(b), 3(b), 4(1)(b), 5; CTR 13(b), 14(b), 15(1)(b), 16(b), 17(b), 18(1)(a), 19, 21(2),(6),(7)

16.26   CTP sch 1 para 5; CTR 19

16.27   CTP sch 1 para 5(2)(c),(d),(2A)-(2F),(3B)-(3G)

16.29   In Wales, you can only get CTR during absences outside Great Britain and Northern Ireland for up to 52 weeks to attend a training course or for the conditions in para 16.26(a).

Migrants

16.30   You are excluded from main CTR, SAR and local CTR/CTR classes if you (the claimant) are a migrant or have recently arrived in the UK, unless you are on UC, SPC, JSA (IB), ESA (IR) or IS, or in one of the eligible groups in table 20.1.

Full-time students

16.31   You are excluded from main CTR (but not SAR) if you (the claimant) are a working age full-time student in Scotland or Wales, unless you are on SPC, JSA (IB), ESA (IR) or IS (or in Scotland, UC), or are in one of the eligible groups. These are normally the same as in UC (table 2.3) and the full details are as in HB (volume 2 chapter 2). But note that the rules can differ for local CTR/CTR classes, and also that students can be exempt or a disregarded person for council tax purposes (tables 15.3, 15.4) whether or not eligible for benefits.

CTR claims and changes

16.32   The rules in this section apply to main CTR and SAR. In England and Wales councils can have their own rules for local CTR/CTR classes and discretionary CTR.

Claims

16.33   To get CTR you have to make a claim to the council that sends your council tax bill. This is the case even if you are claiming UC or SPC at the same time. If you are a renter, you can usually claim CTR at the same time as HB. (In CTR law claims are called 'applications' and the claimant is called the 'applicant'.)

Advance claims

16.34   You can make an advance claim for CTR:

   (a)   up to 17 weeks (in Wales, 13 weeks) before your 66th birthday; or

   (b)   up to 17 weeks (in Wales, 13 weeks) before you expect to qualify for pension age CTR;

   (c)   up to 13 weeks before you expect to qualify for working age CTR; or

   (d)   in England, up to eight weeks before you expect to become liable for council tax.

In (a)-(c) for example, this could be because you know your income will go down.

How to claim

16.35   You can claim CTR on your council's claim form or in most areas by telephone or online [www]. If you are in a couple, one of you ('the claimant') makes the claim for you both.

16.30   CTP 12, 13; CTR 21, 22

16.31   CTR 20, 24, 75(1),(2)

16.33   CTP sch 1 paras 2(f), 3(g), 4(1)(e), sch 7 paras 2, 3, 9, sch 8 paras 3, 4
         CTR 13(f), 14(g), 15(1)(e), 16(f), 17(g), 18(1)(e), 109, sch 1 paras 2, 3, 11

16.34   CTP sch 8 para 5(6),(7); CTR 110(6),(7)

16.35   CTP sch 7 paras 2, 3, sch 8 para 4(1); CTR 109(1), sch 1 paras 2, 3 www.gov.uk/apply-council-tax-reduction

Help with claiming

16.36   You can ask the council or an advice organisation to help with your claim, or you can ask a family member or friend. If you can't manage your financial affairs, an attorney can claim for you, or the council can appoint someone to do this.

Information and evidence

16.37   You should provide the information and evidence the council reasonably needs, including personal, family and household details and your (and your partner's) capital, income and (except in Scotland) national insurance number. The council can request this when you claim or at any time during your CTR award, and should allow you at least one month to provide it.

Decisions about your CTR

16.38   Chapter 18 gives the rules about decision notices, reconsiderations and appeals.

The date your CTR starts

16.39   Your CTR starts:

(a) in England and Scotland, on the Monday following your date of claim or backdated date of claim (paras 16.41-43); or

(b) in Wales, on your exact date of claim or backdated date of claim.

16.40   But your CTR starts on the day your council tax starts if that is in the same benefit week (para 17.2) as your date of claim or backdated date of claim.

Date of claim

16.41   Your date of claim is the earliest of the following dates:

(a) the day the council received your CTR claim;

(b) the day you told the council you want to claim CTR, so long as the council received your CTR claim within one month;

(c) the day your partner died or you separated from them (if they were previously the CTR claimant), so long as the council received your CTR claim within one month;

(d) the day your UC or guarantee credit of SPC began, as long as the council received your CTR claim within one month of the DWP receiving your UC/SPC claim;

(e) the day your council tax started if you are on UC or guarantee credit of SPC, so long as the council received your CTR claim within one month of that.

16.36   CTP sch 8 para 4; CTR 109

16.37   CTP sch 8 para 7; CTR 113

16.39   CTP sch 1 para 45(1); CTR 106(1)

16.40   CTP sch 1 para 45(2); CTR 106(2)

16.41   CTP sch 7 paras 2-7, sch 8 para 5; CTR 110, sch 1 paras 2-7

Backdating

16.42 For pension age CTR claims, your date of claim (para 16.41) is backdated for three months in all cases. For working age CTR claims, it is backdated for up to six months in Scotland or three months in Wales (or longer: para 16.7), but only if you have 'good cause'. In England, some councils include similar working age rules in their local CTR scheme.

16.43 'Good cause' is decided in the same way as in HB (volume 2 chapter 16). You may qualify if you were too ill to claim, were wrongly advised, or had some other good reason for not claiming CTR earlier.

The date your CTR changes or ends

16.44 You should tell the council about any change that could affect your CTR. Your CTR changes when there is a change in your income, capital, family, household, or other circumstances. It only ends when:

(a) your liability for council tax ends;

(b) you move out of the council's area;

(c) you stop meeting the conditions for CTR (e.g. you are excluded: para 16.24); or

(d) the CTR calculations give a figure of nil or a negative figure.

16.45 In most cases, your CTR changes or ends:

(a) in England, on the Monday following the change;

(b) in Scotland, on the Monday of the week in which the change occurs; or

(c) in Wales, on the exact day of the change.

But changes in your council tax take effect the exact day, and some changes relating to non-householder contributions or finding a job are delayed (paras 17.14, 17.36).

Payments and overpayments

16.46 Your CTR is awarded (or 'paid') by crediting it to your council tax account – so you have less council tax to pay. The council normally corrects any errors by:

(a) crediting your council tax account if you've been paid too little CTR; or

(b) deducting CTR from your council tax account if you've been paid too much – so you have more council tax to pay.

16.42   CTP sch 8 para 6; CTR 111, 112

16.44   CTP sch 1 para 46(1); CTR 107(1)

16.45   CTP sch 1 para 46(1),(3),(4); CTR 107(1),(3),(4)

16.46   LGFA 13A(1)(a); CTP sch 8 para 14; CTR 118
         CT(A&E) 1(2) definition: 'discount', 20 as amended by SI 2013/3086

Chapter 17 **Main CTR and SAR**

- ■ Main CTR: see paras 17.4-17.
- ■ Second adult rebate: see paras 17.18-25.
- ■ Capital and income for main CTR: see paras 17.26-36.

17.1 This chapter explains who can get main CTR and SAR and how they are calculated. It gives the national rules (table 16.1). But for working age claims in England, local CTR sometimes has different rules (paras 16.11-12).

Benefit weeks

17.2 Main CTR and SAR are awarded for benefit weeks which always start on a Monday, or on a daily basis if you only qualify for part of a benefit week.

Conversion to weekly amounts

17.3 To obtain weekly figures to use in CTR:

(a) divide annual council tax by 365 (or 366 in a leap year) and multiply by 7;

(b) multiply calendar monthly earnings or other income by 12 and divide by 52.

Main CTR

17.4 Main CTR applies:

(a) in Scotland and Wales whether you are working age or pension age;

(b) in England if you are pension age.

Working age claims in England sometimes have different rules (paras 16.11-12).

Who can get main CTR

17.5 You can get main CTR if:

(a) you are a resident who is liable for council tax (para 15.6);

(b) you aren't excluded due to an absence (para 16.25);

(c) you aren't an excluded migrant or student (paras 16.30-31);

(d) you don't have capital over £16,000 (paras 17.31-32); and

(e) your income is low enough (para 17.6).

17.2   CTP 2(1) definition: 'reduction week'; CTR 2(1)
17.3   CTP sch 1 paras 7(1), 17(1); CTR 29(1), 40(1), 49(1), 50(1),(2)
17.4   CTP 11(1), 14, sch 1 paras 1-4; CTR 13, 14, 16, 17
17.5   CTP 14(2), sch 1 paras 2, 3; CTR 13, 14, 16, 17

Amount of main CTR

17.6   To calculate your weekly main CTR:

(a) start with your weekly council tax (para 17.7);

(b) if you have one or more non-dependants, subtract the amounts they are expected to contribute (para 17.13); and

(c) if you have excess income (paras 17.8-11), subtract 20% of it.

See also para 17.16 if you are jointly liable for council tax and para 17.17 for council tax bands E to H in Scotland.

Weekly council tax for main CTR

17.7   For main CTR, your weekly council tax means the amount due on your home in the current benefit week (para 17.2) after any disability reduction or discount that applies.

Excess income for people on UC

17.8   If you get maximum UC (para 9.7), you don't have excess income. But if you get a lower amount of UC, your excess income equals:

(a) your weekly net income (para 17.9)

(b) minus the weekly equivalent of your maximum UC;

(c) minus, in Scotland only:

- £17.15 for each child/young person you get a child element for (para 9.15), and

- £54.60 for each child/young person you don't get a child element for due to the two-child limit (para 9.17).

17.9   In this case, income means the DWP's figures for your earned income (after it has deducted a work allowance if you qualify for one (para 10.11)) and unearned income. The council adds your UC to the DWP's income figures and converts the total into a weekly figure by multiplying by 12 and dividing by 52. The council uses the DWP's figure for your capital to calculate the tariff income (para 17.33) but apart from this it makes no other adjustments (other than as required by its local scheme rules).

Excess income for people not on UC

17.10   If you get the guarantee credit of SPC, JSA(IB), ESA(IR) or IS, you don't have excess income. But if you don't get these benefits (or UC), your excess income equals:

(a) your net weekly income (para 17.11);

(b) minus your applicable amount (para 17.12).

17.6   CTP sch 1 paras 2(c),(e), 3(c),(e),(f), 7, 10(2),(3); CTR 13(c),(e), 14(c),(e),(f), 16(c),(e), 17(c),(e),(f), 29, 32(2),(3)

17.7   CTP sch 1 para 7(1),(2); CTR 29(1),(2)

17.8   CTR 16(e), 17(e),(f), 28, 32(2),(3), 37

17.9   CTR 37(1)-(4)

17.10   CTP sch 1 paras 10(2),(3), 13; CTR 32(2),(3), 35, sch 7 para 14, sch 8 paras 8, 9

17.11   In this case, the council makes its own assessment of your earned and unearned income and capital (para 17.34 and table 17.3). But if you are on savings credit, see para 17.29.

Applicable amounts

17.12   If you aren't on UC, your applicable amount represents your weekly living needs and those of your family (which means the same as 'benefit unit': para 3.46). It is made up of personal allowances plus additions for disability, carers and people with a limited capability for work. Appendix 2 give the current figures. The detailed conditions are the same as in HB (volume 2 chapter 12) unless the council's local CTR scheme differs (paras 16.7-12).

Non-dependant contributions

17.13   Non-dependants are adult sons, daughters, other relatives, or friends who live with you (para 15.9). They are expected to contribute towards your council tax (which means you get less CTR) unless one of the exceptions applies. Table 17.1 gives the current figures and table 17.2 lists the exceptions.

Delayed non-dependant contributions

17.14   If you or your partner are 66 or over in England (or 65 or over in Scotland), new contributions or increases in contributions during your award of CTR are delayed for 26 weeks.

Non-dependant's gross weekly income

17.15   A non-dependant's gross weekly income includes all types of earned and unearned income, with only the following being disregarded:

(a) SPC;

(b) JSA(IB), ESA(IR) and IS;

(c) PIP, DLA, attendance allowance and equivalent benefits (para 10.37); and

(d) payments from government sponsored trusts and funds relating to certain diseases, independent living for disabled people, and the London or Manchester bombings.

No deductions are made for tax, national insurance or pension contributions.

Examples: Main CTR

1. A single person on UC

Davina is on UC and doesn't have any other income. Her council tax is £24 per week. She doesn't have excess income (para 17.8).

■ Weekly council tax	£24.00
■ Equals weekly main CTR	£24.00

17.11   CTP sch 1 paras 14, 15; CTR 36, 38

17.12   CTP sch 1 para 6, sch 2; CTR 25, 26, sch 2, sch 3

17.13   CTP 9, sch 1 para 7(1), 8; CTR 9, 29(1), 30

17.14   CTP sch 1 para 46(10)-(13); CTR 107(10)-(13)

17.15   CTP sch 1 para 8(8)(a),(c),(9),(10); CTR 30(9)

2. A single person on SPC with a non-dependant

Darra lives in England and is on SPC. His council tax is £30 per week. He has one non-dependant, his daughter. She works full-time and has gross income of £500 pw, so her non-dependant contribution is £12.45 pw (table 17.1).

■ Weekly council tax	£30.00
■ Minus non-householder contribution	−£12.45
■ Equals weekly main CTR	£17.55

3. A couple on UC with earnings

Dean and Dora live in Wales and are on UC. Their council tax is £24 per week. Dora works and has net earnings of £260 per month (£60 pw) but doesn't qualify for a work allowance.

(a) Calculating UC (para 9.8)

■ Maximum UC (monthly)	£594.04
■ Minus 63% of net earnings (monthly)	−£163.80
■ Equals amount of UC (monthly)	£430.24

(b) Excess income for CTR (para 17.8)

■ Net earnings (weekly)	£60.00
■ Plus UC (weekly equivalent)	£99.29
■ Equals net weekly income	£159.29
■ Minus maximum UC (weekly equivalent)	£137.09
■ Equals weekly excess income	£22.20

(c) Calculating main CTR (para 17.8)

■ Weekly council tax	£24.00
■ Minus 20% of £22.20	−£4.44
■ Equals weekly main CTR	£19.56

4. A band H home in Scotland

Dolores and Diane live in a band H home in Scotland. Their council tax is £45 per week. They have net income of £500 pw. For the ordinary main CTR calculation, this is too high for them to qualify (para 17.6). But for the alternative calculation, it is £21 above the threshold of £479 (para 17.17).

■ 22½% of weekly council tax	£10.13
■ Minus 20% of £21	−£4.20
■ Equals weekly main CTR	£5.93

Table 17.1 **Main CTR: weekly non-dependant contributions**

(a) Non-dependants working at least 16 hours per week

Contributions are based on gross weekly income (para 17.15)

England		Scotland		Wales	
Income	*Contribution*	*Income*	*Contribution*	*Income*	*Contribution*
At least £469.00	£12.45	At least £458.00	£12.90	At least £469.00	£15.35
At least £377.00	£10.40	At least £370.00	£10.80	At least £377.00	£12.85
At least £217.00	£8.30	At least £213.00	£8.50	At least £217.00	£10.20
Under £217.00	£4.05	Under £213.00	£4.30	Under £217.00	£5.10

(b) Other non-dependants

England	£4.05	**Scotland**	£4.30	**Wales**	£5.10

(c) Non-dependant couples

There is one contribution per couple: (a) applies to combined gross weekly income if one or both work at least 16 hours pw; (b) applies otherwise.

Table 17.2 **Main CTR: no non-dependant contributions**

Your circumstances

No contributions apply for any non-dependants in your home if you or your partner are:

(a) on the daily living component of PIP;

(b) on the middle or highest rate of the care component of DLA;

(c) on attendance allowance or an equivalent benefit (para 10.37);

(d) on an armed forces independence payment (AFIP);

(e) entitled to (a), (b), (c) or (d) but not receiving it because of being in hospital; or

(f) certified as severely sight impaired or blind by an ophthalmologist or have regained your sight in the last 28 weeks.

Non-dependant's circumstances

No contribution applies for any single non-dependant who is, or any non-dependant couple who both are:

T17.1   CTP sch 1 para 8(1),(2); SI 2021/29, reg 6a; CTR 30(1),(2)

T17.2   CTP sch 1 para 8(6)-(8),(11),(12); CTR 30(6)-(8)

(g) under 18;

(h) on UC without any earned income;

(i) on SPC;

(j) on JSA(IB), ESA(IR), or IS;

(k) a youth trainee getting a training allowance;

(l) a full-time student;

(m) a disregarded person in table 15.4 (other than a student, youth trainee or an apprentice) – this includes education leavers, care leavers and people who are severely mentally impaired;

(n) a hospital in-patient for 52 weeks (including two or more periods in hospital separated by 28 days or less)

(o) in England and Scotland, a member of the armed forces who is away on operations.

Note:

■   There is no non-dependant contribution for someone who doesn't 'normally live' with you even if they eventually return (paras 3.71-72).

Main CTR if you are jointly liable

17.16   If you are jointly liable for council tax with someone other than your partner (para 15.16), the main CTR calculation (para 17.6) uses your share of the weekly council tax and of any non-dependant contributions:

(a) the weekly council tax on your house is shared equally between the jointly liable people except for any who are excluded students (para 16.31) – e.g. if there are three this is one third each, or if one is an excluded student it is half each for the other two;

(b) each non-dependant contribution is shared equally between whichever of you the non-dependant lives with – if they live only with you it applies wholly to you.

Main CTR for bands E to H in Scotland

17.17   If your home is in Scotland and in council tax band E to H, the following calculation is used (instead of the calculation in para 17.6) when it would give you more main CTR:

(d) start with:

■   7½% of your weekly council tax (para 17.7) if your home is in band E,

■   12½% if it is in band F,

■   17½% if it is in band G, or

■   22½% if it is in band H;

(e) if you have one or more non-dependants, subtract the amounts they are expected to contribute (para 17.13); and

---

17.16   CTP sch 1 paras 7(1),(3)-(5); CTR 29(1),(3)-(5)

17.17   CTS 14A; CTS66+ 14A

(f) if your net weekly income (para 17.34) is above the threshold of:

■ £321 (single people with no children of young persons), or

■ £479 (others),

subtract 20% of the excess.

Scotland has this rule because its council tax proportions are higher for these bands (table 15.1).

Second adult rebate

17.18   SAR applies:

(a) in Scotland whether you are working age or pension age;

(b) in England if you are pension age.

It doesn't apply in Wales (para 16.8) and working age CTR in England usually has different rules (paras 16.9-12).

Who can get SAR

17.19   You can get SAR if:

(a) you meet the liability condition (para 17.20);

(b) you have at least one second adult with a low enough income (paras 17.21-23);

(c) you don't have any lodgers who pay a commercial rent to live in part of your home;

(d) you aren't excluded due to an absence (para 16.25);

(e) you aren't an excluded migrant (para 16.30).

If you qualify for both main CTR and SAR, you get whichever of them is worth more.

SAR liability condition

17.20   You meet the SAR liability condition if:

(a) you are a sole householder (para 15.14); or

(b) you are a householder couple or two joint householders (paras 15.15-16) and:

■ one of you is a disregarded person (table 15.4), or

■ both of you are; or

(c) you are three or more joint householders (para 15.16) and:

■ all but one of you are disregarded persons, or

■ all of you are.

17.18   CTP 14(2), sch 1 para 4; CTR 15, 18

17.19   CTP sch 1 paras 4(1),(2), 9(1); CTR 15(1),(2), 18(1),(2), 31(1)

17.20   CTP sch 1 paras 4(2),(3), 9(2),(3); CTR 15(2),(3), 18(2),(3), 31(2),(3)

Second adults

17.21   A second adult is an adult (over 18) in your home who:

(a) is a non-dependant (para 15.9); but

(b) isn't a disregarded person (table 15.4).

Amount of SAR

17.22   If your second adult is on SPC, JSA (IB), ESA (IR) or IS your SAR is:

(a) 25% of your weekly council tax (para 17.24); or

(b) 100% of your weekly council tax if you (the claimant) are an excluded student (para 16.31).

When you have more than one second adult, they must all be on the benefits mentioned.

17.23   Otherwise, your SAR is:

(a) 7½% of your weekly council tax if your second adult's gross weekly income is below £279 pw in England or £273 pw in Scotland; or

(b) 15% of your weekly council tax if it is below £215 pw in England or £209 pw in Scotland.

A second adult's gross weekly income is worked out in the same way as in para 17.15. When your second adult is in a couple, both their incomes are combined. And when you have more than one second adult, all their gross weekly incomes are combined.

Weekly council tax for SAR

17.24   For SAR, your weekly council tax means the amount due on your home in the current benefit week (para 17.2) after any disability reduction but before any discount. (This ensures that discounts and SAR calculations are based on the same amount.)

SAR if you are jointly liable

17.25   If you are jointly liable for council tax with someone other than your partner (para 15.16), the result of the SAR calculation (paras 17.22-23) is shared equally between all of you. So, if there are three jointly liable people and two are a couple, the couple's share is two thirds.

Examples: Second adult rebate

1. A single person with one second adult

Dorinder has too much capital to qualify for main CTR. Her council tax is £36 per week. She has one second adult, her son, who works full-time and has gross income of £240 pw.

■ Weekly SAR of 7½% of council tax   £2.70

17.21   CTP sch 1 para 4(2),(3), sch 3 para 1(1); CTR 15(2),(3), 18(2),(3), sch 4 para 1(1)

17.22   CTP sch 1 paras 9(1), 10(4), sch 3 paras 1, 3; CTR 31(1), 32(4), sch 4 paras 1, 3

17.23   CTP sch 3 paras 1, 3; CTR sch 4 paras 1, 3

17.24   CTP sch 3 para 1(2); CTR sch 4 para 1(2)

17.25   CTP sch 1 para 9(2),(3) ; CTR 31(2),(3)

2. Discount plus SAR

Dan is a carer (table 15.4(g)). He cares for his mother who is a second adult and is on SPC. His council tax is £30 per week.

- Weekly discount of 25% of council tax   £7.50
- Plus weekly SAR of 25% of council tax   £7.50

Capital and income for main CTR

17.26   This section summarises the rules about assessing capital and income for main CTR. (For SAR, see instead para 17.15.) The full details are the same as HB (volume 2 chapters 13 to 15 and appendix 3) unless:

(a) you are on UC (para 17.9); or

(b) you have a working age claim in England and the council's local CTR scheme differs (paras 16.9-12).

Whose capital and income counts

17.27   If you are a single person, your own capital and income are taken into account. If you are a couple, your partner's capital and income are included with yours.

How capital and income are assessed

17.28   All your capital and income are disregarded (or you have no excess income: para 17.6) if you get:

(a) maximum UC; or

(b) the guarantee credit of SPC; or

(c) JSA(IB), ESA(IR) or IS.

17.29   The council uses the DWP's capital and income figures if you get:

(a) UC that is lower than the maximum; or

(b) the savings credit of SPC – but in this case the council adjusts the figures to take account of the higher income disregards in CTR (for the details, see volume 2 chapter 13).

17.30   In any other case, the council assesses capital and income as in paras 17.31-36.

Your capital

17.31   Capital means savings, investments, and other holdings. Some kinds are disregarded and in most cases, these are as in UC (table 10.6). The full details are the same as in HB (volume 2 chapter 15 and appendix 3).

17.32   If your capital is over £16,000 (the capital limit), you can't get main CTR.

17.27   CTP sch 1 para 11; CTR 33

17.28   CTP sch 1 para 13, CTR 28, 35, 37, sch 7 para 14, sch 8 paras 8, 9, sch 10 paras 8, 9

17.29   CTP sch 1 para 14(2) CTR 36(2), 37(1),(6)

17.30   CTP sch 1 para 15; CTR 38, 52(1), 54(1), 57(1), 61(1), 63

17.32   CTP 11(2),(3), sch 1 paras 2(d), 3(d), 4(d), sch 6 para 27; CTR 13(d), 14(d), 15(1)(d), 16(d), 17(d), 18(1)(d), 20, 23, sch 9 para 27, sch 10 para 49

17.33   If your capital is £16,000 or less, it is treated as giving you an assumed weekly income (tariff income) as follows:

   (a) for working age main CTR, deduct £6,000 and divide the remainder by 250;

   (b) for pension age main CTR, deduct £10,000 and divide the remainder by 500;

   (c) if the result of (a) or (b) isn't a multiple of £1, round it up to the next whole £1.

Your net weekly income

17.34   Your net weekly income is made up of:

   (a) earned income from employment or self-employment;

   (b) state, occupational and private pensions;

   (c) the savings credit of SPC;

   (d) JSA(C), ESA(C) and WTC;

   (e) CTC in working age claims; and

   (f) any other unearned income you have.

The amounts in table 17.3 are then disregarded.

Changes in income and capital

17.35   Changes in your income and capital are usually taken into account:

   (a) in England and Scotland, from the Monday following the change;

   (b) in Wales, from the exact day of the change.

Starting work and extended CTR

17.36   But in Scotland and Wales, you get four weeks' extended CTR if:

   (c) you have been on JSA, ESA or IS (not UC or SPC) for at least 26 weeks; and

   (d) this ends because you start work or increase your hours or earnings.

During those four weeks, your main CTR continues at the level it was beforehand.

17.33   CTP sch 1 para 37; CTR 71, 72

17.34   CTP sch 1 paras 14(2)(a), 16(1)(a)-(d),(j), 17(11),(13); CTR 36(2)(a), 39(1)(a)-(d),(j), 40(11),(13), 49(1), 54(1),(2)

17.35   CTP sch 1 para 46(1); CTR 107(1)

17.36   CTR 95-98

Table 17.3 **Main income disregards in main CTR**

Earned income

Your earned income is taken into account after deductions for tax, national insurance and 50% of any pension contributions you pay. The following amounts are then disregarded.

(a) A standard amount of:
- £5 for single people;
- £10 for couples;
- £20 for many disabled people; or
- £25 for lone parents.

(b) An amount for childcare costs of up to:
- £175 for one child; or
- £300 for two or more.

(c) An additional amount of £17.10 if:
- you work at least 30 hours a week; or
- you have one or more children/young persons or are disabled, and work at least 16 hours a week.

Unearned income

Your pensions, benefits and other unearned income are taken into account after any tax you pay on them. The following amounts are then disregarded.

(d) The guarantee credit of SPC.

(e) JSA(IB), ESA(IR) and IS.

(f) PIP, DLA, attendance allowance and equivalent benefits (para 10.37).

(g) CTC in pension age claims.

(h) Child benefit, guardian's allowance and widowed parent's allowance.

(i) HB and most other council payments.

(j) £10 of war disablement and war bereavement pensions – and many councils disregard part or all of the remainder.

T17.3(a)-(c) CTP sch 1 paras 19(2), 24(1)(c),(3), 29(2), 30(3), sch 4 paras 1-5, 8, 10;
CTR 42(2), 52(3), 57(1)(c),(3), 61(3), 62(3), sch 5 paras 1-5, 8, 10, sch 7 paras 4, 5, 11, 18

T17.3(d)-(n) CTP sch 1 para 17(13), CTR 40(13), sch 8 para 4

T17.3(d)-(h) CTP sch 1 paras 13, 16(1)(j)(i)-(vii); CTR 35, 39(1)(j)(i)-(vii), sch 8 paras 8, 9, 11, 14, 21, 52, 66

T17.3(i)   CTP sch 1 para 16(1)(j)(ix)-(xi); CTR 39(1)(j)(ix)-(xi), sch 8 paras 30-34, 37, 42, 64, 65

T17.3(j)   CTP sch 1 para 16(1)(e),(f),(l),(m), sch 5 paras 1-5, 13; CTR 39(1)(e),(f),(l),(m), sch 6 paras 1-5, 13, sch 8 para 20, 53-56

(k) If you have children/young persons:

  ■ maintenance you receive for them, and

  ■ £15 of maintenance you receive for you/your partner.

(l) £20 of rent you receive from a lodger in your home, and 50% of the remainder if you provide them with meals.

(m) Compensation payments for personal injury, charitable payments, and expenses payments for charitable or voluntary work.

(n) Payments from government sponsored trusts and funds relating to certain diseases, independent living for disabled people, and the London or Manchester bombings.

Note: For full details, see volume 2 chapters 13, 14.

T17.3(k)   CTP sch 1 para 16(1)(o), sch 5 para 20; CTR 39(1)(o), sch 6 para 20, sch 8 paras 49, 50

T17.3(l)   CTP sch 1 para 16(1)(p),(v), sch 5 paras 9, 10; CTR 39(1)(p),(v), sch 6 paras 9, 10, sch 8 paras 26, 27

T17.3(m)   CTP sch 1 paras 16(1)(s), 18(2)(f), sch 6 paras 12, 14, 15; CTR 39(1)(s), 41(2)(f), 51(2)(d), sch 6 paras 12, 14, 15, sch 8 paras 5, 6, 19

T17.3(n)   CTP sch 1 para 16(1); CTR 39(1), sch 8 para 41

Chapter 18 **CTR appeals and further reviews**

- How to get a CTR decision reconsidered in England and Wales: see paras 18.2-8.
- How to appeal to a Valuation Tribunal in England or Wales: see paras 18.9-18.
- How appeals are dealt with by the Valuation Tribunal and what happens afterwards: see paras 18.19-22.
- How to get a CTR decision reconsidered in Scotland: see paras 18.23-24.
- How to appeal to a CTR Review Panel in Scotland: see paras 18.25-29.
- How further reviews are dealt with by the Review Panel: see paras 18.30-38.

18.1 This chapter describes the different arrangements for appealing CTR decisions that apply in England, Scotland and Wales. See paras 18.2-22 for England and Wales and paras 18.23-38 for Scotland.

CTR appeals in England and Wales

Decision notices should include appeal rights

18.2 The CTR decision letter you get from the council should tell you how to appeal and point you to the appeal rules in your council's local CTR scheme (paras 16.16 and 18.6). In England and Wales CTR law refers to a person who has the right of appeal as a 'person aggrieved' and this reflects the fact that CTR appeals are dealt with in a similar way to appeals about council tax generally.

Getting a written explanation of the council's CTR decision

18.3 You can write to the council to ask for a written statement that sets out the reasons for any decision in its decision letter. Your request should be made within one month of the date of the council's decision letter. The council should send you its written statement of reasons within 14 days – or as soon as reasonably practicable after that.

Appealing to the council

18.4 A CTR decision is appealable if it affects:

(a) your entitlement to a reduction under the scheme; or

(b) the amount of any reduction that you are entitled to.

18.2   CTP sch 8 para 12(4),(7)-(8); CTR 117(4),(7)-(8); CTPW sch 14, para 3, sch 13 para 9(7)-(8); CTRW sch 10, para 3, 115(7)-(8)

18.3   CTP sch 8 para 12(5)-(6); CTR 117(5)-(6); CTPW sch 13 para 9(5)-(6); CTRW 115(5)-(6)

18.4-5 LGFA 16; CTP sch 7 para 8(1); CTR sch 1 para 8; CTPW sch 12 para 8(1); CTRW sch 1 para 8(1)

18.5   If you want to appeal you should write to the council identifying the matter in dispute. You should also say why you are appealing, e.g. the council has established the wrong facts, considered the wrong law (including the rules in its own local scheme), has misapplied the law to the facts, etc. To avoid any doubt that you are appealing, your letter should ask the council to treat your request as a 'notice of appeal under section 16 of the Local Government Finance Act 1992'.

Time limit to appeal to the council

18.6   CTR law in England (para 16.15) doesn't set a time limit in which your appeal should be made but there may (or may not) be a time limit in your local scheme rules.

18.7   In Wales your appeal should reach the council within one month of the date it issued its decision or, where you requested a statement of reasons, within one month of the date the statement of reasons was issued.

The council's response to your appeal

18.8   The council must consider the matters raised in your appeal. It should then write to you describing the steps it has taken to deal with the grievance. But if it thinks that the grounds for the grievance are not well founded, it should give you its reasons for thinking this.

Appealing to the Valuation Tribunal

18.9   If you are still dissatisfied with the council's response (para 18.8) you can appeal directly to the Valuation Tribunal. You can also do this if the council fails to respond to your appeal within two months from the date the council got it.

18.10   Guidance issued by the Valuation Tribunal in England is clear: you can appeal a decision about discretionary CTR to a valuation tribunal in the same way as any other kind of CTR [www] (and the same is true for Wales).

The Valuation Tribunal for England and the Valuation Tribunal for Wales

18.11   The administrative arrangements for valuation tribunals in England and Wales are slightly different:

   (a)   in England, CTR appeals are considered by the Valuation Tribunal for England and administrative arrangements are the responsibility of the Valuation Tribunal Service (paras 18.12-21);

18.7   CTPW sch 12 para 8(2); CTRW sch 1 para 8(2)

18.8   CTP sch 7 para 8(2); CTR sch 1 para 9; CTPW sch 12 para 9; CTRW sch 1 para 9

18.9   CTP sch 7 para 8(3); CTR sch 1 para 10; CTPW sch 12 para 10; CTRW sch 1 para 10

18.10   Council Tax Guidance Manual para 16.3.4
         https://tinyurl.com/CT-GM-2018
         Consolidated Practice Statement for the Valuation Tribunal for England (2017), PS 6
         https://tinyurl.com/VT-CPS-2017

(b) in Wales, appeals are considered by, and administered by, the Valuation Tribunal Service for Wales (paras 18.12-21).

More details can be found online [www]. In both England and Wales a further appeal (on a point of law if given permission) may be considered by the High Court.

18.12   The Valuation Tribunal is a free service and cannot award costs against you or the council. Members of the tribunal are volunteers and don't have to have any special qualifications, but they should have received training. Normally two or three members sit on a hearing. A clerk who is a paid official advises on points of law and procedure.

18.13   In England, a First-tier Tribunal (para 14.31) can act as members of the Valuation Tribunal in a CTR appeal on issues that relate to the assessment of income, capital or the right of residence (and sometimes in other cases involving difficult points of law). In these cases a First-tier Tribunal member sits with a senior member of the Valuation Tribunal to consider the appeal. Most other CTR appeals in England are normally considered by two Valuation Tribunal members.

Appeals about discretionary CTR

18.14   If you appeal a decision about discretionary CTR the tribunal isn't confined to making decisions solely within judicial review principles (due process, reasonableness, proportionality, legality, etc) and can substitute its view for that of the council provided it is 'soundly and solidly based': SC v East Riding of Yorkshire Council [www]. Even if the council's decision complies with its own published policy, this does not stop the tribunal from allowing the appeal, although it does make it less likely. (See Council Tax Guidance Manual [www].)

Procedural rules and practice statements/protocols

18.15   The tribunal's procedures are set out in the same regulations that govern appeals about other council tax matters (para 15.33). In England the regulations are supplemented by practice statements and in Wales by practice protocols. The details and further information are:

(a) In England, the Valuation Tribunal for England (Council Tax and Rating Appeals) (Procedure) Regulations SI 2009 No 2269 (as amended) and (for CTR appeals) SI 2013 No 465. Practice statements can be found online [www]. In particular, Practice Statement VTE/PS/A11 contains important information and standard directions for both you and the council.

(b) In Wales, the Valuation Tribunal for Wales Regulations SI 2010 No 713 (as amended) (and for CTR appeals) SI 2013 No 547. Practice protocols can be found online [www].

18.11   www.valuationtribunal.gov.uk/ www.valuationtribunal.wales

18.13   Local Government Finance Act 1988 s136, sch 11 para A18A (as amended by Local Government Finance Act 2012, sch 4 para 2)

18.14   SC v East Riding of Yorkshire Council [2014]) EW Misc B46 (UT) www.bailii.org/ew/cases/cases/Misc/B46.html
        Council Tax Guidance Manual para 16, Consolidated Practice Statement, PS6, PS10, PS11 (see footnote 18.10)

18.15   See Consolidated Practice Statement (footnote 18.10)
        www.valuationtribunal.wales/best-practice-protocols.html

The time limits in which to make your appeal to the tribunal

18.16   You should normally make your appeal to the tribunal within:

(a) the two months following the date the council responded to your initial appeal; or

(b) the four months following the date your initial representation is made if the council fails to respond to it.

Your appeal may be allowed out of time appeal if your failure to make it was due to circumstances beyond your control such as illness, absence from home or bereavement. A practice statement and protocol sets out how your application should be made and the relevant considerations [www].

Making an appeal

18.17   You appeal to the tribunal by writing directly to it. Appeal forms and guidance notes are available online [www]. Further details about how and where to appeal are in table 18.1.

Table 18.1 **How and where to appeal CTR**

England	
How:	In writing by post or by email
Where:	Valuation Tribunal CTR Team
	Hepworth House
	2 Trafford Court
	Doncaster DN1 1PN
	appeals@vts.gsi.gov.uk
Contact for administrative matters:	0300 123 1033
Wales	
How:	Online form (or downloaded)
Where:	The appropriate regional office (if downloaded)
Contact for administrative matters:	See guidance notes (para 18.17)
Scotland	
How:	In writing by post. (Download form recommended)
Where:	CTR Review Panel
	4th Floor, 1 Atlantic Quay
	45 Robertson Street
	Glasgow, G2 8JB.
Contact for administrative matters:	0141 302 5840
	CTRRPAdmin@scotcourtstribunals.gov.uk

18.16   SI 2009/2269 reg 21(2)-(3),(6); SI 2010/713 reg 29(1)-(2),(5)
         https://tinyurl.com/VT-CPS-2017 PS1 (Extension of time)
         www.valuationtribunal.wales/best-practice-protocols.html

18.17   www.valuationtribunal.gov.uk/forms/appeal-forms/council-tax-reduction-2/
         www.valuationtribunal.wales/council-tax-reduction.html

18.18 Your appeal should include the following information:

(a) your full name and address;

(b) the address of the relevant chargeable dwelling – if different from your address;

(c) the relevant council's name – and the date on which your initial appeal was served on it;

(d) the date, (if any) that you were notified of the council's response;

(e) the grounds on which you are aggrieved;

(f) brief reasons why you think that the decision or calculation made by the council is incorrect.

If you have also appealed your HB about the same matter to the First-tier Tribunal, you should tell the Valuation Tribunal about this when you appeal your CTR. In Wales your HB appeal letter should be included with your CTR appeal. The clerk should acknowledge receipt of your appeal within two weeks and send a copy of it to the council.

How appeals are dealt with

18.19 Appeals are normally heard unless you and the council agree agree it can dealt with on the papers and the tribunal considers it appropriate. You should normally be given at least 14 days (in Wales four weeks) notice of the time and place of hearing. In England shorter notice than the 14 days may be given in urgent or exceptional circumstances. Hearings are normally held in public so it is possible for you to attend a hearing as an observer to see a tribunal in action. You may be accompanied to your own hearing by someone else. That other person may act as your representative or otherwise assist you in presenting your case. The tribunal itself decides what form the hearing should take (subject to the rules of natural justice). It may give a decision orally at a hearing.

Decision notice and statement of reasons

18.20 The tribunal should provide you with a notice of its decision as soon as reasonably practicable. It should also explain your right to request a written statement of reasons (if not given with the decision) and any right of appeal. In Wales the decision notice should be accompanied by a statement of reasons.

18.21 In England, if you want to ask for a statement of reasons (and it has not been supplied with the decision notice) the tribunal should get your request within two weeks of the date of its decision notice (although it does have the power to extend this period). The statement of reasons should be sent to you (and the council) within two weeks of the request being made or as soon as reasonably practicable thereafter.

18.18　England: SI 2009/2269 regs 20A, 28(2)
　　　　Wales: SI 2010/713 reg 30(1),(2),(5)

18.19　England: SI 2009/2269 regs 2, 29, 30, 31, 36(1)
　　　　Wales: SI 2010/713 regs 33(1),(6); 34(1); 36, 37, 40(2)

18.20　England: SI 2009/2269 reg 36(2)
　　　　Wales: SI 2010/713 reg 40(3)

18.21　SI 2009/2269 reg 37(3)-(7)

After the decision

18.22   The tribunal has the power to correct clerical mistakes, accidental slips and omissions and also to review its decision in specific circumstances. A further appeal to the High Court may only be made on a point of law (para 14.63). It should normally be made within four weeks of the decision notice being issued or, in England, within two weeks of the statement of reasons being issued if later. You should get legal advice before embarking on this course of action.

Scotland: CTR reviews and further reviews

Asking the council to review its decision

18.23   In Scotland if you are dissatisfied with your council's decision about your CTR you can write to it and ask it to review its decision. Your request should get to the council within two months of the date its decision was sent to you. You should set out what you are dissatisfied with and why.

The council's actions on receipt of your review request

18.24   On receipt of your review request the council should:

   (a) consider the issue(s) identified in your request,

   (b) decide if it is going to change the decision you are dissatisfied with (this should be done within two months of getting the request from you);

   (c) tell you in writing about its decision; and

   (d) tell you that if you remain dissatisfied you can request a further review, the address to which this should be sent, and the time period in which this must be done (42 days from the date of the council's letter).

Requesting a further review by the CTR Review Panel

18.25   If you are dissatisfied with the council's decision following its review (para 18.24) you, or your representative, can request a further review by writing directly to the CTR Review Panel (table 18.1). Application forms, are available online [www], or from the Review Panel itself (table 18.1) and the Review Panel strongly recommends that you use the form provided to make your application. Your application must be received within six weeks (42 days) from the date of the council's written response to your review request.

18.26   You can also ask for a further review if the council fails to respond to your initial review request and more than two months have passed since they got it. In these circumstances, your

---

18.22   SI 2009/2269 regs 39, 40; SI 2010/713 regs 43(1)-(2); 42, 44(1)-(2)

18.23   CTS 90A(2)-(3); CTS66+ 70A(2)-(3)

18.24   CTS 90A(4); CTS66+ 70A(4)

18.25   https://counciltaxreductionreview.scotland.gov.uk/apply.htm
         CTS 90B(1); CTS66+ 70B(1)

18.26   CTS 90B(2)-(3) (5); CTS66+ 70B(2)-(3) (5)

request for a further review should be sent in writing to the council. The council cannot write to you about any decision on your initial review and must pass on your request for a further review to the CTR Review Panel as soon as possible.

18.27   Your request for a further review should set out the matter(s) you are dissatisfied with, the reasons why and include a copy of the authority's CTR internal review decision notice (if there is one).

The CTR Review Panel

18.28   The Review Panel is appointed by a Scottish Cabinet Secretary. One of the panel must also be appointed as senior reviewer. To be appointed, members of the panel have to be solicitors or advocates with at least five years' experience. A further review is normally carried out by a single member Review Panel, though in particular circumstances a three member Review Panel may undertake the review. Administrative arrangements are by the Scottish Courts and Tribunal Service.

The council's response to your further review application

18.29   If the Review Panel decides that your application is complete and valid, it writes to the council, informing it of your request. The council's response should normally be submitted within six weeks (42 days). It should contain all the material it wishes the Review Panel to consider. The council should also forward a copy of its submission to you at this time. If the Review Panel does not get a response from the council within the six weeks, it has the power to exclude the council from any further participation in the proceedings and allow your   · application [www].

How further reviews are dealt with

18.30   The responsible panel member:

  (a) decides the procedure to be adopted for the further review (having regard to any guidance issued by the senior reviewer);

  (b) can hold any oral hearing in public or private;

  (c) can ask for, but has no power to require, the production of documents or the attendance of anyone as a witness;

  (d) can refuse to allow a particular person to represent you at an oral hearing if there are good and sufficient reasons for doing so.

18.31   The further review should be by way of an oral hearing unless you, the council and the panel member agree that it should be dealt with on the papers. If the panel member asks you about it being dealt with this way, you and the council must tell them whether you both

---

18.27   CTS 90B(4); CTS66+ 70B(4)

18.28   CTS 90C(1)-(2), 90D(1), 90D(8) ; CTS66+ 70C(1), 70C(8)
         https://counciltaxreductionreview.scotland.gov.uk/

18.29   CTS 90D(4); CTS66+ 70C(4)
         https://tinyurl.com/CTRP-LA-Guidance-Note-2020

18.30   CTS 90D(6); CTS66+ 70C(6)

18.31   CTS 90D(2)-(3); CTS66+ 70C(2)-(3)

agree to it or not. You should also tell the panel member if you have disputed the equivalent housing benefit decision and if it has already been decided on appeal.

18.32 If you or the council are asked by the panel member to provide documents or information and fail to respond within the time limits set, the panel member may draw any inference from this failure they see fit. This can include allowing or refusing the further review.

Withdrawing your request for further review

18.33 You can withdraw your request for further review only with the permission of the senior reviewer.

The decision

18.34 The panel member reaches a decision in private after the hearing. The decision can be to allow or reject your request, in full or in part. It is either given on the day or sent out in the post, depending on the circumstances of the case. Any re-calculation of your CTR entitlement is carried out by the council.

18.35 If you had an oral hearing, a letter setting out the panel member's decision is given or posted to you and to the council on the day of the hearing. If your case has been decided on the papers, you should get a letter through the post a day or two after the decision has been made. A copy of the decision is also sent to the council.

18.36 Both you and the council are entitled to a full statement of reasons for the decision. You can request this by writing to the Review Panel, at the address above, within 14 days of the date on which the decision was given. You should quote your CTR RP reference number [www]. You or the council may also request a set-aside of the decision in the interests of justice. This should be done within 14 days of the date the decision was made. You should give reasons for the request. Where a panel member decides to set aside the decision the further review must be carried out again.

After the Review Panel's further review

18.37 The council should carry out any necessary re-calculation of the amount of your CTR entitlement and put into effect the Review Panel's decision as soon as reasonably practicable. Any queries you have about how the decision is implemented should be addressed to the council [www].

18.38 There is no right of appeal against the Review Panel's decision [www] but it would presumably be susceptible to judicial review. You should get legal advice about this.

18.32   CTS 90D(4); CTS66+ 70C(4)

18.33   CTS 90D(5); CTS66+ 70C(5)

18.34   CTS 90D(6)(e); CTS66+ 70C(6)(e)

18.36   CTS 90D(6)(f),(6A)-(6C); CTS66+ 70C(6)(f),(6A)-(6C)
          Guidance note for Local Authorities (see footnote 18.29)

18.37   CTS 90D(7); CTS66+ 70C(7)
          https://tinyurl.com/CTRP-FAQ-2020

18.38   https://tinyurl.com/CTRP-FAQ-2020

Chapter 19 **Rate rebates**

- Rates, exemptions and disability reductions: see paras 19.1-10.
- Rate rebates general rules: see paras 19.11-17.
- UC rate rebates: see paras 19.18-35.
- HB rate rebates: see paras 19.36-57.

Rates

19.1 This chapter describes who is liable for domestic rates and the different ways your rates bill can be reduced. Rates only apply in Northern Ireland and are administered by Land and Property Services (LPS).

Dwellings

19.2 There is one rates bill per dwelling. A dwelling means a single residential property, for example a house, flat, a houseboat or a mobile home.

Who is liable to pay rates

19.3 The rates bill for your home goes to:

(a) you if you are an occupier or shared owner;

(b) your landlord if you are an NIHE or housing association tenant;

(c) your landlord if you are a private tenant and the dwelling you live in:

- is a house in multiple occupation (HMO), or
- is let as separate lodgings or apartments, or
- has a capital value less than (or equal to) £1,500,000;

(d) you if you are a private tenant in any other case.

19.4 If you are a tenant and the rates bill goes to your landlord, your rent is treated as including rates even if your landlord hasn't said this.

The amount of your rates bill

19.5 Rates bills are issued by LPS and run from 1st April to 31st March. The bill for your home is calculated using:

(a) its rateable value if you are an owner occupier, shared owner or private tenant – this is based on its purchase price in January 2005, capped at £400,000; or

(b) its social sector value if you are an NIHE or housing association tenant – this is assessed by DFC based on the rent you pay.

19.2   RO 4, sch 5 para 1
19.3   RO 20, 25 sch 8
19.4   RO 23A, 24, 25

The annual amount equals (a) or (b) multiplied by the rate poundage for the district you live in. Or if you are only liable for part of a year this is calculated on a daily basis. Your rates bill shows these figures along with any reduction or rebate you qualify for.

Reducing your rates

19.6   You can get help with your rates if you qualify for:

(a) an exemption (para 19.8);

(b) a disability reduction (para 19.9)

(c) a rate rebate (para 19.11).

19.7   All these apply whether you are an owner occupier, shared owner or tenant (paras 19.3-4). If you are a tenant, you can get a rate rebate towards your rates as well as UC or HB towards your rent.

Exemptions

19.8   The main kinds of exemptions are for:

(a) occupied dwellings whose landlord is a registered charity;

(b) some unoccupied dwellings.

In these cases, no-one has to pay rates on the dwelling. An unoccupied dwelling is exempt in similar circumstances to those in table 15.3(d),(h),(j) for council tax (and some other situations). In any other case the rates payable are half for unoccupied dwellings.

Disability reductions

19.9   You qualify for disability reduction equal to 25% of your rates bill if:

(a) you are disabled, or at least one disabled adult or child has their home with you; and

(b) your home provides:

  ■ an additional kitchen or bathroom for the disabled person's use; or

  ■ an additional room (not a kitchen, bathroom or toilet) used predominantly to meet their special needs; or

  ■ sufficient floor space to use a wheelchair if they need one; and

(c) this is of major importance to them, taking account of the nature and extent of their disability.

Your home doesn't need to have been specifically adapted. For example, it could be that the disabled person has to have a separate bedroom or a bedroom downstairs.

19.5   RO 6(1),(3), 17(1)(b), 18(2), 23A, 39(1A)-(1C), sch 12 paras 7-12, 16
         The Rates (Social Sector Value) Regulations (Northern Ireland) 2007 No. 86
         The Rates (Maximum Capital Value) Regulations (Northern Ireland) 2007 No. 184; NISR 2009/77
         Rateable value: https://lpsni.gov.uk/vListDCV/search.asp?submit=form
         https://www.finance-ni.gov.uk/topics/property-rating/rate-poundages

19.6   RO 30A, 31A, sch 7 paras 1(b), 2(2)

19.8   RO 25A, 41 sch 7 paras 1(b), 2(2), 3, sch 8A paras 1(1)-(3), 2(2)
         The Rates (Unoccupied Hereditaments) Regulations (Northern Ireland) 2011 S.R. 2011 No. 36, reg 3, sch paras 6, 10, 11, 12, 17

19.9   RO 31A(2),(3),(10)

Reconsiderations and appeals

19.10   You can ask LPS to reconsider any decision it has made about your rates, e.g. whether you are liable and whether you qualify for a disability reduction. You normally have 28 days to do this. After that you can appeal to a Valuation Tribunal about most decisions and should normally do this within one month.

Rate rebates

19.11   Rate rebates are divided into:

(a) UC rate rebate; and

(b) three kinds of HB rate rebate:

   ■   standard rate rebate,

   ■   supplementary rate rebate, and

   ■   lone pensioner rate rebate.

The law refers to some of these as different types of 'rate relief'.

Who can get a rate rebate

19.12   The main rules are:

(a) if you have a working age claim and are on UC, you can get a UC rate rebate (para 19.18); or

(b) if you have a working age claim and aren't on UC, you can't get any kind of rate rebate unless you have an old claim (para 19.46);

(c) if you have a pension age claim, you can get one or more of the HB rate rebates (para 19.36).

The detailed conditions are in the rest of this chapter.

Working age and pension age claims

19.13   You have a working age claim if you are under 66 or are in a couple and at least one of you is. You have a pension age claim if you are aged 66 or over, or in a couple and both of you are.

19.10   RO 31(11A),(12),(12A),(12B)
         The Valuation Tribunal Rules (Northern Ireland) 2007 No 182, Reg 5(b)

19.11   RO 30A, NICBA 129

19.12   RO 9(1)(b),(2), NICBA 129, RR 10, NIUC 3, NIUCTP 3-6, NIHB 12, NIHB66+ 12; RRLPA 3(1),(3)

19.13   State Pension Credit Act (Northern Ireland) 2002, 1(6); NIHB 5(1); NIHB66+ 5(1)

Your home

19.14   You can only get a rate rebate on:

(a)   your home – this means the dwelling where you live or mainly live (paras 5.16, 5.19 for UC rate rebates; volume 2 chapter 3 for HB rate rebates); or

(b)   two homes if you have a large family and rent from a social landlord or in other limited situations (para 5.31 for UC rate rebates; volume 2 chapter 3 for HB rate rebates). But you can only get a lone pensioner allowance on one home.

However, only (a) applies in the case of lone pensioner rate rebate.

Your monthly/weekly rates

19.15   Rate rebates are based on:

(a)   the monthly or weekly rates on your home (para 19.16) after any disability reduction that applies; or

(b)   your share of (a) if you are a joint householder or have a resident landlord or tenant – this is decided by the number of people, how much each pays and other relevant factors; or

(c)   the domestic share of (a) if your rates bill also includes business premises (e.g. if you live over your shop) – this is decided by floor areas.

19.16   For UC rate rebates your monthly rates equal the annual amount divided by 12. For HB rate rebates, your weekly rates equal:

(a)   the annual amount divided by 365 and multiplied by seven; or

(b)   if your landlord gets the rates bill (para 19.3), the annual amount divided by 52.

Example: Annual and weekly rates

A dwelling has a capital value of £135,000 in an area where the rate poundage is £0.0057777 per £1 of capital value. Capping does not apply so the annual rates (paras 19.5, 19.16) are:

$$£135,000 \times 0.0057777 = £780.00$$

The weekly eligible rates (to the nearest 1p) are therefore:

£780.00 ÷ 365 × 7	£14.96 if paid separately from rent or
£780.00 ÷ 52	£15.00 if paid along with rent

Excluded groups

19.17   Except for a lone pensioner allowance you can't get a rate rebate if:

(a)   you are an excluded migrant (para 20.2); or

(b)   you are an excluded student (para 2.19 for UC rate rebates; volume 1 chapter 2 for HB rate rebates); or

---

19.14   RR 10(1)(a), 28-35; NIHB 7; NIHB66+ 7; RRHB 11; RRHB66+ 11; RRLPA 3(2),(4)

19.15   RR 11(2),(3), NIHB 12(2)-(6); RRHB 14; NIHB66+ 12(2)-(6); RRHB66+ 14

19.16   RR 12; NIHB 78, 79; RRHB 24; NIHB66+ 59, 60; RRHB66+ 23

(c) you are absent from home or from Northern Ireland for longer than the time limits – these range from one to 12 months for UC rate rebates (paras 2.29-35, 5.18-25) or from 13 to 52 weeks for HB rate rebates (volume 2 chapter 3); or

(d) you are a tenant and have a resident landlord who is your close relative (table 5.4(k): terminology); or

(e) your rates liability was contrived to obtain an increase in your rate rebate; or

(f) your home is a care home or independent hospital.

However, none of these apply in the case of lone pensioner rate rebate.

UC rate rebates

19.18   UC rate rebates are for people on UC. They are awarded for monthly assessment periods (para 19.29) and are based on UC law.

Who can get UC rate rebate

19.19   You can get a UC rate rebate if:

(a) you are on UC;

(b) you are liable for rates on your home (paras 19.3-4); and

(c) you aren't in an excluded group (para 19.17).

How much UC rate rebate

19.20   To calculate your monthly UC rate rebate:

(a) start with the monthly rates on your home, or your share of them (para 19.15);

(b) if you have excess income (para 19.21) subtract 15% of it.

Non-dependants aren't expected to contribute.

Excess income for UC rate rebates

19.21   You only have excess income if you have earnings. Your excess income equals:

(a) 37% of your earnings, after deducting a work allowance if you qualify for one (para 10.13);

(b) plus 50% of your work allowance if you qualify for one;

(c) minus any payment in lieu of notice or holiday pay (i.e. when notice is not worked or holidays not taken).

LPS always uses the DFC's figures for (a) and (b), but you need to tell LPS about (c).

19.17   IAA99 115; NIWRO 8-10; NICBA 129; RR 10(1),11(4), 28-35; NIHB 7, 9, 10, 53; RRHB 11-13, 21; NIHB66+ 7, 9, 10; RRHB66+ 11-13

19.19   RO 30A(3)(a); RR 10(1)-(3), 28(1)

19.20   RR 10(3)(b)

19.21   RR 10(7); NISR 2020/308

Examples: UC rate rebates

1. A single person on UC with no other income

Leon is on UC and has no other income. His rates are £780.00 for the year.

■	Monthly rates	£65.00
■	Equals monthly rate rebate	£65.00

2. A couple on UC with unearned income

Eleanor and James are on UC and Eleanor receives a private pension. The pension is ignored for UC rate rebate (19.22). Their rates are £840.00 for the year.

■	Monthly rates	£70.00
■	Equals monthly rate rebate	£70.00

3. A couple on UC with earnings (no work allowance)

Vijay and Kelly are on UC and have earnings. They don't qualify for a UC work allowance. Their earnings are £600 per month, and their rates are £1020.00 for the year.

■	37% of earnings above the work allowance (para 19.21)	£222.00
■	Equals excess income	£222.00
■	Monthly rates	£85.00
■	Minus 15% of excess income	−£33.30
■	Equals monthly rate rebate	£61.70

4. A single person on UC with earnings (and work allowance)

Cherelle is on UC and has earnings. She has two children so qualifies for a UC work allowance of £293. Her earnings are £693 per month (too low for tax or national insurance), leaving £400 after the work allowance is deducted. Her rates are £600.00 for the year.

■	37% of earnings above the work allowance (para 19.21)	£148.00
■	Plus 50% of work allowance (para 19.22)	£146.00
■	Equals excess income	£294.00
■	Monthly rates	£50.00
■	Minus 15% of excess income	−£44.10
■	Equals monthly rate rebate	£5.90

19.22   The excess income calculation in para 19.21:

(a) uses 37% of your earnings because the other 63% is used in your UC (para 9.8);

(b) adds back 50% of the work allowance because all of it is allowed in UC but only half is allowed in UC rate rebates;

(c) doesn't use any of your unearned income because all of it is used in your UC (para 9.8).

19.23   Rate rebate law expresses this in a more complicated way, saying your excess income equals:

(a)   your earnings (after the work allowance), unearned income and UC; minus

(b)   your maximum UC.

But because of how UC and maximum UC are calculated (paras 9.8, 9.4), the calculation method in para 19.21 gives the same result with fewer steps.

Claims

19.24   To get a UC rate rebate you have to make a claim to Land and Property Services (LPS). This is the case even if you are claiming UC at the same time. If your entitlement to rebate changes before LPS decides your claim you are treated as having made multiple claims.

19.25   You make your claim by creating an online rate rebate account [www], giving your name and address and agreeing LPS can obtain your earnings and other information from DFC. If you are a couple, one of you makes the claim on behalf of you both.

19.26   If there are breaks in your UC, your rate rebate claim covers each period you are on UC, but only until LPS confirms your rate rebate award. After that you have to reclaim rate rebate each time you go back on UC.

Information and evidence

19.27   If LPS needs any further information and evidence, it can request this when you claim or at any time during your rate rebate award. You have one month to provide it or longer if LPS agrees.

Help with claiming

19.28   You can ask LPS or an advice organisation to help with your claim or ask a family member or friend [www]. If LPS believes you need support it must arrange to assist you. If you can't manage your financial affairs an attorney can claim for you.

Assessment periods

19.29   UC rate rebates are calculated and paid for monthly assessment periods (in rate rebate law called 'attribution periods'). The first one begins on the day your rebate starts, so UC and UC rate rebate assessment periods are often the same (para 19.30(a)).

19.24   RR 3

19.25   RR 3(2), 36
         https://www.nidirect.gov.uk/services/create-or-log-in-to-a-rate-rebate-account

19.26   RR 5(6), sch para 2(6)

19.26   RR 5(12)

19.27   RR 3(3), 4
         https://www.nidirect.gov.uk/articles/getting-help-your-rate-rebate-claim

19.28   RR 5(1), 6, 12

The date your rate rebate starts

19.30   Your UC rate rebate starts:

(a)   on the same day your UC starts, if you make your rebate claim:

■   within three months of your first payment of UC, or

■   within 48 hours of the LPS computer system becoming available, if it wasn't available on the last day of the three months;

(b)   on the first day of a new rates bill that follows the death of your partner, if you make your rebate claim within one month of it being issued;

(c)   on the day you make your rebate claim in any other case.

The date your rebate changes or ends

19.31   Table 19.1 shows when your UC rate rebate changes or ends. This can be at the beginning of an assessment period or it can be part way through, in which case it is calculated daily both up to and after the change occurs (see examples).

Examples: UC rate rebate changes and revised awards

1. Increase in earnings

A single claimant with earned income is awarded a UC rate rebate from 15th June 2021. Based on the DFC's income figures, she is awarded a rebate of £30.00 per month. On 23rd September her earnings increase; based on the new DFC income figures her rebate would be £15.00 per month. Her UC rate rebate does not change until the next assessment period following the anniversary date of her claim: 15th July 2022.

2. Award of HB

A single claimant claims and is awarded a UC rate rebate on 1st April 2021 when she claims UC. Her rates are £840 per year. On 13th November she reaches pension age and claims SPC and HB rate rebate. Her HB rate rebate starts on Monday 17th November. Her UC rate rebate ends on 16th November and for the assessment period 1st-31st November is

£70 x 16/31 = £36.13.

Table 19.1 **When UC rate rebates change**

Specific change (increase or decrease)

(a) A change in earned income	The start of the assessment period that immediately follows the anniversary date of claim
(b) UC award ends	The day after your last day of entitlement to UC

19.30   RR 5, 6
19.31   RR 14,16

(c) Change in rateable value notified within three months of the revaluation	The date the new rateable value applies from
Other changes resulting in a higher award	
(d) Official error or the wrong UC figures	Date of the original decision
(e) Error due to a mistaken fact notified within three months or which the authority already had sufficient information to identify it	Date of the original decision
(f) Other changes in your circumstances (except as in (g))	Date the change occurs
(g) Other changes that are notified later than three months or that you fail to notify	Date you notify LPS of the change or the date it is first identified
Any other change resulting in a lower award	
(h) Error due to mistaken fact	Date of the original decision
(i) Any other change of circumstance (i.e. reduced award)	Date the change occurs

Payments and overpayments

19.32   Your UC rate rebate is awarded (or 'paid') by crediting it to your rates account if you get the rates bill, or your landlord's if your landlord does (para 19.3) [www]. LPS normally corrects any errors by:

(a) crediting that rates account if you've been paid too little rebate; or

(b) deducting rebate from that rates account if you have been paid too much – so you have more rates to pay.

Decision notices

19.33   LPS provides an online decision when your circumstances change. This says how much you qualify for (or that you don't qualify).

Reconsiderations and appeals

19.34   You can ask LPS to reconsider any decision it has made about your UC rate rebate, e.g. whether you qualify and how much for. You normally have three months to do this.

T19.1   RR 14

19.32   RR 21-27 https://tinyurl.com/UC-rate-rebates

19.33   RR 17(1)

19.34   RR 17(2)

19.35   After that you can appeal to a valuation tribunal and should do this within three months. But your appeal can only be about whether you occupy somewhere as your home in the situations in paras 5.21-23, 5.30-31. This is because other UC rate rebate matters (e.g. your earnings) are decided as part of your UC, so you need to use the UC appeal procedure about them (para 14.31).

HB rate rebates

19.36   HB rate rebates are for people who have a pension age claim (para 19.13) or an old working age claim (para 19.46). They are awarded for benefit weeks (para 19.52) and are based on HB law.

Kinds of HB rate rebate

19.37   HB rate rebates are made up of:

  (a) standard rate rebates (para 19.38;

  (b) supplementary rate rebates (para 19.41); and

  (c) lone pensioner rate rebates (para 19.44).

Some people qualify for one or two of these and some people qualify for all three. They are calculated in the order shown and your HB rate rebate is the total of (a), (b) and/or (c).

Who can get standard rate rebate

19.38   You can get a standard rate rebate if:

  (a) you have a pension age claim (para 19.13) or an old working age claim (para 19.46);

  (b) you are liable for rates on your home (paras 19.3-4);

  (c) you aren't in an excluded group (para 19.17); and

  (d) your capital isn't over £16,000.

How much standard rate rebate

19.39   To calculate your weekly standard rate rebate:

  (a) start with the weekly rates on your home, or your share of them (para 19.15);

  (b) if you have one or more non-dependants, subtract the amount they are expected to contribute (para 19.47);

  (c) if you have excess income (para 19.40) subtract 20% of it.

19.35   RR 18

19.36-37 NICBA 129; RO 30A; NIUCTP 3-6; NIHB 12; RRHB 7, 14; NIHB66+ 12; RRHB66+ 7, 14; RRLPA 3(1),(3)

19.38   IAA99 115; NICBA 129(1),(3), 130; NIHB 7, 9, 10, 12, 40, 53; NIHB66+ 7, 9, 10, 12, 41

19.39   NIHB 12, 68, 69, 78, 79; NIHB66+ 12, 48, 49, 59, 60

19.40   For standard rate rebates, your excess income equals:

(a) your weekly income;

(b) minus your weekly applicable amount.

Your applicable amount, income and capital are assessed in the same way as for HB (volume 1 chapters 12-15).

Who can get supplementary rate rebate

19.41   You can get a supplementary rate rebate if:

(a) you have a pension age claim (para 19.13) or an old working age claim (para 19.46);

(b) you are liable for rates on your home (paras 19.3-4);

(c) you aren't in an excluded group (para 19.17); and

(d) your capital isn't over £50,000 (pension age claims) or £16,000 (old working age claims).

How much supplementary rate rebate

19.42   To calculate your weekly supplementary rate rebate:

(a) start with the weekly rates on your home, or your share of them (para 19.15);

(b) if you qualify for standard rate rebate (para 19.39) subtract that;

(c) if you have one or more non-dependants, subtract the amount they are expected to contribute (para 19.47);

(d) if you have excess income (para 19.43) subtract 12% of it.

19.43   For supplementary rate rebates, your excess income equals:

(a) your weekly income;

(b) minus your weekly applicable amount adjusted as follows:

- if you or your partner are aged 66 or over, the personal allowance is £219.82 for a single person or £314.66 for a couple,

- the carer premium is £45.24

Apart from the adjustments in (b), your applicable amount, income and capital are assessed in the same way as for HB (volume 2 chapters 12-15).

19.40   NICBA 129(3)(b)

19.41   IAA99 115; RO 30A; NISR 2008/68; RRHB 7, 9-13, 19(1)(q); RRHB66+ 7, 9-13, 19(1)(o)

19.42   RRHB 22, 23; RRHB66+ 21, 22

19.43   NISR 2011/43 regs 2(3)(b), 3(3)(b); RRHB 17(2)(g), 23; RRHB66+ 17(2)(c),(e), 22; NISR 2007/244 reg 2

Who can get a lone pensioner rate rebate

19.44   You can get a lone pensioner rate rebate if:

(a)   you are aged 70 or over;

(b)   you live alone, apart from anyone who:

- is aged under 18, or

- is a young person aged 18-20 years (para 3.64), or

- has a medical certificate confirming they have a severe impairment of intelligence and social functioning, or

- is providing you with care or who is receiving care from you and you both meet the conditions in table 15.4(g));

(c)   you are liable for rates on your home (paras 19.3-4);

(d)   you make a claim for it; and

(e)   you still have some rates to pay after deducting any standard and/or supplementary rate rebate you qualify for (para 19.45).

There is no capital limit; your income and capital are ignored.

How much lone pensioner rate rebate

19.45   To calculate your weekly lone pensioner rate rebate:

(a)   start with the weekly rates on your home, or your share of them (para 19.15);

(b)   if you qualify for standard and/or supplementary rate rebate (paras 19.39, 19.42) subtract them;

(c)   multiply the remainder by 20%.

Examples: HB rate rebates

1. Standard rate rebate

Charlie and Miriam are on SPC. Their rates are £18.00 per week. They have one non-dependant, their son, who works full time and has gross income of £250.00 per week.

- Weekly rates   £18.00

- Minus non-dependant contribution   −£6.55

- Equals weekly standard rate rebate   £11.45

Charlie and Miriam are on a 'full rebate', so they don't get a supplementary rate rebate.

2. Standard and supplementary rate rebate

Josef is a single person who works part time during his retirement. His rates are £22.00 per week. He has one non-dependant, his sister, who has a private pension and doesn't work. Josef's excess income is assessed as being £27.00 per week. First, he is considered for a standard rate rebate:

19.44   RO 30A; RRLPA 3(1),(3), sch paras 1-7

19.45   RRLPA 8

- Weekly rates   £22.00
- Minus non-dependant contribution   −£3.30
- Minus 20% of excess income   −£5.40
- Equals weekly HB rate rebate   £13.30

Then he is considered for a supplementary rate rebate:

- Weekly rates   £22.00
- Minus standard rate rebate   −£13.30
- Minus non-dependant contribution   −£3.30
- Minus 12% of excess income   −£3.24
- Equals supplementary rate rebate   £2.16

Josef's total weekly HB rate rebate is:

- £13.30 + £2.16   £15.46

3. Lone pensioner rate rebate

Enda is aged 70 and lives alone. Her rates are £17.00 per week. She has capital of over £50,000 so can't get a standard or supplementary rate rebate.

- 20% of weekly rates   £3.40
- Equals lone pensioner rebate   £3.40

Old working age claims

19.46   Until 5th December 2018, people of any age could get HB rate rebates. If you are working age and claimed before that date:

(a) you continue to be eligible for any of the kinds of HB rate rebate for as long as you are getting at least one of them;

(b) you stop being eligible for all of them if:

- they all end, or
- you are awarded UC, or
- you claim UC and meet its basic conditions (table 2.1) but don't qualify due to the level of your income.

Non-dependant contributions

19.47   Non-dependants (para 19.48) are expected to contribute towards your standard and supplementary rate rebate unless one of the exceptions applies. Table 19.2 gives the current figures and table 19.3 lists the exceptions. A non-dependant's gross weekly income is assessed the same way as in para 17.15.

19.46   NIUCTP 3-6; RR 38; RRHB 7; RRHB66+ 7; NISR 2018/138 reg 3

19.47   NIHB 68(b); RRHB 22(1)(e); NIHB66+ 48(b); RRHB66+ 21(1)(e)

19.48   A non-dependant is an adult who:

(a) lives in your home (para 3.71) – for example a daughter, son, other relative or friend; but

(b) isn't a member of your benefit unit (para 3.46), a joint householder, a lodger or your landlord.

Table 19.2 **HB rate rebates: weekly non-dependant contributions**

(a) Non-dependants working at least 16 hours per week

Gross weekly income	Contribution
At least £394.00	£9.80
At least £316.00	£8.25
At least £183.00	£6.55
Under £183.00	£3.30

(b) Other non-dependants

Regardless of income	£3.30

(c) Non-dependant couples

There is one contribution per couple: (a) applies to combined gross weekly income if one or both work at least 16 hours per week; (b) applies otherwise.

Table 19.3 **HB rate rebates: no non-dependant contributions**

Your circumstances

No contributions apply for any non-dependants in your home if you or your partner are:

(a) on the daily living component of PIP;

(b) on the middle or highest rate of the care component of DLA;

(c) on an armed forces independence payment

(d) on attendance allowance or an equivalent benefit (para 10.37);

(e) entitled to (a), (b) or (c) but not receiving it because of being in hospital; or

(f) certified as severely sight impaired or blind by an ophthalmologist or you have regained your sight in the last 28 weeks.

19.48   NIHB 3; RRHB 3(a); NIHB66+ 3; RRHB66+ 3(a)

T19.2   NIHB 72(1)(a)(ii),(b)(ii),(2)(f)-(h),(3); RRHB 22(1)(i); NIHB66+ 53(1)(a)(ii),(b)(ii),(2)(f)-(h),(3); RRHB 21(1)(j)

T19.3   NIHB 72(6)-(10); RRHB 22(1)(i); NIHB66+ 53(6)-(9); RRHB 21(1)(j)

Non-dependant's circumstances

No contribution applies for any single non-dependant who is, or any non-dependant couple who both are:

(g)   on SPC;

(h)   on UC with no earnings;

(i)   on JSA(IB), the assessment phase of ESA(IR), or IS;

(j)   aged under 25 on a training allowance;

(k)   a full-time student (except during the summer vacation if the student is working at least 16 hours per week and the claimant and their partner are both aged under 65); or

(l)   a member of the armed forces away on operations.

Who administers HB rate rebates

19.49   HB rate rebates are administered by:

(a)   Land and Property Services (LPS) if you are an owner occupier, or the owner's partner, former partner or former non-dependant;

(b)   the Northern Ireland Housing executive (NIHE) if you are a social or private tenant, or have a life interest or are in a co-ownership or rental purchase scheme.

Claims

19.50   To get an HB rate rebate you must make a claim to LPS/NIHE (para 19.49). You can do this online, by telephone or on a written application form, and in each case you have to give your personal, financial and household details. You are considered for all three kinds of HB rate rebate (para 19.37) unless you say otherwise.

19.51   If you are a couple, one of you makes the claim on behalf of you both. If you are a tenant, you can usually claim an HB rate rebate and HB for rent at the same time. The rules about information and help with claiming are the same as in paras 19.27-28 and apply to both LPS and NIHE.

Benefit weeks

19.52   HB rate rebates are calculated and paid for benefit weeks that always run from Monday to Sunday.

19.49   NIAA 126; RRHB 6; RRHB66+ 6; RRLPA 4

19.50   NIHB 81; RRHB 26(1), 27; NIHB66+ 62; RRHB66+ 25(1), 26; RRLPA 5

19.51   NIHB 80; RRHB 26(1); NIHB66+ 61, 25(1)

19.52   NIHB 2(1) – definition 'benefit week', RRHB 2(2) – definition 'rate relief week'; NIHB66+ 2(1); RRHB66+ 2(2)

The date your rate rebate starts

19.53   Your HB rate rebate normally starts on the Monday following the date of your claim. But it starts when your HB starts if you claim your UC rate rebate within one month of receiving the decision on your HB claim. And it is backdated for up to three months automatically if you have a pension age claim.

Payments, overpayments and decision notices

19.54   The rules about payments (except as in para 19.55), corrections and decision notices are the same as in paras 19.32-33 and apply to both LPS and NIHE.

Paying HB rate rebates with HB for rent

19.55   If you are a tenant and your HB for rent is paid as a rent allowance, your standard rate rebate can be added to it. So you or your landlord receive a single payment, usually four weekly or monthly, covering both. Further details are the same as in HB (volume 1 chapter 18). But this rule doesn't apply to supplementary rate rebate and lone pensioner rate rebate, which are always paid separately.

Reconsiderations and appeals

19.56   You can ask LPS/NIHE (para 19.49) to reconsider any decision about your standard rate rebate and supplementary rate rebate. You normally have one month to do this. After that you can appeal to an Appeal Tribunal about most decisions and you should normally do so within one month. You make your appeal to LPS/NIHE who forward it to the Appeal Tribunal if they still disagree with any part of your appeal. The procedures, including how to appeal and when the time limit can be extended, are the same as HB for rent: see volume 2 chapter 20 for further details.

19.57   You can ask LPS/NIHE (para 19.49) to reconsider any decision about your lone pensioner rate rebate. You must do this within 28 days of the decision notice issued by LPS/NIHE. After that you can appeal to the Valuation Tribunal: you must do this within 28 days using Form 5.

19.53   NIHB 74, 81(12); RRHB 25, 41-44; NIHB66+ 55, 62(1); RRHB66+ 24

19.54   NIHB 86, sch 10; RRHB 30, ; NIHB66+ 67, sch 9; RRHB66+ 29, 40-43; RRLPA 9

19.55   NIHB 88; RRHB 31(e); NIHB66+ 69; RRHB66+ 30(e); RRLPA 7

19.56   RRHB 41-43; RRHB66+ 40-42; The Housing Benefit (Decisions and Appeals) Regulations (Northern Ireland) 2001, No 213, regs 4, 20

19.57   RRLPA 9, 10(1); The Valuation Tribunal Rules (Northern Ireland) 2007, No 182, reg 5(e), sch Form 5; NISR 2008/153 regs 4, 7, sch

Chapter 20 **Migrants and recent arrivals**

- The rules that apply to migrants: see paras 20.1-14.
- How the decision is made: see paras 20.15-22.
- The immigration control test, asylum seekers and refugees: see paras 20.23-37.
- Habitual residence and the right to reside: see paras 20.38-52.

20.1 This chapter is about when you are eligible for UC, housing benefit (HB) or CTR if you have recently arrived in the UK. It covers everyone, whether you are from the British Isles, Europe or the rest of the world, and whether you are arriving in the UK for the first time or returning after a time abroad.

Which rules apply

20.2 If you have recently arrived in the UK, there are three main rules which affect whether you are eligible for UC/HB/CTR:

(a) the immigration control test;

(b) the right to reside test; and

(c) the habitual residence test.

We avoid using the term 'person from abroad' because in HB law it only means a claimant who fails (b) or (c).

20.3 You must pass all three tests to be entitled to UC/HB/CTR but in practice if you pass the immigration control test you also have a right to reside (and before 1st January 2021 the reverse was also true). In the law the right to reside test is part of the habitual residence test and this is reflected in the way the DWP notifies its decisions (para 20.40).

The UK's departure from the European Union: law changes

20.4 The law has changed because of the UK's exit from the European Union (EU). EEA nationals could continue to use their free movement rights during the 'implementation period' (which ended on 31st December) and were exempt from immigration control.

20.5 From the 1st January 2021, you must satisfy the immigration control test unless you are:

(a) a British citizen;

(b) a Commonwealth citizen with the 'right of abode' (table 20.2); or

(c) an Irish citizen.

20.2   IAA 115(1),(3); UC 9(1),(2); HB 10(1)-(3); HB66+ 10(1),(3); NIUC 9(1),(2); NIHB 10(1)-(3); NIHB66+ 10(1)-(3)

20.4   Immigration and Social Security Co-ordination (EU Withdrawal) Act 2020, s1, sch 1 para 2(2); SI 2020 No. 1279, reg 4

20.5   IAA 115(9); Immigration Act 1971, s 2(1)(a),(b), 3ZA; SI 2020 No. 1279 reg 3; SI 2020 No. 1309 reg 12(7)

20.6   But if you are an EEA national and you entered the UK before 1st January 2021, you can continue to use your EU free movement rights to qualify for UC/HB/CTR (and the immigration control test does not apply to you):

(a) until 30th June 2021 (whether you have applied to the EU settlement scheme or not); and

(b) after then, but only if you have EU pre-settled status.

These transitional rules are described in chapter 21, including how they apply to EEA family members.

20.7   Table 20.1 summarises how the three tests apply to all new claims from 1st January 2021.

Eligibility of nationals of different parts of the world

20.8   This section identifies which rules apply to you depending on your nationality, followed by a straightforward example of each.

Nationals of the British Isles (the Common Travel Area)

20.9   The 'British Isles' (a geographical term, roughly meaning all the islands off the North-West of the continent) is also called the 'Common Travel Area'. Both terms mean:

(a) the United Kingdom (England, Wales, Scotland and Northern Ireland);

(b) the Republic of Ireland;

(c) the Isle of Man; and

(d) the Channel Islands (all of them).

If you are a citizen of any part of the British Isles you only have to show that you are 'habitually resident' there (paras 20.43-52) to be entitled to UC/HB/CTR. If you are the family member of a 'person born in Northern Ireland' (paras 21.64-65) you can apply to the EU settlement scheme in which case your rights to UC/HB/CTR are the same as a person who is an EEA family member (paras 20.6, 20.12).

Nationals of the European Economic Area

20.10   Table 21.1 lists all the countries in the European Economic Area (EEA) plus Switzerland which for UC/HB/CTR purposes UK law treats as being part of the EEA. The EEA includes all the EU states plus some others.

20.6   Immigration and Social Security Co-ordination (EU Withdrawal) Act 2020, s5; SI 2020 No. 1209 regs 3, 11, 12(1)(i);
           SI 2020 No. 1309, regs 12(7), 83, sch 4 paras 1-3

20.9   UC 9(1); HB 10(2); HB66+ 10(2); NIUC 9(1); NIHB 10(2); NIHB66+ 10(2); CTP 12(2)

20.10   EEA 2(1) definition: 'EEA state'

Table 20.1 **Migrants: who can get UC/HB/CTR**

Nationality/date of entry	Test	Expires
British and Irish citizens		
Any date	Habitual residence	No limit while met
EEA and EEA family members		
Entered UK after 31 December 2020	Immigration control and habitual residence	No limit while met
Entered UK before 1 January 2021 and granted EU settled status	Habitual residence	No limit while met
Entered UK before 1 January 2021 and granted EU pre-settled status	Right to reside and habitual residence	When granted EU settled status
Entered UK before 1 January 2021, no application to EUSS by 30 June 2021	Right to reside and habitual residence	1 July 2021
North Macedonia/Turkey		
Entered UK and claimed UC before 1 January 2021	Right to reside and habitual residence	When UC ends
Entered UK or claimed UC after 31 December 2020	Immigration control and habitual residence	No limit while met
Claimed HB/CTR (any date)	Right to reside and habitual residence	No limit while met
Rest of the world		
On entry to the UK	Immigration control and habitual residence	No limit while met

Notes

- In law the claimant must pass all three tests but in practice it is either one or two (paras 20.38, 20.41).
- For EEA family members the entry date applies to the person they accompany (para 21.7).
- Different rules apply to claimants who have applied for asylum (para 20.34).

20.11   If you are an EEA national (or family member) the rules in this chapter apply to you in the same way as a national of the rest of the world if:

(a) you first entered the UK after 31st December 2020; or

(b) from 1st July 2021 onwards if:

■ you have EU settled status (which ends your EEA rights), or

■ you failed to apply to the EU settlement scheme by the 30th June 2021 deadline. You are not entitled to UC/HB/CTR and you are (likely to be) an overstayer (table 20.2) who is resident in the UK unlawfully.

20.12   But if you entered the UK before 1st January 2021 you can use your EU free movement rights to qualify for UC/HB/CTR at least until 30th June 2021, and after then if you have EU pre-settled status. These rules are described fully in chapter 21.

Nationals of the rest of the world

20.13   In this guide this means any country not mentioned above (paras 20.9-10). It also applies to you if you are from an EEA member state but you don't have preserved rights (para 20.11) or if you have applied for asylum (para 20.31) whether your application has been decided or not.

20.14   If you are a national of the rest of the world you must satisfy the immigration control test (paras 20.23-37) and the habitual residence test (paras 20.38-52) to be entitled to UC/HB/CTR.

Examples: Eligibility for UC

1. A British citizen

A British citizen has been living abroad for 12 years. During that time, she gave up all her connections in the UK. She has now just come 'home' and has rented a flat here.

The only test that applies to a UK national is the habitual residence test. It is unlikely that she satisfies that test to begin with but she probably will after (say) three months or possibly a shorter period (para 20.47). So, for the time being she can't get UC.

2. National of the EEA who entered the UK before 1 January 2021

An Italian national has been working in the UK for several years. He applied to the EU settlement scheme before 1st July 2021 and has EU pre-settled status. He has recently taken a more poorly paid job. He passes the right to reside test because he is working. So he can get UC.

3. National of the rest of the world

An Indian national arrived in the UK six months ago to be with her family. She was given leave to enter by the Home Office without a 'no recourse to public funds' condition, so she is able to claim benefits. She now claims UC.

The two tests that apply to a national of the rest of the world are the immigration control test and the habitual residence test. She passes both tests. So she can get UC.

20.11-12   IAA 115(1),(3),(9); SI 2020 No. 1209 regs 3, 11, 12(1)(i); SI 2020 No. 1309, regs 12(7), 83, sch 4 paras 1-3

20.14   IAA 115(1),(3),(9) as amended by SI 2020 No. 1309 reg 12(7)

Decision-making

20.15   This section covers general matters relevant to this chapter and chapter 21, including decision-making and claims, and how the law and terminology work.

DWP and council decisions

20.16   If you are claiming UC the DWP decides whether you satisfy each of the three tests (para 20.2) and can get UC. If you are claiming HB and/or CTR your council decides this, but the law says you pass the habitual residence and right to reside test if you get one of the following DWP benefits:

    (a)   income-based jobseeker's allowance (but see para 21.24 for exceptions);

    (b)   income-related employment and support allowance;

    (c)   income support;

    (d)   state pension credit (guarantee credit or savings credit).

(And in practice your council will also accept that you pass the immigration control test (HBGM para C4.33)).

20.17   The rule in para 20.16 about HB/CTR only applies if the DWP has decided (in full possession of the facts) that you can get JSA(IB)/ESA(IR)/IS/SPC and not, say, where you wrongly continue to get it. If the DWP has decided that you cannot get one of these benefits, your council is not compelled to make the same decision – but a considered decision by the DWP carries weight.

Claims and couples

20.18   If you are a couple you usually claim UC jointly (para 3.3), but if only one of you is eligible that person can get UC as a single person (paras 2.7-8). You are eligible if you (or you and your partner if you are a joint-claim couple) pass each of the three tests (para 20.2).

20.19   If you are a couple and claiming HB/CTR it can matter which partner makes the claim (because only one of you can be the claimant). The rules in this chapter apply to each partner individually. If partner A is eligible, but partner B is not, partner A must be the claimant to get benefit. In these cases:

    (a)   if the 'wrong' partner claims the council must give you a 'not entitled' decision (but it is good practice to explain this and invite a claim from the other partner);

    (b)   if the claim is made by the 'correct' partner, it is assessed (e.g. income, applicable amount, etc) in the usual way, so you get a couple personal allowance even though only one of you is entitled (HBGM para C4·218). But if your partner is subject to immigration control, they should get advice before you make a claim, because it may affect their immigration status (para 20.21).

20.16   HB 10(3B)(k),(l); HB66+ 10(4A)(k); NIHB 10(5)(l),(m); NIHB66+ 10(5)(l); CTP 12(4)(h),(ha)

20.18   UC 3(1),(3); NIUC 3(2)

20.19   HB 8(1)(b), 10(1); HB66+ 8(1)(b), 10(1); NIHB 8(1)(b), 10(1); NIHB66+ 8(1)(b), 10(1); CTP sch 8 para 4(1)

National insurance numbers

20.20　　If you are claiming UC you must provide your national insurance number (or have applied for one) to complete your claim (para 3.28). If you are a couple this applies to both of you (unless you are claiming as a single person (para 20.18).

20.21　　If you are claiming HB/CTR and you are:

(a) single or a lone parent, you must provide your national insurance number (or have applied for one) to complete your claim;

(b) a couple, the rule in (a) applies to both of you except that:

- if only one of you needs 'leave' from the Home Office (table 20.2) to be in the UK but does not have it (for example, if you have not applied for it or if it has expired) then the requirement does not apply to that person and the DWP advises councils to assign a dummy number (GM D1·284-286);

- it is not a legal requirement if you (or your partner) are claiming CTR in Scotland (para 16.37).

This rule (and the rule in para 20.19) is only about who can get HB/CTR. It does not mean that it is safe for your partner in terms of their immigration status to be part of your HB/CTR claim (the higher couple personal allowance counts as 'public funds'). The council may inform the Home Office, although it is not obliged to do so (HBGM para C4·219).

Making a claim

20.22　　Your online UC claim asks you:

(a) if you are British, Irish or a citizen of a different country; and

(b) if you have been out of the UK or Ireland in the past two years.

Most HB/CTR claim forms ask similar questions. Both questions are intended to act as a trigger for further investigation in appropriate cases. If you are British/Irish and have not been out of the UK/Ireland in the past two years, the DWP/council will normally assume you pass all three tests (para 20.2).

The immigration control test

Table 20.2 **Simplified immigration law terminology**

EU settled and pre-settled status

EEA nationals (and their family members) who entered the UK before 1st January 2021 can apply to the EU settlement scheme (EUSS) to get 'leave' under the immigration rules. Applications to the EUSS must be made by 30th June 2021. EU settled status is a form of 'indefinite leave' and is usually granted after five years lawful residence. EU pre-settled status is granted for lawful residence of less than five years and can be converted to settled status once five years have been completed.

20.20　　AA 1(1A),(1B),(4)(za); NIAA 1(1A),(1B),(4)(za)

20.21　　HB 4(c); HB66+ 4(c); NIHB 4(c); NIHB66+ 4(c); CTP 15, sch 8 para 7(2)-(3)

Immigration rules

The legal rules approved by parliament which UKIV officers use to decide whether a person should be given permission ('leave') to enter or remain in the UK.

UK Immigration and Visas (UKIV)

The Home Office agency responsible for immigration control and determining asylum applications (including asylum support).

Leave and temporary admission

Leave is legal permission to be in the UK. Leave can be for a fixed period (limited leave) or open ended (indefinite leave). Both can be granted with or without a 'no recourse to public funds' condition, and this nearly always applies if you have been given limited leave. Leave can be varied, provided the application is made before it has expired (para 20.27).

A person who is granted leave because they are the partner of a British citizen (or a person with 'settled status') usually gets it in two consecutive blocks of 30 months after which they can apply for settled status.

A person who has been granted open ended leave without any conditions is said to have 'indefinite leave to remain' (or, if granted to a person outside the UK, 'indefinite leave to enter') also known as 'settled status'.

Temporary admission isn't a form of leave, it is merely the discretion allowed by UKIV which allows time for you to do something – such as apply for asylum or leave – without falling foul of the law. Since it isn't 'leave', it does not confer a right to reside.

Public funds

Nearly all tax credits and non-contributory benefits (including UC/HB/CTR and legacy benefits) count as public funds. So does a local authority homelessness duty or acceptance on its housing waiting list.

Sponsorship and maintenance undertaking

These terms go together. Someone (typically a partner or elderly relative) may be granted leave to join a family member on the understanding that this 'sponsor' will provide for their maintenance and/or accommodation.

Some (but not all) sponsors are required to sign a written agreement (a maintenance undertaking) as a condition of granting leave and if they do the person they sponsor cannot get UC/HB/CTR (but see para 20.28 for exceptions).

Illegal entrant and overstayer

These both refer to someone who needs leave to be in the UK but does not have it and has not been granted temporary admission. An illegal entrant is someone who entered the UK without applying for leave and an overstayer is someone who was granted leave which has since expired.

> **Right of abode and right to reside**
>
> 'Right of abode' is a term that describes someone who is entirely free of any kind of immigration control. It applies to all British citizens and some citizens of Commonwealth countries, but not necessarily to other forms of British nationality. Non-British nationals can apply for a certificate in their passport to confirm this [www].
>
> 'Right to reside' is a wider term that describes anyone who has legal authority to be in the UK. It includes anyone who has the right of abode, any form of leave (including leave with a 'no public funds' condition), or who has an EEA right to reside (para 20.41).

20.23   From 1st January 2021, if you are from a country other than the UK or Ireland (para 20.5) you must pass the immigration control test to get UC/HB/CTR. (You must also pass the habitual residence test: paras 20.38-52.) A basic understanding of immigration law terminology is useful to understanding UC/HB/CTR decisions. Table 20.2 explains the key terms.

20.24   The immigration control test stops you getting UC/HB/CTR if:

(a) you require 'leave' but do not have it – e.g. you are an illegal entrant or overstayer (table 20.2); or

(b) you have been granted leave but with a 'no recourse to public funds' condition (but see paras 20.28-29 for exceptions); or

(c) you have been granted leave as a result of a maintenance undertaking (i.e. you are a sponsored immigrant, but see paras 20.28-29 for exceptions); or

(d) you have been granted temporary admission while your application to the Home Office is being decided – for example if you are an asylum seeker.

People who pass the immigration control test

20.25   Having limited leave does not of itself exclude you from UC/HB/CTR but rather the fact that it is nearly always granted with a 'no public funds' condition. However, UKIV officers can in certain situations grant limited leave without one. Examples include the destitution domestic violence concession (para 20.36), the initial period of leave following an application for asylum (para 20.35), or five years leave granted to a stateless person on humanitarian grounds [www].

20.26   You pass the immigration control test regardless of your nationality if:

(a) you hold a passport containing a certificate of entitlement to the 'right of abode' (table 20.2) in the UK;

(b) you have 'indefinite leave to remain' (also called settled status), including EU settled status;

T20.2   www.gov.uk/right-of-abode/apply-for-a-certificate-of-entitlement

20.24   IAA99 115(9); SI 2020 No. 1309 reg 12(7); CTP 13(2)

20.25   Home Office 30th October 2019, stateless guidance, p25 www.gov.uk/government/publications/stateless-guidance

(c)	you have EU pre-settled status (but in this case you must have a qualifying right to reside or be exempt from the habitual residence to be entitled to UC/HB/CTR);

(d)	you fall within one of the exceptions described in paras 20.28-29);

(e)	you applied for asylum and you have been granted refugee status, humanitarian protection or discretionary leave (paras 20.34-35).

The DWP/council normally needs to see your passport or other Home Office documentation to confirm the above.

Entitlement when leave starts and ends

20.27	Your entitlement to UC/HB/CTR doesn't always coincide with the date of your leave as follows:

(a)	your UC/HB/CTR starts from the date you receive your Home Office confirmation letter or the date your passport is endorsed, and not from the date the Immigration Appeal Tribunal allowed your appeal, even though that means confirmation of your leave will inevitably follow: [2011] UKUT 373 (AAC);

(b)	if your leave was granted for a set period you can apply for it to be extended before it expires. Provided your application is made in time and in the correct form, you are still treated as having leave until 28 days after the decision is made on your application, and so you pass the immigration control test until then; but

(c)	if your application for leave was refused or the leave you are applying to extend didn't allow you to claim benefit (e.g. if it had a 'no public funds' condition), you aren't entitled to UC/HB/CTR while you appeal the Home Office decision, even if that appeal was made in time: [2018] UKUT 418 (AAC).

Exceptions to the immigration control test

20.28	The law allows the DWP to set out in regulations exceptions to the general rule that if you fail the immigration control test you are excluded from benefit (para 20.24). The only exceptions are in paragraph 20.29.

20.29	You are not affected by the general rule (para 20.28) and pass the immigration control test if:

(a)	you are a national of a European Convention on Social and Medical Assistance (ECSMA)/ European Social Charter (ESC) treaty member state (para 20.30) and you have leave with a 'no public funds' condition;

(b)	you were admitted to the UK as a result of a maintenance undertaking (a 'sponsored immigrant'), but you have been resident for at least five years beginning with the date of your entry or date the undertaking was signed, whichever is the later;

(c)	you were admitted to the UK as a 'sponsored immigrant' and have been resident for less than five years and your sponsor (or all your sponsors if there is more than one) has died.

20.27	Immigration Act 1971 s3C

20.28	IAA99 115(4)

20.29	SI 2000 No. 636 reg 2(1),(1A), sch paras 2-4; NISR 2000 No. 71 reg 2(1), sch paras 2-4; CTP 13(1A)

Nationals of ECSMA or ESC treaty states

20.30   If you are a national of an ECSMA or ESC member state and have 'leave' (albeit with a 'no public funds' condition ([2015] UKUT 438 (AAC)), and you are habitually resident, you are entitled to:

(a)   HB and/or CTR;

(b)   UC but only if:

- you live in Great Britain and you claimed it before 1st January 2021 (and once your entitlement ends it cannot be restored), or

- you live in Northern Ireland (even if you claim it after 31st December 2020).

The ECSMA/ECS member states are all the EEA member states (table 21.1) other than Bulgaria, Liechtenstein, Lithuania, Romania, Slovenia and Switzerland, plus North Macedonia and Turkey.

Asylum seekers

20.31   You are an asylum seeker if you have applied to be recognised as a refugee (para 20.34) under the United Nations Convention because of fear of persecution in your country of origin (typically on political or ethnic grounds).

20.32   While your asylum application is being processed you fail the immigration control test and are disqualified from UC/HB/CTR (and most other benefits), although there are some limited exceptions (para 20.33). If you are disqualified, you may be able to get help with your maintenance and accommodation from the Home Office asylum support scheme [www].

20.33   The exceptions to the general rule in para 20.32 apply if:

(a)   you are a couple, and your partner is eligible (paras 20.18-19) (and in this case if you are claiming HB/CTR any payment you get from the Home Office for support counts as income: HBGM para C4.128); or

(b)   you have been granted discretionary leave (para 20.34) (e.g. if you are aged under 18 and unaccompanied by an adult: but see para 2.10 for UC).

Refugees and others granted leave on humanitarian grounds

20.34   Following your asylum application the Home Office may:

(a)   recognise you as a refugee (i.e. accept your claim for asylum) and grant leave; or

(b)   refuse asylum but grant humanitarian protection (which is a form of leave) or discretionary leave (see circular HB/CTB A16/2006 for details of when these might apply); or

(c)   refuse asylum and not grant leave.

20.35   If leave is granted it is normally for an initial period of 30 months, and then one further period of 30 months, after which you can normally apply for settled status (table 20.2). Refugee status, humanitarian protection and discretionary leave are usually granted without

---

20.30   SI 2000 No. 636 reg 2(1),(1A), sch paras 2-4; SI 2020 No 1505 regs 1(2), 2(2)(a); NISR 2000 No. 71 reg 2(1), sch paras 2-4; CTP 13(1A)

20.32   www.gov.uk/asylum-support

20.35   UC 9(4)(d),(e)(i),(f); NIUC 9(4)(d),(e)(i),(f); HB 10(1),(3B)(g),(h)(i),(hh); HB66+ 10(1),(4A)(g),(h)(i),(hh); NIHB 10(1),(5)(g),(h)(i),(i); NIHB66+ 10(1),(5)(g),(h)(i),(i); CTP 12(5)(d),(e)(i),(f)

a 'no public funds' condition and in either case you are exempt from the habitual residence test (para 20.40) so you are entitled to UC/HB/CTR from the date your status is confirmed (para 20.27(a)). If you are granted refugee status (but not in other cases) then your dependants are granted leave as well, so they are also entitled to UC/HB/CTR.

Destitution domestic violence concession

20.36   If you were granted limited leave as the partner of a British citizen or a person with settled status (table 20.2) but your relationship has broken down because of domestic violence, you can apply for up to three months leave outside the Immigration Rules without a 'no public funds' condition [www]. This should allow you enough time to make an application to the Home Office to settle in the UK.

20.37   This is known as the 'Destitution Domestic Violence Concession' (ADM C1674-76; HB circular U2/2012 [www]). If your application for DDVC is approved, you can get UC/HB/CTR until your application to settle is decided (para 20.39). The DDVC is not available to EEA family members who entered the UK before 1st January 2021 under the free movement rules but you may have a right to reside under the EEA regulations instead (para 21.58).

The habitual residence test

What is the habitual residence test

20.38   In law the habitual residence test has two parts:

(a) you aren't entitled to UC/HB/CTR unless you are 'habitually resident' in the British Isles – this is decided according to the particular facts in your case (paras 20.43-52); and

(b) you cannot be treated as being habitually resident unless you have a 'right to reside' there – this is decided according to immigration status (e.g. British citizen, paras 20.40-42).

It applies to you regardless of your nationality (including if you are British) – but people with certain kinds of status are exempt (para 20.39). Its purpose is to ensure that someone with the right to take up residence here cannot receive benefit immediately or shortly after their arrival.

Who is exempt from habitual residence test

20.39   You are exempt from both parts of the test – and so entitled to UC/HB/CTR – if:

(a) you applied for asylum and have been granted:

 - refugee status,
 - humanitarian protection, or
 - discretionary leave (paras 20.26 and 20.34);

20.36   UC 9(4)(e)(ii); NIUC 9(4)(e)(ii); 10(3B)(h)(ii); HB66+ 10(4A)(h)(ii);
        NIHB 10(5)(h)(ii); NIHB66+ 10(5)(h)(ii); CTP 12(5)(e)(ii);
        www.gov.uk/government/publications/application-for-benefits-for-visa-holder-domestic-violence
        See Home Office Guidance (2018), DDV concession, page 5 https://tinyurl.com/DDVC-Feb-2018

20.37   https://tinyurl.com/HB-U2-2012PDF

20.38   UC 9(1),(2); HB 10(2),(3); HB66+ 10(2),(3); NIUC 9(1),(2); NIHB 10(2),(3); NIHB66+ 10(2),(3); CTP 12(2),(3)

(b) you have been granted limited leave under the destitution domestic violence concession (para 20.36);

(c) you are an EEA national with preserved rights (para 20.6) who is a worker, frontier worker, self-employed person, retired worker or retired self-employed person or the family member of such a person (para 21.23);

(d) you are the family member of a 'person who was born in Northern Ireland' (para 21.64), if that person would be a worker etc if s/he was an EEA national;

(e) you are a British Citizen, a Commonwealth Citizen with the right of abode or a person with settled status and you have been deported to the UK from another country; or

(f) for HB/CTR only, you get one of the DWP benefits in para 20.16.

How habitual residence (HR) decisions are made and notified

20.40   When the DWP considers the habitual residence test it decides if you have a right to reside as the first stage (para 20.38(b)). If you fail this stage your decision notice usually just says that you are not entitled because you aren't habitually resident. Decisions about the right to reside for EEA nationals are often very complex (paras 21.29 onwards); if this applies to you it may be helpful to ask for a statement of reasons before you ask for a reconsideration or appeal (para 14.8).

Habitual residence stage one: the right to reside

20.41   You must have a right to reside the UK, Ireland, the Channel Islands or the Isle of Man. This is straightforward if you are a British Citizen, Irish Citizen or a Commonwealth Citizen with the 'right of abode' (table 20.2). You also have a right to reside if you have indefinite leave to remain (including EU settled status: para 21.18) and (presumably) limited leave provided you comply with any conditions: Abdirahman v SSWP. But if you have temporary admission (table 20.2) this isn't enough to be a right to reside: Yesiloz v Camden LBC.

20.42   If you are an EEA national or family member with preserved rights (para 20.6) or, in certain circumstances, the family member of a British or Irish citizen with preserved rights you have a right to reside so long as:

(a) you have EU settled status (para 21.18);

(b) you have indefinite leave to remain (21.15);

(c) you have a right of permanent residence (paras 21.45-53, 21.56);

(d) you are a 'qualified person' (para 21.48);

(e) you are the family member of someone above;

(f) you have some other EEA right to reside (paras 21.70-82);

20.39   UC 9(4)(a)-(c),(ca)-(cc),(d)-(g); HB 10(3B)(za)-(zf),(g),(h),(hh),(i),(k),(l); HB66+ 10(4A)(za)-(zf),(g),(h),(hh),(i),(k);
            NIUC 9(4)(a)-(c),(ca)-(cc),(d)-(g); NIHB 10(5)(za)-(zf),(g),(h),(i),(j),(l),(m);
            NIHB66+ 10(5)(za)-(zf),(g),(h),(i),(j),(l); CTP 12(5)(a)-(c),(g),(h),(ha)

20.41-42   Abdirahman v SSWP [2007] EWCA Civ 657 www.bailii.org/ew/cases/EWCA/Civ/2007/657.html
            Yesiloz v Camden LBC [2009] EWCA Civ 415 www.bailii.org/ew/cases/EWCA/Civ/2009/415.html

(g) you are the family member of a person who was born in Northern Ireland (paras 21.64-65); or

(h) you are the family member of a British citizen who has returned to live in the UK after s/he exercised his/her free movement rights (before 1st February 2020) in another member state.

But in the case of (d) to (f) you aren't entitled to UC/HB/CTR if the right you are using is excluded (para 21.24), for example a 'jobseeker' etc, including also if you have EU pre-settled status.

Habitual residence stage two: based on your facts

20.43   What counts as habitual residence is a 'question of fact'. It is decided by looking at all the facts in your case; no list of considerations can be drawn up to govern all cases. The DWP gives general guidance on this (ADM C1946-70; HBGM paras C4.87-106).

20.44   There are two elements to 'habitual residence':

(a) 'Residence': you must actually be resident, a mere intention to reside is insufficient; and mere physical presence is not residence.

(b) 'Habitual': there must also be a degree of permanence in your residence in the British Isles (HBGM para C4.80), the word 'habitual' implying a more settled state in which you are making your home here. There is no requirement that it must be your only home, or that it is permanent, provided it is your genuine home for the time being.

Losing and gaining habitual residence

20.45   Habitual residence can be lost in a single day. For example, if you leave the UK intending to take up long-term residence in another country. But if you have recently entered the UK from another country with the intention to settle here you don't become habitually resident immediately on arrival. Instead, there are two main requirements (R(IS) 6/96):

(a) your residence must be for an 'appreciable period of time'; and

(b) you must have a 'settled intention' to live in the UK.

'Appreciable period of time' and 'intention to settle'

20.46   There is no fixed period that amounts to an appreciable period (CIS 2326/1995). It varies according to the circumstances of your case and takes account of the 'length, continuity and nature' of your residence (R(IS) 6/96).

20.47   Case law (CIS 4474/2003) suggests that, in general, the period lies between one and three months, and a decision maker needs 'powerful reasons to justify a significantly longer period'. But that time must be spent making a home here, rather than merely studying or on a temporary visit.

20.48   As suggested by the DWP (ADM C1965-69 HBGM C4.85-86), factors likely to be relevant in deciding what is an appreciable period of time include:

(a) the length and continuity of your residence;

(b) your reasons for coming to the UK;

(c) your future intentions;

(d) your employment prospects (para 20.49); and

(e) your centre of interest (para 20.50).

The relative weighting given to each will depend on the facts in your case but no one factor is ever decisive.

20.49   In considering your employment prospects, your education and qualifications are likely to be significant (CIS 5136/2007). An offer of work is also good evidence of an intention to settle. If you have stable employment it is presumed that you reside here, even if your family lives abroad (ADM C1969).

20.50   Your centre of interest is concerned with the strength of your ties to this country and your intention to settle. As suggested by the DWP (ADM C1966; HBGM C4.105), this can be shown by:

(a) the presence of close relatives;

(b) decisions made about the location of your family's personal possessions (e.g. clothing, furniture, transport);

(c) substantial purchases, such as furnishings, which indicate a long-term commitment; and

(d) the membership of any clubs or organisations in connection with your hobbies or recreations.

Temporary absence and returning residents

20.51   Once your habitual residence has been established, it resumes immediately on your return from a single short absence (such as a holiday or visiting relatives).

20.52   In considering whether you regain your habitual residence following a longer absence, or repeated absences, the following points need to be considered:

(a) the circumstances in which your habitual residence was lost;

(b) your intentions – if your absence was always intended to be temporary (even in the case of longer absences) you are less likely to lose your habitual residence than someone who originally never had an intention to return;

(c) your continuing links with the UK while abroad;

(d) the circumstances of your return. If you slot straight back into the life you had before you left, you are likely to resume habitual residence more quickly.

Chapter 21 **EEA nationals**

- When this chapter applies: see paras 21.4-14.
- The EU settlement scheme: see paras 21.15-20.
- EEA nationals entitled to UC/HB/CTR: see paras 21.21-28.
- EEA self-employed and worker status: see paras 21.29-44.
- The right of permanent residence: see paras 21.45-53.
- EEA family member rights: see paras 21.54-62.
- Family members of British citizens who can apply for settled status: see paras 21.63-69.
- Other EEA rights to reside (derivative rights, self-sufficient persons and students): see paras 21.70-82.

21.1 This chapter describes your right to reside if you are an EEA national or an EEA family member and exercised your European Union (EU) free movement rights before 1st January 2021. It describes how and when you can continue to use these rights after 31st December 2020 to qualify for UC/HB/CTR.

Who is an EEA national or EEA family member

21.2 You are an EEA national if you are a citizen of an EEA member state or of Switzerland. Table 21.1 lists EEA member states. You are an EEA family member if you are the partner, close relative or dependant of an EEA national as described in table 21.2.

21.3 In certain circumstances if you are the family member of a British citizen you may be able to apply to the EU settlement scheme to get EU settled status (paras 21.63-69).

EEA nationals with preserved rights

21.4 This section (paras 21.5-14) describes how EEA rights to reside are changing following the UK's exit from the European Union (Brexit) and when this chapter applies to you (or chapter 20 applies instead).

The UK's exit from the EU and the end of EEA rights

21.5 The UK left the European Union (EU) on 31st January 2020 (EU exit day). EU free movement and residency rights (para 21.29 onwards) ceased at the end of the 'Implementation Period' on 31st December 2020 (in law at 23:00 hours) and except as described in paras 21.6-14 cannot be used to qualify for UC/HB/CTR (or to enter the UK).

21.2   EEA 2(1) – definitions: 'EEA national', 'EEA State'

21.5-7 The Immigration and Social Security Co-ordination (EU Withdrawal) Act 2020, s1, sch 1 para 2(2); SI 2020/1279 reg 4

When this chapter doesn't apply – UK entry after 31st December 2020

21.6   If you are an EEA national who is entering the UK for the first time on or after 1st January 2021, you must go through immigration control and get 'leave' from UK Visas and Immigration (table 20.2) to be lawfully resident in the UK. This chapter does not apply to you and your entitlement to UC/HB/CTR is described in chapter 20.

21.7   If you are an EEA family member chapter 20 also applies to you if the EEA national you accompany first entered the UK on or after 1st January 2021.

When this chapter applies – UK entry before 1st January 2021

21.8   You can only use the rights described in this chapter if you (or the EEA national you accompany) entered the UK before 1st January 2021 using your (his/her) free movement rights (para 21.29 onwards) and you meet the conditions in para 21.9.

21.9   If you meet the initial condition in para 21.8 you can use the rights described in this chapter to qualify for UC/HB/CTR as follows:

(a)   during the 'grace period' (para 21.10); or

(b)   after the grace period but only if you have EU pre-settled status.

The grace period

21.10   The grace period runs from 1st January 2021 until midnight on 30th June 2021. It gives you extra time to make an application to the EU settlement scheme so you can continue to reside in the UK lawfully.

Using your EEA rights during the grace period

21.11   During the grace period you can use your EEA rights to reside (paras 21.29 onwards) whether you have applied to the EU settlement scheme or not, or if you have and you are granted EU pre-settled status. But if you are granted EU settled status you can no longer use your EAA rights to reside and the rules in chapter 20 apply instead (but you will pass the immigration control and right to reside tests).

What happens when the grace period ends

21.12   If you don't apply to the EU settlement scheme (para 21.15) before the grace period ends all your EEA rights including the right of permanent residence (paras 21.45, 21.56) expire on 1st July 2021. If this happens you become an overstayer (table 20.2) and you are no longer lawfully resident in the UK. You should get advice immediately from a OISC registered adviser [www]. If you applied to the EU settlement scheme on time you can continue to use your EEA/EEA family member rights as described in para 21.13.

21.9   The Citizens' Rights (Application Deadline and Temporary Protection) (EU Exit) Regulations 2020, No 1209, regs 3, 11
          The Immigration and Social Security Co-ordination (EU Withdrawal) Act 2020 (Consequential, Saving, Transitional and Transitory Provisions) (EU Exit) Regulations 2020, No 1309 reg 83, sch 4 paras 1-2

21.10   SI 2020/1209 reg 2

21.11   SI 2020/1209 regs 3(3),(6),11

21.12   The Immigration and Social Security Co-ordination (EU Withdrawal) Act 2020, s1, sch 1 para 2(2); SI 2020/1279 reg 4
          www.gov.uk/find-an-immigration-adviser

When this chapter applies: using your EEA right from 1st July 2021

21.13   If you applied to the EU settlement scheme before 1st July you can continue to use the rights to reside for as long as you have EU pre-settled status. Once you have EU settled status your EEA rights expire and cannot be used again. But you are entitled to UC/HB/CTR provided you are habitually resident (paras 20.26, 20.41).

How the law works from 1st January 2021

21.14   The Immigration (European Economic Area) Regulations 2016 are revoked from 1st January 2021 but are saved in modified form for UC/HB/CTR purposes while you have EU pre-settled status. This chapter describes the modified rules.

Examples: Applying for settled status during the grace period

Isabella is a Spanish national who entered the UK before 1st January 2021. She is working 35 hours a week. She has applied to the EU Settlement Scheme. During the grace period while she waits for a decision she does not have to prove she is habitually resident to be entitled to UC because she is a worker and is exempt (para 21.23). So she can get UC (paras 20.6, 20.39).

Alejandro is a Spanish national. He has lived in the UK for four and a half years. He has been registered unemployed at the jobcentre for the last eight months. He applied to the EU settlement scheme in January 2021 and is granted EU settled status from May 2021 (once he completes his five years). When he gets his EU settled status he qualifies for UC whether he continues to register as unemployed or not.

The EU Settlement Scheme (EUSS)

21.15   This section (paras 21.16-20) tells you how the EU settlement scheme ensures you can continue to live, work, and get UC/HB/CTR lawfully once the grace period ends.

21.16   The EU Settlement Scheme is part of the UK's Immigration Rules ('Appendix EU') [www]. The scheme is free of charge and opened to EEA citizens on 30th March 2019 [www]. It also applies to EEA family members (including family members who aren't EEA nationals: table 21.2). A separate application is required by each family member. If you are eligible you have until 30th June 2021 to apply.

21.13   SI 2020/1309, sch 4 paras 1-3

21.14   SI 2020/1309, sch 4 paras 3, 4

21.16   www.gov.uk/guidance/immigration-rules/immigration-rules-appendix-eu
www.gov.uk/settled-status-eu-citizens-families
www.gov.uk/view-prove-immigration-status
SI 2020/1209, reg 2

Table 21.1 **The European Economic Area (EEA)**

This table shows the EEA members from 20th July 1994 (when the EEA free movement rights began), the dates member states joined and any transitional period of worker registration/authorisation. For the rules about worker registration/authorisation, see previous editions of this guide.

Member states/date of joining	Transitional period/description
(a) Member states joining before 20th July 1994	
Belgium, Denmark, France, Germany, Greece, Hungary, Iceland, Ireland, Italy, Luxembourg, Netherlands, Norway, Portugal, Spain	**No**
(b) 1st January 1995	
Austria, Finland, Sweden	**No**
(c) 1st May 1995	
Liechtenstein	**No**
(d) 1st June 2002	
Switzerland	**No**
(e) 1st May 2004	
Cyprus, Malta	**No**
Czech Republic, Estonia, Hungary, Latvia, Lithuania, Poland, Slovakia, Slovenia	**Yes** – 1st May 2004-30th April 2009 (see note): Worker Registration Scheme
(f) 1st January 2007	
Bulgaria, Romania	**Yes** – 1st January 2007-31st December 2013: Worker Authorisation Scheme
(g) 1st July 2013	
Croatia	**Yes** – 1st July 2013-30th June 2018: Worker Authorisation Scheme

Note: The extension of the worker registration scheme in (e) between 1st May 2009 and 30th April 2011 was ruled unlawful by the Supreme Court (SSWP v Gubeladze).

T21.1(a)-(f) **The Immigration (European Economic Area) Regulations:**
    20/07/1994 - 01/10/2000: SI 1994/1895
    02/10/2000 - 29/04/2006: SI 2000/2326
    30/04/2006 - 31/01/2017: SI 2006/1003
    01/02/2017 onwards: SI 2016/1052

T21.1(d) SI 2002/1241

Worker Registration/Authorisation Regulations
T21.1(e) SI 2004/1219
T21.1(f) SI 2006/3317
T21.1(g) SI 2013/1460

T21.1 note   SSWP v Gubeladze [2019] UKSC 31 https://www.bailii.org/uk/cases/UKSC/2019/31.html

Family members of British citizens who can apply for EU settled status

21.17   In certain circumstances you can apply for EU settled status as the family member of a British or Irish citizen as follows:

(a)   you are the non-EEA parent of a British child (para 21.28);

(b)   you are the family member of a person from Northern Ireland (paras 21.64-65); or

(c)   you are the family member of a British citizen who exercised his/her free movement rights in another member state before 1st February 2020 (paras 21.66-69).

EU settled status and pre-settled status

21.18   If your application is successful you will be given:

(a)   indefinite leave to enter/remain ('settled status'); or

(b)   limited leave to enter/remain ('pre-settled status');

in either case without a 'no public funds' condition (paras 20.24-25). EU settled and pre-settled status are kinds of indefinite and limited leave granted under the Immigration Rules (table 20.2). You can use the online service to view, prove and share your settled or pre-settled status with others (e.g. the DWP) [www].

21.19   You are eligible for settled status if you have completed a continuous qualifying period of five years residence and certain other conditions are met. This is not dependent upon you having met any EEA right of residence conditions (paras 21.29 onwards).

21.20   You are eligible for pre-settled status if you would be eligible for settled status but for the fact that you have not yet completed the five-year qualification period. Once you have completed your five years you can reapply to get settled status.

EEA nationals entitled to UC/HB/CTR

21.21   This section tells you when you are entitled to UC/HB/CTR from 1st January 2021 if you have preserved EEA rights (paras 21.8-14). You are an EEA national if you are a citizen of a country in table 21.1. You are an EEA family member if you meet the conditions in table 21.2.

EEA rights and entitlement to UC/HB/CTR

21.22   You are entitled to UC/HB/CTR using one of your EEA rights if you:

(a)   you are in the 'grace period' or you have EU settled status (paras 21.9-10);

(b)   are exempt from the requirement to be habitually resident (para 21.23); or

(c)   you have some other right to reside (para 21.45 onwards); and

■   your right to reside isn't of the type that is excluded (paras 21.24-28), and

■   you are habitually resident (on the facts) in the British Isles (paras 20.43-52).

If you are a couple, see paras 20.18-21 for how all these rules apply to you.

21.18   www.gov.uk/view-prove-immigration-status

21.22   UC 9(1),(2); HB 10(2),(3),(3B); HB66+ 10(2),(3),(4A); NIUC 9(1),(2); NIHB 10(2),(3),(5); NIHB66+ 10(2),(3),(5); CTP 12(2),(3),(5)

Claimants exempt from the habitual residence test

21.23   You are exempt from the habitual residence test if your EEA right to reside is:

(a) as a worker, frontier worker or self-employed person (paras 21.30-44);

(b) a right of permanent residence acquired through retirement (paras 21.50-53);

(c) as a 'family member', as defined in table 21.2(a)-(c), of a worker or self-employed person; or

(d) a right of permanent residence as a family member which you acquired because the EEA national you accompanied:

   ■   retired or ceased working due to incapacity (para 21.56(c)), or

   ■   died (para 21.56(d)).

EEA rights to reside excluded from UC/HB/CTR

21.24   You aren't entitled to UC/HB/CTR if your only EEA right to reside is due to:

(a) your first three months residence in the UK;

(b) as a jobseeker or as a family member of a jobseeker (para 21.27);

(c) as a 'Zambrano' carer (para 21.28); or

(d) EU pre-settled status either on its own (para 21.26) or with one of (a)-(c) above.

Although you can't get UC/HB/CTR these rights to reside can help you qualify for EU settled status (paras 21.19-20). If your partner has a right to reside, see paras 20.18-19.

Using your pre-settled status on its own

21.25   If you have EU pre-settled status as the family member of a 'relevant person of Northern Ireland' (para 21.64-65) you have a right to reside for UC/HB/CTR purposes so long as the Northern Irish person you accompany would have the right to reside had s/he been an EEA national themself. You are also exempt from the habitual residence test if the person you accompany is a worker, frontier worker, retired worker or self-employed person or would be but for the fact that s/he is not an EEA national.

21.26   In Scotland you are entitled to CTR if you have pre-settled status and you are habitually resident. In any other case the Court of Appeal decided that pre-settled status should be enough to get UC/HB/CTR without relying on another right to reside (Fratila and Tanase v SSWP). However, the DWP believes this doesn't apply to any period from 1st January 2021 (ADM memo 02/21). It also advised decision makers to 'stay' any appeals (para 14.46) that relate to period before 1st January 2021 until the issue is decided by the UK Supreme Court (expected hearing date May 2021).

21.23   UC 9(4)(a)-(c); HB 10(3B)(za)-(zc); HB66+ 10(4A)(za)-(zc); NIUC 9(1),(2); NIHB 10(5)(za)-(zc); NIHB66+ NIHB 10(5)(za)-(zc); CTP 12(5)(a)-(c)

21.24   UC 9(3); HB 10(3A),(3AA); HB66+ 10(4),(4ZA); NIUC 9(3); NIHB 10(4),(4A); NIHB66+ 10(4),(4A); CTP 12(4),(4A)

21.25   UC 9(3A),(4)(ca); HB 10(3AB),(3B)(zd); HB66+ 10(4ZB),(4A)(zd); NIUC 9(3A),(4)(ca); NIHB 10(4B),(5)(zd); NIHB66+ 10(4B),(5)(zd)

21.26   Fratila and Tanase v SSWP [2020] EWCA Civ 1741 https://www.bailii.org/ew/cases/EWCA/Civ/2020/1741.html

EEA jobseekers

21.27   You are an 'EEA jobseeker' if:

(a) you entered the UK looking for work and registered as unemployed; or

(b) you have been registered unemployed as a retained worker for the maximum period of six months after having worked in the UK for less than a year (para 21.41(a)).

You are a jobseeker for as long as you can show you have 'genuine prospects of work' (ADM C1403-50) up to a maximum period of 91 days. Any previous period as a jobseeker is deducted from the 91 days unless it is separated by an absence from the UK of at least 12 months (but after which you would not be able to re-enter using your EEA rights). After 91 days your right to reside ends but if you have EU pre-settled status (para 21.18) you can continue to live in the UK lawfully.

Non-EEA parent of British child ('Zambrano' carer)

21.28   If you are a non-EEA national who is the parent of a child who is a UK citizen you have a right to reside in the UK under the EEA regulations. This right is sometimes referred to as a 'Zambrano' right after the case that established it (and is another kind of 'derivative right to reside': para 21.71). However, unlike other derivative rights it doesn't entitle you to UC/HB/CTR, but it can help you qualify for EU settled or pre-settled status (paras 21.18-20) and you may qualify for other financial support from social services: Sanneh v SSWP.

EEA self-employed and worker status

21.29   This section (paras 21.30-44) describes who has the right to reside as a self-employed person or a worker and how that status can be retained during temporary periods of sickness or unemployment, etc. You can continue to use the rights in this section at least until 30th June 2021 and from 1st July 2021 onwards for as long as you have EU pre-settled status (para 21.13).

Self-employed people

21.30   You have the right to reside if you are an EEA national engaged in self-employed business in the UK. Your self-employment must be 'real', and have actually begun, but the ten-hour threshold (para 21.36) does not apply and your self-employed status can continue even where there is no current work, provided you continue to look for it: [2010] UKUT 451 (AAC). A seller of The Big Issue who buys the magazine at half price and sells it has been found to be in self-employment: [2011] UKUT 494 (AAC). But your self-employed income must provide a real contribution to your required income: [2017] UKUT 155 (AAC).

21.27   EEA 6 as modified by SI 2020/1309, sch 4 para 4(e)

21.28   EEA 16(5) UC 9(3)(b),(c); HB 10(3A)(bb),(3AA)(b); HB66+ 10(4)(bb),(4ZA)(b);
         NIUC 9(3)(c),(d); NIHB 10(4)(bb),(4A)(b); NIHB66+ 10(4)(bb),(4A)(b); CTP 10(4)(b),(4A)(c)
         Sanneh v SSWP [2015] www.bailii.org/ew/cases/EWCA/Civ/2015/49.html

21.30   EEA 6(1)(c), 14(1)

21.31   You have a legal duty to register with HMRC within three months of starting your business – even if you think you won't earn enough to pay tax/national insurance. However, the mere fact of being registered does not determine your self-employed status nor does it necessarily mean that HMRC accepts you are self-employed. On the other hand, the fact that you have not registered doesn't mean that you aren't self-employed: CIS/3213/2007.

Workers

21.32   You have the right to reside as a 'worker' if you are an EEA national in paid employment in the UK provided your work meets the minimum requirements (paras 21.34-37).

Frontier worker

21.33   You are a frontier worker if you are a worker or self-employed in the UK, but you are not 'predominantly resident' here. You can retain your frontier worker status in a similar way to a worker while you are temporarily out of work.

Deciding worker status

21.34   To decide whether you are a worker the DWP applies a two-tier test:

(a) you are 'automatically' considered to be a worker/self-employed (ADM C1487) if your average gross earnings from employment/self-employment:

-   are at least equal to the national insurance primary threshold (£797 per month/ £184 per week in 2021-22), and

-   were at least that level for a continuous period of three months immediately before you claimed UC; or

(b) if the above criteria aren't met the DWP decides the matter according to your individual circumstances by considering:

-   whether you are exercising your EU free movement rights (ADM C1495-96), and

-   if you are, whether you are engaged in 'remunerative' work which is 'effective and genuine' (para 21.35) and not 'on such a small scale to be purely marginal and ancillary'.

Test (a) has no basis in law, so if you fail it the DWP must properly consider part (b) before concluding that you aren't a worker: [2019] UKUT 52 (AAC).

21.35   'Remunerative' has its ordinary English meaning: broadly payment for services you provide. The following are relevant to whether your work is 'effective and genuine' (ADM para C1499):

(a) the period of employment;

(b) the number of hours worked;

(c) the level of earnings; and

(d) whether the work is regular or erratic.

21.32   EEA 6(1)(b), 14(1)

21.36   The number of hours worked is not conclusive of your worker status, but it is relevant: CH/3733/2007. The European Commission considers ten hours to be enough [www] although this may not be enough when the other factors here are considered – and not doing ten hours does not automatically exclude you. The factors must always be considered together. DWP guidance notes that work that is part-time or low paid is not necessarily always marginal or ancillary – and gives the example of working three hours a day, five days a week for the last four months as being enough (ADM C1501 and example 4). But if you work full time (other than a fixed-term contract) you could acquire worker status in as little as two weeks: Tarola v Minister for Social Protection.

21.37   The fact that your job is poorly paid or the fact that you need to claim UC, is not enough on its own to stop you from qualifying as a worker. You can be a 'worker' even if your work is paid 'cash in hand': [2012] UKUT 112 (AAC).

Examples: Right to reside as worker

A Spanish national works in the UK as a cleaner in a garage for two hours a night on two nights a week. He is mainly in the country to study English. So he probably does not pass the right to reside test as a worker.

An Icelandic national works in the UK as a legal translator doing variable hours but averaging six hours a week over the year. She has been doing this for three years, and her hourly rate is substantial. It is therefore quite possible that she passes the right to reside test as a worker.

Retained worker/self-employed status: temporary incapacity for work

21.38   You retain your EEA worker or self-employed status if you are temporarily unable to work due to sickness or injury. What counts as being temporary isn't defined and there is no set maximum period. Provided your incapacity isn't permanent and there is a realistic prospect of you being able to return to work within the foreseeable future you retain your worker status ([2016] UKUT 389 (AAC), De Brito v SSHD). You do not have to show you have 'limited capability for work' (para 2.47) – the test is whether you would be able to do the work you were doing (CIS/4304/2007, [2017] UKUT 421 (AAC)). If your incapacity is permanent see para 21.52.

Retained worker/self-employed status: pregnancy and childbirth

21.39   If you are a worker and stop working because of pregnancy or recent childbirth you retain your worker/self-employed) status as follows:

(a)   (as a worker) while you are still under contract, such as on maternity leave even if it isn't paid (CIS/1042/2008);

21.36   European Commission Communications COM (2002) 694, p5 https://tinyurl.com/EC-COM-2002-694
        Tarola v Minister for Social Protection Case C-483/17 www.bailii.org/eu/cases/EUECJ/2019/C48317.html

21.38   EEA 6(2)(a),(4)(a); De Brito v SSHD [2012] www.bailii.org/ew/cases/EWCA/Civ/2012/709.htm

21.39   Saint Prix v SSWP [2014] AACR 18; www.bailii.org/eu/cases/EUECJ/2014/C50712.html

(b) (as self-employed) if you stop work for maternity leave provided you intend to resume your business (CIS/731/2007);

(c) (as a worker) if you gave up work or seeking work due to the physical constraints of the late stages of pregnancy or the aftermath of childbirth, provided you start work/ seeking work again within a 'reasonable period' after the birth – this usually means up to 52 weeks, starting with 11 weeks before your due date: Saint Prix v SSWP and [2015] UKUT 502 (AAC).

Retained worker status: vocational training

21.40   You retain your worker status or self-employed status while you are undertaking vocational training that is related to your previous employment (or any work if there is no work available that is reasonably equivalent to your last job).

Retained worker status: registered unemployed

21.41   You retain your worker status or self-employed status during a period of registered unemployment:

(a) for up to six months if you were employed (in the UK) for less than a year (which could have been for as little as two weeks: para 21.36); or

(b) without time limit if you were employed for at least a year.

21.42   The one year's employment need not be continuous: [2015] UKUT 128 (AAC). Small gaps (probably no longer than three months) between leaving your employment and registering as a jobseeker can be ignored: [2013] UKUT 163 (AAC).

21.43   The easiest way to register as a jobseeker is to make a claim for UC, JSA(C) or national insurance credits (although it is not strictly necessary that you qualify for these to count as being 'registered unemployed' (CIS 184/2008)). Even if you don't qualify for UC/JSA/HB for the time being you should keep 'signing on' because it can help you qualify for EU settled status (para 21.20).

The old genuine prospects of work test

21.44   The DWP used to apply the 'genuine prospects of work test' (GPoW) (para 21.27) to everyone after six months registered unemployment but now only does this if you have worked in the UK for less than one year (paras 21.27, 21.41). The DWP now accepts that if you have worked in the UK for at least one year you can retain your worker status for long as you are registered unemployed and the GPoW should not be applied to you ([2020] UKUT 50 (AAC), ADM memo 31/20). This change is confirmed in the modified EEA regulations (para 21.14).

The right of permanent residence

21.45   This section (paras 21.46-53) describes who has an EEA right of permanent residence. A different set of rules applies to EEA family members (para 21.56).

21.40   EEA 6(2)(d),(e),(4)(d),(e)

21.41   EEA 6(2)(b),(c),(3),(4)(b),(c),(4A); SI 2020/1309, sch 4 para 4(e)

21.46   Even though it is called 'permanent' you won't be able to use it once EEA freedom of movement rights end. If you acquired permanent residence under the five-year rule it expires on 1st July 2021 if you don't apply for EU settled status before then, or if you do because you get EU settled status instead (para 21.19).

21.47   Apart from that, once you have acquired a permanent right of residence (paras 21.48-53 and 21.56) you only lose it after an absence from the UK of more than two years.

Right of permanent residence: the five-year rule

21.48   If you have lived in the UK continuously for five years while using your free movement rights you have a permanent right to reside and you are entitled to UC/HB/CTR provided you are also habitually resident (para 21.22). You are using your free movement rights during any time in which you had the right to reside as a 'qualified person'. This means you are:

(a)   a worker or a retained worker (paras 21.32-41);

(b)   a self-employed person;

(c)   a jobseeker (whether you receive JSA or not) (para 21.27);

(d)   a student (para 21.78); or

(e)   a self-sufficient person (para 21.80).

21.49   A period of residence counts as 'continuous' despite a period of absence from the UK if:

(a)   in any one year, the total length of your absence(s) is no more than six months, and this can be longer if your absence is due to compulsory military service; or

(b)   the total period of absence is not more than 12 months – so long as the reason is pregnancy, childbirth, serious illness, study, vocational training, a posting in another country, or some other important reason.

Right of permanent residence: retired workers

21.50   You get the right of permanent residence without having to complete five years residence if you qualify as a retired worker/self-employed person (paras 21.51-53). You are exempt from the habitual residence test and entitled to UC/HB/CTR (para 21.23). If you are the family member of a retired worker see para 21.56.

Retirement due to old age

21.51   You have a right of permanent residence due to old age (ADM C1799-1802) if:

(a)   you have retired as a worker before or after reaching pension age, or as a self-employed person after reaching pension age: and

■   you worked in the UK as a worker or self-employed person for at least 12 months before you retired; and

---

21.47   EEA 15(3)

21.48   EEA 6(1) – definition: 'qualified person', 14(1), 15(1)(a)

21.49   EEA 3(2)

21.50   EEA 5(1), 15(1)(c)

- you had been continuously resident in the UK for more than three years before you
  retired; or

(b) you have retired after reaching pension age (whether you have worked or not) and
your spouse or civil partner is a British citizen.

Retirement due to permanent incapacity

21.52   You have a right of permanent residence due to incapacity (ADM C1799-1802) if:

(a) you have ceased working because of permanent incapacity; and

(b) either:

- your incapacity is the result of an accident at work or an occupational disease
  which entitles you to ESA, incapacity benefit, industrial injuries benefit or some
  other pension payable by a UK institution (private company or the DWP); or

- you had resided continuously in the UK for more than two years immediately
  before you stopped working; or

- your spouse or civil partner is a British citizen.

Retired workers: qualifying periods of work and UK residence

21.53   In deciding whether you meet employment condition (para 21.51(a)) a period of
inactivity in which you are unable to work due to illness, accident or some other reason 'not of
[your] own making' is counted as a period of employment/self-employment. If you are a
worker, any period of inactivity in which you retained your worker status while unemployed
(paras 21.41-44) is also counted as a period of employment. Qualification for the residence
conditions (paras 21.51-52) is counted in the same way as para 21.49.

EEA family member rights

21.54   This section describes who has the right to reside as an EEA family member (paras
21.55-56) and who can retain their family member rights when the relationship ends (paras
21.57-62).

21.55   You are an EEA family member if you satisfy the conditions in table 21.2. You do not
need to be an EEA national yourself (although you can be). Your right to reside lasts for as long
as you remain a family member, so if you aren't married or in a civil partnership it usually ends
when you separate unless you have a permanent right to reside or you meet the conditions to
retain your family member rights (para 21.57).

Right of permanent residence: family members

21.56   You get a right of permanent residence as a family member if:

(a) you are a non-EEA national who has resided in the UK for a continuous period of five
years as an EEA family member;

21.51   EEA 5(2),(6)

21.52   EEA 5(3),(6)

21.53   EEA 3(2), 5(7)

21.55   EEA 14(3)

(b) you have resided in the UK for a continuous period of five years as a qualified person or as an EEA family member and at the end of that period you were a family member who had a retained right of residence (para 21.57);

(c) the EEA national you accompany has the right of permanent residence through retirement or incapacity (paras 21.51-53) and:

■ you were his/her family member at the point s/he stopped working, and

■ at that point you enjoyed the right to reside on the basis that you were his/her family member;

(d) the family member you accompany is a worker or self-employed person who has died, and:

■ you were living with them immediately before their death, and

■ s/he had lived continuously in the UK for at least the two years immediately before their death or s/he died as a result of an accident at work or occupational disease.

Table 21.2 **Who is an EEA family member**

You are an EEA family member if you accompany an EEA national who is self-employed, a worker, a student or a self-sufficient person and you are:

(a) their spouse or civil partner (until divorce/dissolution, not mere separation or estrangement);

(b) a direct descendant of that person (e.g. a child or grandchild) or of their spouse or civil partner, and you are

■ aged under 21; or

■ dependent on them or their spouse or civil partner (for example, because you are studying or disabled);

(c) a dependent direct relative in ascending line (e.g. a parent or grandparent) or of their spouse or civil partner;

(d) some other family member (an 'extended family member') who has been admitted to the UK on the basis that you are:

■ their partner (in the benefit sense, instead of being their spouse or civil partner),

■ a dependent household member of that person in their country of origin, or

■ a relative who is so ill that you strictly require personal care from that person,

and you have been issued with a residence card, family permit or registration certificate by the Home Office.

Note: If the EEA national you accompany is a student without any other right to reside you are only treated as their family member if you are their spouse/civil partner or dependent child (i.e. under 18 or dependent in other ways).

21.56   EEA 15(1)(b),(d)-(f)

T21.2   EEA 7(1)-(3), 8(2)-(5)

Former EEA family members with retained rights

21.57   If you are a former EEA family member (FM) you retain your family member rights if you satisfy any of the conditions in paras 21.58-62.

Retained FM: termination of marriage or civil partnership

21.58   You retain your family member status if:

(a) your marriage or civil partnership to the EEA national is terminated; and

(b) s/he had the right to reside at least until the termination proceedings began; and

(c) either:

  ■ before the termination started (which must occur while the EEA national is in the UK), the marriage/civil partnership must have lasted for at least three years with both of you residing in the UK for at least one of those, or

  ■ you have custody of the EEA national's child, or

  ■ your continued right of residence is warranted by particularly difficult circumstances, for example if you or another family member were the victim of domestic violence during the marriage/civil partnership; and

(d) either:

  ■ you are not an EEA national yourself, but if you were you would be a worker, a self-employed person or a self-sufficient person, or

  ■ you are the family member of such a person (in the bullet above).

Retained FM: a child in education

21.59   You retain your family member status if:

(a) you are the EEA national's child or grandchild (or the child or grandchild of his/her spouse or civil partner);

(b) the EEA national you accompanied was a 'qualified person' (para 21.48);

(c) you were attending a course of education in the UK when s/he left the UK; and

(d) you are still attending that course.

21.60   You also retain your family member status as in para 21.59 above if condition (b) is read as if it said a 'qualified person' or a person with a right of permanent residence; and condition (c) is read as if it said you were attending a course of education when the family member you accompanied died.

Retained FM: parent of a child in education

21.61   You retain your family member status if you are the parent with custody of a child who satisfies either of the two paras above.

21.57   EEA 10(1)

21.58   EEA 10(5),(6)

21.59-60   EEA 10(3)

21.61   EEA 10(4)

Retained FM: bereavement

21.62   You retain your family member status if:

(a) the EEA national you accompanied was a worker, self-employed, self-sufficient, a student or a person with a right of permanent residence;

(b) you had resided in the UK for at least a year immediately before s/he (the person in (a)) died; and

(c) either:

- you are not an EEA national yourself, but if you were you would be a worker, a self-employed person or a self-sufficient person, or

- you are the family member of such a person (in the bullet above).

Family members of British citizens and the EUSS

21.63   This section describes which family members of British citizens can apply to the EU settlement scheme and deadlines for making an application (paras 21.64-69).

Family members of a relevant person of Northern Ireland

21.64   If you are not a British or EEA citizen and you are a 'family member' (para 21.65) of a 'relevant person of Northern Ireland' you can apply to the EU settlement scheme (paras 21.15-20). You have until 30th June 2021 to apply and if you are granted settled or pre-settled status you are entitled to UC/HB/CTR (para 21.25). A 'relevant person of Northern Ireland' is person who was born in Northern Ireland to mother or father who was (at that time):

(a) a British citizen;

(b) an Irish citizen; or

(c) a person with settled status.

21.65   You are the 'family member' of a person of Northern Ireland if you are:

(a) his/her spouse or civil partner;

(b) aged under 21 and you are the child, grandchild or great grandchild of that person or of his/her spouse or civil partner; or

(c) his/her child, grandchild, great grandchild, parent or grandparent or that of his/her spouse/civil partner and you are dependent on that person's support for your essential living needs.

21.62   EEA 10(2),(6)

21.64-65   Immigration Rules, Appendix EU, EU11, Annex 1 – 'EEA citizen', 'Relevant person of Northern Ireland', 'relevant EEA citizen (where, in respect of the application under consideration, the date of application by the relevant EEA citizen or their family member is on or after 1 July 2021)' https://tinyurl.com/EUAppendix

Family members of British citizens with 'Surinder Singh' rights

21.66   A British citizen who exercised his/her EU free movement rights in another member state before 1st February 2020 can in certain circumstances, bring his/her family members back to the UK to live here. These are sometimes called 'Surinder Singh' rights after the case that established it (Surinder Singh v SSHD). The British citizen you accompany must have returned to the UK before 1st January 2021.

21.67   'Surinder Singh' family members can enter the UK, live here, and apply to the EU settlement scheme. But there are complex deadlines that depend on your relationship to the UK national:

(a) you must have arrived in the UK on or before 31st December 2020, apply to the EU settlement scheme on or before 30th June 2021 and be related to the UK national in one of the ways in para 21.68; or

(b) you can arrive and apply to the EU settlement scheme at any point up to and including 29th March 2022, if you are related to the UK national in one of the ways in para 21.69.

Surinder Singh family members arriving on or before 31st December 2020

21.68   You are a qualifying family member for the purposes of para 21.67(a) if:

(a) you are the UK national's spouse/civil partner or unmarried partner, the marriage/civil partnership was entered into or relationship started between 1st February 2020 and 31st December 2020, and that relationship continues at the date you apply;

(b) you are a child, aged under 21 of the UK national's spouse/civil partner of a marriage/partnership that was entered into between 1st February 2020 and 31st December 2020;

(c) you are a dependent parent or grandparent of the UK national's spouse or civil partner (where the marriage/civil partnership was entered into between 1st February 2020 and 31st December 2020), and you were a dependant of theirs on 1st February 2020 and continue to be; or

(d) you are a dependent child, parent or grandparent of the UK national, or of his/her spouse/civil partner (where the marriage/civil partnership was entered into on or before 31st December 2020) and your dependent relationship to them existed before you returned to the UK with the UK national, or before 31st December 2020, and you are still their dependant on the date you apply.

21.66-69   Singh v SSHD [1992] EUECJ C-370/90 https://www.bailii.org/eu/cases/EUECJ/1992/C37090.html
            Immigration Rules Appendix EU, EU12, Annex 1 – 'family member of a qualifying British citizen', 'specified date'
            https://tinyurl.com/EUAppendix

Surinder Singh family members arriving up to 29th March 2022

21.69   You are a qualifying family member for the purposes of para 21.67(b) if:

(a) you are the spouse/civil partner or unmarried partner of the UK national and the relationship started before 1st February 2020 and it continues at the date you apply; or

(b) you are child, aged under 21, of the UK national (or of his/her spouse/civil partner of a marriage/civil partnership that was entered into before 1st February 2021 or after then if they were in a durable relationship before); or

(c) you are a dependent parent or grandparent of the UK national (or of his/her spouse/civil partner of a marriage/civil partnership that was entered into before 1st February 2021 or after then if they were in a durable relationship before) and all of those relationships continue to exist when you apply.

Other EEA rights to reside

21.70   This section describes other EEA rights to reside you may have other than those acquired through being economically active (e.g. worker, jobseeker etc) or as an EEA family member.

Primary carer of a child in education in the UK

21.71   You have a right to reside if:

(a) you are the 'primary carer' (para 21.73) of a child/young person; and

(b) that child (now or at any time in the past) has resided with either one of his/her parents at the same time during which that parent was a 'worker' (para 21.75); and

(c) that child is in 'education' in the UK (para 21.76); and

(d) that child would be unable to continue their education here if you left the UK; and

(e) you and the child you care for don't possess any other 'right to reside' (other than EU pre-settled status) (paras 20.41-42).

This right to reside is sometimes called an 'Ibrahim/Teixeira' after the case that established it or (in the EEA regulations) a 'derivative right to reside'. Note that because of condition (e) it only usually applies if the child and parent are non-EEA nationals. To be entitled to UC/HB/CTR you must also be habitually resident (paras 20.38-52). For guidance see ADM C1827-39 and HB Circular A10/2010.

21.72   Your right to reside continues until the child completes their education. The guidance states that your right to reside normally ends when the child reaches 18 but 'it can continue beyond that age if the child continues to need [your] presence and care [...] in order to be able to complete their education' (ADM para C1835).

21.71   EEA 16(1),(3),(4)

21.73   You are the child's 'primary carer' if:

(a)   you are their 'direct relative' or legal guardian; and

(b)   either

- you have primary responsibility for their care, or

- you share responsibility equally with one other person. In this case the rule in para 21.71(d) is read as if it said the child couldn't continue their education if both of you left the UK. But if that person's only right to reside in UK is as a primary carer and they acquired it before you became a joint carer, the rule is read in the normal way.

The issue as to who is the child's primary carer mustn't be decided solely on the basis of the financial contribution a person makes towards the child's care.

21.74   The law doesn't define 'direct relative' but it probably means parent, grandparent, etc. DWP guidance (ADM C1832) states that a 'direct relative' can only be the parent and not a grandparent, but the law doesn't say this.

21.75   This right to reside can't be established through being self-employed ([2018] UKUT 401 (AAC)): one of the child's parents must be/have been a worker who was exercising their EU freedom of movement right to work in the UK (paras 21.32-43). A person can't be a worker during a period of employment before his/her country joined the EU (table 21.1), but employment during the worker registration/authorisation scheme does count, whether s/he completed 12 months in continuous employment or not (ADM para C1837).

21.76   Nursery education doesn't count as 'being in education' but being in a reception class or any education received before compulsory school age that 'is equivalent to' compulsory education does (ADM para C1835). It doesn't matter that the child started their education after the EEA national parent finished work – only that the child lived with that parent during a time when they were a worker (ADM para C1833.2).

Students and self-sufficient persons

21.77   If you aren't engaged in the labour market (including if you are a student) you have a right to reside as an EEA national if you entered the UK on the basis that you were 'self-sufficient' – in other words you had your own resources: [2014] UKUT 32 (AAC).

21.78   If you are an EEA student you have the right to reside if:

(a)   you are currently studying on a course in the UK;

(b)   you signed a declaration at the beginning of the course that you were able to support yourself without social assistance (which means UC and any legacy benefit); and

(c)   the declaration was true at the time it was signed and for the foreseeable future; and

(d)   you have comprehensive sickness insurance for the UK (para 21.82).

21.73   EEA 16(8)-(11)

21.76   EEA 16(3)(b),(7)(a)

21.77   EEA 6(1)(d),(e), 14(1)

21.78   EEA 4(1)(d),(3)

21.79 In practice, this means that if you are an EEA student you are unlikely to get UC/HB/CTR. However, it is possible to get UC/HB/CTR if your circumstances have changed since you started your course (e.g. your source of funds has unexpectedly dried up) – provided you satisfy the other student entitlement rules (table 2.3, para 16.31).

21.80 If you are not a student you have the right to reside as a self-sufficient person if you:

(a) have enough resources not to be an 'unreasonable burden' on the benefits system; and

(b) have comprehensive sickness insurance (para 21.82).

21.81 The fact that your income is so low that you qualify for UC does not automatically mean you are not self-sufficient (although in most cases you will be) and the DWP has discretion to decide otherwise given your circumstances (ADM C1729.2). The fact that you have been able to manage without claiming UC until now is a relevant consideration in deciding whether you are an 'unreasonable burden' as is the length of time you are likely to be claiming (HBGM para C4.123). For example, if your funds have been temporarily disrupted the decision maker may decide you are self-sufficient.

21.82 The requirement for comprehensive sickness insurance isn't met by access to NHS free treatment but you are likely to satisfy this condition if you receive a pension or invalidity benefit from your own country (provided it is an EEA member state) (ADM C1730). Detailed guidance on the meaning of comprehensive sickness insurance and related evidence is set out in the Home Office publication *EEA nationals: qualified persons* p38 [www].

21.80   EEA 4(1)(c),(3)

21.81   EEA 4(4)(b)

21.82   Ahmad v SSHD [2014] EWCA Civ 988 www.bailii.org/ew/cases/EWCA/Civ/2014/988.html
         https://tinyurl.com/EEAGuidance

Appendix 1 **UC/CTR legislation**

UC: England, Scotland and Wales

Main primary legislation (Acts)

The Social Security Administration Act 1992

The Welfare Reform Act 2012

The Welfare Reform and Work Act 2016

Main secondary legislation (regulations and orders)

SI 2013/376	The Universal Credit Regulations 2013
SI2017/725	The Loans for Mortgage Interest Regulations 2017
SI 2013/380	The Universal Credit, Personal independence Payment, Jobseeker's Allowance and Employment and Support Allowance (Claims and Payments) Regulations 2013
SI 2013/381	The Universal Credit, Personal Independence Payment, Jobseeker's Allowance and Employment and Support Allowance (Decisions and Appeals) Regulations 2013
SI 2013/382	The Rent Officers (Universal Credit Functions) Order 2013
SI 2013/383	The Social Security (Payments on Account of Benefit) Regulations 2013
SI 2013/384	The Social Security (Overpayments and Recovery) Regulations 2013
SI 2013/386	The Universal Credit (Transitional Provisions) Order 2013
SI 2014/1230	The Universal Credit (Transitional Provisions) Regulations 2014
SI 2012/1483	Social Security (Information-sharing in relation to Welfare Services etc) Regulations 2012
SI 2017/725	The Loans for Mortgage Interest Regulations 2017

Recent amending regulations and orders

SI 2020/522	The Universal Credit (Coronavirus) (Self-employed Claimants and Reclaims) (Amendment) Regulations 2020
SI 2020/618	The Social Security (Income and Capital) (Miscellaneous Amendments) Regulations 2020
SI 2020/655	The Universal Credit (Persons who have attained state pension credit qualifying age) (Amendment) Regulations 2020
SI 2020/677	The Universal Credit (Northern Ireland Reciprocal Arrangements) Regulations 2020
SI 2020/683	The Social Security (Income-Related Benefits) (Persons of Northern Ireland – Family Members) (Amendment) Regulations 2020
SI 2020/989	The Social Security (Scotland) Act 2018 (Young Carer Grants, Short-Term Assistance and Winter Heating Assistance) (Consequential Provision and Modifications) Order 2020

SI 2020/1156	The Social Security (Coronavirus) (Prisoners) Amendment Regulations 2020
SI 2020/1201	The Social Security (Coronavirus) (Further Measures) (Amendment) and Miscellaneous Amendment Regulations 2020
SI 2020/1209	The Citizens' Rights (Application Deadline and Temporary Protection) (EU Exit) Regulations 2020
SI 2020/1309	The Immigration and Social Security Co-ordination (EU Withdrawal) Act 2020 (Consequential, Saving, Transitional and Transitory Provisions) (EU Exit) Regulations 2020
SI 2020/1372	The Immigration (Citizens' Rights etc.) (EU Exit) Regulations 2020
SI 2019/1314	The Social Security (Capital Disregards) (Amendment) Regulations 2019
SI 2020/1519	The Rent Officers (Housing Benefit and Universal Credit Functions) (Modification) Order 2020
SI 2021/162	The Social Security Benefits Up-rating Order 2021
SI 2021/313	The Universal Credit (Extension of Coronavirus Measures) Regulations 2021

Recent transitional regulations: universal credit

SI 2021/4	The Universal Credit (Transitional Provisions) (Claimants previously entitled to a severe disability premium) Amendment Regulations 2021

CTR: England, Scotland and Wales

Main primary legislation (Acts)

The Local Government Finance Act 1992

The Local Government Finance Act 2012

Main secondary legislation England

SI 2012/2885	The Council Tax Reduction Schemes (Prescribed Requirements) (England) Regulations 2012
SI 2012/2886	The Council Tax Reduction Schemes (Default Scheme) (England) Regulations 2012
SI 2013/215	Council Tax Reduction Schemes (Transitional Provision) (England) Regulations 2013
SI 2013/501	Council Tax Reduction Schemes (Detection of Fraud and Enforcement) (England) Regulations 2013
SI 1996/1880	Local Authorities (Contracting Out of Tax Billing, Collection and Enforcement Functions) Order 1996
SI 2013/502	Local Authorities (Contracting Out of Tax Billing, Collection and Enforcement Functions) (Amendment) (England) Order 2013
SI 2009/2269	Valuation Tribunal for England (Council Tax and Rating Appeals) (Procedure) Regulations 2009
SI 2013/465	The Valuation Tribunal for England (Council Tax and Rating Appeals) (Procedure) (Amendment) Regulations 2013

Recent amending secondary legislation England

SI 2021/29	The Council Tax Reduction Schemes (Prescribed Requirements) (England) (Amendment) Regulations 2021

Main secondary legislation Scotland

SSI 2012/303	The Council Tax Reduction (Scotland) Regulations 2012
SSI 2012/319	The Council Tax Reduction (State Pension Credit) (Scotland) Regulations 2012
SSI 2013/87	Council Tax (Information-sharing in relation to Council Tax Reduction) (Scotland) Regulations 2013

Recent amending secondary legislation Scotland

SSI 2020/413	The Council Tax Reduction (Scotland) Amendment (No 4) Regulations 2020
SSI 2021/12	The Council Tax Reduction (Scotland) Amendment (Coronavirus) Regulations 2021
SSI 2021/51	The Council Tax Reduction (Scotland) Amendment (No 2) Regulations 2021
SSI 2021/137	The Council Tax Reduction (Scotland) Amendment (No 3) (Coronavirus) Regulations 2021

Main secondary legislation Wales

SI 2013/3029	The Council Tax Reduction Schemes and Prescribed Requirements (Wales) Regulations 2013
SI 2013/3035	The Council Tax Reduction Schemes (Default Scheme) (Wales) Regulations 2013
SI 1993/255	Council Tax (Demand Notices) (Wales) Regulations 1993
SI 2013/63	Council Tax (Demand Notices) (Wales) (Amendment) Regulations 2013
SI 1996/1880	Local Authorities (Contracting Out of Tax Billing, Collection and Enforcement Functions) Order 1996
SI 2013/695	Local Authorities (Contracting Out of Tax Billing, Collection and Enforcement Functions) (Amendment) (Wales) Order 2013
SI 2013/588	Council Tax Reduction Schemes (Detection of Fraud and Enforcement) (Wales) Regulations 2013
SI 2013/111	Council Tax Reduction Schemes (Transitional Provisions) (Wales) Regulations 2013
SI 2010/713	The Valuation Tribunal for Wales Regulations 2010
SI 2013/547	The Valuation Tribunal for Wales (Wales) (Amendment) Regulations 2013

CTR recent amending secondary legislation Wales

SI 2021/34	The Council Tax Reduction Schemes (Prescribed Requirements and Default Scheme) (Wales) (Amendment) Regulations 2021

UC: Northern Ireland

Main primary legislation (Acts and Orders)

Northern Ireland (Welfare Reform) Act 2015

The Welfare Reform (Northern Ireland) Order 2015 SI 2015 No 2006 (N.I. 1)

The Welfare Reform and Work (Northern Ireland) Order 2016 SI 2016 No 999 (N.I. 1)

Main secondary legislation (statutory rules)

NISR 2016/216   The Universal Credit Regulations (Northern Ireland) 2016

NISR 2017/176   The Loans for Mortgage Interest Regulations (Northern Ireland) 2017

NISR 2016/220   The Universal Credit, Personal Independence Payment, Jobseeker's Allowance and Employment and Support Allowance (Claims and Payments) Regulations (Northern Ireland) 2016

NISR 2016/221   The Universal Credit, Personal Independence Payment, Jobseeker's Allowance and Employment and Support Allowance (Decisions and Appeals) Regulations (Northern Ireland) 2016

NISR 2016/222   The Universal Credit Housing Costs (Executive Determinations) Regulations (Northern Ireland) 2016

NISR 2016/226   The Universal Credit (Transitional Provisions) Regulations (Northern Ireland) 2016

NISR 2016/178   The Welfare Supplementary Payments Regulations (Northern Ireland) 2016

NISR 2016/56   The Social Security (Information-sharing in relation to Welfare Services etc) Regulations (Northern Ireland) 2016

NISR 2017/176   The Loans for Mortgage Interest Regulations (Northern Ireland) 2017

Recent amending regulations and orders

The following is a list of orders bringing UC provisions into force since 9th April 2018. This list is up to date as at 5th April 2020.

NISR 2020/85   The Universal Credit (Coronavirus) (Self-employed Claimants and Reclaims) (Amendment) Regulations (Northern Ireland) 2020

NISR 2020/108   The Social Security (Income and Capital) (Miscellaneous Amendments) Regulations (Northern Ireland) 2020

NISR 2020/119   The Universal Credit (Persons who have attained state pension credit qualifying age) (Amendment) Regulations (Northern Ireland) 2020

NISR 2020/129   The Universal Credit (Great Britain Reciprocal Arrangements) Regulations (Northern Ireland) 2020

NISR 2020/149   The Social Security (Income-related Benefits) (Persons of Northern Ireland – Family Members) (Amendment) Regulations (Northern Ireland) 2020

NISR 2020/227   The Social Security (Coronavirus) (Prisoners) (Amendment) Regulations (Northern Ireland) 2020

NISR 2020/242   The Social Security (Coronavirus) (Further Measures) (Amendment) and Miscellaneous Amendment Regulations (Northern Ireland) 2020

NISR 2021/14   The Housing Benefit and Universal Credit Housing Costs (Executive
                Determinations) (Modification) Regulations (Northern Ireland) 2021

NISR 2021/67   The Universal Credit (Extension of Coronavirus Measures) Regulations
                (Northern Ireland) 2021

NISR 2021/82   The Universal Credit (Extension of Coronavirus Measures) Regulations
                (Northern Ireland) 2021

Recent transitional regulations: universal credit

NISR 2021/2   The Universal Credit (Transitional Provisions) (Claimants previously entitled to a
                severe disability premium) (Amendment) Regulations (Northern Ireland) 2021

Rate rebates: Northern Ireland

Main primary legislation (Acts and Acts of Northern Ireland Assembly)

The Social Security Contributions and Benefits (Northern Ireland) Act 1992

The Social Security Administration (Northern Ireland) Act 1992

The Rates (Northern Ireland) Order 1977 SI 1977/2157

The Rates (Amendment) (Northern Ireland) Order 2006 SI 2006/2954

The Welfare Reform (Northern Ireland) Order SI 2015/2006

The Welfare Reform and Work (Northern Ireland) Order 2016 SI 2016/999

Main secondary legislation (Statutory Rules and Orders)

NISR 2006/405   The Housing Benefit Regulations (Northern Ireland) 2006

NISR 2006/406   The Housing Benefit (Persons who have attained the qualifying age for state
                pension credit) Regulations (Northern Ireland) 2006

NISR 2007/203   The Rate Relief (Qualifying Age) Regulations (Northern Ireland) 2007

NISR 2007/204   The Rate Relief (General) Regulations (Northern Ireland) 2007

NISR 2008/124   The Rate Relief (Lone Pensioner Allowance) Regulations
                (Northern Ireland) 2008

NISR 2017/184   The Rate Relief Regulations (Northern Ireland) 2017

Main amending regulations: rate relief

The following is a list of amendments to the main rate relief regulations from 1st April 2007.
(For a list of recent amending legislation to housing benefit see *Guide to Housing Benefit*,
appendix 1).

NISR 2007/244   The Rate Relief (Qualifying Age) (Amendment) Regulations (Northern
                Ireland) 2007

NISR 2011/43   The Rate Relief (Amendment) Regulations (Northern Ireland) 2011

NISR 2018/109   The Rate Relief (Amendment) Regulations (Northern Ireland) 2018

Recent amending regulations: rate relief

NISR 2020/308   The Rate Relief (Coronavirus) (Amendment) Regulations
                (Northern Ireland) 2020

Appendix 2 **Weekly CTR applicable amounts: 2021-22**

Personal allowances

Single person	pension age rate	£191.15
	working age rate	£74.70
	working age rate (Wales)	£79.60
	lower rate	£59.20
	lower rate (Wales)	£63.05
Couple	pension age rate	£286.05
	working age rate	£117.40
	working age rate (Wales)	£125.05
Polygamous spouse	pension age rate	£94.90
	working age/lower rate	£42.70
	working age/lower rate (Wales)	£45.45
Child or young person	each (in England up to two only)	£68.60
	each (Scotland)	£85.75

Additional amounts: any age

Disabled child premium	each child/young person	£65.94
Enhanced disability premium (child)	each child/young person	£26.67
Severe disability premium	single rate	£67.30
	double rate	£134.60
Carer premium	claimant/partner/each	£37.70

Additional amounts: working age only

Disability premium	single person	£35.10
	couple	£50.05
Enhanced disability premium (adult)	single person	£17.20
	couple	£24.60
Support component	single person/couple	£39.40
WRA component	single person/couple	£29.70

Appendix 3 **Selected weekly benefit rates from April 2021**

Attendance allowance

Higher rate	£89.60
Lower rate	£60.00

Bereavement benefits

Widowed parent's allowance (standard rate)	£122.55
Bereavement allowance (standard rate)	£122.55
Bereavement support payment (higher rate)	£80.77
Bereavement support payment (lower rate)	£23.08

Child benefit

Eldest/only child	£21.15
Each other child	£14.00

Carer's allowance

Claimant	£67.60

Disability living allowance

Care component

Highest rate	£89.60
Middle rate	£60.00
Lowest rate	£23.70

Mobility component

Higher rate	£62.55
Lower rate	£23.70

Employment and support allowance (new style)

Under 25	£59.20
25 or over	£74.70
Work-related component	£29.70
Support component	£39.40

Guardian's allowance £18.00

Housing benefit applicable amounts

Personal allowance for child/young person	£68.60

All other HB figures are the same as in main CTR (appendix 2), but using the Scotland person allowances throughout the UK.

Industrial injury disablement pension

20% disabled	£36.58
For each further 10% disability up to 100%	£18.29
100% disabled	£182.90

Jobseeker's allowance (new style)

Single under 25	£59.20
Single over 25	£74.70

Maternity and paternity pay and allowance

Statutory maternity, paternity and adoption pay	£151.97
Maternity allowance	£151.97

Personal independence payment

Daily living component

Enhanced	£89.60
Standard	£60.00

Mobility component

Enhanced	£62.55
Standard	£23.70

Retirement pension

New state pension (full rate)	£179.60
Old state pension single (basic rate)	£137.60
Old state pension spouse or civil partner's insurance (basic pension)	£82.45

Severe disablement allowance

Basic rate	£81.25

Age-related addition

Higher rate	£12.15
Middle rate	£6.75
Lower rate	£6.75

Statutory sick pay

Standard rate	£96.35

Appendix 4: **Equivalent footnote references for Scotland and Wales**

Council tax and council tax rebates

This table shows the equivalent footnote references in chapters 15 to 17 for the law on council tax and council tax rebates in Scotland and Wales. 'Not Scotland' means there is no equivalent law in Scotland. For abbreviations see the key to footnotes at the front of this guide.

	Wales	**Scotland**
15.2	LGFA 1(1),(2)(b)	LGFA 70
15.3	LGFA 5(1A),(3)	LGFA 74(1),(2); SSI 2016/368
15.4	See text	LGFA 72
15.5-6	See text	LGFA 99(1) – definition – 'resident'
T15.1	LGFA 5(1A),(3),36(1)	LGFA 74(1),(2),93(1); SSI 2016/368
15.11	See text	LGFA 75(2)(a)-(e)
15.13	See text	LGFA 75(4), sch 1 paras 2, 4
15.14	See text	LGFA 75(1),(2)(a)-(e)
15.15	See text	LGFA 75(3),(4), 77
15.16	See text	LGFA 75(3),(4)
15.17	LGFA 8, The Council Tax (Liability for Owners) Regulations 1992, No 551	LGFA 76, The Council Tax (Liability of Owners) (Scotland) Regulations 1992, No 1331
T15.2(a)-(g)	LGFA 8(1),(3),(6); The Council Tax (Liability for Owners) Regulations 1992, No 551, reg 2, Classes A to F	LGFA 76(1)-(3), The Council Tax (Liability of Owners) (Scotland) Regulations 1992, No 1331, sch paras 1-7
T15.2(a)	Class C substituted by SI 1993/151, amended by SI 1995/620 reg 2	para 3 substituted by SSI 2003/137
T15.2(b),(c)	Class A substituted by SI 2004/2920	para 1
T15.2(d)	Class E amended by SI 1995/620 reg 3	para 5
T15.2(e)	Class B	para 2
T15.2(f)	Class D	para 4
T15.2(g)	Class F added by SI 2000/1024	para 7 added by SI 2000/715
T15.2(h)	LGFA 6(1),(2)(f)	LGFA 75(1),(2)(f)(iii)
15.18	Table 15.2 Class C as amended by SI 1993/151 and SI 1995/620	SI 1992/1331, sch para 3 as substituted by SSI 2003/137
15.20	Table 15.2 Class A; definition 'hostel', in DDO 6 as substituted by SI 2004/2921 art 4	LGFA sch 1 para 8, definition of 'hostel' repealed by Regulation of Care (Scotland) Act 2001, sch 3 para 18
15.21	LGFA 11(2), 12, 12A, 12B, The Council Tax (Exceptions to Higher Amounts) (Wales) Regulations 2015, No 2068	Local Government in Scotland Act 2003, s33; The Council Tax (Variation for Unoccupied Dwellings) (Scotland) Regulations 2013, No 45, regs 2-4
15.22	LGFA 4, 11, 13, 13A	LGFA 72, 79, 80
15.23	LGFA 4(1)-(4)	LGFA 72(1),(6)
T15.3	The Council Tax (Exempt Dwellings) Order 1992, SI 1992/558, reg 3, Classes A to X	The Council Tax (Exempt Dwellings) (Scotland) Order 1997, No 728, reg 3, sch 1 paras 1-25

T15.3(a)	Class N substituted by SI 1993/150, amended by SI 1995/619, SI 2004/2865; Class U substituted by SI 1999/536; Class S added by SI 1995/619; Class X added by SI 2019/432	sch 1 paras 10, 18, 23; SI 1999/757; SSI 2018/45
T15.3(b)	Class K substituted by SI 1993/150	sch 1 paras 11-12; SI 1998/561
T15.3(c)	Class M amended by SI 1993/150 and SI 1994/539	sch 1 para 16
T15.3(d)	Class I substituted by SI 2004/2921	sch 1 para 5
T15.3(e)	Class B, amended by SI 1994/539; SI 2003/673, regs 3, 4	sch 1 para 3
T15.3(f)	Class A substituted by SI 2000/1025; Class C substituted by SI 1993/150	sch 1 paras 2, 4; SSI 1999/140; SSI 2012/339
T15.3(g)	Class H	sch 1 para 9
T15.3(h)	Class Q added by SI 1993/150, amended by SI 1994/539	sch 1 para 21
T15.3(i)	Class L	sch 1 para 13
T15.3(j)	Class G	sch 1 para 7
T15.3(k)	Class O amended by SI 1992/2941	sch 1 para 17
T15.3(l)	Class P added by SI 1992/2941	sch 1 para 22
T15.3(m)	Class V added by SI1997/656, definition of dependent relative in class amended by SI 1998/291	Not Scotland
T15.3(n)	Class R added by SI 1994/539	Not Scotland
T15.3(o)	Class T added SI 1995/619	Not Scotland
T15.3(p)	Class W added by SI1997/656, definition of dependent relative in class amended by SI 1998/291	Not Scotland
15.24	LGFA 13(1),(4),(6),(7); The Council Tax (Reductions for Disabilities) Regulations 1992 No 554, reg 4 as amended by SI 1999/1004	The Council Tax (Reductions for Disabilities) (Scotland) Regulations 1992 No 1335, reg 4 as amended by SI 1999/756
15.25	The Council Tax (Reductions for Disabilities) Regulations 1992 No 554, reg 3(1),(3)	The Council Tax (Reductions for Disabilities) (Scotland) Regulations 1992 No 1335, reg 3(1),(3)
15.26	LGFA 11(1)-(3),12	LGFA 79(3); The Council Tax (Variation for Unoccupied Dwellings) (Scotland) Regulations 2013, No 45, reg 2
15.27-30	LGFA 11(1)-(3)	LGFA 79(1)-(3)
T15.4(a)-(m)	LGFA 11(5), sch 1	LGFA 79(5), sch 1
T15.4(a)	LGFA sch 1 paras 4, 5, 11; DDO art 4, sch 1 paras 2-7; DDR reg 5, class C; SI 2019/431	LGFA sch 1 paras 4, 5, 11; SI 1992/1409, reg 3, sch para 3; SSI 2003/176 art 6, 7; SSI 2011/5; SSI 2014/37
T15.4(b)	LGFA sch 1 para 2, DDO art 3; SI 2013/638; SI 2013/1048	LGFA sch 1 para 2; SSI 2003/176 art 4; SSI 2008/1879 reg 39; SSI 2013/65; SSI 2013/137 reg 14; SSI 2013/142 reg 8
T15.4(c)	LGFA sch 1 para 3	LGFA sch 1 para 3
T15.4(d)	LGFA sch 1 para 11; DDR reg 5, class G; SI 2019/431	LGFA sch 1 para 11; SI 1992/1409 reg 3, sch para 6; SSI 2018/39
T15.4(e)	LGFA sch 1 para 4; SI 2003/673 art 3	LGFA sch 1 para 4; SSI 2003/176 art 8
T15.4(f)	LGFA sch 1 para 4; DDO art 4, sch 1 para 1; SI 2007/580	LGFA sch 1 para 4; SSI 2003/176 art 5; SSI 2007/214
T15.4(g)	LGFA sch 1 para 9; DDR reg 2, sch paras 3, 4; SI 2013/639; SI 2013/1049	LGFA sch 1 para 9; SI 1992/1409 reg 2(3); SSI 2013/65; SSI 2013/142 reg 2

	Wales	**Scotland**
T15.4(h)	LGFA sch 1 para 9; DDR reg 2, sch paras 1, 2; SI 2007/581	LGFA sch 1 para 9; SI 1992/1409 reg 2(2); SSI 2007/213 reg 2
T15.4(i)	LGFA sch 1 para 10	LGFA sch 1 para 10
T15.4(j)	LGFA sch 1 paras 6, 7; DDO 6(b); SI 2004/2921 art 4	LGFA sch 1 para 8, as amended by Regulation of Care (Scotland) Act 2001, sch 3 para 18
T15.4(k)	LGFA sch 1 para 1; DDO arts 2,5; SI 2009/2054, sch 1 para 13; SI 2004/2921 art 4	LGFA sch 1 para 1; SSI 2003/176 art 3; SI 2009/2054, sch 1 para 23
T15.4(l)	LGFA sch 1 para 11; DDR reg 5, Class B; SI 2019/431	LGFA sch 1 para 11; SI 1992/1409 reg 3, sch para 2
T15.4(m)	LGFA sch 1 para 11; DDR reg 5, Class E; SI 2019/431	LGFA sch 1 para 11; SI 1992/1409 reg 3, sch para 1
T15.4(n)	LGFA sch 1 para 11; DDR reg 5, Class A, D, F; SI 2019/431	LGFA sch 1 para 11; SI 1992/1409 reg 3, sch para 1
15.31	See text	CT(A&E)S 10, 15
15.32	See text	LGFA 71
15.33	See text	LGFA 81, 82
15.34	See text	CT(A&E)S 7, 12
15.35	See text	See text
T16.1	LGFA 13A(1)(c),(2), sch 1B paras 3(1)-(3), 4; CTPW 21-25; CTRW 13-16	LGFA 80; CTS 14(1),(3)-(6), 14A; CTS66+ 14(1),(3)-(6), 14A
16.2	LGFA sch 1B para 3(7)(a)-(c); CTPW 22(a), 23(a), 24(a), 25(a); CTRW 13(a), 14(a), 15(a), 16(a)	LGFA 80(1); CTS 14(3)(a), 14A(3)(a); CTS66+ 14(3)(a), 14A(3)(a)
16.3	LGFA sch 1B para 3(7)(e); CTPW 9; CTRW 9	CTS 3; CTS66+ 3
16.4	CTPW 2(1); CTRW 2(1)	CTS 2(1) definition – 'qualifying age for state pension credit'; CTS66+ 2(1)
T16.2	CTPW 3, 22(f), 23(g), 24(f), 25(g), sch 13 para 1; CTRW 3, 13(f), 14(g), 15(f), 16(g), 107(1)	CTS 7, 12, 14(3)(c), 14A(3)(c), 82; CTS66+ 7, 12, 14(3)(c), 14A(3)(c), 61
16.5	LGFA 13A(4),(5), sch 1B paras 1-4; CTPW 11, 12, 14, 15, 32, 33	LGFA 80; CTS 14, 14A; CTS66+ 14, 14A
16.6	Not Wales	LGFA 80(1),(2); CTS 12, 14(1), 14A(1), sch 4 paras 12, 19; CTS66+ 12, 14(1), 14A(1), sch 3 paras 1-2
16.7	LGFA 13(1)(b),(c),(4),(5), sch 1B paras 2(1), 3, 4; CTPW 14, 21-24, 32, 33, 34(4),(5)	Not Scotland
16.8	LGFA 13A(1)(b),(4),(5), sch 1B paras 3-5; CTPW 3-10, 12, 14-18, 27-29	Not Scotland
16.9-12	Not Wales	Not Scotland
16.13	LGFA sch 1B para 3(5),(7)(a),(b),(e); CTPW 12(1), 14(b), 15(2),(3)	Not Scotland
16.14	See text	Not Scotland
16.15	LGFA sch 1B paras 3-5; CTPW 3-10, 27-31, 34(1)-(3)	Not Scotland
16.16	LGFA sch 1B paras 2, 6; CTPW 13, 17, 18	Not Scotland
16.17	Not Wales	Not Scotland
16.18	Not Wales	Not Scotland
16.19	LGFA sch 1B para 4(4),(5)	Not Scotland
16.20	LGFA 13A(1)(c),(6),(7)	Not Scotland
16.21	LGFA 13A(1)(c),(6), sch 1B para 4(1),(2)	Not Scotland
16.22	LGFA 13A(1)(c),(6); CTPW sch 12 para 11(2)	Not Scotland
16.23	Not Wales	Not Scotland
16.24	LGFA sch 1B para 3(1)(b); CTPW 21-31, sch 11 para 3(1),(2); CTRW 13-22, 72(1),(2)	CTS 14(3)(b), 14A(3)(b), 15-20, 42; CTS66+ 14(3)(b), 14A(3)(b), 15-19, 40

16.25	CTPW 22(b), 23(b), 24(b), 25(b), 26, 28(2),(6),(7); CTRW 13(b), 14(b), 15(b), 16(b), 17, 19(2),(6),(7)	CTS 15, 16(1), 17; CTS66+ 15, 16(1), 17
16.26	CTPW 26; CTRW 17	CTS 15; CTS66+ 15
16.27	Not Wales	Not Scotland
16.28	Not Wales	CTS 16(1), 17; CTS66+ 16(1), 17
16.29	CTPW 26(1),(3),(3)(c)-(e),(g); CTRW 17(1),(3),(3)(c)-(e),(g)	Not Scotland
16.30	CTPW 28, 29; CTRW 19, 20	CTS 16, 19; CTS66+ 16, 19
16.31	CTPW 31, sch 11 para 3(1),(2); CTRW 18, 22, 72(1),(2)	CTS 20(1)-(3)
16.33	CTPW 22(f), 23(g), 24(f), 25(g), sch 12 paras 2, 3, 11, sch 13 para 1; CTRW 13(f), 14(g), 15(f), 16(g), 107, sch 1 paras 2, 3, 11	CTS 7, 14(3)(c), 14A(3)(c), 83, 84, 91; CTS66+ 7, 14(3)(c), 14A(3)(c), 63, 64, 71
16.34	CTPW sch 13 para 2(7); CTRW 108(7)	CTS 85(5),(6); CTS66+ 65(2),(3)
16.35	CTPW sch 12 paras 2, 3, sch 13 para 1(1); CTRW 107(1), sch 1 paras 2, 3	CTS 7, 82-84, 91; CTS66+ 7, 61, 63, 64, 71
16.36	CTPW sch 13 para 1; CTRW 107	--
16.37	CTPW sch 13 para 5; CTRW 111	CTS 86; CTS66+ 66
16.39	CTPW sch 1 para 39, sch 6 para 45; CTRW 104(1)	CTS 80(1); CTS66+ 58(1)
16.40	CTPW sch 1 para 39, sch 6 para 45; CTRW 104(2)	CTS 80(2); CTS66+ 58(2)
16.41	CTPW sch 12 paras 2-7, sch 13 para 2; CTRW 108, sch 1 paras 2-7	CTS 85, 91; CTS66+ 65, 71
16.42	CTPW sch 13 paras 3, 4; CTRW 109, 110	CTS 85(7),(8); CTS66+ 62
16.44	CTPW sch 1 para 40(1), sch 6 para 46(1); CTRW 105(1)	CTS 81(1); CTS66+ 59(1)
16.45	CTPW sch 1 para 40(1),(3),(4), sch 6 para 46(1),(3),(4); CTRW 105(1),(3),(4)	CTS 81(1)-(3); CTS66+ 59(1)-(3)
16.46	LGFA 13A(1)(b); CTPW sch 13 para 10; CTRW 116; CT(A&E) 1(2) definition – 'discount', 20 as amended by SI 2013/62	CTS 20A, sch 7; CTS66+ 19A, sch 7
17.2	CTPW 2(1) definition – 'reduction week'; CTRW 2(1)	CTS 2(1) definition – 'reduction week'; CTS66+ 2(1)
17.3	CTPW sch 1 paras 2(1), 11(1) sch 6 paras 4(1), 13(1),(2); CTRW 27(1), 37(1), 46(1), 47(1),(2)	CTS 31(1), 33(1),(2); CTS66+ 31(1), 47(1)
17.4	CTPW 22-25; CTRW 13, 14, 15, 16	CTS 14(1)(a),(3)-(5); CTS66+ 14(1)(a),(3)-(5)
17.5	CTPW 22-25; CTRW 13, 14, 15, 16	CTS 14(1)(a),(3)-(5); CTS66+ 14(1)(a),(3)-(5)
17.6	CTPW 22(c),(e), 23(c),(e),(f), 24(c),(e), 25(c),(e),(f), sch 1 paras 2, 4(2),(3), sch 6 paras 4, 6(2),(3); CTRW 13(c),(e), 14(c),(e),(f), 15(c),(e), 16(c),(e),(f), 27, 29(2),(3)	CTS 14(4),(5),(8)(a),(b), 66(1),(2); CTS66+ 14(4),(5),(8)(a),(b), 47(1),(2)
17.7	CTPW sch 1 para 2(1),(2), sch 6 para 4(1),(2); CTRW 27(1),(2)	CTS 66(1); CTS66+ 47(1)
17.8	CTPW 24(e), 25(e),(f), sch 6 paras 3, 6(2),(3), 9; CTRW 15(e), 16(e),(f), 26, 29(2),(3), 34	CTS 23(2A)(c), 26(1)-(5), sch 1 para 3; SSI 2021/51 reg 3
17.9	CTPW sch 6 para 9(1)-(4); CTRW 34(1)-(4)	CTS 26(3)-(5)
17.10	CTPW 22(e), 23(e),(f), 24(e), 25(e),(f), sch 1 paras 4(2),(3), 5(1), 7, 9, sch 6 paras 6(2),(3), 7(1), sch 8 para 14, sch 9 paras 8, 9; CTRW 13(e), 14(e),(f), 15(e), 16(e),(f), 29(2),(3), 30(1), 32, 35, sch 6 para 14, sch 7 paras 8, 9	CTS 14(5),(8)(a),(b); CTS66+ 14(5),(8)(a),(b)

	Wales	**Scotland**
17.11	CTPW sch 1 para 5(1), sch 6 para 7(1); CTRW 30(1)	CTS 24(1),(2), CTS66+ 21(1),(2)
17.12	CTPW sch 1 para 1, sch 2, sch 6 para 1, sch 7; CTRW 23, 24, sch 2, sch 3	CTS 21, sch 1; CTS66+ 20, sch 1
17.13	CTPW 9, sch 1 paras 2(1), 3 sch 6 paras 4(1), 5; CTRW 9, 27(1), 28	CTS 3, 66(1), 67; CTS66+ 3, 47(1), 48
17.14	Not Wales	CTS66+ 59(10)-(13)
17.15	CTPW sch 1 para 3(9) sch 6 para 5(9); CTRW 28(9)	CTS 67(9); CTS66+ 48(9)
T17.1	CTPW sch 1 para 3(1),(2) sch 6 para 5(1),(2); CTRW 28(1),(2)	CTS 67(1),(2); CTS66+ 48(1),(2)
T17.2	CTPW sch 1 para 3(6)-(8) sch 6 para 5(6)-(8); CTRW 28(6)-(8)	CTS 67(6)-(8); CTS66+ 48(6)-(8)
17.16	CTPW sch 1 para 2(1),(3)-(5), sch 6 para 4(1),(3)-(5); CTRW 27(1),(3)-(5)	CTS 67(1),(2); CTS66+ 47(1),(2)
17.17	Not Wales	See text
17.18	Not Wales	CTS 14(1)(b),(3),(6); CTS66+ 14(1)(b),(3),(6)
17.19	Not Wales	CTS 14(1)(b),(3),(6),(8)(c), sch 5 para 49; CTS66+ 14(1)(b),(3),(6),(8)(c), sch 4 para 27
17.20	Not Wales	CTS 14(1)(b),(3),(6),(7), 78(2),(3); CTS66+ 14(1)(b),(3),(6),(7), 56(2),(3)
17.21	Not Wales	CTS 14(1)(b),(3),(6),(7), 78(2),(3), sch 2 para 1(1); CTS66+ 14(1)(b),(3),(6),(7), 56(2),(3), sch 5 para 1(1)
17.22	Not Wales	CTS 14(8)(c), 78(2),(3), sch 2 paras 1, 3; CTS66+ 14(8)(c), 56(2),(3), sch 5 paras 1, 3
17.23	Not Wales	CTS sch 2 paras 1, 3; CTS66+ sch 5 paras 1, 3
17.24	Not Wales	CTS sch 2 para 1(2); CTS66+ sch 5 para 1(2)
17.25	Not Wales	CTS 78(2),(3); CTS66+ 56(2),(3)
17.27	CTPW sch 1 para 5, sch 6 para 7; CTRW 30	CTS 24; CTS66+ 21
17.28	CTPW sch 8 para 14, sch 9 paras 8, 9, sch 10 paras 8, 9; CTRW sch 6 para 14, sch 7 paras 8, 9, sch 9 paras 8, 9	CTS sch 3 para 14, sch 4 paras 7, 8, sch 5 paras 7, 8
17.29	CTPW sch 1 para 8(2),(3), sch 6 para 9(1),(6); CTRW 33(2),(3), 34(1),(6)	CTS 26(1),(6); CTS66+ 25(2),(3)
17.30	CTPW sch 1 para 5(1), sch 6 para 7(1); CTRW 30(1)	CTS 24(1); CTS66+ 21(1)
17.31	CTPW sch 1 para 25(1),(2), sch 5, sch 6 para 26(1),(2), sch 10; CTRW 60(1),(2), sch 8, sch 9	CTS 43(1),(2), sch 5; CTS66+ 41(1),(2), sch 4
17.32	CTPW 22(d), 23(d), 24(d), 25(d), 27, 30; CTRW 13(d), 14(d), 15(d), 16(d), 18, 21, sch 8 para 27	CTS 14(3)(b), 42, sch 5 para 49; CTS66+ 14(3)(b), 40
17.33	CTPW sch 1 para 31, sch 6 para 33; CTRW 68, 69	CTS 51; CTS66+ 27(2)
17.34	CTPW sch 1 paras 8(2)(a), 10(1)(b)-(d),(j), 11(11),(13), sch 6 paras 12(1), 17(1),(2), sch 9 para 4; CTRW 33(2)(a), 36(1)(b)-(d),(j), 37(11),(13), 46(1), 51(1),(2), sch 7 para 4	CTS 31(1), 39(1),(2), sch 4 para 3; CTS66+ 25(2)(a), 27(1)(b)-(d),(j), 31(10),(12)
17.35	CTPW sch 1 para 40(1), sch 6 para 46(1); CTRW 105(1)	CTS 81(1); CTS66+ 59(1)
17.36	CTPW sch 6 paras 34-37; CTRW 93-96	CTS 68-71

T17.3(a)-(c)	CTPW sch 1 para 18(1)(c),(3), sch 3 paras 1-5, 8, 10, sch 6 para 20(1)(c),(3), sch 8 paras 4, 5, 11, 18; CTRW 54(1)(c),(3), sch 4 paras 1-5, 8, 10, sch 6 paras 4, 5, 11, 18	CTS 27(1)(c),(3), sch 3 paras 4, 5, 11, 18; CTS66+ 28(1)(c),(3), sch 2 paras 1-5, 8, 10
T17.3(d)-(h)	CTPW sch 1 paras 7, 10(1)(j)(i)-(vii), sch 9 paras 8, 9, 11, 14, 21, 52, 66; CTRW 32, 36(1)(j)(i)-(vii), sch 7 paras 8, 9, 11, 14, 21, 52, 66	CTS sch 4 paras 7, 8, 10, 13, 20, 51, 64; CTS66+ 24, 27(1)(j)(i)-(viii)
T17.3(i)	CTPW sch 1 para 10(1)(j)(ix),(xi), sch 8 paras 30-34, 37, 42, 64, 65; CTRW 36(1)(j)(ix),(xi), sch 7 paras 30-34, 37, 42, 64, 65	CTS sch 4 paras 29-33, 37, 42, 62, 63; CTS66+ 27(1)(j)(xi),(xiii)
T17.3(j)	CTPW sch 1 para 10(1)(e),(f),(l),(m), sch 4 paras 1-5, 13, sch 9 para 20, 53-56; CTRW 36(1)(e),(f),(l),(m), sch 5 paras 1-5, 13, sch 7 para 20, 53-56	CTS sch 4 para 19, 52-55; CTS66+ 27(1)(e),(f),(l),(m), sch 3 paras 1-4, 12
T17.3(k)	CTPW sch 1 para 10(1)(o), sch 4 para 20, sch 9 paras 49, 50; CTRW 36(1)(o), sch 5 para 20, sch 7 paras 49, 50	CTS sch 4 paras 48, 49; CTS66+ 27(1)(o), sch 3 para 19
T17.3(l)	CTPW sch 1 para 10(1)(p),(v), sch 4 paras 9, 10, sch 9 paras 26, 27; CTRW 36(1)(p),(v), sch 5 paras 9, 10, sch 7 paras 26, 27	CTS sch 4 paras 25, 26; CTS66+ 27(1)(p),(v), sch 3 paras 8, 9
T17.3(m)	CTPW sch 1 paras 10(1)(s), 12(2)(f), sch 4 paras 12, 14, 15, sch 6 paras 14(2)(d), sch 9 paras 5, 6, 19; CTRW 36(1)(s), 38(2)(f), 49(2)(d), sch 5 paras 12, 14, 15, sch 7 paras 5, 6, 19	CTS 51(2)(d), sch 4 paras 4, 5, 18; CTS66+ 27(1)(s), 32(2)(f), sch 3 paras 11, 13, 14
T17.3(n)	CTPW sch 1 para 10(1), sch 9 para 41; CTRW 36(1), sch 7 para 41	CTS sch 4 para 41; CTS66+ 27(1)

Index

References in the index are to paragraph numbers (not page numbers), except that 'A' refers to appendices, 'T' refers to tables in the text and 'Ch' refers to a chapter.